War & Peace in The Balkans

War & Peace in The Balkans

The Diplomacy of Conflict in The Former Yugoslavia

IAN OLIVER

I.B. TAURIS

LONDON · NEW YORK

In association with
New European Publications

To my wife Allison and my two children Thomas and Harriet for their continued love and understanding, and for enduring my long absences – "saving Bosnia" but neglecting them.

And lest we forget: To my friends and former colleagues who risked, and in too many cases, gave up their lives for the people of Bosnia i Hercegovina.

Published in 2005 by I.B.Tauris & Co Ltd
6 Salem Road, London W2 4BU
175 Fifth Avenue, New York NY 10010
www.ibtauris.com

In the United States and Canada distributed by St. Martin's Press
175 Fifth Avenue, New York NY 10010

In association with New European Publications
14-16 Carroun Road, London SW8 1JT

International Library of War Studies 4
ISBN 1 85043 889 7
EAN 978 1 85043 889 2

A full CIP record for this book is available from the British Library
A full CIP record for this book is available from the Library of Congress

Library of Congress catalog card number: available

Typeset by www.orbitgraphic.co.uk
Printed and bound in Great Britain by MPG Books Ltd, Bodmin, Cornwall
from camera-ready copy edited and supplied by the author

Contents

Preface

The title that I originally chose for my book was 'On a Field of Blackbirds'. There are strong historical reasons for such title, but unfortunately they are largely unknown outside the Balkans. The image is also a powerful one, conveying the intense, austere beauty and mysterious power of this corner of Southeast Europe. It resonated with me throughout my time there, and during the making of this book.

In Serbo-Croat, 'Kos' means blackbird and 'Polje' means field. 'Kosovo,' that much disputed and still divided Southern province of Serbia, is named after the blackbirds that plague the skies of the region whilst 'Kosovo Polje,' -literally 'Field of Blackbirds,' is but a small hamlet Southwest of the capital Pristina. At one end of that field, at Gazimestan, is a monument to one of the largest battles ever fought in medieval Europe, a battle which even today is central to Serbian history, culture and the nation's psyche.

It was on this "Field of Blackbirds," that a Serbian Christian Army tried in vain to block the northward advance of the invading Ottoman Turks. On the 28 June 1389, both Armies joined battle. Losses on both sides were appalling and the outcome inconclusive although the Serbs never fully recovered and the battle spelt the end of the once powerful Serbian Empire of the time. It took the Turks another seventy years before they occupied the land they'd fought for. After the battle, legend has it that blackbirds tore at the corpses for weeks. Among the dead were both leaders, Sultan Murad I and Serbian Prince Lzar. The Turks went on to conquer significant parts of the Balkans establishing Islamic law and spreading the Islamic faith throughout the region. When the Turks were finally forced by the Serbs and Montenegrins, during the Balkan Wars of 1912-13, to withdraw towards Constantinople ending their five hundred year rule in Southeast Europe, they left behind a cultural, religious and economic rift across what was later to become Yugoslavia.

On 28 June 1989, the 600th Anniversary of the Battle, a relatively unknown party functionary and former bank clerk, Slobodan Milosevic took to the same field to proclaim his nationalist credentials and to exploit this rift. Several hundred thousand Serbs assembled below the monument to hear him speak. Milosevic told the crowd;

> 'After six centuries we are again engaged in battles and quarrels. They are not armed battles, but this can not be excluded yet.'

His speech that day was a turning point; the spectre of Pan-Serb Unity had been rekindled with all its previous malevolence and enmity. As Milosevic whipped up Serb nationalist fervour, the idea that the other states were better off on their own took root. The disintegration of Yugoslavia had begun.

The Gazimestan Monument to the Battle of Kosovo Polje (1389): This picture taken in 1999, shows the monument under the protection of KFOR troops following NATO's Kosovo campaign. The final outcome of Milosevic's adventurism was a far cry from what he envisioned during his speech here in 1989.

Blessed are the poor in spirit, for theirs in the kingdom of heaven.

Blessed are those who mourn, for they shall be comforted.

Blessed are the meek, for they shall inherit the earth.

Blessed are those who hunger and thirst for righteousness,
for they shall be satisfied.

Blessed are the merciful, for they shall obtain mercy.

Blessed are the pure in heart, for they shall see God.

Blessed are the **Peacemakers**, for they shall be called sons of God.

Blessed are those who are persecuted for righteousness' sake,
for theirs is the kingdom of heaven.

Beatitudes: Matt. 5: 3-11

Acknowledgements

I would like to thank all those who inspired, helped and encouraged me to write this book. In particular, I would like to thank Tony Cripps for providing me with the initial impetus to put pen to paper, John Durnin for help with my research, and Tom Mouat who assisted me with his comments on the text.

Glossary

ABiH	Army of Bosnia i Hercegovina
AoR	Area of Responsibility
ARRC	Allied Rapid Reaction Corps
BCP	Border Crossing Point
BMM	Border Monitor Mission
BSA	Bosnian Serb Army
CAFAO	Customs and Fiscal Advisory Office
CAO	Chief Administrative Officer
CAPSAT	Data-link satellite system
CC	Co-ordinating Centre
CCP	Controlled Crossing Point
CFE	Conventional Forces in Europe
CO	Commanding Officer
COMDIFOR	Commander Implementation Force
COS	Chief of Staff
CP	Close Protection
CRHB	Croatian Republic of Herceg Bosna
CSCE	Conference on Security and Co-operation in Europe
CTO	Compensatory Time Off
DCOS	Deputy Chief of Staff
DDT	Defence Debriefing Team
DEM	Deutschmark
DFID	Department for International Development
DHOS	Deputy Head of Sector

DP	Displaced Person
DPA	Dayton Peace Agreement
EAU	Eastern Adriatic Unit
EBRD	European Bank for Reconstruction and Development
EC	European Commission
ECMM	European Community Monitor Mission
EEC	European Economic Community
ERIC	Election Results Implementation Committee
EU	European Union
EUAM	European Union Administrative Mission (in Mostar)
FCO	Foreign & Commonwealth Office
FoM	Freedom of Movement
FRY	Federal Republic of Yugoslavia
GFAP	General Framework Agreement for Peace
GPS	Global Positioning System
HCC	Head of Co-ordinating Centre
HDZ	Croatian Democratic Union
HGV	Heavy Goods Vehicle
HOD	Head of Delegation
HOM	Head of Mission
HOS	Head of Sector
HQ	Headquarters
HRC	Head of Regional Centre
HRCC	Human Rights Co-ordinating Centre
HRTF	Human Rights Task Force
Hv	Croatian Army (Hrvatska Vojska)
HVO	Bosnian Croat Army (Hrvatska Vijece Odbrane)
IC	International Community
ICFY	International Conference on the Former Yugoslavia
ICOM	International Customs Observer Mission
ICRC	International Committee of the Red Cross
ICT	Information and Communications Technology
ICTY	International Criminal Tribunal for the Former Yugoslavia
IEBL	Inter Entity Boundary Line
IFOR	Implementation Force
IFRC	International Federation of the Red Cross
IHL	International Humanitarian Law
IMF	International Monetary Fund

INF	Intermediate-range Nuclear Forces
INMARSAT	International Marine Satellite
IPTF	International Police Task Force
ISP	Internet Service Provider
JCC	Joint Civilian Commission
JIC	Joint Interim Commission
JMC	Joint Military Commission
JNA	Yugoslav People's Army
KOALICIJA	Coalition for a Single and Democratic BiH
LAN	Local Area Network
LEC	Local Election Commission
MLRS	Multi-Launch Rocket System
MND	Multi-national Division
MOU	Memorandum of Understanding
MPRI	Military Professional Resources Incorporated
MRE	Meal, Ready to Eat
MUP	State Security Police
NATO	North Atlantic Treaty Organisation
NERIC	National Election Results Implementation Committee
NGO	Non Governmental Organisation
NRC	Norwegian Refugee Council
ODA	Overseas Development Agency
OHR	Office of the High Representative
OP	Observation Post
Ops	Operations
OSCE	Organisation for Security and Co-operation in Europe
PBX	Telephone Exchange
PEC	Provisional Election Commission
PIC	Peace Implementation Council
PTT	Postal, Telegraph & Telephone
R&R	Rules and Regulations
RC	Regional Centre
RERIC	Regional Election Results Implementation Committee
RoM	Restriction of Movement
RPV	Remotely Piloted Vehicle
RS	Republika Srpska
RSK	Republic of Serb Krajina (Republika Srpske Krajine)
RSNA	National Assembly of Republika Srpska

SACEUR	Supreme Allied Commander in Europe
SAMCOM	Sanctions Administrative Mission
SAS	Special Air Service
SDA	Party of Democratic Action
SDS	Serb Democratic Party
SFOR	Stabilisation Force
SFRY	Socialist Federal Republic of Yugoslavia
SHAPE	Supreme Headquarters Allied Powers Europe
SNS-BP	Serb People's Alliance – Biljana Plavsic
SNSD	Party of Independent Social Democrats
SOP	Standard Operating Procedure
SPAS	Serb Patriotic Party
SPRS	Socialist Party of Republika Srpska
SPS	Socialist Party of Serbia
SRS	Serb Radical Party
SRT	Serb Radio Television
UN	United Nations
UNCHR	United Nations Centre for Human Rights
UNESCO	UN Economic, Scientific and Cultural Organisation
UNHCR	United Nations High Commission for Refugees
UNMiBH	UM Mission in Bosna i Hercegovina
UNMO	United Nations Military Observer
UNPROFOR	United Nations Protection Force
UNSC	United Nations Security Council
UNSG	United Nations Secretary General
UNTAES	United Nations Transitional Administration in Eastern Slavonia
USAF	United States Air Force
USAID	US Agency for International Development
VIREP	Violation Report
VJ	Yugoslav Army (Vojska Jugoslavije)
VJLO	Yugoslav Army Liaison Officer
VOPP	Vance-Owen Peace Plan
VRS	Bosnia Serb Army (Vojska Republika Srpska)
VRSK	Army of the Republic of Serb Krajina
WAN	Wide Area Network
YAT	Yugoslav Airlines
ZOS	Zone of Separation

Introduction

The pilots completed mapping out their routes poring over the 1:50,000 scale maps that were strewn across the planning tables and entered the data in to the navigation computers. Each one programmed in their Way-Points along the route, the IP or Initial Point from which they would make their final approach, and finally designated their targets calculating a final bearing, range and time of flight from the IP to the weapons release point at which they would release their pay load. All the flight information was transferred by data cassette to the on-board navigational computer in each aircraft and once all pre-flight checks had been completed, the pilots slowly and carefully manoeuvred their multi-million dollar weapons platforms out from underneath the relative protection of their Hardened Aircraft Shelters and in to the bright Italian sunshine. As each aircraft emerged from its hide away, the pilots armed their ejector seats, removing the yellow and black striped safety pins securing the release handles between their legs and held them up for the chief ground crew Master Sergeant to see. A quick thumbs-up from the Sergeant followed by a smart salute and each of the F16s purposefully made their way out on to the runway.

Less than two KMs to the West of Sarajevo, the Bosnian Serb Army was dug-in in defensive positions surrounding the town of Hadzici, protecting the Serb population of the town and the ammunitions complexes that were so vital to their war effort. Milenko had been a Naval Officer in the JNA before the war but now he found himself commanding a Bosnian Serb Tank Battalion equipped with the latest Yugoslav version of the Soviet designed T72 Main Battle Tank. He was now a Colonel in the Bosnian Serb Army and with his long black beard, dirty sheepskin waistcoat and cloth cap, looked every bit the sinister and archetypal Chetnik.

Less than twenty minutes after leaving their bases in Southern Italy, the F16s approached their targets deep inside Bosnia. Flying low to avoid Serb anti-aircraft batteries, the aircraft each turned at their respective IP and made to execute their final 'approach to target.' The attack was to be NATO's first ever use of force outside of its own borders and was being made in retaliation against the Serbs for their continuing violations of the ceasefire agreement not to bombard Sarajevo. Within seconds of leaving their IPs, the F16s were screeching low over their targets releasing their deadly payload aimed directly at Milenko's positions and the Bosnian Serb Army just below them.

Several bombs had found their targets and the sound of huge explosions briefly muffled the screech of the jets loitering overhead seeking out new targets before making another attack run on top of Milenko's hapless troops. Smoke was now pouring out of the ammunition depot immediately behind him as he screamed to make his orders heard above the deafening commotion of battle. Milenko was frantic to get some return fire going in the other direction as the Americans had had it all their way so far, but no sooner had he organised his troops, than the F16s departed leaving the Serb positions surrounding Hadzici a smouldering ruin.

Milenko looked at me for quite a long time before speaking. When he did, all he could muster was, 'Fucking Americans.' He was clearly moved and very emotional, he had tears in his eyes as he stared transfixed at the destruction in front of him. He drained his beer before passing me another can and then opened a new one for himself. We were sat together on his sofa in Trebinje, a hard-line nationalist stronghold in the mountainous Southeast of the country bordering Montenegro and Croatia. It was quite bizarre to sit here with him now watching a videotape of a Serb Radio-Television documentary of the war and to watch him and his men get the shit kicked out of them by 'my own' pilots. The attack had been part of a much larger effort that day by ninety NATO aircraft, which struck Bosnian Serb targets in and around Sarajevo. It had taken place on 5th September 1995, when I had been in the relative safety of Montenegro before the war had finally been brought to a close. It was now October 2000, and the beard, uniform, sheepskin, and the M70-AKM 'Kalashnikov' assault rifle had all gone. Indeed Milenko now worked for the international community as an elections officer in the municipality's Political Resource Centre and I was working with him helping the Municipal Elections Commission stage the latest in a series of democratic political elections at national and presidential level. But this story is not about those elections, it is about the war, how it was brought to an end and moreover it is about the efforts of ordinary people from around the world who devoted, and in some cases lost their lives in the service of others trying to rebuild a country ravaged by fours years of war. This is not the story of a senior diplomat or politician, nor is it the story of an Army General. It is the everyday story of an ordinary person's efforts to better the lives of four and a half million Bosnians.

PART ONE

THE INTERNATIONAL CONFERENCE ON THE FORMER YUGOSLAVIA (ICFY): JUNE 1995 - FEBRUARY 1996

1

The Background

The war in Bosnia[1] was a modern human tragedy without comparison, it was the most brutal and savage war in Europe since the end of the Third Reich and many of the consequences remain extant today. There was the wholesale destruction of property, industry, basic infrastructure and the total collapse of the social, economic and political systems, albeit these were already outdated before their destruction reflecting as they did, old communist doctrine. In addition there was the massive displacement of peoples both within and out of the country and the widespread genocide of whole sections of the population. But the war in Bosnia was not the only war fought in the Former Yugoslavia during the last decade, it was in fact only one of four[2] wars fought during the 1990s that saw the wholesale disintegration of Yugoslavia. Moreover, war was not new to Yugoslavia, as the area had been engulfed by conflict on three previous occasions[3] during the last century.

These four most recent wars were incredibly complex as they were fought for political, religious, economic, ethnic and historical reasons. Some say that from an historical point of view, these wars were inevitable and that the war in Bosnia was a continuation of age old religious animosities and ancient ethnic hatreds which Tito had kept in check, but which gave way to violence following his death. This is an overly simplistic view that many commentators promote, but which ignores centuries of peaceful cohabitation. Any animosities that did arise did so largely in and after the First World War and during the four years of fighting during the Second World War.[4]

A detailed history of Yugoslavia, covering the migration of the Illyrians, Vlachs and other Slavonic tribes and the rivalries that existed between the two opposing empires of the time, the Ottoman and the Austro-Hungarian Empires, is beyond the scope of this book. Nevertheless some background is helpful. The area of Former Yugoslavia lies on an historic fault line, not only between these two great empires, but also between three of the world's great religions; namely Christianity, Islam and Orthodoxy. To understand the conflict that exists between the different ethnic groups and their religions one must go back to 1389, to the Battle of Kosovo Polje – the Field of Blackbirds, one of the largest battles ever fought in medieval Europe. Here a Serbian Christian Army tried in vain to block the northward advance of the invading Ottoman Turks. On the 28 June 1389 both Armies joined battle. Losses on both sides were appalling and the outcome inconclusive although the Serbs never fully recovered and the battle spelt the end of the once powerful Serbian Empire of the time. It took the Turks another seventy years before they occupied the land they'd fought for. After the battle, legend has it that blackbirds tore at the corpses for weeks. Among the dead were both leaders. Monuments to each leader, Sultan Murad I and Serbian Prince Lzar stand near the hamlet of Gazimestan in Kosovo, Southern Serbia and both the date and the battleground remain sacred in Serb history. The Turks went on to conquer significant parts of the Balkans establishing Islamic law and spreading the Islamic faith throughout their Sandzaks.[5] When the Turks grudgingly withdrew towards Constantinople after severe losses inflicted by the Serbs and Montenegrins during the Balkan Wars of 1912-13, their five hundred year rule in South Eastern Europe left a cultural and economic rift across what later became Yugoslavia. The victorious Serbs, who had nearly doubled their territory, believed in the ideal of Pan-Serb Unity and longed to unite all ethnic Serbs in one nation state where ever they currently lived. To this end they had designs on the territories of Bosnia i Hercegovina with its large Bosnian Serb population. In fact there is little to support the notion that the 'Serbs' in Bosnia are indeed from the same ethnic origins. For sure there were numerous periods of migration between Serbia and its neighbour, Bosnia; but Bosnia's Serbs do not have the same tribal ancestry as Serbia's Serbs. Indeed the main link between the two peoples is the Orthodox religion, which remains common to both. The same can be said for the Bosnian Croats whose main link with proper ethnic Croats remains the Catholic faith and not tribal and ethnic ancestry. In fact all the peoples of Bosnia have common roots and any identification with nations outside of Bosnia are purely modern and artificial.

> 'The Turks had in fact used a word meaning 'Bosnians' (bosnaklar) to refer to all those who lived in Bosnia; but in Serbo-Croat the only people who had traditionally called themselves 'Bosnians' were the Bosnian Muslims. The Catholics had referred to themselves as 'krscani,' a word for 'Christians' and the Orthodox had called themselves 'Vlasi' – Vlachs, or 'hriscani,' another word for 'Christian.' ...... during the Ottoman centuries there were separate religious identities in

Bosnia, and those identities could indeed have political implications: many Bosnian Catholics had looked to the lands beyond
the Croatian and Dalmatian border for support or even liberation. But that was a matter of religion not nationhood........ Only
in the mid-nineteenth century at the earliest did the modern idea
of nationhood begin to spread from Croatia and Serbia to the
Catholics and Orthodox of Bosnia. Of the three basic criteria by
which the Croat and Serb Nations established themselves during
this period – history, language and religion – only religion could
apply in Bosnia, a country which had its own separate history
and in which the contours of the linguistic map cut across all religious boundaries.'[6]

Nevertheless despite these tenuous links, the myth of Pan-Serb unity
remains central to Serb culture and mindset and has been a central cause of
numerous conflicts. The Serbs however, were unable to capitalise elsewhere
on their 1912-13 victories against the Turks in the Southeast, as Bosnia i
Hercegovina had been annexed by the Austrians in 1908. Instead they
agitated against Habsburg rule, a policy which ultimately led to the assassination of Archduke Franz Ferdinand, the Habsburg heir, shot dead by a
young Bosnian Serb nationalist, Gavrilo Princip, when the Archduke was
visiting his subjects in the Bosnian capital Sarajevo in 1914. Austria responded by invading Serbia, World War I commenced and the rest is history.

During the war, plans were made for a Slavic union. In 1918 following the
end of hostilities and the dissolution of the two great empires, Yugoslavia
was formed as a Kingdom of Serbs, Croats and Slovenes although it
included both Montenegro and Bosnia. But unity did not bring an end to
animosity as the Kingdom was ruled by the Serbian monarch, King
Alexander whose despotism soon alienated both the Croats and the
Slovenes. In 1929 he formally changed the country's name to Yugoslavia, the
'Land of the Southern Slavs.' Following his own assassination in 1934 in
Marseilles, at the hands of a Croatian separatist, the country slowly began to
disintegrate. Throughout World War II, not only did the different ethnic
groups fight against occupation, but they also fought against each other and
against themselves.

'The history of the Second World War in Yugoslavia is the story
of many wars piled one on top of another. First, of course, there
was the initial war conducted by Germany and Italy against
Yugoslavia itself. Some territory was annexed: half of Slovenia by
Germany, the other half of Slovenia and parts of Dalmatia by
Italy, and other areas by Hungary, Bulgaria and Italian controlled Albania. The truncation of Serbia was punitive, but the
main aim was merely subjection and control. Then there was the
continuing Axis war effort against the Allies: for this purpose

Yugoslavia was important for communications, and for the supply of raw materials and labour. There was also the war of the Axis occupiers against Yugoslav resistance movements; this war was always subsidiary to the wider aims of Axis strategy against the Allies. And then there were at least two civil wars. One was a war conducted by Croatian extremists against the Serb population of Croatia and Bosnia, a war of aggression on one side and sometimes indiscriminate retaliation on the other. And finally there was a war between the two main resistance organisations in which the Serbs from those areas enlisted: the Cetniks and the communist Partisans. Both movements, as time went on, gathered in members of other ethnic groups as well. It is not possible to disentangle all these strands when looking at the total number of deaths in Yugoslavia during those terrible four years. But it is clear that at least one million people died, and it is probable that the majority of them were Yugoslavs killed by Yugoslavs.'[7]

The modern Yugoslavia that existed in 1992 at the start of these latest conflicts was formed by a Croatian guerrilla leader called Josep Broz who emerged from the ashes of World War II as Marshall Tito. Tito, who led the Partisans, declared the Socialist Federal Republic of Yugoslavia (SFRY) during the Second World War[8] and became its leader 'for life' afterwards. Tito's Yugoslavia comprised six Republics. Serbia, the largest republic, contained two provinces which Tito gave greater autonomy to in order to prevent Serbian domination of the entire country. These were the Vojvodina in the North of Serbia with a large Hungarian population where seas of yellow wheat sweep northwards from the Sava and Danube Rivers towards the Great Hungarian Plain and secondly Kosovo in the South of Serbia with a large Albanian population. Croatia to the North and West of Yugoslavia, with its tourist industry is mostly known for its fabulous Adriatic coastline, which runs for three thousand eight hundred miles along spectacular rugged and mountainous scenery, formed by the backdrop of the Dinaric Alps. Montenegro, the smallest of the six, is a tiny republic infamous for smuggling and banditry and which for centuries had existed as a theocracy ruled by Bishops. Slovenia in the far North was perhaps the most forward and Western of all the republics and contained most of Yugoslavia's industry due to its closeness to trading partners in Europe. Bosnia, centrally located and populated by a mixture of all ethnic groups was truly multi-cultural and prided itself on religious tolerance. Finally Macedonia in the far South, existed in an area disputed by Greece and is now known officially as FYROM, the Former Yugoslav Republic of Macedonia, in order to appease Greek sensitivities. Perhaps the most telling testament to Tito, is that he was the only man who has ever been able to make these hostile peoples that populated the six republics be civil to one another.

As communism began to wane in Yugoslavia following Tito's death in 1980, the voice of nationalism began to rise. After more than forty years in which tribal and ethnic rivalries were held at bay, a former bank president emerged and tapped these latent passions for his own ends. He didn't find it difficult, for the county had no tradition of democracy and it was often rhetoric rather than the truth that people preferred to believe. Slobodan Milosevic went from obscurity to dictator, to President of Serbia by riding on the back of one issue, an issue which was largely of his creation and which he manipulated and exploited to the full; namely the persecution of minority Serbs in the Southern province of Kosovo. In a county where the press was and remains rigidly controlled, people believed what they were told and he told them that Serbs were being persecuted and their women raped by the Kosovar Albanians. At the same time as he was stirring ethnic tensions in Kosovo, Milosevic was manoeuvring himself up the ladder within the communist party to become the undisputed leader of Serbia. Milosevic hijacked genuine discontent within the country, which was impoverished by government austerity measures and hyperinflation[9] and used them for his own ends. In March 1989 the Serbian Assembly abolished the political autonomy that Tito had given to the two provinces of Kosovo and Vojvodina. With the voting rights from these provinces now his own and assured of Montenegrin support, Milosevic now controlled four out of the eight votes in the Federal government. By reducing Macedonia to puppet status, he was able to do what he wanted with the Federal Constitution and ensure the dominance of Serbia throughout Yugoslavia. On 28 June 1989, several hundred thousand Serbs assembled on the Field of Blackbirds at Gazimestan for the 600th anniversary of the Battle of Kosovo Polje. Milosevic told the crowd – 'After six centuries we are again engaged in battles and quarrels. They are not armed battles, but this can not be excluded yet.' This was a turning point. The spectre of Pan-Serb Unity had been rekindled with all its previous malevolence and enmity. As Milosevic whipped up Serb nationalist fervour, the idea that the other states were better off on their own took root. The disintegration of Yugoslavia had begun.

2

The Disintegration

When people refer to the war in Bosnia, they refer, probably without knowing it, to the last of the three wars waged between June 1991 and November 1995 that saw the break-up of Tito's Socialist Federal Republic of Yugoslavia. The three wars were fought successively in Slovenia, Croatia and then in Bosnia i Hercegovina. Each war was very different. The first lasted only ten days during June 1991 and was essentially a straightforward war of secession. It was successful because Slovenia was essentially allowed to secede and because the vast majority of Slovenia is Slovenian and is thus 'ethnically homogeneous'. The second war, fought in Croatia, was also one of secession. What made it different to the war in Slovenia however, was that although the principal of secession was not disputed, the idea that Croats could control all of the territory of Croatia was. This was because Croatia's population was not largely homogeneous as there were eight hundred thousand Croatian Serbs; ethnic Serbs with Croatian passports, living in Serb dominated regions within the country. These Croatian Serbs were living in two main regions known as the Serb Krajina and Eastern Slavonia. Eastern Slavonia is bounded by the River Danube to the North and borders with Serbia proper in the East. To the South, across the water of the River Sava lies Bosnia. The main city in Eastern Slavonia is Vukovar, a beautiful city which was soon to be laid waste by the advancing Serb led Yugoslav People's Army (JNA).[10] The Krajina however refers to the border areas between Croatia and Bosnia in the Western part of Yugoslavia. The word Krajina derives from the word Kraj, which means 'end'. The Krajina marks the end or rather the extent to which the Ottoman Empire existed in Europe for five centuries and it marks the actual fault line where Habsburg fought Ottoman and defended Christendom from the invading Muslim armies. During this period of confrontation, parts of Croatia came under direct Hungarian rule and the dangerous border areas of the Krajina largely became populated by volunteer Serb militias who fought for the Austro-Hungarian Empire against the Turks in exchange for land rights. In 1991, the descendants of these Serb Militias wanted to become part of a new resurgent Serbia and did not want to become an ethnic minority within an independent Croatia. This was all part of Milosevic's grand strategy of uniting all the Serbs in Croatia, and ultimately in Bosnia as well, with Serbia itself. Clearly this was something that Croatia could never allow, not just from a point of principle, but also from an economic imperative. Croatia's economic prosperity was heavily dependent on tourism. The main supply route between the tourist areas on the Dalmatian Coast and the Croatian capital Zagreb, was the railway line that ran through the Serb controlled fortress town of Knin. Croatia simply could not allow Knin to fall outside of her control, yet as the regime embarked on more and more acts of ethnic discrimination against their minority ethnic Serb population, that is precisely what happened. Serbs in Knin started the war in Croatia. It started with logs being laid across the entrances to villages as Serbs barricaded themselves in to protect themselves from the Croatian police and municipal authorities. In Serb folklore, these early days are recalled as the 'war of logs,' but such actions soon escalated into war proper. War erupted in June 1991 following the Croatian declaration of independence. It lasted six months before the first cease fire, by which time one third of Croatia, namely Eastern Slavonia and the Krajina, lay in Serb hands.[11] These two areas were later proclaimed by the Croatian Serbs as autonomous republics and became known collectively as the Republic of Serb Krajina (RSK). To secure their gains, the Croatian Serbs even established their own Army, the VRSK, to defend themselves from the fledgling Croatian Army (Hv)[12] following the departure of the JNA which had actively assisted them in defeating the Croats. Meanwhile Milosevic's grand design was to link these two areas of Croatia together and then to join them to Serbia proper by carving out a swathe of land running through Northern Bosnia, a republic both he and Croatia's President Tudjman, had in their sights. At the beginning of 1992, the United Nations (UN) moved in to the Former Yugoslavia to keep the peace. They deployed into Croatia, not Bosnia and conducted operations in four UN Sectors known as Sectors North, South, East and West. UN Sector East covered Eastern Slavonia whilst the other three UN Sectors covered the Krajina. Peace however was short lived. It was only a year before the Croatian Army crossed the Blue UN lines and attacked the Serb controlled areas in January 1993. Limited, set objectives were achieved, but the stalemate was to continue until the autumn of 1995, when the Croats launched two offensives known as 'Storm' and 'Flash' which completely over ran the UN positions and largely ousted the Croatian Serbs from their homelands in Croatia. At least one hundred and fifty thousand refugees crossed in to Serbia and Bosnia where they mostly remain today, both disenfranchised and stateless, as Croatia only now slowly starts to reverse its position on ethnic cleansing. These stateless Croatian Serbs, known by the International Community (IC) as either 'Croatian' or 'Krajina Serbs' will crop up throughout this account of the conflict in Bosnia, as they remain a key factor in the overall equation. Long lasting peace in Bosnia will never be achieved without addressing the issue of the Krajina Serbs from Croatia.

The third war was fought in Bosnia and started in 1992, during the pause in the second war. Unlike the two previous wars, it was not a straightforward war of secession by a single Bosnian people. This was because historically, the people of Bosnia never regarded themselves as a single nation although they all shared a common history and language, and before the arrival of Christianity to the region, one could also argue that they all shared a common religion, albeit a religion based on tribal and pagan beliefs. Instead, the people of Bosnia chose to identify with the religions of their neighbours, which they gradually adopted, and to refer to themselves as either being of Serb or Croatian decent, something which simply was not true. Both these groups then chose to believe that under Ottoman rule, many of their ethnic group, often referred to as the 'weaker' element, were converted to the Muslim faith. True, Catholics and Orthodox in Bosnia were converted to the Muslim faith, but this was a religious conversion and does not negate the fact that we are still talking about a singular Bosnian people, now practising three different religions. Yet traditionally it is only the Muslims of Bosnia who have called themselves Bosniaks with both the Orthodox and Catholic believers referring to themselves as Serbs and Croats respectively. Ironically this concept of Bosnia containing three different ethnic groups rather than just one with three religions, was reinforced by Tito, when in passing the new Constitution in 1974,[13] he granted 'Nation' status to Bosnia's Muslim population. Consequently the war in Bosnia was not about the self-determination of a single national group but was more about the conflicting views of three so called 'national' groups, at a time when the whole of Yugoslavia was breaking up.[14]

Bosnia had supported both Slovenia and Croatia in their quest to change the previous Federal structure to a far looser confederation, but had not supported their full independence, as their succession would have left her, along with Macedonia, under Serb dominance. Now that both Slovenia and Croatia had left the Federation, Bosnia had little choice but to follow suit, unfortunately such action did not fit in with Milosevic's plans. To add further complication to an already complex situation, the war that was to ensue in Bosnia was not wholly the result of internal conflict between these three groups and so one cannot simply refer to it as a civil war either. Bosnia was divided from within as a result of Milosevic's systematic plan to unite the Serbs. The tactics used by the Bosnian Serb leader, Radovan Karadzic, mirrored those employed by Milosevic in Croatia; – the setting up of autonomous regions, the arming of the Serb population, non-stop propaganda, staged managed local incidents and the request for JNA protection; – to create the tensions and conditions that led to war. When war finally broke out, it wasn't as the vagaries of the western press so often put it, that "fighting had broken out between the warring factions," but rather that Bosnia had been systematically dismantled and then invaded by a third country – Yugoslavia. This was all part of Milosevic's plan yet the point seems to have been missed by so many commentators and politicians alike, that the war in Bosnia was not a civil war; Bosnia had been invaded.

On 14 October 1991, Bosnia declared her independence, and on 6 April 1992, the then European Economic Community (EEC), decided to recognise that independence marking Bosnia's first appearance as an independent state since 1463. Many commentators remarked that Bosnia could never remain a viable state, since it contained three ethnic groups and that history had shown that Bosnia could only exist as part of a larger whole. In this sense, they argue that Bosnia had brought the war on itself by insisting on her independence. The first claim implies that only nation-states are viable states, in which case most of the one hundred and eighty odd nations of the UN must be considered nonviable. The second claim misses the point. Bosnia was never kept in check by a larger external power to prevent it destroying itself from within. What had endangered Bosnia were never genuine internal tensions, but the aspirations of neighbouring and occupying states. Those earlier conflicts which had erupted in Bosnia's history were largely a result of economic strife between landowners and peasants, and the so called historical tradition of inter-ethnic conflict, was newly inspired by Serbia and Croatia's desire to persuade the Orthodox and Catholic Bosnians that they should think of themselves as Serbs and Croats. With the recognition of Bosnia's independence, Serbia had become yet another external power attempting to manipulate Bosnian internal tensions for its own ends. When Milosevic ordered the JNA into Bosnia in support of the Bosnian Serbs, he was acting to complete the carve up and to realise his aim of Pan-Serb unity. Milosevic's pretext that the JNA was merely acting to defend the Federation lacks plausibility and when Serbia and Montenegro decided on 27 April 1992, to form a new country, the Federal Republic of Yugoslavia (FRY),[15] the pretence was over. Milosevic had to rethink his strategy, as he could no longer pretend that the JNA was simply acting to maintain the integrity of a county that no longer existed. The JNA was now very much a foreign army in occupation of whole sections of Bosnia. Milosevic's solution came in early May, when he announced that he would withdraw the JNA but in doing so he would release all those soldiers who were citizens of Bosnia. Those who were Bosnian Serb would simply be transferred to the Bosnian Serb Army (BSA) along with all their equipment and supplies and placed under the command of General Ratko Mladic who was appointed personally by Milosevic. The war began in earnest.[16]

Numerous attempts were made by various mediators to broker a peace. In August 1992, the International Conference on the Former Yugoslavia (ICFY) was set up by the IC to focus world attention on Bosnia and to help efforts to reach a settlement. With its Headquarters (HQ) in the UN Palais des Nations in Geneva, it was co-chaired by the UN Secretary General

(UNSG) and the Head of State of the county holding the European Presidency and its activities were supervised by a steering committee co-chaired by their representatives. The cause of peace attracted many former statesmen to the ICFY Mission including such personalities as the former Swedish Prime Minister Carl Bildt, Thorvald Stoltenberg, Lord Owen and Cyrus Vance. Pressure was brought to bear on the FRY President, Slobodan Milosevic to stop supporting the Bosnian Serbs and to withdraw the JNA. The UN first refused to recognise the FRY and to grant it Yugoslavia's seat at the UN. Sanctions were then applied to Serbia & Montenegro, and in surrounding countries, SAMCOM[17] teams were deployed to implement these measures by ensuring that no proscribed trade took place.

By the middle of 1994, the sanctions against the FRY were biting and political divisions were emerging between Milosevic and the Bosnian Serb leader, Radovan Karadzic. As the FRY was being bought to its knees, Milosevic agreed to cut support to the Bosnian Serb Republic in return for a limited lifting of sanctions.[18] Despite these improvements, the FRY would remain politically and economically isolated and the SAMCOM teams in place in case of serious violations, which might necessitate the re-imposition of the previous measures. In order to verify his stated intent to stop all support to the Bosnian Serbs, Milosevic 'invited' the IC to establish a Border Monitor Mission (BMM) in the FRY to ensure that these supply lines were cut and remained so. By the beginning of 1995, the new teams known as the ICFY Border Monitor Mission or simply as 'ICFY' were in place along the whole border between the Bosnian Serb Republic and the FRY. Geographically the River Drina marks this border and so the mission to cut the supply lines between the FRY and the Bosnian Serb Republic became known colloquially as the 'Drina Sanctions'.

At the same time as the initial ICFY teams were arriving in theatre, I was looking for something worthwhile to do. I'd spent the last fifteen years in the Army serving for the most part with the 1st Battalion, The Parachute Regiment. I'd ended my career in Berlin as a Staff Officer working in the Joint Intelligence Staff and was finding normal work in a suit and tie to be utterly unbearable and pointless. My greatest fear was having a grandchild sat on my knee and being asked what I'd done with my life. Up until the age of thirty-four the answer would have been fine, but since leaving the Army I had achieved little unless of course one considers obtaining a company car and a nice monthly salary to be an achievement. The Officers' Association, which is run by the Royal British Legion, is a font of information on employment opportunities open to retired military officers from all three services. The Services Employment Network does a similar job for the enlisted ranks and both provide an excellent service to those looking for mainstream and off beat opportunities. In my case I obtained the name of the desk officer in the Foreign and Commonwealth Office (FCO) who regularly trawled the Officers' Association for suitable people to staff their operation in Yugoslavia with the European Community Monitor Mission

(ECMM). It seemed to me that obtaining some sort of post with the FCO out in Yugoslavia would fulfil my need to do something worthwhile. After all, what could be more rewarding and exciting, than helping to stop a war and all the inherent suffering that war brought. After submitting my application, I was short-listed to attend an interview with the Eastern Adriatic Unit (EAU) at the FCO in London. The selection procedure was demanding and the interview board, which consisted of two FCO officers and an Intelligence Corps officer from the Defence Debriefing Team (DDT), quite gruelling. Thankfully I was well prepared having obtained and swotted up beforehand on lots of briefing documents and articles about the conflict. Although primarily concerned with the ECMM operation, the EAU was now running the UK end of the ICFY operation and were keen to place as many suitable 'Brits' in to theatre as soon as possible. Within hours of arriving home from the interview, I got a telephone call telling me that I'd been successful at interview and two days after that another call asking me to deploy immediately. It was all a bit of a blur really. It took just over two weeks from flash to bang, from making an application to sitting on a YAT[19] 737 on the flight to Belgrade.

3

Belgrade

On 19 June 1995, as part of the UK Foreign and Commonwealth Office Delegation to ICFY, I arrived in Belgrade, the Serbian capital at the start of my first mission in the Former Yugoslavia. Little did I know at that stage, that I'd end up staying in theatre for over three years, work in three different missions and play a more than significant part, not only in stopping the war but in building the peace. I'd been in some pretty unsavoury places in my time, especially with the Paras. But this was the first time that I was going anywhere hostile as an individual – even when working as an intelligence officer, we used to work in pairs in case anything went wrong. That was not to say that I wasn't prepared, just that it was a bit unusual, although I have to add, I also felt a little uncomfortable. I was already upset from having left my family behind. My wife Allison was fairly used to me disappearing at frequent intervals but my two small children, Thomas who was five and Harriet who was three, were not used to me going away although thankfully the significance of where I was going to, had not yet registered with them. As the aircraft approached Belgrade airport I had butterflies in my stomach. I had no idea what to expect other than the picture which one drew from the press and general media coverage of the war and from the short briefing I'd received at the FCO from Phil Figgins, a retired Royal Marine officer who had completed one tour with ICFY already. I'd operated in Eastern Europe before and knew what a communist state, with its military, police and security apparatus, was like. As a member of ICFY, I would eventually have diplomatic immunity to protect me from the excesses that such a state often dispenses on its own people. Unfortunately, I wouldn't get the immunity until I'd been issued with my ICFY ID Card following my arrival at the Mission HQ and, unlike other internationals, Her Majesty's Government didn't concern itself with issuing us with proper British Diplomatic Passports. Just to add to the apprehension, I didn't even have a

Yugoslavian visa. The brief had been to, 'Just get out there' and that it would, 'all be sorted out on arrival.' Its bad coming back in to a UK airport, wondering whether the taxi you ordered so long ago would be there waiting for you. But to arrive in a foreign airport in a communist 'police state,' when there was a war going on in the neighbouring country and to do so without a visa, is quite nerve racking. As I walked through the concourse towards the customs booths, my eyes were fixed on several Serbian police officers that were checking passengers' documentation. They all wore the traditional Serbian militia uniform of camouflage blue – almost purple, and black. All brandished weapons. What was I to say to them, how did I explain that I didn't really need a visa, did they speak English? To my utter relief, at the bottom of the stairs leading to the check point, stood Bisa, affectionately known throughout the Mission as 'Bisa the Visa'. Bisa, like most Yugoslavian women in their twenties, was tall, slim, extremely attractive and dressed very elegantly. Her most important attribute however, was that she was carrying a board with my name on it.

Processing through the airport took several minutes, infinitely quicker than processing through London Heathrow. Bisa had been meeting people off planes for several months now and all the authorities knew her and what the incessant stream of foreigners were doing coming to Belgrade. We had no difficulties and soon I'd boarded a car for the trip down the motorway in to Belgrade, some thirty minutes away to the East. Belgrade is the largest Serbian City in the world, the 'second biggest' being Chicago in the United States. The city was established on the confluence of the Sava and Danube Rivers on the site of an ancient stronghold. The name Belgrade means white fortress and a medieval citadel, the Kalemegdan still stands today. From the third century BC to the seventh century AD, Belgrade was fought over and occupied successively by Celts, Romans, Huns, Sarmatians and Goths. It has also fallen to the Byzantines, the Franks and the Bulgars. Throughout the Middle Ages, the city continued to be fought over due to its important position on the trade route between Constantinople and Vienna and was occupied by Greeks, Magyars and Turks. Austrian troops twice held the city during World War I and German troops occupied it throughout most of the Second World War. Today, modern Belgrade is a sprawling city, still retaining much of its history and character in the old town on the East Bank of the Sava. Novi Beograd – New Belgrade – with its modern hotel complexes and the famous Sava Shopping Centre, was sprouting up on the West Bank. As we drove through Novi Beograd on our way to the Mission HQ in the Hotel Hyatt Regency, we passed through the residential areas of Belgrade where normal Serbs lived huddled together in their communist flats in row after row of drab tower blocks. It looked as if nothing was finished, an image projected in part by neglect and squalor, and in part by the fact that the international sanctions were biting hard and construction work had largely stopped. Street vendors stood on every street corner. Some were in orange coloured kiosks about the size of Dr Who's Tardis. Many were just stood around with their wears, usually cigarettes, on the floor at their feet. By far the biggest trade was in petrol. For some reason this seemed sinister. Perhaps it was the fact that every corner seemed to sprout a clapped out Lada or Zastava[20] with dirty plastic bottles of siphoned petrol on their roofs and bonnets, or perhaps it was the sight of unkempt grown men lurking in the shadows plying the black market or 'grey economy' as it was known locally. At the time I remember thinking how glad I was to be in the car and not on the streets, but as time progressed, my fear; undoubtedly born from American TV images of gangs hanging around crime torn city streets; was replaced by empathy for a population reduced to such activities by world sanctions. It was after all, normal Serbs who were being punished for their leader's actions. Whilst one could argue that a leader in a democracy is accountable to his people and therefore the blame (and punishment) for wrong doing must be shared, one starts to question whether Serbia's population, constantly being fed false information by a controlled press, had the inclination let alone the means to replace their leader. Against this backdrop of dreariness, the Hyatt Regency seemed quite opulent and would not have been out of place in London, Paris or any other West European city. It just looked out of place in Belgrade. It stood alongside the Hotel Intercontinental, which similarly stuck out like a sore thumb. Most of the area surrounding these two hotels was a building site but without workers and without materials. Inside the Hyatt, the Mission completely occupied both the fifth and sixth floors. The former was used as office space whilst the latter was used as accommodation space, either for the permanent HQ Staff or for transiting Mission personnel like me. Armed bodyguards dressed in smartly pressed dark suits permanently controlled access to either floor. It was all very efficient and functional and whilst it appeared at first to be slightly ostentatious, it was probably the only workable solution as Belgrade simply didn't offer an abundance of alternative office space nor 'secure' private living accommodation. The Hyatt hotel chain was struggling to maintain its presence in Belgrade after such a huge capital investment in the building. They needed guests and were keen to offer competitive rates to the Mission in return for the block bookings of the two floors. Without us they would not have survived for long. In return, the Mission had secure office and living accommodation with the benefit of having all of its people altogether under one roof in case they needed to get out in a hurry. Having been dropped off by Bisa, I was met by Tim Stanning, an ex Royal Navy helicopter pilot who was the 'senior' member of the British Delegation by virtue of his time in theatre and current job in the mission rather than by any other criteria. Tim had previously served with the ECMM in Bosnia and knew the score. His expertise was being put to good use as ICFY's Senior Operations Officer. It was Tim's job to brief me on not just the British requirements of the Mission but on all the operational aspects as well.

I was to spend three days in Belgrade, slightly longer than normal due to difficulties in obtaining internal flights and some indecision as to where I was going to go. Having been issued with my ID Card at the American Embassy, my passport was sent off to have a three-month multiple entry and exit visa stamped in it. Normally Yugoslavian Visas were valid for only one month and for only one trip. We were to get the more flexible versions thus allowing us to go home on leave and to return later on. We also got a paper from the Federal Customs Bureau Director Mihalj Kertes, saying that we were exempt from the currency restrictions which stopped normal travellers from leaving Yugoslavia with foreign, i.e. their own, currency. Tim also took me to the British Embassy in the old part of Belgrade so that I could book in and pick up some allowances towards in-theatre expenses. The signing in book was amusing. Just in front of where I put my own signature was that of Ian Mcleod, one of my first bosses in the Paras over twelve years ago. It's a small world and Yugoslavia was to prove that to be the case more than once and in some quite bizarre ways. With the normal welcome, administrative and personnel briefings out of the way, the remaining briefings centred on the Mission's organisation, role, deployment and tasks with some formal albeit brief training on the specialist communications equipment which we were to use.

The Mission contained about two hundred international 'observers' in total, quite a small number considering the length of the border that needed to be sealed. The Federal Republic's self-imposed embargo on the Bosnia Serb Republic had managed to get the UN to agree to an initial one hundred-day suspension of sanctions on sporting and cultural links, international flights in to Belgrade airport and the use of the Bar-Bari ferry.[21] In return the FRY had agreed to the closure of its border with Bosnia to all goods except foodstuffs, medical supplies and clothing needed for essential humanitarian purposes. The Mission's role was to monitor the effectiveness of the border closure and to report its findings to the co-chairmen of ICFY, Lord Owen and Thorvald Stoltenberg, who would in turn report to the UN Security Council every thirty days, on whether the border was closed. If at any time the border was not closed, then full sanctions would be re-imposed; there was no provision under the existing UN Security Council Resolution to have sanctions lifted completely. After the first one hundred-day suspension had elapsed, the UN had decided that since there had been no serious violations of the embargo, the suspension of sanctions could continue for a second period of one hundred days. This pattern had been repeated into 1995, and the ICFY Mission continued to observe the agreement. Apart from the political, command and administrative functions of the HQs, there were four main areas of work that the Mission conducted in the field to achieve its aim. Essentially these involved observing and checking all vehicles at recognised Border Crossing Points (BCPs); observing the loading and sealing of heavy goods vehicles going in to Bosnia from Belgrade and from Niksic in Montenegro; observing the loading and sealing of trains from Serbia into Bosnia and verifying that all other potential crossing points were sealed and not in use. For operational purposes, the

Mission was divided up into five sectors. 'Sector Belgrade' was co-located with the HQ in the Hyatt and was responsible for checking heavy goods traffic and humanitarian convoys alongside FRY customs officials. 'Sector Alpha' was the most Northerly sector with its Sector HQ based in Loznica. The sector covered several recognised crossing sites including those at Mali Zvornik and at Sremska Raca near the Croatian border. To the South of Alpha was 'Sector Bajina Basta.' Originally the area that this sector now covered, was an integral part of the next sector, 'Sector Bravo,' but the area had proved too large to control and the sector had been split up. Bajina Basta was not only concerned with observing recognised BCPs but also with observing and sealing trains departing from the main railway station at Uzice. 'Sector Bravo' had its HQ in Priboj and was the last sector in Serbia covering five recognised BCPs. The final sector was 'Sector Charlie' whose Area of Responsibility (AoR) covered all of Montenegro and extended to the sea at Herceg Novi. Sector Charlie had its HQ in Niksic, a town described by Misha Glenny as, '... a miserable industrial wasteland in northern Montenegro, and fabled as one of the most primitive and violent towns in Yugoslavia.'[22] I'd read Glenny's book before starting the Mission and also knew from the Foreign Office briefings that one of the sectors was based in the town. Sitting in the luxury of the Hyatt and being told that everything they said about Niksic was true – and much worse, was not reassuring. Only a day in to my Mission and I'd already picked up vibes that Sector Charlie was definitely not the place to be sent. All other sectors allowed their teams to live amongst the local community in nearby rented accommodation that individuals negotiated and paid for themselves. In Sector Charlie, all Mission members including the Serb drivers and interpreters lived under one roof in the local state owned hotel for their own protection. Rumour was rife about Montenegro; about how tall the people were, how violent and primitive their culture was and how there was constant gunfire and explosions with at least two murders a night in Niksic. All through my military career I'd been given some of the worst jobs, the ones that nobody else wanted, very few understood and nobody thanked you for, but which were actually central to operations. Somehow, as I listened to all these stories, I just knew where I was going to be sent.

4

Sector Charlie: Niksic, Montenegro

The flight from Belgrade to Podgorica, the capital of Montenegro took only forty minutes. There were only two flights a day, one very early in the morning and the other in the early evening, I was on the latter. I'd spent my third day in Belgrade trying not to think too much about where I was going and had been out and about sightseeing. I'd been up to the fortress of Kalemegdan and I'd taken some photos of the River Sava with all the boats moored up along the pathway on the West Bank – not going anywhere – now exclusive restaurants and night clubs. But the view from the window of the twin turbo-prop YAT aircraft which was taking me South to Crna Gora – Serbo-Croat for Montenegro, was breathtaking. As we flew over Lake Scutari which marks part of the border between Montenegro and Albania, the sun was just setting and snow was still visible on the highest mountain tops. The orange hew from the dimming sun glistened on the waters of the lake far below and was reflected in the colours of the mountain ranges. This was a spectacular countryside, rugged and largely unspoilt where man was still at the mercy of the elements. As the plane banked for its final approach, I caught sight of Podgorica itself lying in the long flat plain which extended Northwest from the lake, through the city and up towards Niksic, my ultimate destination. This small area, visible almost in its entirety, was one of only a handful of fertile patches of land in Montenegro on which it was possible to cultivate anything. In this case, the lowlands surrounding Podgorica were almost totally given over to vineyards. Montenegro makes some of the best wines that you can find anywhere in the Former Yugoslavia and they are all from these vineyards. In Serbo-Croat, if you were to ask for a red wine – Crven Vino, you would be understood to have wanted a rosé. To get a true red wine you have to ask for a 'black wine' – Crno Vino. These vineyards produced two excellent 'black' wines; a rather nice Merlot and a very tasteful local variety called 'Vranac.'

In addition, they produced a very good white variety known as 'Krstac.' During the communist era of the SFRY, Podgorica had been re-named Titograd[23]. It had now reverted back to its original name but the legacy of the period still remained. As the plane came to a halt on the tarmac, the name TITOGRAD was clearly visible on the terminal building, welcoming visitors to this country's capital. The fact that no one had bothered to change the name, summed the place up to a 'T.' The building was a dilapidated single story concrete affair of the sort that film directors search for when trying to depict some fictitious tin-pot banana republic. Unfortunately this was not a film set, it was for real and the rows of Russian MI-8 'Hip' helicopters, and MIG 21 'Fish Bed' fighters did much to reinforce my first impressions of a banana republic. As we sauntered across the pan towards the terminal, I also caught sight of an Anglo-French Gazelle helicopter and several ground attack fighters that looked from a distance like Jaguars. Clearly the Royal Air Force hadn't just popped in for an open day but quite what these aircraft were doing here was a mystery which I later learnt the answer to. The Gazelles were built under license in Yugoslavia by a company called Soko, an arrangement dating back to the days when the West supported Tito's non-aligned status and the Jaguar look-a-likes were a Yugoslav copy called the Orao. The 'Arrivals Terminal' consisted of a narrow corridor, down one side of which was a metal conveyor belt that looked as if it should be conveying sacks of flour or concrete, but certainly not passengers' luggage. After a few minutes, a red agricultural tractor and trailer pulled up by the open door and a man started to bundle cases on to the conveyor. It all looked pretty Micky Mouse and I was desperate to find my contact. Milenko, who had come to pick me up, was affectionately known as 'The Professor.' He was one of only two Montenegrins serving in the Sector, since the rules were that all local staff, that is drivers and interpreters, were not allowed to work where they lived. This rule was simply there to protect them and their families from local recriminations. Milenko however, came from the hills around Scepan Polje, the Sector's Northern most BCP and was widely known and hugely respected. He was as big and as strong as an ox and with his dark complexion and weather beaten face, had an air of authority about him which instantly drew respect. In real life he was a history teacher and as time went by we spent many an evening discussing the local tribal history and customs of his proud nation. The ride to Niksic took an hour and for that whole period I had that horrible feeling in my stomach again. We arrived in the dark, parking the car outside the hotel and leaving it to be guarded by an armed security guard whose diligence ensured that we never lost a vehicle throughout the whole period of the Mission. I was met by Archie, a Brit who had served in the Army as a Officer in a Highland Regiment and who had been in on this Mission from the start. Archie was the DHOS, Deputy Head of Sector, and was really the man who ran the place. After dumping my kit in my room, I went up to the office on the fifth floor for a quick briefing with Archie to cover the

'Ground,' 'Situation' and 'Mission' parts of the standard NATO briefing format before joining those members of the sector who were not deployed, for a mid-summers party. It was a warm welcome and a good start.

'Sector Charlie' was by far the biggest sector in ICFY with an AoR covering the entire territory of Montenegro, which lay in the South of what remained of Yugoslavia. Montenegro itself was a small country covering an area of about 5,300 square miles and with a population of only just over 600,000, sixty-two per cent of whom were ethnic Montenegrin, fifteen per cent Muslims, nine per cent Serbs, seven per cent Albanians and the remaining 7%, 'others.'. At the beginning of the twentieth century its borders were undefined and its status in relation to the Ottoman Empire was unclear. Montenegrins maintain that they were always independent; the Ottomans in contrast, strongly insisted that this area was an integral part of their Empire. For centuries the country was run as a theocracy[24] with a Bishopric in Cetinje[25], the ancient capital which lies to the South of the current capital, Podgorica and in which can still be seen the abandoned embassies from an age gone by. Despite the rule of the bishops and an office of a governor, real authority lay with the tribes that continue to make up Montenegro's population to this day. Loyalty was to the local leadership and to family based groups and despite a central system of (communist-style) government today, little had changed. When both Serb and Croat tribes migrated from the area of modern day Iran and began to settle in the Balkans, they encountered a large Slav population already in place. This substratum of Slavs cannot be broken down into separate sub-ethnic groups but nevertheless it would have consisted of peoples whose ancestors may have originally been Illyrian, Celt or Roman. As Milenko was able to tell me later on, this Celtic connection is still very much alive today, especially in the far North of the country in the region lying along the Tara River Canyon. As the Serbs extended their rule further South, they eventually moved into the territory of 'Duklje' – (Montenegro) where they began to mix with these existing Slav peoples but they never fully assimilated them. To this day, Montenegrins retain their own identity and refute that they are Serbs. By the Middle Ages, the region formed the province of 'Zeta' and was part of the Serbian Kingdom in the Balkans. Throughout this period, local Slav populations were organised on a traditional tribal basis. The hierarchy of tribal rule started with the family, more often than not – an extended family. This concept is fiercely alive today with 'the family' remaining the single most important concept in everyday life. Within the family itself, men dominate in what is very much a patriarchal society. Women will support the family and the home but they play little part in making decisions and their role is very much secondary. By the time a young boy reaches the age of ten, his mother is no longer entitled to tell him what to do, he is now considered an adult male and therefore cannot be directed by a female. Groups of families were then united together as clans and separate clans were united together as tribes or 'plemena.' In Montenegro there were thirty-six such tribes each of which inhabited its own territory known as a zupa, which was ruled by a zupan. Today, modern Montenegrins will still be able to tell you which tribe they belong to. Tribal rivalries still exist as does the concept of the 'blood feud' where it is incumbent on the tribe to exact revenge on another for the killing of one of its own members. This primitive cycle of violence is one reason why even the Serbs remain fearful of their Southern brethren today.

Everyday life in Montenegro has always been harsh. The extreme poverty of the land is due to its mountainous and rugged character with heights from 762 to 2438 metres above sea level and the remaining countryside strewn with rocks and stone with only a few arable regions lying in river valleys, mainly along the Zeta River, on the plain around Lake Scutari and near the town of Cetinje. The most famous peak is Mount Loven (1749m), called the 'Black Mountain' for its basaltic rock, from which the country's name is derived. Since few areas are available for cultivation, much of the economy was traditionally derived from agriculture and small scale animal husbandry concentrating mainly on the raising of small animals like goats and sheep and the production of vegetables, grapes, figs and olives. The pattern remains the same today, supplemented only by the ugly industrial megaliths of modern communist planners and an industrial base concentrating on lumbering and on iron and tobacco processing. Raiding and cattle rustling were an established part of the economy for centuries and, as I was to learn later on, this practice – albeit with different commodities – continues to this day with smuggling and Mafia related activities permeating through all levels of society from the very top, down. Because the land was too poor to support its population, Montenegro was faced with the need to expand. At the beginning of the nineteenth century, the country had no access to the sea and was surrounded by quarrelling Muslim Beys[26] who continued to resist the rule of Constantinople. Whilst the Montenegrins could, to some extent, play between these rival groups, the problem came when Ottoman reform succeeded in uniting these groups raising the sceptre of possible Ottoman occupation. The poverty from within and the constant threats from without had the effect of virtually compelling the Montenegrin tribes into accepting a single authority. Uniting was not easy, apart from a Bishop and a Governor in Cetinje, the 'Central Government' consisted of very little else. Normal functions of state were not conducted. Taxes were not raised, there was no standing army, no system of justice and essentially no administration – everything was administered by the tribes.

Traditionally the dual offices of the Bishop and the Governor were held by the Petrovic and the Radonjic families respectively. The position of Bishop was passed from uncle to nephew since Bishops were required to be celibate[27]. In 1830, when the bishopric passed to Rade, a seventeen-year-old without formal training and who was not yet even a monk, open feuding broke out between the Petrovic and the Radonjic families. Despite claiming that his powers were equal to that of the Bishop, the Governor – Vuk Radonjic was unable to win over the support of the clan chiefs who instead backed the Petrovic family. As a result, the office of the Governor was abolished and the members of the Radonjic family were either killed or banished. Rade Petrovic had thus become the undisputed secular and religious leader of Montenegro. But Rade, who had assumed the title 'Peter II' was never to be remembered for uniting the tribes as he was never fully successful in this aim. Despite heavy Russian subsidies that paid for a centralised administration, he was never able to raise taxes or to raise a standing army. Despite his failed attempts at internal consolidation, Peter carried out an active foreign policy hoping to attain a port on the Adriatic and to push out his borders in the East to Podgorica and in the Northwest to Grahovo. He met with limited success but is best remembered for creating a Senate, opening schools, trying to abolish the blood feud and finally for his writings. Peter also went by the name 'Njegos' and was considered one of the greatest Serbian poets. Concerned mainly with the problems of humanity, Njegos wrote passionately about the Serbian (Montenegrin) past. Buried in a mausoleum overlooking Kotor Bay, his lasting legacy is that the tradition of writing poetry in Montenegro is still very much alive today. I was soon to spend many long evenings sat on the borders of the country drinking rakija[28] and listening to stories and poetry which belied the rough appearance of the storyteller. Something which remains with me to this day is the paradox of how it is possible for such a lawless, primitive and at times exceedingly cruel people, to sit down and discuss poetry and the problems of humanity. Yet there was no dichotomy, no paradox in their minds; they saw life with a single clarity that we no longer can in the West. Life was harsh for these people, yet despite their adversity they retained a code of honour and an integrity centred around their past, their culture and around traditional family values. It was as if the clock had been turned back to Victorian times and I wondered who was better off whilst at the same time remaining fearful that someday 'progress' would destroy all these values too.

Peter died in 1851 and the Bishopric passed to his nephew, Danilo. But Danilo did not want to be a Bishop; he wanted to marry and so in 1852 he secularised the office, separating the church from the state and proclaimed himself a prince. He too had problems in containing the tribes but was able to fend off Ottoman advances albeit with Habsburg assistance. In 1852 a Montenegrin force finally took Grahovo after exploiting a Christian uprising in Hercegovina at the time. Today Grahovo still marks the border between Montenegro and Bosnia, but whilst the significance of this dirty village cum town seems lost in the past, its strategic importance is clear for all to see. The town lies at the Northern tip of a fertile valley which runs Northeast from the coast at Risan on Kotor Bay extending up and into Bosnia running along the spectacular Nudo Valley. The whole area was to be heavily patrolled by ICFY, not just because of its proximity to the Bosnian Serb Republic, but because the valley line was one of only a handful of passable routes between the two countries and, as I was to observe later, one of the hamlets in the valley regularly had a Gazelle helicopter parked outside.

In 1860, Danilo was assassinated and was succeeded by Nicholas I, who was to rule until the end of World War I. Nicholas also conducted an active foreign policy in an attempt to enlarge the Principality and to enable it to feed itself. Heavily reliant on the Russian subsidies, the administration in Cetinje continued, giving rise to the joke that the capital consisted of thirteen foreign consulates and a hotel. Nicholas also had to contend with the fractious tribes and with a war against the Turks who were again attempting to exert their control over the area. This time both Serbia and then later Russia entered the war and the Ottoman attempt to conquer Montenegro failed allowing Nicholas the opportunity to occupy an area of coastline for the first time. In the Treaty of Berlin[29] that followed, Montenegro effectively doubled in size although in return the Principality did have to accept some Habsburg supervision. Despite these territorial gains, the country still could not support itself and most of the population lived in extreme poverty. Whilst an increasingly autocratic Nicholas had proclaimed Montenegro a Kingdom and himself the King in 1910, it was estimated that at least a third of all able working men had to leave the county to find work. Many emigrated to the United States and sent money back to their families, but the stark reality at home was that the country was impoverished and without the means of feeding or clothing its people properly. The Kingdom needed to expand again but with the Habsburgs to the North in the Sandzak and also to the Northwest in Bosnia i Hercegovina, the only direction in which Montenegro could expand, was southwards into Albanian territory. The Turkish revolution of 1908-1909, and the Turko-Italian War of 1911-1912, presented the Balkan states with an opportunity to retaliate against the Turks for their five hundred year occupation of Southeast Europe. In March and May 1912, Serbia and Greece respectively, formed an alliance with Bulgaria. In August, Bulgaria demanded that the Turks grant autonomy to Macedonia and on 8 October, Montenegro declared war on the Ottoman Empire. Ten days later, the Balkan allies entered the war on the side of Montenegro, precipitating the First Balkan War. The Balkan Alliance won a series of decisive victories over the Turks during the next two months, forcing them to relinquish Albania, Macedonia as well as most of their other holdings in Southeast Europe. The Turks sued for an armistice but Greece continued to fight on. Representatives of the belligerents later met with the major European Powers in London to decide terms, but the Turks rejected the demands and the conference failed. In the subsequent fighting, the Turks lost considerable territory to both Greece and Bulgaria before again suing for peace in April 1913. The Treaty of London[30] however, caused considerable friction between the Balkan allies, especially between Serbia and Bulgaria. Serbia had laid claim to an area of Macedonia, which was now held by Bulgaria, and in addition Serbia was resentful for failing to obtain territory along the Adriatic. In June 1913, the Second Balkan War started when Serbia and Greece declared war on Bulgaria. Within two weeks, Montenegro, Rumania and the Ottoman

Empire had also entered the war along side Serbia and Greece. Within a month, Bulgaria requested and received an armistice. By the ensuing peace agreement,[31] Bulgaria lost considerable territory including most of Macedonia to Serbia and Greece. The two Balkan Wars profoundly influenced the course of European history. The immediate effect concerning Montenegro was that the country had almost doubled in size. The wider effects were that the wars created a strong and ambitious Serbia whilst the peace settlements engendered fear and anti Serbian sentiments in the neighbouring Habsburg Empire. The dismantling of the Ottoman Empire and Bulgaria also gave rise to dangerous tensions throughout the whole region, all of which greatly intensified the forces that ultimately led to the First World War.[32]

When World War I was declared, the Kingdom of Montenegro joined its traditional allies, Serbia and Russia, against the Central Powers. However, fears that an Allied victory might lead to territorial adjustments and the end of their dynasty, led Nicholas and his sons to conspire with the Habsburgs. In late 1915, Montenegro was occupied by the Austro-Hungarians but in 1916, Montenegrin patriots met with Serbs, Croats and Slovenes on the Greek island of Corfu and voted to unite in a single Slav kingdom. This pact was endorsed by the Allies and following their victory in 1918, the Kingdom of Serbs, Croats and Slovenes was proclaimed with Montenegro becoming a constituent part and known as the Province of Zeta. The Kingdom was ruled by the Serbian monarch, King Alexander, until his assassination in 1934. In 1929 he formally changed the Kingdom's name to Yugoslavia, the 'land of the Southern Slavs' but the country never became truly united. When Axis troops invaded the Balkan Peninsular in 1941, during World War II, Italian forces occupied much of Montenegro until their capitulation when they were replaced by German troops. In 1945, Yugoslavia became a Socialist Federal Republic under communist rule and Montenegro became one of the six constituent republics. In line with the rise of nationalism during the late 1980s and early 1990s, and with the general break up of Yugoslavia which followed, Montenegro adopted a new constitution in 1990, and established an eighty-five member National Assembly which was empowered to make legislative decisions on the basis of a simple majority vote. Executive power was held by the President who is elected for a four year term. In the 1993 elections, Momir Bulatovic from the Socialist (former communist) party was re-elected president for a further four year term. Bulatovic, a staunch supporter of Milosevic, was still in power when I arrived in 1995, but lost to Milo Djukanovic in the 1997 elections, having been held responsible for bringing his country to ruin through his support of Milosevic and his war aims. Milosevic rewarded Bulatovic for his loyal support by appointing him Federal Prime Minister, a move that Montenegro considers illegal and which has resulted in a major divide between the two Federal partners. In early 1992, after Slovenia, Croatia and Macedonia had all declared their independence from Yugoslavia, a referendum was held in Montenegro to decide its future within the Federation. Two-thirds of the voters chose to remain in the Federation and when Bosnia i Hercegovina declared their independence, Serbia and Montenegro announced on 27 April 1992, the formation of a new country which they called the Federal Republic of Yugoslavia (FRY). However, the international community refused to recognise Serbia and Montenegro as a new country, preferring to call the union by the term 'Rump Yugoslavia,' and denied it Yugoslavia's existing seat at the United Nations. Both Montenegro and Serbia then became actively engaged in the war in Croatia as the JNA fought in support of the Krajina Serbs. At their request, Montenegrin reservists were switched from the Northern front in Slavonia and were instead allowed to push a new front through from the South along the Dalmatian coast where Croat resistance was virtually non existent. Most of these reservists were from Niksic and as they moved up towards Dubrovnik from Herceg Novi on the coast and in from Trebinje in Eastern Hercegovina, they sliced through the Croat defences with ease. The marauding reservists plundered anything and everything. 'Videos, televisions, furniture, jewellery and material goods of all other kinds flooded into Niksic and Titograd where the going price for a brand new video recorder was between fifty and seventy-five German marks.'[33]

Although the Montenegrin reservists withdrew from Croatia and took no overt part in the war in Bosnia, the UN sanctions imposed in 1992, were placed on the whole of the Rump Yugoslavia including Montenegro. When these were scaled back in October 1994, Montenegro – like Serbia, was subject to international review. My job, having arrived in Niksic amongst these primitive and violent people who still held onto their clan based patriarchal and intolerant social system, was to review their intent to remain out of the war in Bosnia. It was to be one of the greatest challenges of my life so far and certainly one of the most enjoyable.

5

Operations

At any one time, there were about one hundred people serving in the Sector. Fifty per cent of these were locally employed staff, that is to say, they were Yugoslavians from Belgrade, with the odd exception like Milenko who was truly local and from Montenegro. The local staff fell into two categories, they were either drivers – all men; provided by the Belgrade authorities and to a man, all ex-police or customs officers. Whilst the argument from Belgrade was that these drivers could also provide us with some level of protection, and indeed most of them did carry a gun, clearly the overriding factor behind their selection was that they provided the Belgrade regime with a set of eyes and ears within the Mission. The other half of the local staff was employed as interpreters, often affectionately known as 'interrupters.' This group of local staff remained distinct from the drivers for several reasons. Firstly they were a mixed group, male and female and they were all significantly younger than their driver colleagues. Secondly, interpreters were selected by an agency in Belgrade and were mostly in their twenties having graduated in English if not several other modern languages as well. None of them had a police or customs background although most of the men had served their conscription with the JNA and several had fought in either Croatia or Bosnia during the JNA intervention there. Whilst it was accepted that all the drivers would be 'de-briefed' by the authorities in Belgrade each time they returned home for a spell of leave, it was not widely assumed that this would be the case with interpreters. Whether this was naïve or not, didn't really matter. ICFY was an open, diplomatic Mission without secrets. If the Belgrade regime was intent on breaking the arms embargo on Bosnia, then the only information it needed about the Mission was its operational patrol programme for the immediate future. This information could never be kept secret for long, but the system that was in place when I arrived could nevertheless have been improved upon. Unfortunately I was unable to

do anything about it for several months, until I was promoted to run operations. The other fifty per cent of the Sector was made up from members
drawn from the whole of the IC. Most 'observers' as we were known, had
'Special Forces' or similar backgrounds, although some were police or
customs officers. In Niksic I was working with people from different ends of
the political and cultural spectrum; at one end – American Special Forces
Colonels and at the other end – Russian KGB, GRU and Spetznaz Colonels.
Without doubt this was one of the most fascinating aspects of the mission,
but it added a further complication to an already complex task. Time and
time again in my dealings with local leaders and politicians, the IC was collectively blamed for this or that but what these interlocutors failed to grasp,
or perhaps chose to ignore, was that the IC was not a single entity where all
its constituent parts were in total agreement. The reality throughout the
whole of the war and afterwards, was that the IC more often than not
remained divided on its policy towards any one problem. In this respect you
could almost rely on the Turks to have an opposite opinion to the Greeks, the
Russians to the Americans and indeed the British to that of the Germans. It
was fascinating to be placed into such an environment, knowing full well
what the British line on Bosnia was, and believing you knew what the
Contact Group[34] position was, but to suddenly find yourself at the sharp end
trying to implement what you thought was a simple consensus agreement,
only to find that each nation had interpreted it in their own way. In Sector
Charlie, the only participating nation that was not represented was Germany.
It was Mission policy that no Germans would be deployed to Montenegro
because of latent historical animosities dating back to the Second World War.
Taking into account the Montenegrin concept of the blood feud, it was considered too dangerous for any German to be deployed to the Sector.
Certainly this was the feeling on the street, our presence was not appreciated
anyway and to add in a factor that compounded an already dangerous situation was not considered to be worth the risk. This policy was later to be
reversed due to constant German pressure to 'face their past.' Thankfully no
one died as a result, but there were some serious consequences initially.
Unlike the policy in the other sectors, all Mission personnel in Sector Charlie
were required to 'live-in.' This meant that all staff in Niksic were accommo-
dated in the state owned Hotel Onogost. Unfortunately, like most if not all
state run enterprises in the Former Yugoslavia at the time, the Onogost was
a desperate place to live. Nicknamed the Hotel Holocaust, it was the only
hotel in Niksic. Built probably in the 1960's, it was a modern concrete tower
block that reminded me of North Howard Street Mill, an old industrial mill
in the centre of Belfast which had been taken over by the Security Forces and
used as a fortified barracks. The hotel was the centre of the Mission in
Montenegro. Our offices were located on the fifth floor, we had a TV room
on the third floor and the most popular location of all, a bar located in Room
501. Of the one hundred staff working in the Sector, most were accommo-
dated throughout the building, providing the hotel and hence the state with

a steady source of foreign income throughout the deployment. In addition we had a small detachment permanently based on the coast at Herceg Novi and at any one time we would have twenty-four people deployed on the border with the Bosnian Serb Republic. Any deployment, whether to the border or as part of the mobile patrol plan, was conducted by a team of four travelling in one car. Each team consisted of a driver, an interpreter and two international staff, one of whom was designated as the team leader. In essence the task of these teams was to ensure that the whole of the border between Montenegro and the Bosnian Serb Republic remained sealed to proscribed goods, yet remained open for humanitarian goods and the normal movement of people. One had to remember that this 'border' was largely transparent and had not physically existed six months earlier. When the Mission first deployed just before Christmas 1994, they had to establish joint customs points on all the main roads between the two countries. These Border Crossing Points were the only points where international traffic was allowed to pass. Because much of Montenegro was impassable due to its mountainous nature, all major routes followed river valleys and this limited the number of possible crossing sites considerably. In total there were only six BCPs in the Sector and all these had to be manned twenty-four hours a day by joint teams consisting of Montenegrin customs officers, ICFY monitors and Montenegrin police officers who also acted as personal protection officers; the latter being quite a joke since the majority of incidents involving shooting or grenade attacks on our positions were either carried out by the police or certainly involved them in some way or another! In addition to these permanent positions, all minor roads and every track crossing the border had to be physically severed. This was accomplished by digging huge ditches or by building stone barricades. All such obstacles were manned by the Yugoslav Army (VJ)[35] and had to be patrolled by 'mobile teams' from the Sector. The fact that these patrols were not continuous was a glaring oversight on the part of the Mission and one that I was not able to do anything about until after my promotion. All operations in Montenegro were extremely difficult. Navigation itself was difficult as the only mapping was based on a 1942 German Wehrmacht issue which had been overlaid – updated – in the 1960s courtesy of American satellite surveillance. Most mountain areas were inaccessible and in the border regions most roads were simply rough dirt tracks which hardly featured on the maps at all. Added to this, we were operating amongst a very hostile population. Politically we had been invited into the FRY by Milosevic in order to verify that his own decision to suspend support for the Bosnian Serbs was being implemented in return for a partial lifting of UN sanctions. In reality, the Montenegrins referred to us all as UNPROFOR[36] and at best held us in contempt for stifling their pre-war smuggling routes into Bosnia, whilst at worst saw us as the real face of the outside world which was perceived to have ganged up on the Serbs, and was now dividing them from their brothers in Bosnia. Prior to 1995 there had been no border and even now it was largely artificial. Families and relatives lived either side of the border and for generations had simply crossed over, walking or riding their carts up and down these same roads. Now, the minor roads were blocked or cratered and 'international customs points' had been established on all major crossings.

The four Northern most BCPs were manned by Mission personnel from Niksic whilst the two Southern most BCPs were manned by personnel from our Herceg Novi detachment. This was done for simple logistic reasons. The length of the border which we had to seal was about two hundred KMs from North to South but there was no single road which ran the length of the border. To get from one crossing site to another, you either had to patrol across country on the rough dirt tracks which tended to parallel limited stretches of the border; the task of our mobile patrols; or you had to travel inland, join a North-South route and then branch off again towards the next BCP. This meant that it could take up to 12 hours just to get from the North of the Sector to the South of the Sector calling at BCPs en-route, and for this reason the job of staffing the sites was split in two. Scepan Polje was where Milenko came from. It was about an hour and thirty minutes drive from Niksic on an excellent road which had previously been the main route to and from Sarajevo. It was also our most Northerly BCP and known simply as BCP-1. The drive to Scepan Polje was always wonderful and the scenery spectacular. The main roads throughout the Former Yugoslavia had been some of the best anywhere in Eastern Europe. I could well remember the state of the roads in East Germany in the early days after the Berlin Wall had come tumbling down and these were infinitely better. The drive took you through the mountains of Northwest Montenegro and followed the line of the River Piva. After about forty minutes one came to the Piva Monastery, a small stone structure parked quite unnaturally in a field. The monastery had been founded in 1575, by the Metropolitan, Savatija Sokolovic and contained some wonderful seventeenth century frescos. Further North, the river had been dammed and widened to form a lake by the small town of Pluzine, which had been newly built as a holiday resort, as the old town now lay at the bottom of the man made lake. Pluzine was not pretty, its population had almost trebled and the holiday flats were now overflowing with refugees fleeing from the war in neighbouring Bosnia. The last forty minutes of the drive were perhaps the most spectacular. The translucent turquoise waters of the River Piva cut ever-deepening gorges through the mountains as the river ran its course northwards towards its confluence with the River Tara. The dam, which had caused the lake to form at Pluzine, was truly a feat of Titoist engineering. Protected at either end by Radar installations it was clearly regarded as a strategic site and you were not allowed to stop and look under any circumstances. Needless to say, we often did and were rewarded by a breathtaking view of the dam wall rising some 600 feet above the valley floor below. The road continued northwards along the same line as the river, cutting through sixty-four unlit and leaking tunnels, often strewn with unseen fallen rocks, before reaching the small village which marked the border. Just before the road ended, it bridged the Piva across a narrow gorge. This was one of my favourite places and I always stopped to look at the waters below. You could parachute off this bridge, and thinking about it made you realise just how insignificant man was when compared to the power of nature. But this was not the largest gorge. The River Tara which joined the Piva at Scepan Polje to form the mighty Drina, ran through the second largest canyon in the world, second only to the Grand Canyon in America. On the Montenegrin side, there were no roads along that stretch of the Tara. If you wanted to see the canyon, you had either to fly or to go white water rafting. That is precisely what people used to do before the war. Scepan Polje was a small hamlet consisting of several farm buildings and two restaurants, both of which used to serve the tourists coming for the white water rafting. Nowadays, they had little trade except to fulfil the needs of the police and customs officers manning the crossing point, the odd bus load of travellers which passed through it and of course, members of the Mission. The BCP itself was located by the biggest of these restaurants situated on a sharp left-handed S-bend which dropped away before curving sharp right towards the wooden bridge that physically marked the border and crossed the Tara. The Bosnian Serb checkpoint was clearly visible on the other side of the bridge. The position was surrounded on all sides by hills that cast shadows on the village by late afternoon even in the summer months. On the Bosnian Serb side, for as far as one could see, was a grizzly reminder of why we were there. All the houses that had previously overlooked the river had been destroyed. These had been Muslim homes before the war, but now they were burnt out shells, abandoned by a fleeing population. I always wanted to see what lay on the other side of the bridge but we were forbidden to cross and in any case it would have been too dangerous. Within a year however, I would be able to satisfy my curiosity and travel from Sarajevo to Niksic to revisit the town and the people that I was just getting to know. What would astound me was that the road on the other side had almost ceased to exist. This may have been the main route to and from Sarajevo, but for the next thirty KMs, the road was nothing more than a dirt track, which at times crumbled down steep drops to the Drina below. Yet scheduled buses constantly used it crammed full of passengers and also heavy trucks laden with humanitarian aid throughout the whole period that I was there. Our own presence in the village was limited to two rather nasty caravans that had been plonked outside the first restaurant. The idea of having two vans was that one served as the accommodation for the two local staff whilst the other served as the accommodation for the two international staff and as the team's office. How this worked in practice was always left up to the team. Often the whole team would cook and eat in the former whilst leaving the other van clear of food because of the need to protect the sensitive communications equipment that was inside. Whatever the arrangements, these were determined by the operational needs and not by the niceties of accommodating males and females in separate vans. Because of the travelling distance from Niksic, the BCP duty at Scepan Polje lasted forty-eight hours, after which the team would recover to Niksic, write their report and sort themselves out before joining the daily collective de-brief at 4,30 pm. The following day they would conduct mobile patrols to bolster up the numbers of the main Mobile Section, and the day after that they would re-deploy back out to the BCP. This cycle continued non stop with the only variety being changes in BCP location or leave, known as Compensatory Time Off (CTO). There were no rest days in Sector Charlie unlike in all the other sectors, a fact that often caused friction between the Sector and the Mission Personnel Officer in Belgrade. For the forty-eight hours that a team manned the BCP, they were essentially on their own. Perhaps a mobile patrol, if operating in the local area, would call in to check all was well – indeed it was Standard Operating Procedure (SOP) that they should do so. But if there were no patrols, then there were no visitors and no one to check that the teams were still OK. Communications were therefore vital, not just for reporting, but for safety purposes. Unfortunately Scepan Polje, like most of our BCPs was too far away from any of our UHF repeater sites to reach the HQ in Niksic. Even if it was close by, which it wasn't, UHF communications would almost certainly have been impossible due to the surrounding hills. The only way to communicate with the outside world was to use a satellite system and at Scepan Polje we had two; a Satphone for voice transmissions and a CAPSAT[37] for data transmissions. Both worked off the International Marine Satellite (communications & navigation) system (INMARSAT). But even this system was not perfect. We had a choice of hitting two satellites; one above the East Atlantic or one above the Indian Ocean. We were supposed to be on the latter but due to the size and proximity of the mountains getting the required angle and line of sight to either of these satellites was not easy. Despite the high technology, communications between Niksic and Scepan Polje was always difficult. Thankfully therefore there were few security incidents at this BCP. This was quite surprising really when one considers that the Bosnian Serb police from the other side of the river always used to come across in to Montenegro and take their rest breaks in one or other of the two café-restaurants. Since Milosevic had voluntarily imposed these sanctions which the Montenegrin police and customs officers with us were enforcing, and which we were ensuring was actually happening, we were largely responsible for the economic plight that was developing just across the border. Yet the Bosnian Serb police officers, by and large acted professionally in their dealings with us. I am not sure what would have happened had we crossed over to their territory, but the only real cause of friction between our two sides was that they insisted on bringing their weapons with them when they came across. Strictly speaking this was a violation of the sanctions agreement but in practice we were mainly concerned with arms supplies going in to Bosnia and not an individual carrying their own personal weapon temporarily out of it. Where it did become an issue, was when one of these officers got too drunk and then decided to play up. With a gun culture prevalent throughout the whole of this society, it was not uncommon for the police to simply let off a burst of automatic gun fire right outside one of our vans, only to find out that they had been shooting at stray cats across the road. Whilst Scepan Polje was designated as an international crossing point and was therefore open for the movement of non-proscribed goods, it was not open twenty-four hours a day. Only one of our six BCPs was permanently open day and night and that was BCP-4, at Vilusi, the nearest location to Niksic. Scepan Polje on the other hand, was closed to traffic during the hours of darkness. In theory this meant that there was no work for the teams to do after dark. In practice however, you still had to ensure that nothing went past and that still required at least one of the two international observers to be awake and visibly up and about the whole time. Since this BCP was located on a sharp S-bend which sloped steeply down to the bridge below, it was not impossible for a vehicle to turn its engine off and simply free-wheel past the check point. If the whole team was inside their vans sleeping, then the chances were that the vehicle would pass undetected. There was also a security consideration here too. Our presence was not endearing us to the local population and especially to those who lived just on the Bosnian Serb side of the border, many of whom crossed through the BCP daily. The police were supposed to protect us, but once the border was 'closed', they would start to drink Rakija and were often in no fit state to do anything other than to cause problems themselves. Unfortunately, at the start of my tour, it was the practice for all the teams on the border to assume that nothing would pass once the border was closed. This was both naïve and lazy. The fact that so many observers were content to operate in that way was understandable though. With no rest days after a BCP deployment, teams were reluctant to 'stag-on' for a twenty-four or forty-eight hour shift, knowing that when they came off duty that they would have to go out again on mobile patrol. In all the other sectors, they had rest days, but in Sector Charlie we could only programme in rest days at the expense of mobile patrols. Nevertheless, with so many ex-military personnel employed within the Mission, teams should have known better, but that does not take into account the varying cultural and political views of the different nationalities. It would be equally naïve to expect a Russian to voluntarily remain vigilant all night when Russia had always been a traditional ally of the Serbs and had financially supported Montenegro for centuries. The Russians simply had no interest in maintaining an around the clock vigil unless they had to. Despite these reasons, the practice was poor and potentially negated all our other efforts. Why bother trying to seal the two hundred KMs of border, all the minor roads and tracks that criss-crossed back and forth, when all the VJ had to do, was to drive a munitions convoy right through a manned BCP at 2,00 am in the morning when everyone was asleep? This practice had to be reversed and I would endeavour to do so when I had the opportunity in the autumn.

Our second BCP was located about two KMs beyond the village of Krstac. Unlike at Scepan Polje, there was absolutely nothing to mark the border, no houses, no café-restaurants, no life! The position had been determined by the VJ and confirmed as the official border by the Mission using a Global Positioning System (GPS) satellite navigation aid, but there was no physical landmark to suggest that this was a proper international border whatsoever. The journey to Krstac also took about one hour thirty minutes and therefore the BCP was also manned on a forty-eight hour shift cycle. Getting to and from the BCP was a feat in itself. By and large it was fine during the summer months, but on more than one occasion in the winter we had to abandon the shift change and leave the team in-situ for seventy-two hours. Individuals were responsible for buying their own food and taking it with them on all their deployments, but in case a team ran into difficulties and had to stay longer than planned, each BCP had ten days emergency rations. These were American Army 'Meals, Ready to Eat' (MRE) and consisted of boil in the bag recipes which were infinitely better than any of the British stuff that I had been brought up on. Unfortunately many of these were eaten by unscrupulous observers who then never reported that the items were missing. Often as not, when it came to a real emergency, vital equipment was found missing. The ride out of Niksic initially followed the same road northwards leading to Scepan Polje. Before you got to the lake at Pluzine, you had to turn off Northwest towards the border and follow a dirt track for about an hour. This was an incredible cross-country route through the rocky landscape passing the occasional tiny hamlet and lone farm building. The hills were full of small trees barely six foot tall that gave the area the appearance of scrub land. The soil wasn't deep enough to support any bigger growth and the local Montenegrins were careful never to chop down a whole tree for firewood. Instead it was common practice to cut off parts of branches and allow the tree to recover before harvesting again in a few years time. In this way, the locals were able to sustain an indefinite crop of firewood. The farms, as I refer to them, didn't really match the normal West European concept of farming. A 'farm' often consisted of a few small stone buildings with a couple of windows in each and a single chimney coming from the 'Sporet'[38] In some cases there would only be a single building which was used to house both humans and animals at the same time. A traditional farmer might have one or two cows, several goats and perhaps a pig. I was always surprised by the lack of chickens, as it seemed to me that they would have been easy to farm and would have provided a ready supply of meat and eggs. But this was third world, East European subsistence farming. The farmers lived in poverty, barely able to scratch a living off the rocky landscape. Old women would spend their complete day walking their only cow; a sign of wealth; to and from small patches of edible vegetation. Young children, who should have been at school, would sit by the side of the road all day watching two or three goats, whilst the men-folk would spend their day cutting grass, – which grew in small circular patches of soil that formed naturally between the outcrops of rock, – with razor sharp, long handled scythes. The grass was used as animal feed during the harsh winter months and was made into small haystacks. These man made haystacks were common throughout all Yugoslavia and did not resemble anything like the machinery produced cubic stacks or neat giant sized 'toilet rolls' that adorn the English countryside. Instead the grass was piled onto a wooded frame and ended up resembling a giant sized muffin. They were quite peculiar but somehow they reinforced the over all impression that one got when travelling around; one of time standing still. When you looked at these farms it was difficult to see what, if anything had changed in the last hundred years. The only signs that time had visited these parts, were the power cables bringing electricity into the dwellings and the odd dilapidated Zastava car parked outside by the gate. Other than that, you could still have been in the Middle Ages. After an hour on the dirt track, you reached the village of Krstac. Here the road was metalled and there was some semblance of normal life. The first building you passed was an Army barracks, literally a big house with a small wall marking the perimeter of what might otherwise have been a garden. Inside the compound were usually several dishevelled young conscripts, some trucks and a 'cook's-set' – a trailer based generator cum field kitchen. Further into the village there was a school and a bar from which we collected water for drinking and washing and that was about it. Two KMs further on and you reached the BCP; two caravans dropped at the side of the road with an overhead mains power cable diverted to provide local power. The police and customs officers who controlled the border occupied an old stone building across the other side of the road. Their accommodation sounded nice, but our vans were infinitely more hygienic. As in Scepan Polje, the team's duty was to monitor whether the Montenegrin police and customs officers were doing their job properly to enforce their own government's decision to suspend support to the Bosnian Serb Republic. This did not involve actually doing their job for them, a concept which was sometimes lost on new observers but nevertheless was crucial in order to establish and maintain a good working relationship with these officers. The concept also presented a dilemma since to merely observe a customs officer going through the motions of checking a truck to ensure that it was not carrying proscribed goods, was not the same as knowing that it wasn't carrying proscribed goods. But, if you were to climb all over the vehicle yourself, you wouldn't necessarily be better off as you would offend the officers and then meet with a wall of obstruction for the rest of your duration on the border. Finding the right balance was the key to success and some people were better at it than others. First and foremost, these crossing points were not open to heavy goods vehicles (HGV) and no attempt was ever made by such a vehicle to cross. Only BCP-4 at Vilusi could deal with such traffic. At Krstac, the only trucks that would cross were small 'TAMs' or Zastavas, which were equivalent to an old three Ton Bedford, if you were lucky. These canvas-topped vehicles were owned by either the bigger farmers or by shopkeepers and were not capable of carrying much that would influence the war effort in Bosnia. The danger that these trucks might enhance the Bosnian Serb war machine was groundless, although one had to remain alert to the possibility that small, lightweight and high value items, such as Surface to Air missiles could be concealed in such a vehicle. But there was no way that even a steady stream of these small trucks could bring in enough supplies to run an army even for an hour. By and large, any smuggling that was going on was low level, individual enterprise of a non-military nature. Most 'illegal' activities consisted of shop owners buying goods in the FRY to stock their stores in Bosnia and trying to cross the border carrying too much for individual use. Individuals continued to cross the border to buy food and toiletries and this was not a problem. The difficulty came when a car would repeatedly cross back and forth with supplies, using the excuse that the vehicle was the only car in the Bosnian village and the shuttle runs were to help those families without transport and not to stock a shop. Many shop owners got rich this way but it was difficult to know where the truth lay and whilst you would keep tally of all crossings in order to build up an overview of who was doing what, you were reliant on the police and customs officers to draw the line for you. Another complicating factor was that as the border was essentially a new concept, many farmers owned land either side of the BCP. These farmers crossed back and forth all the time but it was still necessary to check their trucks on every occasion. Perhaps the biggest scam was the smuggling of diesel and petrol as both were in very short supply in Bosnia. In fact both commodities should have been in very short supply in the FRY as well and would have been but for the steady stream of '... oil and other supplies which came overland from Greece and up the Danube from Russia and the Ukraine,'[39] and, as I was to personally witness later, across from Albania. Trucks would pass into Montenegro with empty fuel tanks and simply try to cross back into Bosnia with full tanks. Even a small truck could smuggle three to five hundred litres of fuel at a time in this manner. Whilst such an amount would only run a main battle tank for an hour or so, it would bring in a very tidy profit when sold on to private car owners. Needless to say it was common practice to dip all external fuel tanks on vehicles that entered the FRY and to compare the readings with those when they attempted to leave. Although there was nothing to stop a vehicle leaving by a different crossing point, the distance between them almost negated any benefit that would be gained from filling up with fuel. The only BCPs vulnerable to such activity were BCPs 3 and 4 as these were close together, but these two BCPs also had good radio communications and could alert each other as necessary. Perhaps the best way to build up a good rapport with the customs and police officers was to initially keep a respectful distance. Some teams sat in their van and only came rushing out when the heard the sound of an engine. This always gave the impression that you didn't trust the officials and appeared overly aggressive. By always having one of you out and about, there was no need to go rushing over to the actual barrier to 'supervise' anyone and it did away with the big-brother image that you otherwise created. Secondly, you very quickly learnt which cars were thoroughly searched and which, as a general rule, weren't. The individual Montenegrin officers were not especially interested in whether the Bosnian

Serbs got their goods through or not, at the end of the day, they simply wanted an easy life. This meant that they had to play ball with us to a certain extent so that they didn't get a Violation Report (VIREP)[40] raised against them. It also meant that they didn't want trouble from those trying to cross. It was the cultural norm to accept 'gifts' and most cars would hand over at least one packet of cigarettes to the police or customs officers, and it was not unusual for a whole carton of twenty packets to exchange hands. Sometimes these were freely offered and on other occasions they were just taken. But the hardest thing was to determine the pattern. It didn't necessarily correspond that by offering a whole carton of cigarettes that you got through the border. I often saw such gifts accepted and yet the car turned away. When it came to the 'big fry' however, the story changed. It was clear from very early on, that in each area there would be leading families and individuals who were not to be interfered with. Whether this was the Montenegrin clan system at work, or whether it was just a reluctance to get involved with local 'organised crime' rackets, I was never able to establish. Either way, the effect was the same; some cars got easier treatment than others and it was not beyond the wit of man to work out that it was the high value vehicles that were being allowed through. A good team quickly picked up this pattern and also knew the personalities of the customs and police officials with whom they were working. Putting the two together meant that you could afford for the most part, to hang back somewhat, giving the appearance of trust and respect that was so central to their culture, making small talk, allowing them to get on with their duty. Only when a known 'player' or a 'bad' customs officer appeared, would you, as if by chance, appear to take more notice and perhaps make a random request to look a bit further than normal – perhaps suggesting that since Skodas had their engine in the back, it might be worth looking in the front for a change. This game of cat and mouse more often than not worked since not only would you find what you were looking for, but you and not the customs officer would be the bad guy, thus maintaining the officer's credibility in the eyes of the local crime family. None of this was rocket science. For the most part it was all common sense, yet it was surprising just how many observers got it wrong. Some thrusting observers didn't just observe, they tried to take over the jobs of the officials and hence put themselves and their team at risk. Other teams went completely in the opposite direction and did very little at all, content to sit back and hardly verify anything. Whilst this gave an easy ride to that team on that day, not only was it lazy and unprofessional but it sent the wrong message to the customs team, namely that they had the scope to do as much, or rather as little as they wanted. Over a period of time, this lack of uniformity on the part of the Mission, led to an extremely dangerous situation which nearly cost us the lives of two monitors who were trying to work professionally but who were repeatedly taking over from a shift with exactly the opposite approach. Another weakness of the Mission was that our operations were fairly low tech. It took weeks for a team to get to know all the police and customs officers working a particular crossing, to build up the rapport that was so essential to effective co-operation and to get to know all the players in the area. Whilst each team completed a BCP Report on the conclusion of their duty, there was no proper de-brief by the HQ nor was there any attempt to collate and analyse the data brought back by the teams. If there had been, an overall picture of who was doing what could easily have been built up covering the whole of our AoR. This would also have shown cross BCP patterns, who came in where – yet went out by a different route, or as we were later to determine, who repeatedly came in but never technically went out again – at least not via a legal crossing. As it was, this data remained unrecorded and was rarely passed on.

BCP-3, was located just outside the village of Vracenovici. Situated on a forward slope with commanding views of the border and a beautiful lake that marked the limit of Montenegrin territory, the BCP controlled the main route between Niksic and the East Bosnian town of Bileca in Hercegovina. Unlike BCPs 1 and 2, this BCP was manned on a twenty-four hour basis with teams rotating between Vracenovici and Vilusi, BCP-4. Although working the other BCPs from time to time, I was to spend most of my first two months working between these two. This suited me well, as both locations were far busier than the Northern crossings and this made the time go more quickly. Unlike at the other crossings however, Vracenovici had only one van in which a team of four was supposed to work, rest, cook, eat and sleep. Needless to say, it didn't really work. The first solution was to bin the driver from the team. As the role of the team was essentially that of a static customs post, the driver was not really needed. Instead, the on-coming teams for both Vracenovici and Vilusi were brought out to the BCPs in a mini bus and the off-going teams withdrawn in the same transport. Each BCP was left an old German Army VW Iltis[41] which had been painted bright blue. In theory these vehicles didn't need to go anywhere other than to collect water from the nearest village tap, but nevertheless they were made available as 'escape' vehicles in case the need arose to bug-out in a hurry. Deploying the Iltis's was a good decision as they were in fact used to escape on more than one occasion. With the teams now only being three strong, the van was just sufficient for its purpose, especially if one observer was outside the whole time as one was supposed to be – day and night. The second solution came in about mid July. As there was no political solution to the war in Bosnia in sight, the Mission had obtained from the UN, a number of containers, which they then deployed to the border. This gave the appearance of a far more permanent presence. The containers were the ones that could fit on the back of an articulated lorry or be loaded onto container ships to be transported all around the world. These ones were white, had two windows and a door and internal wall panels to provide some insulation from the extremes of the weather. Sector Charlie was allocated three containers; one was deployed to Vracenovici, one to Vilusi and the other to BCP-6 in the South at Vrbanja. The advantage of these containers was that the team could now present itself in a more professional manner. Our containers were better than the ones which the police and customs had and by doing away with the vans, we no longer looked like a bunch of gypsies camped by the road side. In addition to being able to accommodate four people, we were also able to set up a proper office area and work desk without the need to dismantle it every night in order to make the bed! This of course meant that the communication equipment could be set up properly and remain that way. All in all it was a vast improvement.

The route between Bileca and Niksic was always busy with Bosnian Serbs crossing to shop in the daily market at Niksic. Most of the traffic consisted of small cars or light trucks, but there was a main bus route between the two towns which still operated. The crossing was open during the hours of day light but was supposed to be closed at night, although in practice it was common for a vehicle to be delayed in Niksic and to arrive back at the crossing after it was closed. In these circumstances the teams would often allow the vehicle to pass once it had been thoroughly checked out. There were two main causes for concern at Vracenovici. One concerned the bus traffic and the other, the ability to circumvent the checkpoint. Apart from the fact that the buses which plied back and forth across the BCP were lethal (almost all of them were running on bald tyres and were completely over-crowded) it was Mission policy that observers were not allowed onto them, to search for themselves. This was part of the original negotiated agreement and we couldn't do a thing about it. In practice, it would have been extremely dangerous to board such a bus, full of Bosnian Serbs returning to their war. Certainly our Montenegrin police protection officers would have had an epileptic fit had we tried to get on board. Again, we had to rely on common sense and ones ability to build up a good working rapport with the local customs officers. All buses would be stopped every time. On each occasion the customs and police officers would board the bus to check personal documents and papers of those inside. Meanwhile the driver would always be required to open up the underneath baggage lockers. At this stage we would always be in a position to pay particular attention to what the bus was carrying. Two things could then happen. Either we would point to several items of luggage which would then be off loaded, the owners identified and the cases searched; or several passengers would be selected at random to find their luggage and present it for inspection. During this process we would also be in a position to have the fuel tanks dipped for the same reasons as we examined trucks. This level of co-operation was about the best one could expect to achieve. It was an active deterrent and frequently uncovered minor stashes of cigarettes and the odd additional Jerry can of fuel. But it was never going to establish what was actually on the floor of the bus between the passengers' feet. Unfortunately we were never going to truly answer that question, although I have to say that it is unlikely that we would have uncovered any major – systematic and state sponsored breach of the sanctions. An army requires a mass of supplies to keep its wheels in motion and these buses, despite their frequency, were incapable of carrying such volumes. They were overcrowded, overloaded with personal effects and un-roadworthy. At worst, I believe that our inability to board the buses permitted some low level smuggling of foodstuffs and cigarettes to continue across the border.

Our other concern, the ability to circumvent the BCP, was equally annoying but similarly non-sinister in the overall scheme of things. Behind the BCP was a small rocky outcrop that gave a commanding view down towards the lake to the Southwest and across a small valley, which lay behind the outcrop, to the Northwest. At night, I often used to sit on top of the outcrop, watching and listening to what was happening around me and watching the clear night skies. On these warm summer nights you could clearly see the Milky Way and often caught sight of shooting stars and even the odd satellite passing overhead. There was no light pollution and with little else to do, it was quite pleasant to watch the stars move across the sky. Unfortunately, not many other people did what I did, too many either sat inside or even crashed out completely. What I soon discovered was that cars coming from Niksic would often drive up to the bend in the road above and just short of the BCP and then stop. From on top of the outcrop, you could both hear and see this happening, especially after dark when it was easy to watch for the headlights to go off. After about an hour, the car would then come forward and attempt to cross through the BCP. More often than not it would be allowed through. What was harder to detect, was the reverse. The road on the Bosnian side of the BCP quickly disappeared out of sight round a sharp right-hand bend. From time to time a pattern emerged with some cars passing through our BCP into Montenegro and then stopping at the curve above it. After about half an hour this time, the car would continue on its way. Clearly something was going on, but to wonder off and OP[42] the valley line was not a good option, one – we were unarmed and two the police should technically come with us but in all possibility they might have been part of whatever scam was going on. For these reasons, it took several weeks to build up sufficient a picture to determine what was happening. In the mean time we had managed to obtain several military issue 'image intensifier' night scopes from the Mission HQ in Belgrade. These night scopes intensified the ambient light source and gave a green image of what was otherwise a completely dark area. By listening in the quiet of the night for car engines that suddenly stopped in the middle of nowhere and then waiting and watching the valley from a safe distance with the night scopes, I was able to see that the valley was being used to bypass the BCP. It was fairly low level individual enterprise, but what was happening was that a car and driver would enter Montenegro having dropped off an accomplice out of sight below the BCP. The accomplice would carry empty Jerry cans[43] along the valley into Montenegro and rejoin the car above the BCP. This took about half an hour. On the return journey, both occupants would carry the full cans back into Bosnia, leave them hidden by the sharp right-hand bend and then return to the car to drive through the BCP. This return trip would take about an hour. By sitting out at night, listening and observing the surrounding area, I had stumbled across a hole in our system, one that was mainly being exploited during day light, but one which had only come to light after dark. Whist it appeared that only small amounts of fuel were being smuggled into Bosnia, clearly the route could be used for other items as well and therefore having uncovered the scam, the next problem was finding a solution. The problem lay in the police and customs officers' refusal to respond to our requests for action when we were actually observing an illegal crossing. Although we would naturally raise a VIREP, they were completely unconcerned since they were not responsible for what happened beyond the immediate area of the actual crossing. Sealing the border at points other than at the six recognised BCPs was the responsibility of the VJ. To solve the problem the Sector HQ had to persuade the VJ Liaison Officer (VJLO), Captain Branko Konotar, to deploy a permanent Army OP to the top of the valley. After some tortuous negotiations and a stream of VIREPs, which were raising eyebrows in Belgrade, he reluctantly agreed and the problem went away.

BCP-4, was our main and certainly busiest crossing point. Situated just outside the small village of Vilusi, it had one of the best views I have ever experienced, the sort that tourists would pay a fortune to see just for a few moments. The BCP itself was located at the top of a steep decent that eventually wound itself down to the floor of the Nudo Valley below. The road was cut into the mountainside and afforded incredible views into Bosnia across sheer drops of over one thousand feet. From our container, you could sit outside in the sun and look across the valley below as if you were flying in a helicopter. There were some rock escarpments to the West of our position and it was wonderful to watch the rocks change colour throughout the day as the sun moved across the clear skies. At night, the remoteness and the beauty of the landscape was more apparent. There was almost no visible man made light anywhere except from a few isolated farmhouses. The sound of crickets was constant as if one was in the tropics, and the clear skies and lack of light pollution gave the same views of the Milky Way that you could see at Vracenovici. The crossing was open twenty-four hours a day and was the only one in Montenegro which could be used by HGVs in addition to the normal traffic of farm vehicles, buses and private cars. HGVs were not allowed to cross the border anywhere else because Vilusi was the only location that could deal with the customs procedures involved in allowing them to cross. It was also the nearest crossing point to our HQ in Niksic where we kept our customs office and it was really the only road capable of handling such heavy vehicles. It was not that heavy trucks were themselves proscribed; it was what they were carrying that mattered. Humanitarian goods were allowed to cross and most of the traffic fell under this heading, as regular convoys from the UN High Commission for Refugees (UNHCR) and the International Committee of the Red Cross (ICRC) plied back and forth. Nevertheless, it was our responsibility to ensure that these vehicles were carrying what the paperwork said there were. To ensure that this was the case, every truck had to clear a joint ICFY – Yugoslav customs point in Niksic. Since we always had a core nucleus of customs personnel in the sector, we were always able to provide experts to oversee the inspection and sealing of these vehicles. Each vehicle was thoroughly searched in slow time in the compound that we had set up across from our HQ in the Hotel Onogost. Had we attempted to search these vehicles at the border, we would not have been able to cope with the volume of traffic attempting to pass. It was enough just to monitor and check the small trucks and private cars let alone huge aid convoys. In this respect, the customs team in Niksic ensured that anything arriving at the border on its way to Bosnia, had already been checked and cleared. Trucks arriving to enter Montenegro were not our concern, albeit the Montenegrin customs officers did take a very keen interest in them for their own professional reasons. Our real interest in these vehicles was to ensure that they weren't smuggling fuel out on their return trip and so the tanks were always dipped and the amount of fuel in them recorded. To ensure that the system worked however, we had to be certain that none of the vehicles on their way to Bosnia were tampered with, from the moment that they left the customs compound in Niksic, until the moment when they arrived at the BCP. We ensured this in a number of ways. When the search had been completed in Niksic, the ICFY Team Leader sealed the load with customs seals. These were red plastic ties, of the type used by police as 'plasticuffs,' but with a serial number to individually identify the seal. Whilst the UNHCR vehicles, which were mainly Volvo articulated container lorries, could easily be sealed with one such seal on the lock at the rear of the container, most trucks had canvass or plastic tarpaulin covers over the load carrying area. These vehicles needed ten or more seals, each placed on the tensioning strops along the sides of the cargo box. Whatever the method, the load carrying area was effectively sealed. If a tarpaulin was ripped or a vehicle could not be sealed, then it was rejected. The serial numbers of the seals were recorded on an ICFY Custom's Form as were details of the load and finally the date and time that the vehicle was cleared to proceed. The form, along with all the Yugoslav papers needed to proceed, was handed to the driver to present at the BCP. Any irregularities or apparent amendments could easily be checked by means of the radio between the BCP and Niksic. Officially, the driver had six hours to arrive at the BCP, easily enough time to travel what was only about a thirty to forty minute drive. In practice, if the vehicle had taken more that a couple of hours to arrive, it was subject to very close scrutiny. At the BCP, the seals were checked against the paperwork to ensure that the serial numbers matched and that they were all intact. Fortunately there were never any problems with false serial numbers as this may have implied that our seals were being copied and manufactured elsewhere. Where, on the few occasions, seals were found to have been broken, then the observers either rejected the vehicle or, having assessed the cause and satisfied themselves that there was no fowl play, they then removed all the seals from the vehicle prior to permitting it to cross. The final check was always to confirm that the load still matched that stated on the form. This could never be done as thoroughly as in Niksic and indeed it was never designed to be so. Essentially it just gave us another opportunity to see that nothing had been dropped down the side of the cargo bay and served as a deterrent to others. Once the Montenegrin officers were satisfied with their paperwork, the unsealed vehicle was allowed to cross into Bosnia.

I spent my first two months working between Vilusi and Vracenovici interspersed with the occasional mobile patrol to check the remainder of the border. One quickly settled into the routine of these deployments although to be truthful, no two trips were ever the same. Much depended upon who you were teamed up with and to a certain extent, who you were taking over from. On the morning of a deployment, everyone would go down to the local market and buy sufficient food for the duration of their deployment. This was not like the military where you are simply provided with cooked meals, such as roast beef and Yorkshire pudding, despite being in some far flung corner of the earth. Most of us ate in the hotel where the food was incredibly bad, swimming in grease and fat, and had to supplement our diet with what we could find in the local markets. There was very little to choose from, except domestically grown fruit and vegetables which, thankfully were of good quality and in abundance. The lack of variety, fish, decent fresh meat and the total absence of convenience foods that were suitable to take into the field and cook on camping stoves, was in part due to the undeveloped nature of the economy anyway, and in part due to the international sanctions which we were imposing on the country. Since we represented the IC and were therefore the ones who were imposing the sanctions, we could hardly complain that we couldn't find better food to eat. At least we had the advantage of being able to afford the ever rising prices which were resulting from the effects of the sanctions, whereas the local population largely could not and were suffering badly because of it. I spent much of my time on these two BCPs working with an interpreter known to us all as 'Mother Olga.' Olga's surname was Vukotic and in a country where family, tribe and hence surname meant everything, she was an incredible asset to have along. Olga always told everyone that she was related to the Montenegrin Royal Family although her name was neither Petrovic nor Radonjic, the two families who effectively governed Montenegro for centuries. In 1831 however, the Russian government sent two Montenegrin envoys to assist Njegos, one of whom was Ivan Vukotic and that may well have been where the family connection came from. Nevertheless, regardless of the historic details, where ever Olga went, she always received the greatest of respect that one could possibly imagine. However, the reason why everyone in the Mission called her 'Mother Olga,' was because she was like a mother-hen, always nagging at observers for the slightest of reasons. She used to drive most people mad but I really enjoyed working with her and being naturally clean and tidy, I was rarely subjected to her nagging. Together we used to cook some excellent meals in our small van and we never went hungry. Other observers chose not to cook and simply ate bread and chocolate. This was largely due to laziness, not just in wanting to avoid cooking, but in not being bothered to do the washing up afterwards. I never subscribed to that view and even cooked a breakfast every morning despite knowing that we would soon be relieved and could get something to eat back in Niksic. I used to boil 'Virsle,' the nearest equivalent to a frankfurter and fry eggs and tomatoes, the latter being a real novelty to Olga who had never contemplated doing anything other than making a salad out of a tomato. But the real reason why Olga had got a reputation for nagging was because there was usually something for her to nag about. When you arrived at a BCP to start your shift, it was essential that the off-going team briefed you on the operational events of their shift. By and large this was done quite satisfactorily, but more often than not you would inherit a dirty container. Getting the out-going team to take their rubbish with them often seemed impossible. Leaving uneaten food behind was the usual crime, the problem being that you never knew just how old it was, how many teams had passed it on to the next and therefore whether it was safe to eat. Considering average day-time temperatures of thirty degrees centigrade, there was potentially serious health problems here. Another, and far more significant problem that an out-going team could leave you with, was the ramifications of how they had dealt with their opposite Montenegrin police and customs teams. More often than not, the police and the customs teams worked different shift patterns than we did, usually because they were expected to sit out on the border for far longer periods than we were. It wasn't that we were softer than they were, it was more to do with remaining alert. We considered that variety was essential to staying alert, although by switching people between a pair of BCPs rather than all over the place, we were also able to build up local knowledge at the same time. What this meant in practice, was that an on-coming ICFY team would probably spend part of their shift with the same police and customs officers who had been working with the previous ICFY team. Had an incident, or simply a particular style of working, caused conflict between them, then you would naturally inherit the follow on problems. Major incidents where problems and confrontation had occurred were rare. The most common cause of problems, as already mentioned, was in the different styles of approach between different teams, especially when professional teams followed on from those with 'different agendas.' Thankfully such problems were also rare at Vilusi but the problem of 'hand-overs' between teams still needed to be addressed.

In the valley below Vilusi was our fifth BCP, which we referred to as 'Nudo.' By line of sight it was probably no more than one mile away from Vilusi, although the actual crossing point was obscured by rock escarpments and you couldn't actually see the BCP. However, to get to it was another story. The shortest way was to go down the road past the Vilusi BCP, enter Bosnia and once you'd reached the valley floor, to turn back on yourself and cross back into Montenegro. The total distance this way was no more than five or six KMs, but it entailed crossing into Bosnia, something that was illegal for us to do. It would also have been decidedly unsafe since the Bosnian Serb Republic was after all, the target of our sanctions. The only other route was to enter the same valley floor but from the Southeast at a point where the main fertile plain from Risan on the Adriatic coast passed through Grahovo. This route went past the house with the helicopter parked outside and then crossed into Bosnia winding its way towards Trebinje in Hercegovina. The problem with this route was that it took well over an hour

Trebinje; Bosnian Serb Republic: The first town inside Hercegovina situated below the Vilusi BCP and subject to our blockade.

to drive it. This meant in practice that it took at least ninety minutes, if not up to two hours depending upon road conditions, to get from Niksic to the Nudo BCP despite the BCP being only ten minutes on from Vilusi (via Bosnia). It was for this reason that the Sector was divided into two, with a detachment based on the coast in Herceg Novi. This detachment covered two BCPs, the first being BCP-5 at Nudo and the second being our last crossing point, BCP-6 at Vrbanja at the triangulation of Montenegro, Bosnia and Croatia near the still disputed Prevlaka Peninsular. The detachment conducted no mobile patrol duties, the Nudo valley and Grahovo was covered by Niksic and the sheer scale and impassability of the Dinaric Alps on the

Southern coastline of Montenegro simply meant that traffic was limited to the two main crossings which we had blocked. As a Mission, we spent weeks religiously exploring for other possibilities, driving up inaccessible tracks which appeared to cross the border only to find that they led nowhere. Later on in the year, when I ran operations, we even analysed satellite imagery of the area that we had obtained from the Americans, yet we still couldn't find any other ways across. In the late thirteenth century, Bosnia was a Banate,[44] ruled by the Kotroman family and was repeatedly fought over by both Hungarian and Ragusan[45] powers. Stephen Kotroman was the first Ban to unite both Bosnia and its neighbour, Hercegovina in 1326, having successfully conquered and annexed much of Hercegovina and several hundred miles of the Dalmatian coast between Ragusa and Split. But these gains were cemented by Stephen's successor and nephew, Stephen Tvrtko who in 1377 declared himself King of not only Bosnia, but king of Serbia too. It was King Tvrtko who founded the new trading port of 'Novi' (New) on the Northern side of the Bay of Kotor and he intended it to be a rival to the great port of Ragusa. In 1463, the Kingdom of Bosnia was conquered with great speed by the Turkish Army although in the Northern territories the Hungarians continued to hold on to parts of Bosnia for the next sixty years with Jajce finally falling to the Turks in 1527. In Hercegovina too, resistance continued for a brief spell, albeit only for two years. The Duke (Herceg), who defended this ever-diminishing rump of Hercegovina was Herceg Stephen Vukcic, who eventually took refuge in the fortified port of 'Novi' and died there in 1466, after which the port was renamed Herceg-Novi in his memory. Our detachment in the port lived in a small villa right on the sea front where it would have been an idyllic spot to spend a holiday but for the war raging just across the border to the North. Nevertheless, it was a fantastic place to be based, especially after the privations and open hostility of life in Niksic. The people living on the coast, whilst still being Montenegrin, were far more open to foreigners as there had been quite a tourist industry in this part of Yugoslavia before the war. In fact Montenegro's second airport which largely serviced the tourist industry was located just across the bay at Tivat on the other side of the Kotor peninsular in which the FRY had its main naval facilities. The whole of this area was extremely sensitive. It was from this point that Montenegrin reservists had launched their attack into Croatia in support of the Serb Krajina and had raided and plundered the many villages along the coastline on their way towards the Croatian city of Dubrovnik. All of Serbia and Montenegro's naval forces were now harboured in the bay, yet the outlet into the Adriatic was less than a mile across. Croatian forces, had they occupied the Prevlaka Peninsular on the West of the bay's entrance, would have been in a position to indefinitely blockade these vessels and prevent them from ever setting to sea. For this reason, Prevlaka remained a UN protected zone, as had parts of Eastern Slavonia around Vukovar and United Nations Military Observers (UNMO) patrolled the Peninsular to ensure that the area remained a de-militarised zone. Nevertheless, sensitivities were high and the Yugoslavian Army retained artillery units fully deployed in the field with their guns trained on Croatia throughout the whole of my time in the Mission. Our detachment here was the envy of the rest of the Mission and not without reason. The work schedule was less demanding and there was ample opportunity to enjoy the delights of the Adriatic coastline when one was off duty. It made a welcome break from Niksic, where there was little time for relaxing and in any case, no where to go. For these reasons, we had a policy that observers would only spend about a month at a time deployed to the detachment and that new observers would not be eligible to go there until they had spent at least a month working out of Niksic. The system worked well, but I was not to enjoy a tour there myself and continued to work on the Northern BCPs and on mobile patrols until such time as I was promoted to run overall operations, a post which meant that I was to remain stuck in Niksic.

Vrbanja, our last and sixth BCP was situated high in the hills on what was an old crossing point on the way into Croatia but which was now closed to all but Yugoslav military traffic. This in itself presented a special problem since the teams on the BCP only really ever encountered military vehicles. It was vital that these vehicles were searched since if anyone was going to actually break the embargo and smuggle combat supplies to the Bosnian Serbs, it was the military. Unfortunately, many observers took the opposite view, making the wrong assumption that if one was relying on the Montenegrin customs and police to up hold the sanctions, then surely one could also rely on the army. Clearly this was a rather naïve assumption but one that was fairly well entrenched all the less. Turning the practice around was no easy feat and it took an excellent team consisting of an American, Tim Vandersommen and a half-Brit, half-Aussie, Ken Lindsay, to make the change, but not without cost. The fact that both these observers took their responsibilities properly when many did not, meant that they took the brunt of the backlash when the VJ decided enough was enough and they didn't want to be searched anymore. Having your life threatened when you're in the middle of nowhere, surrounded by a belligerent army which is threatening you without even the basic means of self-defence except a diplomatic ID, takes a certain type of courage. Both these two observers stuck it out whilst hasty attempts were made to address the issue at the highest level. In the end, it all settled down, but it could have been a lot worse. However, by far and large the biggest smuggling operation that was being conducted in the area, had nothing to do with the war and by definition, was therefore outside of our remit. Herceg Novi and the Kotor Bay had long been renowned for the smuggling of contraband, mainly counterfeit cigarettes and on several occasions when I was at Belgrade airport, I witnessed huge Antonov cargo planes full of crates of cigarette cartons. Where these had come from or were eventually destined for is hard to say as the sale of cigarettes is central to most customs rackets throughout the Balkans. What was known however, was that counterfeit cigarettes were being smuggled into Western Europe via

Montenegro. The smugglers used high-powered speedboats to ply between Herceg Novi and Bari on the Italian coast. The Italian 'Garde Finance' spent huge resources trying to stop this trade but it was equally well sponsored on the Montenegrin side. Essentially the local police and customs took absolutely no action whatsoever. Clearly, apart from smuggling being part of the Montenegrin psyche, this operation also involved those in power at the highest level and some even rumoured that Momir Bulatovic, the then Montenegrin president, and Milo Djukanovic, his successor, were involved. Without doubt this was no small scale, half-hearted affair. These were extremely expensive off shore powerboats and they were rumoured to carry shoulder-launched surface-to-air missiles to shoot down the Garde Finance helicopters which tried to intercept them. Since such state sponsored activity was not considered out of the ordinary in Montenegro, I often wondered what we were really trying to achieve and whether we were really up against the impossible. What ever my conclusions, as I continually mused these questions over in my mind, I never lost sight of the fact that it was always worth trying. As long as we could help stop the war in Bosnia and subsequently lift the sanctions off the ordinary people of Yugoslavia, then it simply had to be worth the effort.

In between BCP duty, observers conducted mobile patrols. I much preferred these because I enjoyed the challenge of navigating around the spectacular Montenegrin countryside and stopping off in the villages to meet and talk with people. Other observers preferred BCP duty because they saved on expensive hotel bills, which as foreigners, always cost us twice the local rate. Perhaps it was the primitiveness of the people and the remoteness of the land, I don't know, but whatever the reason, these people had an incredible sense of hospitality and it was ingrained in them. Despite being intrinsically poor, whenever you turned up outside one of their dwellings, you would be welcomed inside, given coffee and offered food. You couldn't help but feel humbled by the experience. As Westerners we were imposing sanctions on these people and were filthy rich in comparison; the average monthly salary in Montenegro was about fifty Deutschmarks (DEM) at the time (less that twenty pounds). We would invariably turn up in a good, if not fairly new 4x4 jeep of some description and yet be hosted by a family with almost nothing material to their name. On one occasion when patrolling high in the hills to the South of the Nudo valley, I remember entering a typical rural dwelling to speak to the family who were living there. The dwelling was built of Breeze Blocks with a tin roof. It consisted of just one room and had a single door with a window either side. Inside it was dark and dank despite the searing temperature outside. At one end of the room was a sofa-bed and a wood burning Sporet on which all the family's food was cooked and which also provided the heating. At the other end of the room were two beds in which the family doubled up, head-to-toe and a collection of enamelled pots and pans hung on the walls. There were three children, all girls, aged five, ten and thirteen. The ten year old was hardly bigger then my three year old daughter at home. Outside there was an animal pen that contained several sheep and a cow. Apart from an old knackered Zastava Fica[46] parked outside, that was all that the family owned. It was difficult to see how the family could earn any income especially as the land surrounding the dwelling was unable to support crops of any description. Yet despite this poverty the whole team were given coffee, cherry juice and Vinjak.[47] Finally we were offered a meal which, had we accepted, would have consisted of meat, the ultimate honour because such families usually only ate meat once a week, as that was all that they could afford. This sort of hospitality was intrinsic throughout not just Montenegro, but throughout Bosnia too, as I was soon to experience. It followed a certain code that was quite alien to the Western approach but one that was central to the local culture. If you failed to grasp the complexities of this code, you could make the most awful gaffs imaginable. Simply put, the code requires the host to offer you what they have. What is theirs', is yours. There are two sides to this simple statement however. Firstly, your actual preferences are almost irrelevant to the process. Rarely will you be offered the choice of say a Vinjak or a beer. This is because the host might not have both and so more often than not you will just be given a Vinjak. Whether you like Vinjak, matters not. The host has done his duty and in many of the dwellings that I was to visit during my time in the country, you had literally been offered everything the person owned. The second side of this ritual is that as the guest, you should never refuse and certainly never, ever ask for something different. I absolutely hated most Rakijas and Vinjaks but frequently had to drink them so as not to cause deep offence to my host despite the fact that I was making myself ill. Had I asked for a beer instead, I could have easily insulted my host had he not been able to give me one. I made that mistake once with a Montenegrin family that I became very attached to and the eldest daughter never really forgave me for it. Certainly it was a mistake that I will never forget. Coupled with this concept of never asking for something different or refusing, is the seemingly impossible task of stopping the host from refilling your glass or plate. It is natural for us in the West to drain our glass before leaving and to clean our plate of every last scrap in a show of appreciation to the cook. Yet both acts of politeness on our part are interpreted the opposite way around in these Balkan communities and can and will have the opposite effect. To empty a glass or a plate implies that your host has not given you sufficient. It will be refilled immediately. If you then struggle to empty it again under the misconception that the last thing you want to do in the presence of such poverty is to waste food, then it will be refilled again. By being polite you are being rude and taking their food in to the bargain. The only way to break this cycle is to leave something on your plate and to try and leave something in your glass (somehow this never seemed to work for me). This might seem wasteful, but it was the way it worked. The other thing that you could never do was to offer any payment in return. This would be an incredible insult to your host and so we had to come to a compromise especially when we returned to an area for a second time. To solve the problem we often used to stop for coffee but state that we had only just eaten in a local Kafana. On a return trip to an area we would often call in at a house and drop off some cigarettes or a bag of coffee whilst feigning that we were en-route to another part of the border and couldn't stop for long. By making such house calls throughout the rural areas, we were able to build up a sound knowledge of what happened there and consequently we were able to spot the unusual from the usual.

The countryside was both beautiful and rugged at the same time. Most of the villages were quite remote from one another and I was always amazed how such isolated communities could survive the harshness of the winter months. Whilst communist rule had provided these peasant communities with electricity, there were few if any phone lines and we frequently met women walking donkeys laden with plastic containers, to and from the local water tap. In town, the story was better but you soon picked out what was missing when compared to a normal town back home. I never saw a supermarket, there were few pavements, roads didn't have curb stones along the side and many were simply gravel tracks. Public telephones did exist but only inside main Post Offices (PTT) and I never saw a telephone kiosk or a post box anywhere on the street. Traffic signals were rudimentary and most road signs, if not all in the rural areas, looked like metal colanders having been shot to pieces by passing motorists with pistols. Crash barriers, which were coloured bright orange, did exist but where these had served their purpose in saving someone's life, the twisted metal rails had been left to rust, a health and safety nightmare. In may cases; and unerringly prevalent along the shear drops and switch-back roads of the Dinaric Alps; these barriers had long since disappeared altogether, a crumbling piece of tarmac the only indication that a barrier had once existed there before it and the vehicle that had demolished it, had disappeared over the edge into oblivion. But all too often, spectacular views were blighted by fly-tipped rubbish left to rot in the baking temperatures. Worse still were seemingly endless skeletons of abandoned cars and old fridges which were strewn across the countryside. For some completely mindless reason, the Montenegrins were intent on ruining the beauty of what nature had given them by rolling their scrap cars over the nearest bank and down into their rivers. It was crass and senseless. People fished these rivers to supplement their diets, not for sport. Yet countless rivers were blighted by rusting cars and discarded refrigerators and cookers. I often wondered what would happen in a few years time, if or when Western culture and materialism invaded their country. How on earth would they deal with the waste generated by modern supermarkets and bulk packaging? This was an environmental disaster waiting to happen.

Driving around this landscape was something that I personally found to be very pleasant. Spotting the difference between the usual and the unusual was an interesting challenge and one that I also enjoyed. A retired American Colonel called Bob Freeman shared my enthusiasm. Unlike most of the other Americans in the mission, Bob did not have a Special Forces background, instead he had spent most of his career in the murky world of military intelligence. Whereas I'd spent my time in the intelligence world working as an operative in the field, Bob had worked at the governmental level and had actually been heavily involved as a negotiator with Paul Nitze during the Intermediate-range Nuclear Forces (INF) negotiations in Geneva during the early nineteen eighties and also as an assistant to the US Secretary of Defence during other negotiations in the late eighties. He had also done a tour as the Army Attaché to Finland in Helsinki and had been the Operations Officer of the American Task Force which had been set up post Glasnost, to search for American prisoners of war held in the Former Soviet Union. What interested both Bob and I, was a segment of track that paralleled the border from a point just behind our BCP at Vracenovici and headed northwards for about twenty kilometres towards, but not joining, our BCP at Krstac. At various points along the track, there were quite a few places where it would have been possible to cross the border, as in parts, this area was reasonably flat. The VJ had responsibility to ensure that nothing crossed; a fact that in itself caused us some concern. In total there were seven places which we considered needed to be blocked, all other areas were considered too difficult to traverse, even by tracked vehicles. Of these seven locations, two points were already listed as Controlled Crossing Points (CCP). These CCPs were manned by the VJ, twenty-four hours a day and were subject to frequent visits by our teams. One of these, CCP-3, just North of a small kasarna[48] at Crkvice, consisted of a small wooden hut and a pole across an isolated track passing through the forested mountain side. Young conscripts were sent here for the duration of their military service, something that I imagined to be quite mind-numbing. The whole scene was quite surreal and reminded me of those old black and white Cold-war spy movies where Michael Caine used to crash through some isolated check point on the Iron Curtain deep inside Czechoslovakia. Local trucks and farmers were allowed to cross the border, but it was the VJ, and not the Montenegrin police and customs authorities who had jurisdiction here. I never trusted the VJ and it always seemed to me that if Milosevic was supplying the Bosnian Serbs, then this was one of the places where it was probably happening. Nevertheless the VJ religiously maintained registers of all vehicles which passed and readily made these available for our inspection upon request. Quite often we used to meet a foot patrol either making its way to or from the CCP. As it was about five kilometres from the kasarna, we often gave the soldiers a ride in the back of our pick-up trucks and plied them for information at the same time. Despite the real opportunity for the VJ to simply drive a military convoy right through the crossing, we never had any real foundation to presume that they had done so, although I very much doubt that the soldiers would have given such information away in any case. One important aspect about the need to work up a good relationship with the conscripts was the fact that they were our only real protection when out in the field. At Crkvice we often called in at the local kafana for a coffee and frequently got chatting to the conscripts. The kafana was the social highlight of the surrounding area for at least a twenty kilometre radius, yet it consisted of one small dark and smelly room, several tables and chairs and a wood burning stove whose flue probably hadn't worked properly since the turn of the century. On entering the place, you immediately started coughing on the wood smoke much to the delight of the locals. Just North of the kafana, the locals weren't quite so hospitable. On two occasions I personally ran into trouble whilst trying to get through to CCP-3. The first incident essentially involved the locals setting up an impromptu roadblock across the track. Although the villagers were hostile and many had decided to sport their Kalashnikovs and point them in the general direction of our heads, their real concern was that we were affecting their livelihoods because the CCP effectively stopped them from obtaining timber (non-humanitarian goods) from across the border in Bosnia. Since the local economy relied on a sawmill, they had a point, but it was one that we could do little about. The second incident occurred in the same place but in the middle of the night and involved a local man who was both drunk and armed with a Kalashnikov, deciding that we really didn't ought to be around any longer. This incident unlike the previous one, which was merely to make a point and to vent some anger at the IC, was actually quite ugly. My efforts to talk the man out of using his weapon were not altogether meeting with much success when fortunately a VJ patrol, which was coming off duty from the checkpoint, came to our aid. Out numbered four-to-one, the man saw that discretion was the better part of valour and eventually was sent packing by the patrol. I have no doubt that had we not previously made concerted efforts to engender good relations with the soldiers from the kasarna, that the outcome that night might have been tragically different.

The remaining five locations which we had identified as potentially troublesome were not manned by the VJ and were therefore not known as CCPs. Since these locations were not designated as 'controlled crossing points' there was no requirement for anyone to control them and check the identity of anyone crossing, indeed the point was that nobody should have been crossing there at all. In this respect what mattered was that these locations were rendered impassable. This was achieved either by cratering the path or by building a huge stone barricade across it. The five check points in question were all serial numbered with the prefix '4' with '4-Bravo in the North and '4-Foxtrot' in the South. The VJ randomly patrolled the area to ensure that these obstacles remained intact and of course we did much the same. At '4-Delta' however, the track that led off to the border passed through a field. As such, digging a ditch or building a barricade across the path had no effect whatsoever. The only way to plug the apparent gap was to insist that the VJ put a permanently manned OP opposite '4-Delta' actually on the main North-South track that linked all these points together and paralleled the actual border. In effect this would up-grade '4-Delta' from a mere checkpoint to a full CCP. As we had no evidence to suggest that this apparent gap in our defences was actually being exploited, the VJ pointedly refused to do so. Getting evidence was not easy. In the heat of the summer the rocky soil left little if no evidence to suggest whether vehicles were crossing the field. Many trucks on both sides of the border still used the same old communist 'Red Star' SFRY number plates and so we couldn't prove whether any vehicle we observed belonged to one side of the border or the other without first checking the relevant paperwork, something which required the presence of a police officer and not a soldier. We tired dropping off a team at night to sit and observe the area, but were warned by the VJLO that, 'The VJ can not guarantee your safety after dark, as there are too many hunters in the hills,' – a euphemism for saying that they were likely to shoot us (by mistake of course) if we continued. So we then tried it during day light instead, but ended up with the team being arrested by the Army for supposedly spying and threatened with deportation as 'persona non grata.' It soon became a game of cat and mouse between the mission and the Yugoslav authorities, but that in itself indicated that something untoward was going on in the area. As Bob and I began to build up the picture frame by frame, Bob coined the phrase, the 'Delta Boulevard' to describe that section of track which paralleled the border and which we believed was being used as a transit route for trucks plying between Niksic and Bileca. We had yet to prove it, but it seemed to us that rather than cross the border at the Vracenovici BCP, smugglers were turning North just short of the BCP, travelling up the 'Boulevard' some ten kilometres until they reached the area of '4-Delta' and were then turning West to cross into Hercegovina with their illegal cargoes. Proving it and getting '4-Delta' upgraded to a CCP was another matter and one that was to take several more months of cat and mouse games to achieve.

The Foreign Office contract, on which all the UK Delegation was employed, ran for seventy-two days. This gave one no sense of job security whatsoever but in a way it was appropriate since our mission existed purely to ensure that Milosevic's self imposed sanctions regime was being adhered to. Should the war end, then external sanctions would automatically become irrelevant, as would our own services. The Foreign Office therefore needed to engage us under terms that allowed them maximum flexibility should they need to get rid of us in a hurry. The system they had devised did just that. It gave them the flexibility to bin us at a moment's notice whilst leaving open the possibility to keep renewing contracts almost indefinitely (subject to good behaviour) up to a maximum of two years (when employment legislation would otherwise kick in protecting our rights as employees – something which they were keen to avoid). The problem with this system however, was that we were never really considered part of the Foreign Office 'club.' In fact, we were often belittled as being, 'in it purely for the money,' and constantly reminded that we were, 'paid far too much anyway.' It is true to say that we were not mainstream FCO employees and we were

all on short-term contracts. As such I certainly regarded myself as a consultant working abroad. But it is also true that whilst we were not treated, paid
or pensioned like main stream FCO personnel, we still had to pay UK
income tax and national insurance contributions as if we were mainstream
FCO 'Crown Servants' which was quite unlike all other expatriates working
abroad in charities and Non Governmental Organisations (NGO). In
essence the FCO had it both ways whilst we had none of the benefits
(pension, job security etc) and all of the down-side (still had to pay UK tax
and national insurance). Whilst this never really gave me cause for concern
what did grate however, was the reference to being 'in it only for the money.'
I, along with many other members of the UK Delegation, had been in perfectly good, well-paid jobs before resigning them in order to take up our
appointments in Yugoslavia. I can well remember the faces of some of my
friends, who when I announced to them that I was leaving my secure job
and handing in my company car to go off to a war zone, gasped with shock
and disbelief. Whilst such action is common in military circles where you
have to go where you are sent, volunteering for such a job as a civilian was
not common place and my friends had found it a little difficult to fathom out
just why I was doing it. My sole motivation was the desire to do something
worthwhile and specifically to help in an international context. Many people
'do their bit' by donating to charity, but I have always felt that I could help
more by being personally involved and so the snide comments from some
FCO officials always got my back up.

During a seventy-two day contract, only fifty-six days were spent in
theatre. Basically this worked out as two months on, two weeks off or to be
precise exactly eight weeks on (fifty-six days continuous duty without rest)
and then sixteen days (the eight Saturdays and the eight Sundays taken at the
end of the tour) back in the UK. In reality there was no annual leave entitle-
ment, you just got your weekends at the end of a two month period giving
rise to the term – a '56-72' day contract. Without doubt, these were good
terms especially when compared to the military, but they did not warrant
the jealousy or comments that they attracted back in London. When I had
originally joined the mission, it was my intention to do just one tour, but as
my first fifty-six days in theatre were coming to a close, I had to decide
whether to continue with another seventy-two day contract and return to
Niksic after my leave, or to gather my belongings and go home to stay. What
had been very easy to decide back in the UK with my wife and family now
seemed somewhat inappropriate. I had only just got to grips with what was
happening and in several areas had seen things that needed major improvement. To leave now, before really being able to move things forward, seemed
like a cop out. Besides which, for the first time since leaving the Paras, I had
truly regained my self-esteem, was personally thriving and doing a job
which I really enjoyed for which there was a clear and over-riding humanitarian purpose. Also, from a purely mercenary point of view, I no longer had
a job to go back to, as my previous employer had no intention of keeping it

open for me. UK legislation lags behind many of our European partners in this respect in that we do not have a system whereby an employer can be compelled to release an employee for humanitarian relief work and to keep their old job open for them on their return. In the UK, the only legislation that provides this sort of protection whilst people to go off and 'do their bit,' is where a member of the reserve forces is mobilised for active military service. In Norway however, the Norwegian Refugee Council (NRC) maintains a list of volunteers who are available to go anywhere in the world on humanitarian service at a moment's notice and employers are compelled by law to keep jobs open for them when they return. In the next three years I would meet many Norwegians throughout the Former Yugoslavia all of whom were professionals in their own fields and who would simply be able to walk back into their old jobs when they finally chose to leave. Unfortunately this was not the case for me, neither was it for Archie, the DHOS who had briefed me on my first night in Niksic and who had just elected to bite the bullet and return home to Scotland to seek work nearer to his family. With Archie's departure, there was a gap in the leadership of the Sector and one that I was called upon to discuss. Archie actually performed three quite separate functions amid the chaos of the Sector's sole office; he ran operations, controlled the budget and personnel issues and finally deputised for the Head of Sector. The situation was intolerable and he was rightly exhausted and in need of calling it a day. He had done far more than what was required of him and had single-handedly managed to keep the Sector together and run operations at the same time. The fact that the HOS, a very likeable Finn called Urpo, had permitted the situation to get like this was unfair and although I was later to regard Urpo as a very good friend, he should have done something about it a long time ago but for some unknown reason had chosen not to do so. To find a replacement for Archie would not be easy, not just because of the skills required, but because of the hard work and thanklessness that went hand-in-hand with the post. During the course of my seventh week, with the Foreign Office needing to know whether I wanted a single or a return air ticket and with my wife wondering how we would manage to get through Christmas if I didn't have a job, I was called into the office along with an American named Bill Feaster, to discuss several issues. Bill was an incredibly nice guy, a retired Colonel (this time with a Special Forces background) who lived in Florida and to the delight of my children, had crocodiles in his swimming pool – although not intentionally. He had come to ICFY to escape the rigours of his current desk job and loved being back out in the field again. Unfortunately for him personally, but of great benefit to the Sector, Bill's days in the field were numbered, as were mine.

6

Autumn - Winter 1995

Operations in Sector Charlie were run from a small room on the fifth floor of the Hotel Onogost – Room 509. The decor was typical modernist-utilitarian, as found throughout the former communist block. The bottom half of the walls were covered with gaudy red wooden panelling and the bathroom was similarly decorated in the same colour but with rough quarry tiles. All the normal bedroom furniture had been removed from the room and replaced by six desks on which the Staff Officers were supposed to work amongst the plethora of satellite communications systems and associated equipment that crowded the room making it almost impossible to work anywhere. To make matters worse in what was already a confined space, the room was also used to store what little supplies we had built up, mostly spare vehicle tyres for the 4 x 4s and incredibly Jerry Cans full of fuel which were kept under our watchful eye to stop them going for a walk in the night. The situation was crazy and quite simply, a health and safety nightmare. Power, computer and communications cables criss-crossed the room whilst drivers lugged fuel cans back and forth hoping not to trip headlong into a pile of tyres. There was no sense of order whatsoever, neither was there any sense of control. Archie, who had previously had to work in this environment, had constantly been doing his nut, trying to work whilst being interrupted all the time, not just by people looking for supplies, but by observers on the scrounge for a cup of coffee from the office percolator, writing their patrol reports on his desk the moment his back was turned and to add insult to injury, playing Space Invaders on the laptop that was supposed to be the direct data entry device for the CAPSAT. With Archie's departure imminent, both Bill Feaster and I had been asked whether we would like to come into the office and assume a staff appointment. Neither of us was keen on the idea and the sight of Archie suffering late into the night whilst those around him did nothing to help, indeed did everything in their power to stop him working, filled both of us with trepidation. What actually annoyed me though was why Urpo the HOS, had allowed the situation to continue like this for so long. But in a way, I suppose the answer to that was that the situation didn't personally affect him. Archie had often been working an eighteen hour day for fifty-six days at a stretch in an unsafe environment that was not conducive to work and had stoically been covering three jobs (although at the time this was not recognised and therefore the posts were not established) whilst Urpo had simply watched from the side lines. As DHOS, Archie had overall oversight of what the Sector did on a day-to-day basis. He also ran operations in detail and finally he looked after the administrative and financial side of the house. Urpo had ultimate responsibility for what went on, but in practice that only amounted to being the Sector's interface with the HQ in Belgrade, and with the outside world and Montenegrin officials. Bill and I were determined that we were not going to follow suit and be taken advantage of like Archie had been. Both of us were keen to stay in the field but at the same time were acutely aware that things needed to be gripped and sorted out. Eventually we both decided that we were up to the challenge and agreed to come in to the HQ. Bill took the more senior position of DHOS and I took the position of Operations Officer. We still hadn't managed to convince Urpo of the need for an administrative post and so Bill reluctantly took this on as well, but at least there were now two of us doing the three jobs Archie had done single-handedly for so long. Sorting things out was quite a challenge in itself but it was one that was compounded by the fact that we had no official hierarchy or seniority and getting people to do what we wanted them to do and to accept the changes we were about to introduce, would all have to be achieved by force of personality alone, something which in itself was further compounded by the different cultural and political background from which we were all drawn.

Bill and I decided that it was no use putting a sign up on the office door saying 'Keep Out,' for two reasons. Firstly, we needed people to come in to the office, albeit to work. We needed observers to talk, we had to debrief them properly and we had to be sensitive to their needs and fears whilst working out in the field and the dangers which that entailed. It is all too easy for Staff Officers to loose contact with reality if they sit in the comfort and relative safety of their HQ and distance themselves from their personnel in the field. Bill and I were both experienced enough to know the pitfalls of such action and always managed to keep an open office policy throughout. Secondly, we decided that the best way to bring about change and to professionalise our operations was to lead by example and set high standards in what we were doing so that observers would feel that they were part of a well oiled machine and hence behave accordingly. After all, they were all capable of doing so by virtue of their backgrounds and previous professional training. With this in mind, we set about sorting ourselves out first. The first thing we did was to get rid of the boss. We hired a second but smaller room across the hallway and gave it to Urpo. It was actually a good idea as not only did it create space for us in the main office, now renamed the Operations (Ops) Room, but it also meant that in Urpo's new office, we now had somewhere private to speak to visitors such as the Police or Army liaison officers whom we constantly summoned. Often as not, observers coming in from the field also used the quiet of the office to write up their reports rather than clamber all over the Ops Room. With more space available for us, we set about redesigning the layout of the desks and all the cabling, a task which took two days due to the amount and confusion caused by the complexity of all the systems. Jerry Cans of fuel were put outside on the balcony along with the tyres and other stores – not an ideal solution as this still entailed drivers coming back and forth with their loads, but at least the stuff wasn't inside the office any longer. The coffee machine was banished to Urpo's office, which was where we now took our own breaks, and playing Space Invaders on the CAPSAT was forbidden, indeed, doing anything in the Ops Room other than working was forbidden period, as should always have been the case. We also managed to obtain another computer from Belgrade, which meant that we could leave the CAPSAT laptop alone and both Bill and I had machines for our own use. This was actually a major achievement for us as although we could usually get resources out of the HQ in Belgrade, the fact that the Mission was not permanent meant that capital expenditure was often discouraged. Slowly Bill and I managed to go through all the files, sorting out what was required from that which was not. We designed and implemented a new system for filing our data, one which would enable us to go back through records and pick up and analyse patterns and so better target our resources in the future. We also set about archiving old data in preparation for the eventual end of the Mission. All our files would need to be kept for prosperity, and we knew that they would eventually have to go off to the ICFY Office in Geneva and so Bill and I set about organising archives for back-loading. Within about a fortnight, Bill and I had completely revamped the way we worked in the Sector HQ and people were beginning to benefit from the difference. By being more organised and by creating a professional working environment around us, people were no longer coming in to the office when they were bored and disturbing us. In turn we were no longer having to work from 7,00 am through to 11,00 pm like Archie had done. Quite often I had completed my own composite report (which I had to send to Belgrade each night) based on all the incoming BCP and mobile patrol reports, by around 9,00 pm and there was still a lot of room for improvement yet. Essentially once the Sector Daily Report had been sent, our work for the day was finished. But it was still a very long day. We took shifts for meal breaks always ensuring that one of us was in the Ops Room during the day and if we needed to do any physical exercise, which we did, then we had to do it outside of these hours. Bill and I often used to run together – for added safety in the town area – around 4,30 am. This was a huge strain on the both of us, but it was the only way at present, that we could get out and stay fit and be back in time for a shower, breakfast and to staff the Ops Room by 7,00 am.

There was one aspect of the routine that we never changed however. Sadly it was a very unpopular one but it was the one aspect that distinguished our Sector from all the others. This was a daily 4,30 pm meeting and it was held every single day that the Mission was in operation including Christmas day. All international staff who were not deployed in the field had to attend these meetings. Those manning the BCPs or conducting patrols could not, but those who had just returned had to attend despite perhaps wanting to sleep or do other personal administration etc. The purpose of these meetings was two-fold. Primarily they were used to disseminate information within the Sector and to provide a vehicle for the cross exchange of information between observers. Secondly they were a method of gelling the Sector together to work as a single team, something that was quite difficult to achieve yet essential to the success of the Mission. Since, for security and safety reasons, we were the only sector whose members had to live together in one place, we had a captive audience but nevertheless it was always difficult getting everyone to attend willingly. Surprisingly enough, most of the opposition to these meetings came from several Americans who lacked the ability to socialise outside of their own small group of fellow countrymen and who failed to grasp the opportunity to experience and absorb different cultural perspectives from their other colleagues. Instead they preferred to spend most of their off-duty time watching trash movies on pirated videos in a shared 'common room', which they had established solely for themselves. I had often worked with Americans before, usually with some of their elite military units, but I have always remained unimpressed. Most of the Americans I'd met were ignorant of world affairs and different cultures save that portrayed by their own media and as far as I was concerned, watching CNN was not the best way to learn. Thankfully Bill didn't fit this mould and where I had expected opposition to the meetings (from the Russians who had a political reason for ensuring that we were not operationally effective) the opposition never materialised. The meetings followed the same pattern every day. Urpo would often start off with any announcements and then Bill would follow on with information taken from the various print media that we received, namely the independent 'VIP News' from Belgrade. I'd follow on with operational updates and then we would go around the room asking each team leader to give a brief summary of their activities describing anything of note that had happened during their last deployment. Finally Bill would conclude with any admin points and then the floor would be open for any final comments. The meeting therefore followed a formal pattern starting with what NATO would refer to as G2 matters (information/intelligence), then G3 matters (operations) and finally concluded with G1/G4 matters (admin/log). In all, the meeting took about thirty minutes a day and was extremely beneficial in sharing operational information; passing administrative, personnel and logistic details, and for briefing everyone on wider matters such as the conduct of the war in Bosnia, which of course, we were trying to starve of its essential supplies. By insisting that the scheduling of these meetings was non-negotiable and that everyone not physically deployed would attend, we actually created the professional ethos and corporate bond that the other sectors could not. The spin off for Bill and I of holding these meetings, was that it was the vehicle by which we exercised our 'command and control' of the Sector. Without them, we would never have got anywhere, we would not have had control and we could never had hoped to raise and then maintain high professional standards, as too many observers would have simply gone about their own or their country's individual agendas. A second spin off of these meetings was the social aspect. It forced the Americans to socialise with the Russians and the rest of us, even if it was only for thirty minutes each day. But for the rest of the Sector, it went beyond that. The daily meeting was held along the corridor from the main office in another room on the fifth floor; namely the bar in 'Room 501.' The significance of this room number, is now known throughout numerous other missions across the Former Yugoslavia. Room 501, or just simply '501' as it was known, was both the Sector's bar and the focal point for all of us; observers, interpreters and drivers alike. We employed three local Montenegrin girls as bar staff; Irene, who ran the accounts for most of the period of the Mission, and two sisters; Biljana, the eldest and Natasa the youngest of the two. All three worked tremendously hard taking it in turns to work the evening shifts and also to help purchase stock during the day and to administer the accounts. Unlike our interpreters, they were not paid for by the Mission but by ourselves from the profits of the bar sales. As such they were paid only a fraction of what the interpreters received, but in my opinion often worked far harder than many of them. As it was considered too dangerous to venture out into the local bars at night, most if not all of the observers (and the interpreters and drivers as well) spent much of their off duty evenings in or around 501. We had built a wooden bar at the back of the room and had acquired a fridge and a portable stereo. Once the daily meeting was over, the bar opened and remained so until everyone had gone to bed. Needless to say, a lot of drinking went on, but there were never any problems of drunkenness whatsoever. The local Niksic beer, Niksicko Pivo, was renowned throughout the Former Yugoslavia as the county's best beer and we were lucky enough to have the brewery right on our door step. Some exceptional evenings were spent in 501 as it was tradition for observers to announce any special occasion that might give rise to a celebration. On Bastille Day we celebrated with the French, likewise with the Finns on their Independence Day and despite my earlier comments, the Americans did us proud on their 'Thanksgiving' Day throwing an excellent party. But any excuse would do, especially Birthdays. I celebrated my thirty-fifth in real style throwing the bar open all night on my tab and quite unexpectedly received a surprise set

of presents from the Russians, a gesture which I shall never forget. Of the
four Russians in the Sector, Vladislav, the youngest, had bought me a
Montenegrin vase, rather like an ancient Greek urn whilst the other three
had bought me three bottles of wine which they aptly labelled 'KGB,'
'GRU,' and 'Spetznas' to reflected their own individual professional backgrounds[49]. It was also tradition for observers to throw a party when they
were leaving the Mission. This was often a very sad occasion as we all built
up a tremendous rapport with each other despite our differing backgrounds
and the odd disagreement. When a departure was announced, the person
leaving would normally open the bar on their account and either Urpo, Bill
or myself – whoever was present at the time – would make a short speech
and vote of thanks, and then formally present ICFY Medals for completing
service in the Mission. These medals had been specially commissioned and
cast for the Mission to acknowledge our efforts in trying to establish peace
and stability to this troublesome corner of Europe. It was really a nice touch
and a far cry of the British 'old school tie' system of Honours and Awards.
Apart from it being a very pleasant social venue, 501 gave us the opportunity to really get to know each other better. This in turn enabled us to create
a very special camaraderie, which no other Sector enjoyed. Even three years
after leaving Sector Charlie, it was still possible to find people, now in other
Missions in other parts of the Former Yugoslavia, who still talked about the
Sector with affection. This alone gives testimony to what the Sector achieved
in Montenegro. It was also fascinating, with countless war stories being told
over the bar like when John Williams (simply known as 'JW'), a retired
Royal Artillery Colonel, recounted how, back in 1963 he had been rescued
from the jungles of Borneo & Sarawak by a young naval helicopter pilot
from 845 Royal Naval Air Squadron who had braved the odds which had
defeated the RAF and managed to reach the patrol and pluck them to safety
– only to find out that the pilot in question was Tim Stanning now Head of
ICFY Ops in Belgrade. But such stories were not confined to the same
nations and many crossed the divide of the Cold War, such as when Mike
Austin recounted the loss of a British helicopter shot down in Aden in
which the helicopter was recovered but the pilot never found. The mystery
was finally explained by one of the Russians, Igor who confirmed that the
pilot had been captured alive (although critically injured) by the Russians
and had been taken from the scene for interrogation and subsequently died.
Despite many such stories, there was never any animosity between former
adversaries. As is so often the case in the military, former warring factions
regarded each other as professionals and left it at that.

Considering that at any one time, there were approximately one hundred
people living and working in the Sector, we didn't have much to entertain
ourselves during our off duty hours. In Belgrade they all had the use of the
hotel's splendid facilities including a gymnasium and swimming pool. In
Niksic we couldn't even go and lose ourselves in the town, as we would
easily have been spotted as foreigners in such a small tight knit community.

So in addition to 501, we also had use of another room, 309 – which was used as a TV room and which was fitted out with a satellite TV system, a video player and several uncomfortable soft chairs. To be frank, it was never used much apart from as another venue for parties when we often set up a small disco in the room for special celebrations like Christmas and New Year. If one wanted to watch a video, then the very latest films were readily available for hire in one of several hire shops in the town. It was always quite amusing for me to know that newly released films were often available in Niksic before they were on general release in the United Kingdom. I recall watching the new James Bond movie, Golden Eye, only about a week after its official release. But the reason these films were available was because they, like many other items widely available in the Balkans, were pirated copies of Western originals. But these weren't copies of the original film, these were terrible Camcorder recordings of the actual film being shown in a cinema somewhere in the United States, a fact that I figured out whilst watching Golden Eye when I saw a member of the audience stand up and walk out! It was really quite amusing and to think that most of the shops would have been stocked with films obtained in a similar fashion said a lot about their attitude towards Western copyright laws.

Niksic itself was a small town in which the local people all knew each other. The Montenegrin dialect of Serbo-Croat[50] is quite distinctive and even our interpreters and drivers who came from Belgrade stood out as 'strangers' when they went into town. Every morning, a whole pile of us would go into the local market to buy bread, fruit and vegetables to take with us on our patrols or to the BCPs. As we walked about the town we were often subjected to the odd heckle by groups of men who always seemed to loiter around all day without anything to do. Usually we were simply referred to as 'UNPROFOR' and I am sure that even today, tourists would be called the same as it was impossible to get it through to even our liaison officers that we were not part of the armed 'UN Protection Force' that was operating inside Bosnia. Observers were required to travel in pairs when they visited the town and one of the pair was always required to have their radio with them. This system worked well and we never really had any major difficulties in Niksic itself, although this was mainly on the count that we generally never gave anyone the opportunity to make trouble with us. But our concerns were well justified. The town was the centre of most of the Mafia and organised crime activity in Montenegro. Apart from this indigenous problem, we also met the same Bosnian Serbs in the market place whom we were restricting at the crossing points. It would have been all too easy for them to take out their frustrations on us if we had been careless in the town. The Montenegrin Police were everywhere, there were as many Police officers on patrol in and around the small town square, as there would have been in the whole of a major UK city. These officers were needed however, as there was an over-riding sense of lawlessness about the town. The sound of gunfire was a daily event, which considering that this country was not at war, was quite disturbing. The Police were attempting to deal with the problem by making it illegal to open fire within the immediate area of the town centre, a statement which in itself acknowledges that trying to stop shooting verbatim, was an impossible aim. Although some of the shooting was directed at fellow Montenegrins, much of the overt violence that we had been warned about was not visibly evident. In the briefing that I had received before arriving in Niksic, I had been told that there were two murders a night. Yes, there was shooting all the time, but it was never clear to me whether there was a correspondingly large pile of bodies at the end of each day as a result of it all. Much of the shooting was connected with celebrations, saints' days, birthdays, weddings and the like. It was traditional for Montenegrins to stand on the balcony of their flats and to fire off long bursts of machine gun fire to celebrate such events. Likewise, in the small open space behind our hotel, guests would assemble outside the Registry Office and await the arrival of the bride and groom before letting off numerous volleys of automatic fire into the clear morning skies. In all these cases, the fact that 'what goes up – must come down' was never a consideration. Meanwhile the Police did their best to limit the shooting whilst at the same time, not wanting to stop the party. What was far more sinister however was the odd 'double-tap' sound of a pistol being fired, often after dark. It was difficult to imagine that these sounds were celebrations and one therefore tended to restrict ones movements after dark, even if you had become accustomed to the sound of shooting during the daytime, as you inevitable did. Added to this backdrop was the sound of explosions. These were not anything like as frequent as the gunfire, but nevertheless it was commonplace for the Montenegrins to use dynamite to blow up each others' shops and kiosks. All in all then, Niksic was not the sort of place you'd want to take your partner for an evening on the town. But we had to go out from time to time, it would have been far too claustrophobic not to have done so. In the summer, every evening started with the traditional 'Korzo,' the evening stroll through the town's main street. It seemed that the whole town would turn out. Older men would sit outside in the bars that lined the street (their womenfolk no doubt kept at home by tradition). Young men, dressed in tacky, dirty nylon shell suits would line the pavements watching the younger women and girls promenade up and down the main street. In stark contrast to their men-folk, Montenegrin women dressed as if they were on a Paris or Milan catwalk. Many of the clothes were home made to a professional standard and based on designs copied straight from fashion magazines. Many came from Italy, whose goods were readily available in the chic boutiques of Montenegro's Adriatic holiday resorts. As a race, the Montenegrins are very tall and because of their lifestyle – a lack of private cars and the absence of junk-convenience foods – they are mostly slim and healthy. The combination of tall, beautiful, slim women dressed in the latest Paris fashions, was one of the only bright spots in what was otherwise a fairly dull routine and many observers took the opportunity to practice their observation skills during the korzo as often as they could. The town itself was fairly nondescript although it was designed around the traditional square – Trg Slobodno – Freedom Square – with rather nice tree lined avenues coming off each corner. Just off the square and down the main street was a Tailor's Shop owned and run by the Brother of Radovan Karadzic, the most wanted war criminal in the world today. The buildings in the centre of town were mainly low, traditional designs made of stone and faced with plaster, but all were in a poor state of repair reflecting both communist neglect and the renowned Montenegrin penchant for laziness. In fact, many of the jokes in the Former Yugoslavia are made at the Montenegrins' expense, rather like the English tell yokes about the Irish, and most of these jokes centre around their laziness which certainly appeared to be national characteristic as far as the men were concerned. Later, I was even given a wooden scroll on which were carved the 'Ten Montenegrin Commandments' all of which followed the same theme such as, 'Why do something today, when it can be put off until tomorrow?' Some of the buildings in the centre of the town were typical communist utilitarian structures that did little if nothing to blend in with their more traditional surroundings. Out in the suburbs there was a mixture of run down, drab apartment blocks, traditional single story buildings grouped together in settlements and some terrible lean-to shacks in what resembled a South African shantytown. All in all it was not a pretty place and although many took immense pride in their immediate surroundings, most areas were drab and strewn with litter and abandoned cars. There were numerous restaurants throughout the town but the security issue restricted our ability to frequent them all. The most friendly and therefore the most used venues were a pizza place in the centre of the town, and a proper restaurant just a few hundred metres away from our hotel. Restaurant 'Arcada' was located at the bottom of a high-rise block of flats in a residential area of town. The Mafia frequented it and so access to it was strictly controlled. To get in to it you had to negotiate a sliding steel door that was opened from the inside and controlled via a CCTV camera. The actual restaurant was down a flight of stairs which meant that it was totally underground giving the impression of entering a bomb shelter. The decor however, was such that it gave the appearance that you were above ground level with subtle lighting hidden behind net curtains giving the impression of normal daylight. The food here was excellent and inexpensive by our standards yet well beyond the pocket of normal Montenegrins, except that is, those powerful families who continued to make money from the country's traditional occupation of smuggling and banditry. It was quite amusing to consider that the safest place for us to eat out was in a restaurant frequented by Mafia gunmen and crime families who simply left us to our own devices.

There was little else to do or see in Niksic and so most of our off duty time was therefore spent in the hotel. Hotel Onogost was dreadful and typified all that was wrong with the state controlled system. Apart from the drab, modernist styling which looked both inappropriate and already dated, the hotel was run by a management that cared little whether the hotel was empty or full. Indeed, as it wasn't run as a business, it didn't matter whether they attracted customers or not and, since it was the only hotel in the whole region, they knew that if people needed somewhere to stay, then they would have to stay at the hotel. As such, customer service was non-existent, but this was not a phenomenon directed just at foreigners. Even fellow Montenegrins were treated in the same shoddy, off-hand manner. At breakfast, the only choice was 'ham and eggs' but you still had to wait ages to have your order taken and then seemingly ages again for it to be delivered. Often it could take forty-five minutes just to be served, even in an almost empty restaurant. When the food did eventually arrive, it would always be swimming in grease as clearly they did not own a spatula and merely poured the contents of the pan, oil and all, onto one's plate. Every morning I had to pin the ham and eggs down to my plate with my fork and pour the oil into a glass ashtray before I could begin to eat anything. Other meals in the hotel were equally bad. This was in part due to the sanctions, but as most other (private) restaurants were able to serve good quality meals, it was not the only reason. For sure, fresh vegetables soon stopped appearing as the autumn and then winter arrived. The Montenegrins could not import fresh supplies, neither did they have a system of tinned or frozen food distribution and so for six months a year had to eat only what they had individually pickled in jars and set aside for the winter. Vegetables and salads gave way to pickled cucumbers and pickled cabbage. It was monotonous in the extreme; everyday the same, ham and eggs for breakfast, pizza for lunch in the town and meat with pickles in the evening. But even under these circumstances, the hotel could have done better but it just didn't care to. Everyone was in the same boat, locals and Mission members alike. It was what people expected from a state run hotel and it was what people got. In the rooms, the service and standard was little better. Whilst we always had running water, a luxury I was to sorely miss several months later amongst the misery of Sarajevo, we often had only cold water for days on end and during the winter it was common place for the heating system to fail completely. Perhaps the most irritating thing however, was the fact that the hotel didn't provide bath or sink plugs. It sounds stupid, but this was a phenomenon that was common to everywhere I stayed during the three years I lived in the Former Yugoslavia. Whether there were plugs in years gone by is hard to say, but I never came across one in any hotel. This of course meant that when there was hot water, you still couldn't take a bath, and when you washed and shaved, the hot water just went down the plughole. Not that this seemed to matter, as environmental conservation was not on anybody's priority list in the Balkans. The solution of course, was to bring your own set of plugs back with you after your first period of home leave. The one area however, in which the hotel tried to do well, was in providing the venue for various concerts and celebrations. At the end of the school year, the senior classes of students throughout Yugoslavia traditionally celebrate their graduation with a Graduation Ball. In Niksic the hotel staged a huge party and dance in their honour, although we all kept well clear. However, the largest event they staged was a traditional Gusle concert. The Gusle, is the national instrument of Montenegro, rather like the Bagpipes are to Scotland. It looks rather like a violin of sorts but is slightly bigger and usually carved from solid wood with a huge ornate eagle or similar on the top of the arm. There is only one string, which is also played with a bow, but the instrument is held vertically like a cello and not under the chin like a violin. The other major difference between the two is that the Gusle sounds like someone murdering a cat. This assault on the eardrums is worsened by the accompanying singing, which similarly sounds like someone else murdering yet another cat. Whilst it is not my intention to be derogatory about a country's national instrument, the description is quite accurate although I am told that the ability to sing in tune with the instrument, is a complex vocal achievement. Needless to say, many observers took a shine to these beautifully hand-made instruments and bought them as souvenirs, although no one really managed to appreciate the music, no matter how long they served in the Sector.

Outside of the hotel and its immediate environs, the countryside provided the greatest attraction. The scenery was breathtaking and one of the best parts of the job was that we were able to absorb this during the normal course of our duties. There were two 'attractions' however, which we always recommended observers visit as part of their 'education' as well as relaxation. Both of these were off our normal patrol routes and near to the capital, Podgorica. The first attraction was the Ostrog Monastery, which was located high above the Zeta valley and cut into the sheer rock face of the mountainside. From the main road that ran between Niksic and Podgorica, you could just make out a tiny spec of white reflecting from the white-washed walls of the monastery high up in the distance. It was a feat of engineering prowess and certainly one of the holiest sites of the Montenegrin Orthodox church as it contained the remains of Saint Vasylius. Vasylius was born in Hercegovina in the small hamlet of Mrkonjic just Northwest of Trebinje but spent much of his time in Montenegro evading the Turks. Quite how the monastery was built in such a precarious position beggared belief as it took almost an hour to drive up the mountainside on the new road that had been made for that purpose. The actual site itself was carved into the side of the rock face and access to it other than by the road would have necessitated abseiling down by rope from the top of the mountain. The second attraction was the district of Tuzi just South of Podgorica. Tuzi had a huge flee market which was well worth a visit and also gave its name to the nearby customs point between Montenegro and Albania which was a few kilometres further South again. Albania was probably the poorest country in Europe and has very little going for it after years of closeted and insular dictatorship. Much of the population scratch a pitiful existence off the land but as in Montenegro, much of the land is too barren to cultivate. Even the rocky landscape of Montenegro looked lush compared to the barren grey rocks of Albania, which were readily visible immediately across the border. It was as if a child had taken a paint brush and had painted one side of the border green and the other side grey, such was the stark difference in landscapes, no doubt caused by over enthusiastic cutting of wood and scrub on the Albanian side. Our mission was to verify that the supply lines to the Bosnian Serbs had been cut. To do this we monitored the River Drina. Meanwhile, the UN was imposing sanctions on the FRY as punishment for previous transgressions and to continue to apply pressure on Milosevic to keep out of Bosnia's affairs. These sanctions involved ensuring that nothing got into the FRY and in theory the SAMCOM Teams which were operating in every country that had a common border with the FRY, were supposed to administer these sanctions and ensure that nothing got through. But it only took a second standing on this border, to know that it wasn't working. The twentieth century hadn't yet reached Albania, most of the population travelled in horse drawn carts yet in 1995, Albania imported more oil than West Germany did. Clearly it was not all for domestic use, it was coming into Montenegro. The actual Montenegrin border post consisted of several small buildings either side of the main road that ran along side Lake Scutari. There was a similar set of buildings about a hundred metres further down the road that marked the Albanian border post. Both sets of officials dutifully went about their business of checking what went through their posts; cars, buses and small lorries were all properly checked and cleared for passage. No one however, took a blind bit of notice of what was happening on the lake only some ten metres away. First of all, there was a roaring trade in goods going on. Huge articulated lorries (clearly trade and therefore proscribed) would drive up to an area of grass which had long been designated as a turning circle and off-loading area. Here they would unload all their cargo and cross deck it onto small boats that would then ply the hundred metres back and forth between the two countries, collecting and dropping off endless quantities of supplies. In return, the Montenegrins received desperately needed supplies of oil. Emanating from the Albanian side was a pipeline that carried the oil across the short strip of water to an endless supply of waiting petrol tankers. These tankers filled up with oil and drove off to Podgorica in a continuous operation which made a mockery of the UN sanctions and which made a farce of the customs inspections which were being rigorously applied to individual citizens only some ten metres away. I brought the matter to the attention of the Foreign Office, as I am sure other observers did as well. But the tide was never stemmed and I understand it was in part due to Albania's reluctance to stop the trade, which it too, sorely needed.

Having started to put our own house in order, Bill and I continued to make gradual improvements to the way in which we and the Sector operated. One thing we were keen to ensure was that the relief teams going out to the BCPs got out on time each morning. This was a simple task of ensuring that one of us was always down stairs out the front of the hotel each morning to castigate those who were not ready to move on time. Often the problem was with the interpreters who really had the least excuse for being late. Sometimes the drivers weren't ready but slowly and surely, we turned this around. Within a month we had drivers doing proper checks of their vehicles each morning and all teams departing on time. We also decided that we needed another office in addition to the extra one that we had acquired for Urpo. The reason was that we needed somewhere for the Customs Team to operate from. The team needed to pop back and forth between the hotel and the customs inspection site across the road on a frequent basis but had to complete all their paper-work back in the privacy of the hotel. We managed to convince Urpo that it was necessary and as part of the deal we hived off some of the administrative and finance work across to the team as well. This was a good deal all round as it divided the work responsibilities more evenly and left each member of the HQ with more time to do what they ought to have been doing all along. We then decided to tackle the subject of general professionalism. This was a tricky area, as at the end of the day, we had no legal powers to enforce anything. Instead we requested, pleaded, cajoled or embarrassed observers into behaving better. By putting our own house in order, we at least now looked the part but we still had to get people to come on board. The first thing we did was to ensure that new arrivals were treated better, welcomed into the Sector properly and briefed thoroughly on what we were about, so as to enable us to set a high standard right at the start of an individual's tour. Previously, how you were treated on arrival had been a hit and miss affair. More often than not your own countrymen would take you aside and fill you in on what was hap-pening and how we went about things. Bill and I decided that every time new arrivals came from Belgrade, that we would ensure that they travelled on the early morning and not the evening flight and that, where possible, they trav-elled in groups rather than trickled into the Sector individually. That way we could devote sufficient time to proper 'in-briefings' and did not have to end-lessly repeat everything every one or two days. Having been picked up at Podgorica airport, arrivals would be taken to their rooms and then for break-fast in the hotel. By 9,30 am they were ready to meet Urpo and then to receive their first briefing from me on Ops. An Admin/Log briefing from Bill followed, and finally we would then attach an observer to give the newcom-ers a quick tour of Niksic and to accompany them to lunch in the pizza place. After lunch, the same observer would take them out to the nearest BCP at Vilusi just to give them a quick taste of what was to come. Finally, they would all be welcomed and introduced to the rest of the Sector at the daily 4,30 pm briefing which was followed by a good session in 501. Having been up since 4,00 am in order to catch the Belgrade to Podgorica plane, this was a very long and tiring day for them especially when one also considers the stress and worry of travelling into the unknown. Nevertheless, it set both the scene and the right tempo for the rest of one's tour.

To ensure that our teams performed properly when out in the field was a far more difficult problem to solve. Clearly, the majority of teams didn't need checking but there are always bad apples in any organisation and we were no different. I started by ensuring that all mobile patrols were given 'out-by' and 'in no earlier than' times, in addition to their routes and objectives. This ensured that they didn't simply race around a given patrol route to get back to Niksic as quickly as they could. I also started to substantially vary patrol timings. Previously, all mobile patrols had been back in by the 4,30 pm briefing, but this routine meant that we hardly ever conducted night patrols and there was a marked sense of predictability about the way we went about our business which could easily have been exploited by the FRY. Patrols now went out day and night around the clock, not a very popular decision but one that was nevertheless professionally necessary. I also got patrols to call in and visit all the BCPs they passed on their route as a matter of SOP (Standard Operating Procedure). By making it SOP, BCP teams could not justifiably get angry and accuse a mobile team of checking up on them – the onus was now on the BCP team to be awake and if they weren't then they only had themselves to blame if they were reported. I altered the mobile patrol 'De-Brief Report' to include a list of what BCPs were visited by the patrol and asked for comments. In practice, fellow observers didn't want to catch their mates out, but neither did they want to be put in an awkward position by lazy colleagues. The system worked well and it became normal practice for a Mobile to call up the BCP on radio before arrival thus ensuring everyone was turned out, even if they hadn't been previously. Tackling BCPs was also a major issue. Again I changed the BCP 'De-Brief Report' to force observers to conduct checks and take certain actions. I added a part that dealt with cleanliness on handover, which asked about when and for how long the generator was tested so that we could programme maintenance work and asked whether the supplies of fuel and MRE Ration Packs were complete. Even if a shift hid the facts, the oncoming shift would report items missing for fear of being accused by the next shift. For the best part of two months, Bill and I put in place minor obstacles to stop people shirking their responsibilities only to see someone find a way of circumventing them. The game never ended. With every new procedure, someone would discover a way around it, but overall there was no doubt that things had become far more professional already. Unfortunately and all too quickly, the time came when Bill and several other Americans had to depart the Mission. Bill had singularly failed in his personal mission to come to Yugoslavia to get 'out of the office.' He had spent most of it in the office working very long hours trying and succeeding to improve things for all of us in the Sector. We all benefited from his efforts, but he did far more than many people realised. Behind the scenes he helped many of us with our personal problems and difficulties; me with some major studying that I was also completing for the Institute of Management and others with counselling which inevitably considerably prolonged his already long day. He was a great loss to the Sector and as with all such departures, his leaving party was a very sad affair.

With Bill's departure, I became the DHOS and a Dane, Andrej Waltenburg, otherwise known, as 'Blood-Axe' became the Ops Officer. Andrej had previously served with the ECMM in Croatia and knew exactly what he was doing. He was a good operator, spoke quite a bit of the local language and was keen to help out in the HQ, something which at that stage was still considered to be a bad option due to the amount of work involved. Customs was now being run by another Brit, Jon Fellows who was seconded to us by HM Customs and Excise having taken a break from his normal job at Luton Airport. Jon was a really sound guy and was doing an excellent job with the Montenegrin customs officers across the way in their compound. His side kick, a Swedish Customs Officer called Lena Larssen, was also now taking on more and more of the administrative tasks which left me in a better position than Bill had been in as DHOS, to get involved more fully in what we were doing on the ground. Finally I convinced Urpo of the need to officially appoint an Admin/Log officer as this job needed doing anyway, and with winter fast approaching, we had to ensure that our vehicles, equipment and BCP containers were up to the job. Finally then we managed to get ourselves properly established and the Sector now sported a HOS, a DHOS, an Ops Officer, an Admin/Log Officer and a Customs Officer. This was a far cry from what I had inherited and things were really beginning to move now. With Jon's departure, Lena took on the Customs duties and a newly appointed 'JW' set about sorting out the admin and logistic arrangements, hiring a proper store room downstairs in the hotel foyer area and implementing a winterisation programme for all our kit and vehicles. We even employed a mechanic cum chief driver to sort out minor problems with our vehicle fleet rather than follow the ridiculous instructions to back-load our cars to Belgrade for minor services etc. To co-ordinate the work of the staff officers in the HQ, I introduced a system of 'morning prayers' which I conducted every day at 9,15 am with the HQ staff. We would all gather in Urpo's office over a coffee whilst the Ops Room and associated radios were monitored by Dragan, the Chief Interpreter. Once JW had ensured all the relief patrols had got underway, he would join us and we would run through the schedule for the day and for the forthcoming days ahead. In this way we co-ordinated transport assets to meet operational and administrative requirements such as mobile patrols and taking people to and from the airport, we allocated interpreters to specific tasks and insured that we addressed the overall needs and concerns of the Sector. We were also able to examine BCP and mobile patrol reports and begin to identify patterns and concerns which we needed to raise with the local Police, customs or military authorities. From these meetings a number of things became apparent. One such problem which we identified was that no matter how well we improved things and motivated people, some observers were still getting lost when out on the ground. Navigation was very difficult and the 1942 Wehrmacht maps didn't help much. We had to devise a system of helping those less able than others to get about and to reach their targets. The solution, which took a lot of time and effort, was to send expert map readers to each target area recording their route on a schematic diagram showing turns, distances and marker points. These had to be very accurate, as the intention was to get the less able navigators to their objectives without the use of a map and solely by means of reading these instruction boards. Distances were recorded from vehicle trip counters and exact positions were registered using Magellan GPS Satellite Navigation Equipment. In all, it took nearly a month to create these boards but in the end they enabled all our teams to be utilised in any role rather than have to rely on the best navigators to get to the remotest targets. Perhaps the most serious concern which we identified however was the fact that we still did not provide twenty-four hour coverage in the Ops Room. I had identified this weakness when I was in the field and now that I was the DHOS, the onus was on me to address it. The simple fact remained that if we had observers deployed to the BCPs and overnight mobile patrols, then we should have someone monitoring the radios back in the Ops Room in case there was an emergency. There was no escaping the logic of this requirement yet it was not Mission practice to staff Ops Rooms after 11,00 pm at night when Archie and latterly Bill and I had been standing down. Our reorganisations in the Sector had cut down our working hours in the HQ quite considerably, but even under the improved system we were still having to staff the Ops Room between the four of us (as well as conduct our normal duties) from 7,00 am until 11,00 pm each day. I was determined to address the issue and to ensure that the place was properly staffed at all times. A compromise half measure was not going to be acceptable operationally and so I was in no doubt that this was going to be an unpopular move, whatever the eventual solution. I broached the subject at one of the 4,30 pm meetings. To my surprise the logic of my argument seemed to carry the day. Most people were happy with the concept and since they were the ones who were out in the BCPs and therefore might be calling for help, there was almost unanimous agreement to the need to find a solution. In order to capture everyone between shift rotations, I repeated the argument at the next two meetings obtaining a similar reaction. My first attempt at reaching a solution was to call for volunteers to do the duty from 9,00 pm until 7,00 am. To my surprise there was no shortage of volunteers despite the fact that those volunteering would probably have just come off BCP duty that same morning. The Americans were the most willing as they all took their work very seriously and it was encouraging to see such a team spirit amongst the Sector. Things had genuinely improved. Unfortunately though, the system soon became unsustainable, as it was always the same few who volunteered each time. I instigated a log of who had done the duty and started to read out the totals hoping to shame those who had not yet volunteered into doing so. But that didn't really work either as some people just didn't care. In the end, we had to bite the bullet and pull an observer off the BCP/Mobile roster – something which we could ill afford to do – and formally schedule the Ops Room 'Watch-keeper' duty as a proper shift. By agreement it was decided to run the duty for a week at a time, thus allowing people to get used to the night-time shift routine and to work the shift from 7,00 pm through to 7,00 am. The system worked well and we made it as easy and as comfortable as possible by obtaining another satellite TV and coffee machine, although we soon had to ban anyone other than the Watch-keeper from watching TV in the room as it would have fast turned in to another 309 and undone all our efforts and gains so far. Providing a Watch-keeper meant that we had proper professional cover for those deployed in the field, twenty-four hours a day. Once I had written the orders for the duty it also had several side benefits, such as ensuring that 501 closed down at midnight and not when the last person had finished drinking, as had previously been the case. It also had the effect of reducing my own working hours from a routine eighteen hours to a more manageable twelve hours per day, although I still had to find time for personal fitness and was still permanently available like Bill before me, to deal with people's problems and concerns.

The Sector was now well deservedly earning itself an extremely good reputation within the Mission. No longer was a posting to Niksic seen as the worst option in the Mission, but increasingly it was seen as the most desirable. When observers past through Belgrade, as they all had to on their way to and from leave, stories of what we were about and the spirit we had engendered inevitably got out. The Mission HQ began paying more interest in what we did and we suddenly began to attract more and more visits from the Head of Mission and his staff. As our professionalism and the interest of the HQ grew, the inevitable poaching began. Belgrade needed good Staff Officers just the same as the Sector HQs did. We were all on the look out for suitably willing and capable staff to fill the various HQ posts but many capable observers still preferred to stay working in the field and so volunteers were still hard to find. The attractions of Belgrade however, were great. Compared to life in Niksic, those living in the Hotel Hyatt lived a life of luxury with excellent accommodation and facilities, good food and the prospects of a normal social life as well. I had been asked to move to Belgrade on several occasions but had always refused. For some reason, I always thought that the luxury of the Hyatt was somewhat incongruous to what the Mission stood for and for that reason preferred to stick it out at the sharp end in Montenegro. Andrej was the first to go, poached to be the Communications Officer in Belgrade. Unlike me, Andrej was a reserve officer in his Air Force and so completing a suitable post in the Mission HQ in Belgrade would have done his proper career wonders, something which I no longer had to worry about. Fortunately, finding a replacement was now becoming easier. As our own HQ was becoming more professional and better organised, observers were now keen to become a part of it and there was no shortage of well-motivated and capable volunteers. Andrej's replacement was an American, Bob Freeman who was still keen to tackle the issue of the 'Delta Boulevard' which we had both become interested in during our time on mobile patrols together and which we still hadn't solved. But this was only one of the issues that we faced. Over the previous few months, there had been such a drastic turn around in professionalism, that I was determined not to let such progress be reversed. Together with Bob, we set about devising ways of sustaining what we had achieved so far. With so many good people coming forward to help in the management of the Sector and with few positions open to them, there was a chance that people might become frustrated. To tackle this possibility, we decided to devolve responsibility down further and to appoint Section Leaders. Our detachment in Heceg Novi had always had someone 'in charge' but this was never a formalised arrangement, rather it was a leadership position assumed by force of personality. It had worked relatively well but we now wanted to use a formally appointed Detachment Leader to conduct more of the routine liaison functions with the Montenegrin Police, and the Yugoslav Navy and Army in that area. Such liaison was infrequent as we conducted it from Niksic during routinely scheduled visits. But this system didn't give us the flexibility to drop in as frequently as we would have liked. Neither did it afford us as a Mission, the ability to build up the necessary rapport with local officials which is so fundamental in any relationship in the Balkans. Urpo, the HOS liked the idea and appointed a Russian to the post, a smart move which went down well with the local military commanders and Police alike. In the Niksic AoR, we appointed a Section Leader to run the two most Northerly BCPs, which were operating on a forty-eight hour basis, and another Section Leader to cover the twenty-four hour BCPs at Vracenovici and Vilusi. Finally we appointed a Section Leader to cover the mobile patrol section. In essence, another four observers, who all remained deployed in the field with their sections, had been given responsibility for working out shift patterns, ensuring that equipment was maintained, working out patrol routes and for overseeing the day to day operations of their sections. To pull all these advances together and to formalise them as the correct and normal way of operating, I set about rewriting the Sector's SOPs. This was a mammoth task, as the SOPs had to reflect all the changes made to the way we operated. In some cases this was simply a matter of changing the BCP and Mobile report formats over to the new ones. But in most cases it involved either rewriting whole sections of operational detail, such as the hand-over routine between BCP shifts and the detailed requirements for checking the inventories, or it involved the writing of completely new sections from scratch, such the Watch-keeper's Orders, 501 Bar Rules, the Role and Organisation of the Sector HQ, Job Descriptions and Orders for the Admin/Log Officer and the Customs Team and special considerations such as 'in-briefings' and formalised Continuation Training on satellite communication systems etc, which we had never previously addressed properly. In all, it took me four months to complete the new SOPs and it was only done that quickly with the help of all the HQ's Staff and with another American, John Arthur, who was an expert on computers and worked diligently in his spare time typing up text and amendments piecing the document together bit by bit. At the end of the four months though, we had an excellent set of SOPs that served as a reference document for the way we went about our business. It covered both operations and administration. It dealt with new issues such as training, discipline, grievance procedures and covered in detail essential aspects which had not been adequately addressed beforehand, such as a proper Sector Evacuation Plan which we also had to write from scratch. But this was not a paper exercise, it was a living document and it had been born from the changes and improvements that had gradually been implemented over the preceding months. It also reflected the way the Sector lived and breathed, encompassing as it did, the professional ethos and enthusiastic team spirit that the Sector now had, the like of which I had rarely seen before or sadly, since.

But whilst all these procedures were being rewritten and these changes were being implemented, life in the real world was continuing unabated and as DHOS, much of my day-to-day work involved dealing with real incidents as and when they occurred in the field. The Delta Boulevard was still attracting our attention and we again turned to John Arthur for help. What we needed was a simple database setting up, to enable us to record all vehicle movements across the border in either direction and at any BCP. We had the data on paper already, BCP reports were now recording the registration numbers of all trucks crossing their checkpoint but we were not able to interrogate this mass of information meaningfully. By putting it all onto a database, we could see that certain trucks came into the country empty – legally – and then came in again and again. We had no record of them ever leaving. From this we could deduce that they had to be crossing back into Bosnia illegally at a point other than a recognised BCP and as such, we could also assume that they were full of contraband. It was then a relatively simple matter of working out the pattern of an individual truck's movements and of looking out for it. Mobile teams were tasked to be at certain points at certain times of the day in order to try and spot the vehicles as they passed. We were not allowed to stop or challenge these trucks; indeed it would have been very dangerous to try to do so out in the wilds of the mountains unarmed and with no back up. Instead we built up a picture of what was happening and presented our findings to the VJLO, Captain Konotar. Konotar was less than impressed, but at first said that he'd look in to it all. For several weeks he came back with little more than denials stating that nothing was happening and that we were all very much mistaken. We presented him with the hard evidence and demanded that the VJ take action. To stress the point, we started to submit VIREPs at an alarming rate as he had already had long enough to deal with the problem but had clearly been stringing us along. This time Konotar reacted, but not to solve the problem. It was normal for him to attend our meetings in uniform, but recently he had started to turn up in jeans wearing a black leather bomber jacket with his pistol tucked down the back of his belt. With short, razor length back hair, dark complexion and often unshaven, he cut a mean figure, made all the more menacing by the Makarov pistol. It wasn't pleasant doing business with him at the best of times, he loathed our presence in his country and never tried to conceal it. Now we had questioned his integrity and found him wanting. Some thing was happening on the 'Boulevard' although just what was still difficult to say. Whether it was an Army operation to break the sanctions or simply local Mafia or villagers running supplies was not yet clear. But whatever it was, Konotar was riled that we had found out about it. In one of the most menacing confrontations I'd been involved in since arriving in theatre, he told Urpo and I to back off. Looking me straight in the eye he warned, 'It's too dangerous to patrol at night, anything could [and probably would] happen if you're not careful'. The VJ patrol the area and they will shoot if necessary,' adding finally, '... and I'm not prepared to guarantee your safety.' The threat was clear. In communist parlance he had just told me that if I wasn't careful and didn't heed his warnings, then some-thing very nasty was likely to happen to me. For the first time, I was seri-ously worried. Whilst Bob and I continued to direct operations including daily patrols on the Boulevard, Urpo did wonders to diffuse the situation. He called General Tauno Nieminen, ICFY's Finnish Head of Mission and had him raise the matter with the VJ General Staff at Army Head Quarters in Belgrade. VIREPs continued to be submitted and the situation remained tense for several weeks before getting worse.

The composition of the Mission was multinational, multi-cultural and multi-political. This wasn't just a matter of the Sector versus the VJ. There were also internal complications. Bob and I had been 'successful' in uncov-ering a small gap in the border, of developing a way to analyse the data and ultimately to detect what was happening there, namely the systematic exploitation of an area which was supposed to have been sealed by the VJ. But the Russians didn't see it as a 'success' at all. To them it was far too effi-cient. For me to be threatened by Konotar was one thing, but to be threat-ened again several days later by a member of my own Mission was quite another. Nikolai was a KGB Colonel and the senior Russian in the field. He was typically 'old school' and frequently travelled to Belgrade for meetings with the Mission's Russian Chief of Staff under the pretence of debriefing him and the Head of Mission on the political aspects of our work in Montenegro. He did this because he held the position of the 'ICFY Special Envoy to Montenegro', a job he generally speaking did very well, as being a Russian he was able to smooth over many matters with the local leadership which we might otherwise have had great difficulties with. Nevertheless, like everyone else, Nikolai visited his embassy each time he was in Belgrade and it was following one of these routine visits that he took me aside and like Konotar, warned me, 'My Embassy is concerned for your safety. We think the night patrols are dangerous and that you should reconsider them before someone gets killed.' And then just like Konotar, he added, 'My Embassy can not guarantee your safety if you continue.' This was a nightmare out of control. I had no doubt that any one of a number of people could easily have topped me if they had been given the go ahead. Furthermore, the chances of anyone being caught were non-existent. Niksic was an extremely dangerous place to start with and now I had the VJ and the Russians threatening me as well. Fortunately for me and just in the nick of time, Urpo's high-level dealings with Belgrade managed to bring about a solution. The VJ at Army level directed that the Mission was right to demand the creation of another permanently manned check point (CCP) on the border at '4 – Delta.' We had won the day but it had been a frightening experience for me and a lesson well learnt on where the boundaries lay and what could and what could not reasonably be expected from an unarmed diplomatic Mission who's remit entailed diplomacy and negotiation and not force and coercion.

As autumn turned to winter, the war in Bosnia was coming to its climax and the effects were becoming more evident on our side of the border as more and more refugees passed into Montenegro towards the town of Pluzine and the sounds of artillery became more frequent and audible from our BCPs. The helicopter at Nudo had been reported several times crossing back and forth between the two countries but finally disappeared for good, only for us to learn later from the newspapers that it had crashed with the loss of four lives whilst on one of its frequent trips to Belgrade. At Scepan Polje, the effects were vividly and tragically brought home to us all when, at the beginning of September, six very young school children were rushed to our BCP caravan by the Bosnian Serbs who appealed to us for help. The children had found a hand-grenade and one of them had taken it into the school playground. Gathering over it to have a closer look, the group of six had either inadvertently or perhaps unknowingly removed the pin. Whatever the cause, the effect was deadly. The six had been huddled together over the grenade when it had exploded. The result was utter carnage. In desperation the Bosnia Serb Police had come to our team for help as at that stage all six were miraculously still alive. The team acted in an exemplary fashion, with their first aid kit they began administering what help they could whilst calling a 'May-Day' on the Satphone. Urpo and I took the call in the Ops Room. We were both quite numb but immediately called the VJLO, State Security Police (MUP), the local Police and the Interior Ministry to scramble assistance. Within minutes they were respond-ing and Police and military helicopters were en-route. We informed Belgrade Ops of the incident and requested airspace clearance for the heli-copters to transit through Bosnian airspace past Foca as this was the shortest route to the main hospital in Belgrade where they wanted to take the children. UN observers at Belgrade Air Traffic Control Centre gave the clearance but by then the helicopters had already over flown Bosnia anyway. Urpo and I kept the BCP informed of what was happening as the rescue operation got underway, but for one child it was too late. The team had done what they could for the children but one of them was so badly injured that he died on the pavement right outside the team's van. It was a tragic day for us all and vividly brought home what the real price of war was. The team was badly shaken by the episode but sadly more was to follow. A week later, NATO launched air strikes against the Bosnian Serb Republic at strategic points designed to inhibit the movement of men and materiel towards the UN save areas and enclaves which were being threatened by the Bosnian Serb Army under the leadership of General Ratko Mladic. The town of Foca, some ten kilometres from the BCP at Scepan Polje was and remains a key interchange with major routes heading South towards the Croatian coast, Northwest towards Sarajevo and North up the River Drina towards Gorazde and Srebrenica. Facilitating freedom of movement in all these directions was a series of major bridges across the River Drina. It was these

Foca / Srbinje: This picture shows one of the bridges blown up by NATO just outside Foca during the air strikes that had caused the widespread panic amongst the bus of school children that had tried to pass the ICFY BCP at Scepan Polje.

bridges, five in all, which NATO destroyed from the air in one of the first displays of NATO's impatience with the ever-faltering peace process and intransigence of the Balkan leadership. With news of the NATO action against Foca reaching us in Montenegro but with little to no details of targets or results, the situation became quite tense on the Northern border. The Bosnian Serb Police and customs officers were talking to their Montenegrin counterparts and if they were to be believed, then Foca had been raised to the ground, which clearly it had not been, at least, not by NATO. With this air of tension and apprehension, the problem was brought to a head when a bus full of school children turned up at the BCP attempting to cross back into Bosnia. The children were accompanied only by their teachers and had just enjoyed a week's holiday on the Adriatic coast, organised by a Greek charity in order to give them a break from the misery of the war. Sadly, all the children were from Foca and it wasn't until they reached the BCP that they learned that NATO had just bombed their town. They were petrified, utterly distraught and had no way of knowing what had happened to their parents and families, who for all they knew, could have been killed in the NATO air raids. To be fair to the Bosnian Serb Police, there was no accurate information available. They weren't deliberately trying to stir up resentment against our presence, they just decided that it was possible that Foca had been destroyed and that these children might not have any homes or families to go back to. The fact that NATO would not have deliberately set out to destroy a populated area of the town, was not something that they considered, and so under these circumstances they refused to allow the coach back into Bosnia. It was an awful and heart rendering situation. Our team had fifty school children stuck at the BCP all under the impression that their parents and families had been killed and their homes destroyed. The Montenegrin officials decided in true style, that the matter had nothing to do with them and that was that. Needless to say, faced with such a traumatic situation, the onus fell on the Sector to sort something out. There were only two other international organisations working in Montenegro who might have been able to help, ECMM which as far as I could discern from several visits to their HQ in Podgorica, did bugger all, and the International Federation of the Red Cross (IFRC) who were also in Podgorica. Their representative, Kari Vanhanen had been a frequent visitor to our HQ in Niksic dealing with various humanitarian issues pertinent to the border and our ability to control passage across it. It was now to him that I turned, asking him for details of what had happened in Foca, information that he could easily obtain from his colleagues in Bosnia. We also asked him to arrange accommodation and feeding for the children until such time as we had established the true facts and had obtained permission from the Bosnian Serbs to allow them through the border. Whilst this was being organised, our team at Scepan Polje was having to deal as best they could with the children and their teachers. JW who'd pulled the BCP duty over this unfortunate period was doing a marvellous job in calming the situation down and passing information to the party as and when we got it to him. But it was not easy for him and I know that the incident caused him much distress, so much so that I mentioned to London that he should be invited to speak with one of the FCO's professional staff counsellors who were available to help us deal with bereavement or other post traumatic stress disorders, when he was next in London. Kari sorted out over-night accommodation and feeding and we managed to establish that NATO had only hit several bridges and not the town itself and that it was therefore safe for the children to return. What we couldn't establish however, was whether all the bridges were down and whether this meant that the bus could actually get anywhere. Unfortunately they would have to find that out for themselves but thankfully we were able to set them on their way the next day knowing that their families and homes were indeed safe.

Although the overall situation was becoming more tense, we were now much better equipped to deal with it. As a Sector, almost everyone was working professionally save but a very small minority who still considered that it was easier to curry favour with the local Police and customs officers rather than take difficult decisions which might not go down too well. We knew who these people were and did our level best to ensure that we never put two of them together on the same shift at the same time. Unfortunately this was not always possible and predictably, the results were dire. At BCP-2 (Krstac), one of the teams had repeatedly allowed the Police to use the VW Iltis escape vehicle to collect water on their own. Where a BCP was several kilometres from the nearest village, the vehicle had to be used to fetch and carry Jerry cans of water, as these were too heavy to lift any other way. Normally, the ICFY driver would be used for this purpose and most teams did not object if members of the Police or customs team hitched a lift with our driver if they wanted to go to the local café for a while. In some cases, perhaps when the weather was bad and where the distance wasn't too great, we would even arrange for the vehicle to go back to the village and collect the officers from the café an hour or so later. What was never allowed was for the vehicle to sit in the village for an hour or two whilst the officers ate their lunch or for the Police to use the vehicle by themselves. An escape vehicle was of no use to anyone if it was several kilometres away, but sadly one of our teams had frequently allowed just that to happen. Because the Police demands to use the vehicle had been so frequent, they'd decided to give the Police the keys to the vehicle. The Police had come to accept this as the norm and indeed had become so friendly with the team that they were now having bar-b-cues together at the BCP. There was absolutely nothing to stop teams socialising with the Police if that helped build up a healthy working relation-ship, indeed to refuse to share a glass or two of Rakija, would certainly have the opposite effect and would create a barrier between them and the Police. But it was a fine line that one had to tread and walking it demanded a certain maturity and level headedness that was not evident in this particular team. The problem arose in mid October when the relief team came on and had to continue working with the existing Police/customs team which was working a seventy-two hour shift system and not a forty-eight hour one. That evening, three observers were leaving the Mission and as Urpo was on leave, I had the task of giving the leaving speeches and of presenting the ICFY Medals. One of those celebrating that evening had previously been responsi-ble on several occasions for giving the keys of the Iltis to the Police and he had also just finished the shift at Krstac that morning. Because it had been his last shift ever, he had held a celebration at the BCP and generally conducted a lax shift. This presented the on-coming team with horrendous difficulties as the Police and customs teams did not want to conduct their duties, instead they simply wanted to continue drinking. Ever increasing demands were placed on the team to free up the vehicle, something that they stoically refused to do. The situation had degenerated throughout the day with the team becoming increasingly more and more isolated. The ICFY driver had attempted on several occasions to defuse the situation. As a retired Police officer, he exerted quite a lot of influence on the younger serving officers but unfortunately he was from Belgrade and not Montenegro and so his interventions were largely ignored. By nightfall, the driver had taken the Police back and forth to the village several times attempting a workable compromise but as the Police became more and more drunk, the atmosphere became more and more sinister. It was forty KMs down a rough track to the main road out of Niksic. No one could help the team in such an isolated position on the Bosnian border. The Police were their protection but as the hours passed, it was the Police who were becoming openly hostile. Finally, around midnight, as the driver eventually recovered a Police team back to the BCP site – having been held at the village for several hours waiting for them to finish drinking – the British team leader, Adam Boys, a former Price Waterhouse accountant, intervened decisively. Adam took the keys to the Iltis and flatly refused to allow the driver to act as a ferry service any longer. The Police were enraged. Cursing the team and shouting that the previous team had allowed them to use the vehicle, the Police detachment leader, Striko drew his pistol, aimed at Adam and pulled the trigger. Adam described the sound as, 'a sickening click' – mercifully Striko didn't have a round up the spout. This was not the first time that a BCP team had been shot at or as in this case, so blatantly intimidated by the Police, but it was the first time it had been done so overtly without any attempt at concealment. Adam was lucky as Striko, in his drunken stupor, hadn't made his weapon 'ready' and the rest of the Police detachment still had the wherewithal to prevent him doing so. Meanwhile back in Niksic, the leaving party was drawing to a close and most of us were fairly well plastered. Fortunately, the duty Watch-keeper system was working well and was soon to prove its worth. A very shaken Krstac team had managed to call through on the Satphone and had alerted the Watch-keeper to the incident. He called for my presence and I took the phone, beer in hand and listened to what Adam had to say. The ten seconds or so that it took me to sober up seemed like an eternity. I remember saying, 'Shit.' There then followed a long pause as my brain raced to come to and focus. I managed a, 'Wait,' as I took several more seconds to form the makings of a coherent plan, breathing in and out deeply gasping at oxygen and holding the phone at arms length whilst I thought through the options. Finally I managed to blurt out instructions for Adam to evacuate the BCP in the infamous Iltis. I told Adam to get out with his kit. He was to take the driver but leave the interpreter and the other observer in-situ, as he assessed that the problem was personal and that as it had in effect already come to a head, nothing else was likely to happen unless Striko decided to have another pot at him. I got the Watch-keeper to fetch the Chief Interpreter, Dragan, and another observer, Kevin Andrews, a very steady and professional American who had served with 'Delta Force', the elite of the American military and their equivalent to the SAS. Within minutes Kevin, nicknamed simply as 'K2' because he was the second American by that name in the Sector, was ready to deploy. With a hastily rounded up driver he was dispatched to meet Adam half way, to swap over vehicles and then travel the remaining way to the BCP in the Itlis with the original driver and take over command of the team and report back. Meanwhile Dragan had got the Chief of the Internal Security Police, Misko, out of his bed and on my instructions, demanded that Striko be removed from the BCP area. Misko was thoroughly professional and he sent up an armed relief team to arrest Striko and bring him back to Niksic. The evacuation went without incident and a very shaky Adam eventually arrived back in the hotel around 1,00 am. Most observers had gone to bed by then but several had kept me, the Watch-keeper and Dragan company whilst we waiting for Adam. Biljana had kept the bar open and once Adam arrived she suitably plied him with several stiff drinks. The next two hours were spent waiting for Adam to write up a very detailed statement of what had happened, which we were later to use as the basis for a Diplomatic Protest against the Yugoslav authorities. I spoke to Belgrade and appraised them of the circumstances and when Adam had finished writing his statement at around 3,00 am, I sat down with him and Biljana in 501 to read it. Adam was still shaking, and both of us were exhausted and quite the worst for wear, albeit for quite different reasons. I read his report through several times, it was a fairly lengthy affair and must have taken me twenty minutes before I'd finished. After the second attempt it was apparent that I hadn't a clue what he written and as I returned to the start of the report for a third attempt, Adam burst out laughing, grabbed the document and offered to read it to me. His laughing was infectious and it started us all off, quickly easing the tensions and tiredness that had built up throughout the night. It was a moment I shan't forget, the three of us sitting there quite drained and exhausted, Adam alive but severely shaken and all of us laughing our heads off unable to read the report he'd just spent two hours drafting. The humour continued the next day as 'Wanted' posters started to spring up all over the hotel offering a reward for the capture of 'Adam – Chetnik – Boys,' who was allegedly, 'Wanted for desertion. Currently absent without leave from the war-zone of Krstac.' The reward was equally droll, 'A weekend in Niksic with Striko the gunslinger.' Unfortunately, the situation in Niksic was deemed too dangerous for Adam to stay in the Sector as Striko was being hauled over the coals for his action and many of his colleagues resented it. It would have been too easy for one of them to get back at Adam and so with much reluctance, we had to move him to Belgrade where he was far safer and later became the Mission Finance Officer.

Timing they say, is everything and one day before the Krstac incident, three German observers came proudly marching into the Sector. To be fair to them, all three were extremely pleasant and professional observers who soon fitted extremely well into the Sector, but it was an assimilation that was not without its difficulties. The Krstac incident served to remind us all of the dangers we faced and the need to maintain a common level of professionalism across the board. Without giving names, I reinforced the lessons-learned from Adam's incident at several of my 4,30 pm briefings. Not that it needed much reinforcing, other than to point out the real cause of the incident and to ensure that Adam's team was not, for some lack of understanding, drawn into the mud as well as those who were truly responsible. The incident scared the hell out of the Germans. For a long time, Germany had been represented in the Mission but had only deployed its observers to the other four sectors. Their presence in Montenegro had always been resisted due to latent animosities dating back to the Second World War. The German embassy had decided that enough was enough and that Germany had both faced and purged itself of its past and that the time was now right for it to fulfil a proper role in world events. I have tremendous sympathy with this view but such subtleties as these held no water with Montenegrin families and tribes who still followed a code which demanded that blood be drawn from those who had killed one of their own. The existence of the blood feud was seen as a very real problem, one that was reinforced in all our meetings with interlocutors where the subject was raised. The three Germans knew all this before they arrived and it was almost as if they were three sacrificial lambs being offered to the slaughter by their Embassy just to make a point. It was also a point that the rest of the Sector felt was a purely German one, and one, which they quite understandably decided, should not involve them. If the Germans wanted to make a point, then fine, but not if it required the rest of the Sector risking their lives as well. And this was precisely how their arrival was viewed in the Sector and indeed there was an element of logic about it all. When the Germans arrived, they had to be deployed with another team member of a different nationality and by definition, the whole team was then at risk. Nevertheless, there was no easy solution but to face the problem and bite the bullet. The Germans had to be deployed and despite the rhetoric from the Police and the VJLO, their passage went largely without incident much to the credit and professionalism of the three concerned.

7

The Road to Dayton Ohio

B y the end of 1995, the Bosnian Serbs were losing the war in Bosnia. It had dragged on for four long years confounding all attempts to bring it to an end by international mediators and governments alike. In effect, the inability of the IC to see the conflict for what it really was, part of a grand strategy by Milosevic to create a greater Serbia, was part of the problem which led to Bosnia's destruction and to the West's inability to stop it. Our belief that the war was essentially a civil war clouded our thinking, played to the script prepared by Milosevic and Karadzic whilst at the same time, tragically led to disastrous consequences. The much vaunted Vance-Owen Peace Plan (VOPP) which was finally tabled in Geneva in January 1993, gave refugees and displaced persons (DP)[51] the right to return, but at the same time gave full executive, legislative and judicial powers to the Cantons which were divided up equally between the three ethnic groups thus making it impossible to believe that one ethnic group would ever wish to return to a Canton ruled by another. But worse still, the areas allocated to each ethnic group were not confirmed, an oversight that incited renewed conflict as each side fought for greater territory. But the consequences didn't end there. The plan incited conflict between Muslim and Croat forces in central Bosnia, an area that up until then had contained a largely mixed population which had not been in conflict with each other.

> 'After the arms embargo, this [the VOPP] was the second most important contribution of the West to the destruction of Bosnia: it stimulated the development of a genuine Bosnian civil war, and in so doing it broke down the Croat-Muslim alliance which had been the only effective barrier to the Serbs.'[52]

As the war continued to rage on in central Bosnia with all its brutality and savagery, it was events on the ground which eventually gave rise to the conditions which would finally lead to peace. On 5th February 1994, a mortar attack on Sarajevo in which sixty-eight people were killed, convinced NATO to declare an 'exclusion zone' for heavy weaponry around Sarajevo and to warn of the threat of air strikes if the Serb commanders did not withdraw their forces from within the zone. Although sniper fire was to continue until the end of the war, General Mladic complied with NATO's demands and the heavy bombardment of Sarajevo ceased but for a few occasional breaches of the zone. But the most important development was a political/military one which finally, one year on, managed to reverse the disastrous effect of the Vance-Owen proposals, namely to stop the civil war between the Croat and Muslim armies. Throughout January and February 1994, Muslim and Bosnian Croat representatives worked on a plan to maintain the territorial integrity of Bosnia and to establish a decentralised system of administration based on Cantons. With American assistance an agreement was worked out to establish a Muslim – Bosnian Croat 'Federation.' Known as the 'Washington Agreement,' it was signed in Washington on 1 March 1994, and established a new constitution based on a series of Cantonal governments throughout all areas of Bosnia which had had a Muslim or Bosnian Croat majority before the war. At the Federal level, a new legislature was created with a one hundred and forty member House of Representatives and a House of Peoples with thirty Muslim and thirty Bosnian Croat members. The agreement was a major political achievement for American policy makers in the Balkans but their euphoria was blind to the reality that the agreement was a military necessity for the two ethnic groups in that it stopped the civil war between them and militarily united their efforts which could now be directed against the Bosnian Serbs in the field. The agreement was not born out of any substantial political desire for the two ethnic groups to live together permanently. The inability and perhaps naïveté of the Americans to grasp this truth was to be carried forward in their thinking some eighteen months later when they were locked into negotiations at Dayton Ohio in peace talks which were to finally bring the war to an end. But to carry over the war time alliance into the permanent peace time structures which now exist, was to build a peace on very shaky foundations and to ignore the desires of many Bosnian Croats and Croatia itself, to play the same game as Milosevic and to try to strive for a greater Croatia. After all, both Milosevic and the Croatian President, Franjo Tudjman had been locked in secret negotiations at Karadjordjeva in March 1991, during which they had discussed possible ways of dividing up Yugoslavia, and the carve up of Bosnia had been on their agenda. Even ignoring these facts, the reality on the ground was that the Bosnian Croat mini state-let, the 'Croatian Republic of Herceg Bosna' (CRHB), still existed with all its trappings; its institutions, flags and currency to name but a few. Nevertheless, despite subsequent difficulties which would arise during 'the peace' which finally emerged following the end of the war in December 1995, the Washington Agreement of 1 March

1994, was a substantial success as it created the conditions which led to the events which began to see the gradual reversal of Bosnian Serb gains so far. By May 1994, a 'Contact Group' consisting of Britain, France, Germany, Russia and America had been set up and had proposed a new peace plan based on a '51:49' per cent territorial division of Bosnia between the Federation and the Bosnian Serb Republic respectively. In August, the Bosnian Serbs finally voted to reject the proposal much to the annoyance of Milosevic who believed that the plan gave them all that they wanted. It was at this point, suffering from international sanctions and in dispute with the Bosnian Serb, leader Radovan Karadzic, that Milosevic took his decision to break off support to the Bosnian Serbs and invite the ICFY Mission into the FRY to oversee this undertaking in return for a loosening of sanctions. Karadzic continued the war unabated and it became clear to the Federation leadership that any real progress could only be made on the battlefield. In October 1994, the Bosnian Muslim Army's (ABiH)[53] 5th Corps, led by the charismatic General Dudakovic, mounted a break out from the Bihac pocket in Northwest Bosnia and drove towards the towns of Sanski Most and Prijedor. Meanwhile, General Alagic's ABiH 7th Corps along with the Bosnian-Croat Army (HVO)[54] conducted a joint offensive against the Bosnian Serbs in central Bosnia capturing the town of Kupres on 4 November. As the war entered in to its last year – 1995, the fighting intensified in may parts of Bosnia. In early April, Bosnian forces made significant gains around Travnik and by taking advantage of heavy snows, succeeded in crossing Serb mine fields on snow shoes to take the commanding heights of Mount Vlasic which dominates the main Zenica – Travnik – Jajce highway. Despite the exclusion zone, the Serbs were again pounding Sarajevo. In the space of six hours on 16 May, UN observers counted eight hundred artillery shells and rockets landing on the city, yet infuriated by the concept of 'dual-key,'[55] NATO commanders were refused permission by the UN civilian leadership to launch air strikes against the Bosnian Serb positions. Finally on 25 May, NATO was eventually given permission to strike in response to the continuing bombardment of Sarajevo by the BSA. NATO jets destroyed two BSA ammunition supply depots near Pale and a further six were destroyed on the following day. The BSA responded by shelling the UN 'Safe Area' of Tuzla killing seventy-one people outright with one rocket and by taking over three hundred and sixty UN personnel hostage. As the stakes were raised and the West became increasingly more frustrated by the UN's apparent inability to take a more robust line, Britain and France decided to deploy a slightly less that Rapid – 'Reaction Force' on to Mount Igman just outside Sarajevo to counter any subsequent BSA bombardments of the capital. As the force was deploying, the critical weaknesses of the UN system and the dual key concept were being graphically demonstrated in the 'Safe Area' of Srebrenica in what must surely go down in history as the blackest moment in the UN's involvement anywhere in the Former Yugoslavia to date. On 9 July, Bosnian Serb forces rolled in to the 'UN Safe

Area' overrunning several UN positions manned by the Dutch UN Contingent. Thirty-two soldiers were taken hostage and instead of acting as a trip-wire for air strikes to counter the attack on the safe area, they became the exact opposite; a shield that gave the BSA the ability to do as it willed. The UN in Zagreb took an unacceptable two days to debate and to decide whether to respond to the Dutch Commanding Officer's (CO) request for air support, whilst all the time the BSA was in action against the enclave. When air strikes were finally authorised on 11 July, two BSA tanks were destroyed before the attacks were called off in fear for the hostages lives. Lacking the 'authority' from the UN command to defend the safe area, the Dutch did little other than to look on whilst the BSA under the direct and personal command of General Ratko Mladic, began the all too familiar and sinister ritual of separating the men (teenagers to pensioners) from the women, and taking them away. Within two weeks reports were emerging of between 2,700 and 4,000 men and boys being slaughtered in cold bold by the victorious Serbs and of many women, children, the aged and the sick being cut down in the hills surrounding the town as they attempted to flee to safety. As part of my next job, I was later to walk these same killing fields with a forensic team during exhumations, picking my way through the dead bodies of small children and women, which even some 9 months after these events took place, were still lying on the ground where they had fallen. Even though I'd spent fifteen years of my life as a British Army paratrooper, these sights were beyond description, these people had fled with all their worldly

Srebrenica: The site of a Serb massacre during an initial visit by the exhumations team. The clothes in the picture contain decomposed bodies.

possessions in small suitcases which now lay broken open where they had fallen with their contents scattered around amongst the leaves. Toys, – an infant's small bootie, – a child's story book – a photograph album, – normal family items that you and I would expect to take with us on holiday. But these cases had been broken open and their contents strewn across the ground by the same shells that had decimated their owners cutting them down like a reaper's scythe. The site was one of many in and around the enclave. A site where innocent people had been caught up in the savagery of what purported to be warfare but which bore no resemblance to the way an Army was supposed to conduct itself on the battlefield within the rules and constraints laid down in International Humanitarian Law (IHL).[56] Most of the bodies lay in a central area that had clearly been used as an overnight camp. Cooking utensils, pots, pans and American MRE ration pack wrappers were still lying on the ground where moments before the shelling had started, their owners had been cooking an evening meal whilst under the misapprehension that they were safe from attack. Unexploded mortar bombs were still stuck in several tree trunks. The attack had been devastating. Caught in the dark where they'd camped for the night within the trees, their position was given away by a combination of their own camp fire lights and probably by the fact that the US Air Force had recently air dropped supplies nearby[57] and had thereby inadvertently given the position away. The BSA had mortared the main body of the camp and then cut down with small arms fire all those who managed to flee the main killing area. The tactics used were deliberate, 'well planned' and murderously executed. Likely escape routes had been determined and 'cut-off groups' deployed to mow down those who made in that far. As a former infanteer, I quickly found the obvious escape routes. I followed them and saw the bodies. They were all civilians, none were in uniform. It must have been terrifying. Mothers with infants and toddlers, small children, the old and the infirm, all camped out in the woods, being hunted down like animals. Trying to cook an evening meal as best they could – and then the mortars, the noise, the confusion. It was dark, panic would have instantly gripped all those caught in the camp, families trying to stay together not knowing where the attack was coming from or which way to run – the darkness of the night being broken by the blinding flashes of the bombs as they impacted, the screams, the sickening noise of incoming fire and the deafening 'Crump' of high explosive. These sights were horrific and the attack should never have been allowed to happen. When you are witness to the effects of such barbarity as occurred at Srebrenica, one can only wonder at the ineptitude of those charged with ensuring that it should never have happened. The UN was all too often ineffective because it could never really resolve many of the academic and moral dilemmas posed by its actions. For example, the UNHCR often refused to bus DPs to safer areas because it did not want to be seen to be aiding ethnic cleansing. Such points are for academics to debate and whilst such actions, or rather inaction might make sense on paper, it

ignores the humanitarian imperative and must be contrary to basic principles of humanity. To simply refuse to help transport thousands of homeless
people trudging down mountain tracks in the middle of winter having been
forced from their homes by a rampaging and undisciplined army, beggars
belief. At Srebrenica, the UN did not give the Dutch Battalion's CO the
authority to defend the enclave. It has long been held that those who
instruct others to commit war crimes, as well as those who 'actively' carry
out the crimes, should be charged and put before a tribunal. Yet what is not
so clear, is whether the same can be said of those who have the means, the
ability and dare I say, the moral responsibility to prevent such atrocities but
who 'passively' stand by and in effect permit such crimes to take place. Are
they not also guilty of some crime against humanity for failing to stop something that was within their power to stop? The defence that 'I was only following orders' will not work for those who 'actively' participate in such
crimes, so why should it for those who 'passively' allow them to happen
when morally they had a duty to prevent them? Over the next two years I
was to work closely with members of the Dutch Army and one thing that is
certain is that the horrendous scars that Srebrenica etched on that Army's
moral and professional standing, will take decades to heal. Surely in the
name of humanity, the Battalion should have stood its ground and fought,
with or without UN authority, to do what was morally required of them as
human beings in the face of such barbarity on the part of the BSA which was
clearly visible to their eyes. Sadly, the ethics of Western liberal democratic
societies whose armies always regard themselves as being subordinate to the
'civil power,' stifle such lateral and radical thinking. It would be a brave
officer who deliberately set about to disobey his orders, and sadly the Dutch
CO put national law and his responsibility to his national chain of
command before his moral 'duty' to uphold the wider ethics of
International Humanitarian Law (IHL).

As the BSA was making gains in the Eastern part of Bosnia i Hercegovina
at Srebrenica and eleven days later, at Zepa – another so-called UN Safe
Area, the Presidents of Bosnia and Croatia met in Split on 22 July and signed
an agreement on military co-operation. The town of Bihac, which now lay
in Bosnian Serb hands, was playing a vital role in allowing the Serbs to
maintain their grip of the rebel 'Serb Krajina' area of Dalmatia around Knin.
President Tudjman of Croatia therefore had a clear interest in aiding the
Bosnian forces in their efforts against the Bosnian Serbs in and around
Bihac. With support from the Croatian Army, the HVO pushed northwards
from Livno, along the Bosnian side of Bosnian-Croatian border and seized
the town of Bosanski Grahovo and in so doing, cut the vital Serb supply
lines to Knin. On 4th August, Tudjman launched a massive offensive code
named 'Operation Storm' against the Serbian Krajina to retake the Knin
area. Aided by Dudakovic's Bosnian 5th Corps,[58] the Croatian Army took
Knin in spectacular time on 5th August and within seventy-two hours were
in almost complete control of the entire region. Croatia's ethnic Serbs fled

the advancing Croatian Army and abandoned their homeland for the relative safety of the Bosnian Serb Republic. Many travelled further, preferring sanctuary in Serbia proper. Over one hundred and fifty thousand of them left in cars and on the backs of tractors and trailers. I was in Belgrade at the time and it too was a pitiful sight to see – literally a sea of humanity on the move. Mile after mile of red tractors clogged the main motorway from Zagreb to Belgrade, as part of this vast exodus of people meandered its way towards the Serbian capital. All the motorway exits had been blocked on the orders of Milosevic to ensure that these peoples were, in the main, relocated to Kosovo in order to 're-dress' the ethnic balance in that formerly autonomous and troubled province. The misery and inhumanity of such a vast movement of people was readily apparent. Whole families were huddled together with all that they could carry loaded on to their tractors and trailers. The plight of these people is intrinsically interwoven in to the overall 'Balkan Problem.' To try to solve the 'Bosnian Problem' without recourse to the plight of the Krajina Serbs is doomed to failure. Yet over the next two and a bit years I was to find that too many negotiators, officials from the IC and Western government ministers were blind to the issue and unprepared to make the link between the two peoples. This failure was in part due to the complexities of the problem. The eventual peace agreement that ended the war in Bosnia was incredibly complicated without drawing in the added complexities of a third external party. But the link was there in reality on the ground for all to see. In essence, the Bosnian Serbs were always going to be reluctant to enter in to a two-way 'returns process' with the Federation when no one was addressing the issue of one hundred and fifty thousand Serbs who had been ethnically cleansed from Croatia. In their eyes, the 'returns process' had always to be a three-way process involving Tudjman's Croatia. Sadly few people grasped this concept until very late in the day. But the failure was also in part due to differing national agendas, sadly even amongst our own Western nations. In my last year in Bosnia I was to work closely with numerous Germans, – diplomatic representatives of their government. Their attitude to this issue is best summed up in the words of one of my former German colleagues, who said quite matter-of-factually (and in front of my Krajina Serb interpreter)' … yes, but of course, when Croatia "liberated" the Krajina from the Serbs…!' But the most striking example of duplicity and the realpolitik of the post Cold-war 'New World Order' was the involvement of America in actually shaping these events in the first place. America does not take action out of some esoteric concept of superpower benevolence, neither does it act solely on humanitarian grounds as it would have us believe was the case with the subsequent NATO intervention against Yugoslavia in Kosovo in 1999. America has never shaken its isolationist tendencies and it only acts to promote its own interests or where its interests are threatened. The ethnic cleansing of one hundred and fifty thousand Krajina Serbs from Croatia was not on the same scale as the Serb expulsion of ethnic Albanians from Kosovo, neither was it anywhere as brutal. Nor did the Croats raise the emptied villages to the ground, yet it was ethnic cleansing on an unprecedented scale. Not only was America conspicuous in its absence from calling the free world to stop these crimes, but America, through an operation involving the US 'company' – Military Professional Resources Incorporated (MPRI), was covertly involved in training the Croatian Army prior to Operations Storm and Flash, which together led to the 'liberation' of the whole RSK. It is little wonder that 'Post-Dayton' American policy in the Balkans did not want to acknowledge the plight of the Krajina Serbs as an integral issue in the post-war recovery of Bosnia; after all, it was they who had helped create the problem.

With the loss of the Krajina and Bihac, the Bosnian Serbs strengthened their stranglehold on Sarajevo despite the 20 KMs UN exclusion zone. On 28th August, a mortar attack[59] killed thirty-seven people and wounded eighty-eight in the small confined market place in the centre of Sarajevo. The world was outraged and the UN and NATO again issued an ultimatum to General Mladic to remove his heavy weapons from the exclusion zone. Mladic called the UN's bluff for the last time. What he had failed to appreciate was a series of key indicators that should have told him that the rules of the game had changed forever. Firstly, the inept system of dual-key control between the UN and NATO had been refined giving NATO more say in the application of its force. Secondly, the Rapid Reaction Force on Mount Igman was ready for action and finally the BRITBAT[60] at Gorazde had withdrawn leaving few if any potential hostages for the BSA to get its hands on. On 30th August, NATO started a series of air strikes against the BSA that lasted for two weeks almost without a break with over three thousand sorties being flown. In the meantime Bosnian forces with Croatian assistance were making huge gains elsewhere. In central Bosnia the towns of Donji Vakuf and Jajce fell on 13th and 14th September respectively. By the 17th Federation forces controlled the main road between Jajce and Bihac which passed close to the Serb controlled town of Mrkonjic Grad and through an area later to be known as the 'Anvil.' Mrkonjic Grad lay only a short distance to the South of the largest Bosnian Serb town of Banja Luka which had so far survived the ravages of war and which was (much) later to become that entity's capital. In the Northwest, their forces were pressing on out of the Bihac pocket towards Bosanski Novi (now known as Novi Grad) and towards the strategically vital towns of Sanski Most and Prijedor. From Prijedor it was only a short forty-minute drive to Banja Luka, this time approaching from the Northwest. By late September, the Bosnian Serbs had lost an area equivalent to fifteen per cent of the country and for the first time in the conflict, it looked like a purely military solution to the war was on the cards; namely a military defeat of the Bosnian Serb Army. But a military defeat rarely brings a lasting and equitable peace and so the negotiators, now led by the Americans, continued to develop the existing 51:49 per cent plan originally introduced by the Contact Group. In early September, Bosnia,

Croatia and Serbia[61] agreed on the basis of this plan and by late September had also agreed to the principle of the preservation of both the Muslim-Croat Federation created at Washington and the Bosnian Serb Republic within the pre-war borders of a single Bosnian state albeit with modified constitutions. In essence, the negotiations which were to last for the next two months were based on the conflicting requirements to maintain the de facto division of Bosnia on the one hand, whilst on the other – ensuring that the country maintained its status as a single sovereign state within its pre-war borders. Following a period of shuttle diplomacy by the US Assistant Secretary of State, Richard Holbrooke, all sides were locked into negotiations lasting for three weeks during November at the US Air Force base at Dayton, Ohio. No side was permitted to leave the negotiations and the Americans applied constant pressure throughout. During the closing session of the talks, negotiators continued working for forty-eight hours without sleep as part of the overall plan to find a solution. Meanwhile on the 19th November, the UN Security Council (UNSC) debated two resolutions aimed at providing both a carrot and a stick to the various delegations. The first resolution, UNSC Resolution 1021, called for the lifting of the 'embargo on delivery of weapons and military equipment imposed by resolution 713 (1991)…' (arms embargo on Bosnia) whilst the second resolution, UNSC Resolution 1022, referring to the international sanctions against the FRY, stated that 'measures imposed by or reaffirmed in previous resolutions are suspended indefinitely with immediate effect subject to …'. On 21 November 1995, the Bosnian, Croatian and Serbian Presidents initialled a peace agreement in Dayton, Ohio often referred to as the Dayton Peace Agreement (DPA) or Dayton Accords, although known officially as the 'General Framework Agreement for Peace' (GFAP). The following day, the UN Security Council passed both Resolutions 1021 and 1022. Work quickly began to iron out the mechanisms by which the agreement would be implemented. During the London Conference (8th - 9th December) the Contact Group met to discuss Bosnia's reconstruction. A Peace Implementation Council (PIC) was established to hold ultimate responsibility for the reconstruction effort, which by definition, was to include both the civilian effort and the post-war military/security framework. The London Conference, much to the irritation of the Americans, appointed a European, the former Swedish Prime Minister and chief ICFY negotiator, Carl Bildt to be the first 'High Representative' and to have overall responsibility for civilian peace implementation in theatre. The GFAP also called for the deployment of an international armed force, under NATO leadership, of sixty thousand troops to supervise the cessation of hostilities and to provide framework security to enable civilian peace implementation. This Implementation Force (IFOR) was to take over from the UN forces on the ground and both Commander IFOR (COMDIFOR) and the High Representative would report directly to the PIC. On 14th December 1995, the formal Peace Agreement was signed by the Presidents of Bosnia, Croatia and Serbia in the

Elysee Palace in Paris; the war had officially ended. On 19th December, Ambassador Robert Frowick, a retired US diplomat, was appointed Head of the Organisation for Security and Co-operation in Europe (OSCE) Mission to Bosnia and charged with holding elections and overseeing changes to the political landscape inside Bosnia. A day later, the NATO led and American commanded 'Implementation Force' took over from UNPROFOR whilst the UN was ordered by the Security Council to prepare a new force for immediate duty in the former Serb Krajina in Eastern Slavonia, the former UN Sector East, in order to provide protection to the remaining Serbs in that area of Croatia and to ensure a smooth transition back to Croatian rule. On 21st December the final piece of the jigsaw was put in place, the UN Security Council authorised the deployment of an 'International Police Task Force' (IPTF) to be deployed within Bosnia to oversee the 'Rule of Law.'

With the adoption of UN Security Council Resolution 1022, the external sanctions on the FRY had been suspended. This was not the same as having them lifted altogether and indeed the Resolution provided a mechanism whereby Carl Bildt could apply to have them reinstated. But in reality it meant the end of the ICFY Mission and it also saw the end of the SAMCOM teams in neighbouring countries. As Christmas approached, we began earnestly to develop a plan for phasing out the Mission. Within the Sector we stopped patrolling the border and checking vehicles at the BCPs although we continued to staff them for security (anti-theft) reasons. It was also far easier to pick up from where you left off if you hadn't completely withdrawn in the first place and as yet we were still uncertain how this peace plan would fare when all others had failed. Christmas itself was a fairly sombre affair. The Sector had built up such a spirit of camaraderie that it was saddening to imagine that we would all inevitably have to go our own separate ways. In many cases the inevitable would mean deep personal loss in terms of personal relationships and also in terms of employment. For those who were not fortunate enough to have work to return to, the new UN Mission in the former UN Sector East, the UN Transitional Administration in Eastern Slavonia (UNTAES), offered the prospect of future employment which many were able to take advantage of later in the new year. We did our best to liven up the festive season, decorating 501 with Christmas decorations donated by Bob Freeman's wife and a tree cut down locally. JW and I toured all the BCPs on a mammoth 'round robin' on Christmas day to deliver Champagne to the troops on duty in the field. In early January, my contract ran out again and I travelled home for a belated and emotional Christmas with my family who had delayed opening some of the presents until my return. It was wonderful to be home, yet at the same time I had no idea what the future was to hold for me. It was a worrying time for all of us. As was usually the case during my short spells at home, I travelled to the Foreign Office in London and met with the senior FCO Officer responsible for the ICFY Mission within the EAU. He was a good man and knew the Mission well having been out to Yugoslavia on more than one occasion to visit and tour the sectors. During the negotiations at Dayton, the Foreign Office delegation had been led by Dame Pauline Neville-Jones and so now the FCO were keen to continue to play a leading role, albeit this time in the implementation of the peace plan, which was rapidly unfolding.[62] However, at this stage in the game, matters were still far from clear. Carl Bildt had yet to arrive in Sarajevo but when he did he would need to establish an office for himself and his staff before things could really begin to get moving. Until that was done and an office set up, it remained unclear as to what any subsequent requirement would be. Nevertheless, I registered my interest, in playing a part in the Bosnian post-war reconstruction effort, with the Foreign Office and left it like that in the certainty that just about all the other Brits in ICFY had already done the same. At that stage, in mid January, I had no idea that I was soon to be the person selected by the British Government to go in to Sarajevo and establish Bildt's Office, the 'Office of the High Representative' (OHR) for him there and to be one of only a small hand full of Brits at the centre of the peace implementation process from the outset. The call came several weeks later having already returned to Niksic. It was a Thursday evening, the FCO must have been working late and the message was simplicity in itself. I was to, 'Get to Sarajevo and set up Bildt's office for him.' Apart from that, there was only one other instruction: I was to start work on Monday morning! Whilst the instruction was clear and simple, carrying it out was not going to be and getting there was only the first of many more problems to come.

PART TWO

THE OFFICE OF THE HIGH REPRESENTATIVE
FEBRUARY - DECEMBER 1996

8

The General Framework
Agreement for Peace

The Bosnian peace agreement, initialled in Dayton on 21 November 1995 and signed in Paris on 14 December, provided the general framework for the post-war effort that was to follow. Signed by the Presidents of Bosnia, Croatia and Serbia, it included a territorial settlement, which maintained the 51:49 per cent division between the Muslim-Croat Federation, and the Bosnian Serb Republic first envisioned by the Contact Group. It established a new constitution (arguably the most complicated one in history to date), set up various mechanisms for the protection of human rights, the Rule of Law, the return of DPs and refugees, planned for the reconstruction of the country and the restructuring of the economy, and finally, under the authority of the UN, it provided for a sixty thousand strong international protection force under NATO leadership, to supervise the cessation of hostilities, to provide security for the beneficiaries i.e. the Bosnian people, and finally to provide the essential security framework for the civilian agencies to operate in.

Whilst the map of Bosnia had been redrawn during the negotiations at Dayton using the latest high-tech computer graphics, the reality on the ground was quite different. The 51:49 per cent division did not reflect where the armies had ended up when the fighting had stopped. The Serbs were occupying large areas around Sarajevo that were now allocated to the Federation. Likewise, the main route between Bihac and Jajce, which Muslim forces had recently taken by force, was under the agreement, to be handed over to the Serbs in an area which was to become known as the 'Anvil' around Mrkonjic Grad. Contentious as these moves may seem, there was only one area which evoked open dispute and which could not be resolved at Dayton. The dispute was over a small town in Northeast Bosnia in an area known as the Posavina corridor. The corridor was a small stretch of land which at one point was only several kilometres wide and which connected the Northwestern part of the Bosnian Serb Republic with the Eastern part. In this sense, it was what the military refer to as 'vital ground.' The town of Brcko lay in the centre of this disputed area. The Serbs had taken Brcko during the war and now refused to negotiate it away despite their pre-war minority status in the town. Dayton was unable to resolve this single issue and the agreement therefore provided for the issue to be submitted to binding international arbitration. The decision was to be announced on the first anniversary of the peace agreement in December 1996. In the end, it wasn't announced until March 1999, and the award, which was less than perfect, created a constitutional crisis in the Bosnian Serb Republic at a time when that entity was already in the grips of a Presidential crisis, arguably also of the IC's making, and at a time when their fellow Serbs in the FRY were about to take on the might of NATO's air forces as a result of continued atrocities in Kosovo.

The agreement set out to establish separate administrative divisions, known as entities, within a single and sovereign Bosnian state. The two entities became known as the 'Federation,' an entity based on the shaky war-time Washington Agreement between the Muslims and the Bosnia Croats, and 'Republika Srpska' – (known simply as the RS and previously referred to as the Bosnian Serb Republic). Each entity was entitled to make special parallel arrangements with neighbouring states; namely Croatia and Serbia proper.[63] This fact, along with the RS concern over maintaining a strategically viable corridor in Posavina, gave the impression that Dayton had set out to create separate independent 'state-lets' rather than merely separate administrative entities within a unified Bosnia. Such ambiguity may have helped the negotiators to find a mutually acceptable agreement at the peace table, but the same ambiguities were to have serious repercussions when it came to the implementation of the agreement as each entity was able to choose how it interpreted what they had signed. Similar doubts over the viability of maintaining a single sovereign state were raised by the new political constitution. Each entity would have its own parliament, government, army and Police. As such, it would carry out most of the normal functions of state within its own territory. The central organs of state, referred to as the 'Common Institutions,' consisting essentially of a Bosnia Parliament, Council of Ministers and a three-person Presidency (one representative from each of the three ethnic groups), would concern itself with foreign policy, trade and monetary policy. In essence, most of the core activities central to rebuilding a single and reconciled state such a media, law and order and education, were left to the separate entities. Likewise, the mechanisms of central government were particularly weak. A quorum was needed for laws to be passed yet if either side walked out, then there would not be a quorum. Additionally, even if a law was passed, the parliament of each entity reserved the right of veto if the law was deemed to be against their 'vital interests.' None of these arrangements made the prospects of civilian peace implementation any the easier.

With such wide spread abuse of human rights evident throughout the war, Dayton naturally provided for the protection of human rights during the peace. A Human Rights Commission was to be set up but there were inadequate enforcement arrangements set in place at the beginning. Likewise an IPTF was to be established to supervise each entity's Police force but it lacked the power to curb abuses or make arrests and had to contend itself with issuing 'non compliance notices.' DPs and refugees were to be encouraged to return and their property was either to be returned to them or they were to be adequately compensated for the loss if they decided not to return. Dayton also made the provision that no one indicted by the International Criminal Tribunal for the Former Yugoslavia (ICTY) for war crimes would be able to hold public office. This provision was eventually to be used to rid the RS of its wartime President, Radovan Karadzic who had already been indicted before the agreement was reached at Dayton, but for the next six months continued to hold on to power. Finally, all the civilian components of the peace plan were to be co-ordinated by the newly appointed High Representative and former Swedish Prime Minister, Carl Bildt. But first the Office of the High Representative had to be created in order to provide the means by which the IC could deliver on its undertaking to help the people of Bosnia. I had been chosen to be a part of that future and to put the OHR on the map. Unlike NATO who simply picked up and moved their existing Allied Rapid Reaction Corps (ARRC) Headquarters from Rheindahlen in Germany and deposited it in the leafy suburb of Ilidza on the Western outskirts of Sarajevo, the OHR didn't exist. It had to be created, staffed and equipped from scratch at a time when you couldn't even buy a ream of paper in Sarajevo let alone a computer. This was my personal challenge. It was to take almost a year of my life and was not without cost in terms of health nor rewards in terms of personal satisfaction and achievement. But whilst my personal challenge was daunting, so were the tasks and challenges ahead for the office and its other members of staff. The OHR had to co-ordinate the work of all the other agencies and organisations that would eventually arrive in theatre to help in the recovery effort. In addition, it led that effort – providing guidance and leadership at the very highest levels of state. The overall task was formidable. Essentially, to establish a sovereign state from scratch with all the institutional paraphernalia which that entails: new laws, new bodies and new institutions. This would be difficult enough under any circumstances never mind after the most destructive and bitter war Europe had seen since the end of the Second World War. Most of the infrastructure had been destroyed. Armies were still deployed in the field. Both sides had yet to withdraw behind the new lines drawn on the map at Dayton. Whole communities would find themselves on 'the wrong side of the line' in another's entity. Half a million people out of a population of only four and a half million had been displaced either internally or externally to other countries. Tens of thousands of refugees had arrived in the country from Croatia with little to no prospect of return.

Millions were traumatised by the events of the war and both entities still operated on a war footing. Politicians were unaccountable to their electorate whilst war-lords; criminals made rich by the pickings of war, still plied their trade at the highest levels of government in both entities. Corruption was rife and Police forces followed the orders of their paymasters rather than uphold the Rule of Law. It was a country of striking differences, of the rich and powerful in Mercedes Benz limousines and of the poor and destitute surviving in abject poverty and depravation amongst the burnt out ruins of their homes. OHR had to change all this, but it wasn't a matter of just reversing the effects of the war, of rebuilding what the bombs had knocked down. The war had been born out of nationalism, which in turn had replaced communism, which in turn had replaced authoritarian monarchism. Bosnia, like the rest of the Former Yugoslavia, born in 1921, had never experienced democracy. This was where OHR's first main task lay – political reform. Political reform was about building a liberal democracy in Bosnia, a country with no traditions or experience of democracy at all. It was about holding and supervising elections and about creating a system of government where the politicians understood that they should be responsible and accountable to their electorate and moreover, the opposite side of the same coin, where the electorate knew that they could and should hold their previously all powerful and aloof politicians accountable. It was about putting in place mechanisms whereby they could bring them to account. In a patriarchal society where to hold power meant that you used it – often for your own personal well-being – this was an alien concept which, despite the trappings and vestiges of democracy, has still not properly registered even today. OHR had to implement the new constitution often imposing its will on the former warring factions whose war time leaders had to remain in power until the first elections could be held in September. It also had to set up the six Common Institutions envisaged by the new constitution, namely the Presidency, the Council of Ministers, the Parliamentary Assembly (House of Representatives and the House of Peoples), the Constitutional Court, the Central Bank and the Standing Committee on Military Matters. Such was the enormity of these tasks, that the original concept of only a one year mandate for OHR was to be blown out of the window and OHR would see the decade out before any real progress was to be evident.

Part and parcel with political reform, OHR's second priority was economic restructuring. Again, it wasn't sufficient to simply reverse the clock and return Bosnia to its pre-war economy. The economy had long been bankrupt and OHR needed to change it from what had previously been a 'command economy' to a 'market' one. But it wasn't as simple as that. Many senior politicians had behaved like war-lords and had become rich on the black market and were therefore opposed to reforms. They controlled the customs laws and ran import-export rackets in fuel and cigarettes which made them millions of Deutschmarks whilst their populations starved. OHR needed to work with other agencies such as the International

Customs Observer Mission (ICOM) and later the Customs & Fiscal Advisory Office (CAFAO) to reform the customs laws, establish joint tariffs and ensure that duties went in to central (and not entity or personal) coffers whilst at the same time it needed to look at new laws to privatise state enterprises (and all the socially owned housing which previously came with the job) and create capital markets. As with OHR's efforts at political reform, the enormity of these tasks were complicated by the sheer obstruction posed by those in power that stood to lose out. Not all politicians were corrupt by any means, but the idea that 'with power came responsibility' and that high office meant that you served rather than benefited as a privileged class, was as alien to many as political accountability. Even those who strove for reform, and there were many honest people in high office, didn't really understand the Western concepts and culture which we were trying to impart. This made OHR's work all the more difficult.

The final main thrust of OHR's work was in post-war reconstruction, i.e. rebuilding the infrastructure which had been so badly damaged or destroyed by the war. There were many facets to this work. The most obvious and most visible was the reconstruction of the housing stock and lines of communications undertaken by aid agencies and IFOR engineers. But OHR did much behind the scenes. Fore example, it co-ordinated loans from the World and European Banks and ensured continued funding via the Contact Group and at regular 'Donor's Conferences' for major approved capital projects such as the reconstruction of the water system in Sarajevo and Bosnia's national telephone infrastructure. Without this effort other aims such as ensuring the return of DPs and refugees would not have been realised.

Whist political reform, economic restructuring and the reconstruction of the basic infrastructure were the main trusts of OHR's activities in the year following Dayton, there were also a whole plethora of other objectives which OHR had to address and which were no less important than the main ones. These other objectives were all inter-related and inter-dependent. For example, basic human rights such as the right to own property, or in this case the right to have your own property returned to you, was a fundamental principle which had a direct influence on the 'returns' process.[64] Likewise, returns were influenced by the concept of sustainability i.e. the likelihood of employment, lack of discrimination and by the overall security situation. Security in itself was influenced by the application of fundamental principles of human rights and the absence of abuses by those in authority especially the Police. Thus, the Rule of Law became a central issue. Abuses by the Police, especially their vehicle 'checkpoint' policies prevented many from travelling in another's entity where technically they were free to travel; it was after all, one state. The OHR had to ensure that each obstacle placed in the way of progress was removed, whether by sanction, enforcement or circumvention such as replacing the three ethnically styled car number plate designs with one common Bosnian design which did not show where the owner came from thus reducing the opportunity for corrupt Police to stop and search on an ethnic basis. This 'game' for want of a better description, went on throughout all aspects of the IC's involvement in Bosnia. Whatever reform the IC wanted to make, it would doubtlessly adversely affect the personal interests of someone in power who then did their utmost to ensure that progress was stifled. The situation was incredibly frustrating and extremely slow. As Admiral Leighton-Smith, COMDIFOR once ill advisedly remarked to Carl Bildt, civilian peace implementation was too slow. But, as a furious Bildt retorted, the IC had given him a budget to rebuild the whole country and all which that entailed, which amounted to the cost of no more than one or two of IFOR's main battle tanks! Progress was slow and difficult but progress was made and it was made for the common good of all of the people of Bosnia.

The basis for the peace effort was enshrined in the eleven articles of the General Framework Agreement for Peace document. The articles, each dealing with a separate component of the peace accord, were set out in separate annexes and provided the legal basis for all activity inside Bosnia following the war. Annex 1, was split in to two parts; 1A dealt with military aspects of the peace settlement and 1B with regional stabilisation. Under 1A, all parties agreed to the deployment of the NATO led force, IFOR, which like OHR initially had only a one-year mandate. IFOR was to take over command from UNPROFOR and had the specific task of ensuring the continued cessation of hostilities, the general compliance with the peace accord by all sides, of establishing lasting security and arms control measures and of promoting reconciliation between the former warring factions. Clearly the force was to be armed and capable of defending itself but nowhere was it stated that its own protection; namely 'Force Protection,' was a principle task of the force albeit it was an implied one. All sides agreed to disarm and disband all armed civilian groups except for authorised Police forces within thirty days of the transfer of authority between UNPROFOR and IFOR. Each side further undertook to withdraw all military forces behind a zone of separation, known simply as the 'ZOS' within the same period. The ZOS was in effect a four KM wide military exclusion zone stretching right across Bosnia, two KMs either side of the agreed cease fire line which was officially known as the Inter-Entity Boundary Line (IEBL). The problem was that the IEBL reflected the new division of Bosnia as drawn up in Dayton (51:49 per cent) and was not where the armies had stopped fighting. All sides therefore undertook to withdraw all their forces from positions where they had stopped fighting but which were now in another entity within forty-five days. There was no compulsion in Annex 1A, for any of the people to move, as this would have been tantamount to ethnic cleansing by the IC. Simply, the Bosnian Serb Army had to withdraw from the Federation and the Federation armies (HVO and ABiH) had to withdraw from the RS within the given time frame. In reality however, there was no way that following the withdrawal of their armies, that people were going to stay put in the other side's entity, and so in effect the agreement sparked off yet another spate of human migration even though the war had finished. IFOR was further tasked to assist all the agencies that would eventually be working in Bosnia by providing a safe and secure environment. It was specifically tasked to help with the elections and to assist in clearing the countless mine-fields, which littered the country. Joint Military Commissions (JMC) were established as a vehicle to discuss military matters such as prisoner exchanges, minefields, the deployment of forces and boundary lines which as yet had to be physically marked out on the ground with bright orange posts.

Annex 1B, set out various confidence building and security measures designed to ensure regional stabilisation throughout the Balkans. One of the main tasks involved regional arms control and concerned not just Bosnia but Croatia and Serbia as well. This task was not assigned to IFOR but to the OSCE, which was originally set up from the Conference on Security and Co-operation in Europe (CSCE)[65] after super power arms control talks in the early 1970s and was therefore well equipped to carry out this task.

Annex 2, set out the agreements on the IEBL and also for the arbitration process on the disputed town of Brcko in the Posavina corridor. Annex 3, in five short articles, defined the role of the OSCE in staging free and fair elections throughout Bosnia which were to be held within six to nine months. From the authority contained in this Annex, a whole series of rules and regulations governing the political landscape of Bosnia was to emerge which would significantly shape the future of the country whilst in Annex 4, the new Bosnian Constitution was laid down defining the powers of each entity and the Common Institutions. In the event of a dispute between the entities, each side agreed in Annex 5, to take the matter to binding arbitration. A Commission on Human Rights was established under Annex 6, consisting of an Office of the Ombudsman and a Human Rights Chamber.

In Annex 7, refugees and DPs were given the right to return freely to their original homes and to have restored to them any property of which they were deprived or to be compensated. The choice of destination was left up to the individual and the UNHCR was tasked to supervise this aspect of the plan. Refugees charged with crimes, other than serious violations of IHL, were to be granted amnesty.

Under Annex 8, a commission was set up under the auspices of the UN Educational, Scientific and Cultural Organisation (UNESCO) to preserve national monuments of historic, religious, cultural or ethnic importance. This part of the agreement might seem rather inappropriate or even vulgar when one considers the human misery caused by the war. But most experts on post-war recovery would argue that it is insufficient to simply rebuild houses and deliver humanitarian relief if you are trying to return people to their former homes and rebuild their lives and livelihoods. Part of the process must involve the rebuilding of the whole community and re-creating community identity. Monuments of any sort play a very significant part in any community's identity and in Bosnia this was especially the case in terms of religious monuments that had been subjected to systematic and planned destruction by all sides. The difficulty here was that whilst each entity would look after sites in its own entity, it would naturally concentrate on those monuments which identified with their own ethnic culture and not those which had probably been destroyed as they had belonged to another's. It was to be almost another two years (following talks with Eric Zivojin, the Bosnian Serb Minister of Science and Culture) before I managed to connect the efforts of the RS Government with their counterparts in the Federation.

Annex 9, addressed the sticky issue of joint-entity public corporations. Primarily it concerned itself with the basic utilities, energy, postal and communications sectors of the economy. For Bosnia to function as a single state, it was vital for example, that there was one telephone system and that postal communications didn't stop at the IEBL. But progress in these aspects was possibly the slowest of any in the recovery effort. Simply, there was no will on the part of the politicians to see it work. Each side played at being part of a single sovereign Bosnian state yet in reality the work of their entity institutions took precedence over all else. It was impossible to make a telephone call from one entity to another without using a SATPHONE. It was even impossible for OHR in Sarajevo to call the RS capital in Pale, only several kilometres away without using an INMARSAT and there was no desire on the part of the authorities to change things. During the war, the Bosnian PTT had retained its integrity and used the prefix 387 as its international code. Croatia used 385 and Serbia 381. The Bosnian Serb Republic however, had ensured that throughout its territory, all calls were made via the Belgrade switch. This meant that both the FRY and the RS had the 381 prefix and calling Belgrade or any town in either Serbia or Montenegro from the RS was classed as a national call whereas calling another Bosnian village, which now just happened to be on the other side of the new IEBL, was classed as an international call. But the problems didn't end there. Whilst subscribers throughout the world could call whoever they wanted in Bosnia as long as they remembered 381 for the RS and 387 for the Federation, no one inside one Bosnian entity could call the other entity's international code as these were blocked, although they could make other normal international calls. In other words, whilst in Sarajevo I could call my wife in the UK or anyone in nearby Croatia, but I could not call any 381 number. Likewise, if I was in Pale or Banja Luka, I could still call home but not Sarajevo. In effect, cross IEBL telephone traffic was impossible whether you tried it nationally or internationally. It was blocked and it was done deliberately. There was a similar story throughout all public corporations in Bosnia and a huge sense of inertia when it came to try and deal with the problems. At the end of the day, officials in both entities did not want to create the conditions which might lead to the realisation of the IC's stated intent, namely of maintaining the territorial integrity of Bosnia as one single sovereign state. They much preferred the concept of separate state-lets protected by the guarantee of their neighbours with whom they intended to establish 'special parallel relations.'

The mandate of the High Representative remains 'to oversee the civilian implementation of the Agreement.' The High Representative's authority and primary guidance is contained in Annex 10, where it directs the High Representative to monitor the implementation process, maintain close contact with all the parties concerned in order to promote full compliance, co-ordinate the activities of all international organisations and agencies, provide guidance to the IPTF and to report periodically on progress. The GFAP made the High Representative the 'final authority' regarding the interpretation of the Agreement on civilian implementation. In essence, this gave Carl Bildt tremendous power over the internal affairs of Bosnia albeit with few weapons to enforce compliance from those who transgressed. It was to be more than a year in to the peace before any real measure were to be agreed by the IC, which would give Bildt real power over the entities to force their compliance. These measures were to be mainly financial; placing conditions on humanitarian aid donations although additional powers such as the ability to strike offending politicians off their party lists and hence from power, were also to become an effective weapon in the IC's arsenal. According to the Agreement, the actual specific tasks of civilian implementation included the establishment of political and constitutional institutions, economic reconstruction and the rehabilitation of the infrastructure, the promotion of the respect for human rights, the encouragement of the return of DPs and refugees, the continuation of humanitarian aid for as long as necessary, and finally the assistance with free and fair elections. In addition to the requirements laid out in the Annex, the London Peace Implementation Conference in December gave further guidance. It established the PIC and also a 'Steering Board' consisting of Britain, France, Germany, Russia, the US, Japan, Canada, Italy, the European Union (EU) Presidency,[66] the European Commission (EC) and finally Turkey on behalf of the Organisation of Islamic Countries. The Conference confirmed OSCE's role in supervising the elections and directed the High Representative to establish a Human Rights Task Force. Meanwhile UNSC Resolution 1031 directed all UN agencies to co-operate with and to accept general guidance from the High Representative. The agreement tasked the High Representative to form and chair several joint bodies that would bring together representatives of the entities and the Government of Bosnia. A Joint Interim Commission (JIC) was to be created at the level of Prime Minister to discuss in advance the establishment of the Common Institutions that would be set up following the first elections. Like IFOR's Joint Military Commissions, the High Representative was also tasked to establish Joint Civilian Commissions (JCCs) which would bring together entity representative with a variety of international agencies and organisations including IFOR. These were not just to be set up in Sarajevo but regionally as well, with a JCC set up in the Northwest, the Northeast and the South. This requirement would soon mean that I would not only need to battle against the odds creating an international diplomatic office for the High Representative in Sarajevo, but also in Banja Luka and Tuzla, and just before I finally completed my contract, to start the process off again in Mostar.

The final annex of the Agreement, Annex 11, dealt with the IPTF. It established a civilian law enforcement task force that was to be headed by a Commissioner, initially Peter Fitzgerald, whose tasks were to monitor, observe and inspect law enforcement activities and facilities including associated judicial organisations, structures and proceedings. In addition it was to carry out training of entity Police forces and generally promote the Rule of Law throughout Bosnia. This was a mammoth task, which the IPTF became more and more proficient at despite their continuous upward battle against the odds.

Not since the end of the Second World War had the IC made such a huge undertaking. The GFAP was not a large document but in obtaining the agreement of all sides, compromises had been made, interpretations were loose and implementation would thus be difficult. No side had won the war and no side had lost either. It was not as if the Agreement had been imposed on the loosing side. The Bosnian Serb Army had been staring defeat in the face but it had not been defeated in the field. The test of this Agreement would be in whether any one side considered itself to have lost the peace having survived the war. If Dayton was to succeed, then all sides, both entities had to feel that they had won, that they got the best deal that they could under the circumstances. For without that feeling, their exhausted yet undefeated armies could so easily take to the field again as they so nearly did on the first anniversary of the Agreement when the Brcko decision was about to be announced. It was a very fragile peace that hung over Bosnia and one that I and many others had a personal interest in ensuring that lasted.

9

ZETRA: Zelena Transferal
The 'Green Route' – to Sarajevo

Having received the telephone call from the Foreign Office on the Thursday evening, I then had to work out how I was going to get from Niksic to Sarajevo by Monday morning. My mind was racing, as there was so much to do never mind the fact that the whole concept was a bit of a shock. Nevertheless I was elated at the prospect of what lay ahead and of having been chosen to take this on in the first place. I immediately called home and told Allison the good news although the uncertainty of when I'd next be home and the prospects of now going right in to the middle of a war zone was not the best news that she could have received. The way I saw it, I had two main tasks to sort out. One was extracting myself out of ICFY in the best possible manner and the other was somehow organising my trip to Sarajevo. At this stage in the proceedings, anyone who was inside Bosnia as part of the new peace plan, was getting there courtesy of NATO, via military flights in and out of Sarajevo airport which was now tentatively open despite the surface to air missile threat which remained extant. These flights on the whole originated from Germany or Brussels and often staged through Zagreb. I didn't know all this yet but even had I known, it would have been of little use as I couldn't get to Zagreb either. I had no choice but to try and sort out a way in to the country over land and that meant driving right through the armies in the field, assuming of course that I could bluff my way across the border in the first place. Whatever the final solution, there was no way that I could sort anything out from Niksic. I had a satphone but I didn't have Bildt's number or any concept of who or where to call for advice. Faced with these seemingly insurmountable obstacles, I decided that the best course of action was to get myself up to Belgrade as quickly as possible and so on Friday I set about trying to put the plan together. With only two flights a day from Podgorica to Belgrade, it didn't come as a surprise to find that I couldn't get on one until 6,00 am on

Tuesday morning. In a way that was much better and certainly a much more realistic timetable as it gave me Friday through to Monday, four clear working days, to sort out my affairs, conduct a proper hand over of my responsibilities as DHOS to Bob Freeman, and of course to throw a cracking good leaving party in 501. Handing over to Bob was painless; he'd been my Operations Officer for several months now and essentially knew what the issues were anyway. Added to that was the fact that we had stopped patrolling and so apart from planning the eventual closure of the Mission and ensuring that our equipment remained operational, there was little to do but wait. I held my leaving party on the Saturday night, opening the bar on my tab for the whole evening. It was an extremely emotional affair. I had previously been the one making countless speeches when others had left and been witness to the sadness in their eyes as they had said their goodbyes to a unique set of colleagues representing as they did, a whole spectrum of the IC. Now it was my turn to depart. I had spent most of my working life within the British Army, an institution envied throughout the world for its regimental system, its local ties and tradition of family bonding within its battalions. Yet I had never experienced such bonding as we had engendered in ICFY, at least in Sector Charlie anyway. The fact that everyone was so different, had different backgrounds, cultures, religions, beliefs, professions and political agendas, made it so incredibly fascinating and the challenge of uniting all these individuals, all special in their own right, in to a small group with a common aim, was so incredibly worthwhile and rewarding that I expect never to be so privileged again. I had made so many friends, not just colleagues but genuine friends that I didn't want to leave either. The sadness was real, you could touch and feel it and it was made worse by the fact that I had no idea at that stage whether I would ever see any of them again. As had become the custom, I gave my speech thanking all the drivers and interpreters for their part in ensuring the success of the Mission and then thanked all the internationals for their support and co-operation. I didn't want to forget the three bar maids; Biljana, Natasa and Irene either (which sadly most if not all of the others had done) as they had worked incredibly hard to ensure that we all enjoyed ourselves in 501 when there was nowhere else to go. They were not officially members of the Mission as we paid their salaries from bar profits, but they were neverthe-less an integral and essential part of the Sector and so I mentioned them in my speech as well and also gave each of them a big box of chocolates as a token gesture of thanks. Urpo made a speech on my behalf, presenting me with my ICFY medal and a humorous certificate listing all the cock-ups I'd made during my tenure in the Sector. It was a wonderful end to a wonder-ful period in my life. I had achieved lots during the last eight months. I'd started as a monitor conducting mobile patrols and sitting in BCPs on the border. I'd spotted numerous problems with the way we conducted our business and set out to rectify them, working my way slowly but surely up the chain of command until I was in a position to act. I'd welded a disparate group of highly professional individuals with different work ethics and differing political agendas, in to a highly motivated team which set the standards for the rest of ICFY despite having to operate over the most difficult terrain in Yugoslavia and amongst the most hostile elements of the population. I had turned the Sector around, from simply 'playing' at it, to becoming the example for others to follow. As sad as it was to be leaving, my reward was being chosen to set up the OHR. To do that, I had to leave and in any case it was just a matter of time before everyone else would have to do the same and it was better to go individually on a high, rather than en-masse on a collective low when the Mission closed. At least I would be spared that.

My transport left the hotel at 4,30 am on Tuesday morning and despite the unearthly time, a small group of drivers, interpreters and internationals had gathered to see me off. This was my last memory of Sector Charlie and it typified the spirit that we had managed to create amongst ourselves. It was a sad trip and one in which the realisation of what now lay ahead was beginning to dawn on me with all the worry and trepidation which that entailed. I settled in to the Hotel Hyatt Regency in Belgrade and took breakfast before turning up in the Mission Ops Room to see JW who was now helping out on the admin-log side having moved from Sector Charlie shortly after Christmas. JW handed me a slip of scrap paper on which he had written a set of instructions. There were just three short bullet points; One – 'Depart Hyatt 0900 hrs for Mali Zvornik to arrive by 1200 hrs.' Two – 'Met by transport officer from Sarajevo.' Three – 'Our vehicle to return to Belgrade with Earle Scarlett.' That was it, slightly better than the Foreign Office instructions, but not a lot. I confirmed the transport for the following morning and learnt that I'd be travelling with Arnold Horowitz who was a political expert from the American State Department who had been with the ICFY HQ in Belgrade for some time and who had been to visit Niksic not long before. Arnold would later join the OHR as a senior political officer but for the moment was only going as far as Loznica, the HQ of Sector Alpha. His intention was to take me to the border and wait for Earle Scarlett to cross over and travel back with him to Belgrade. Earle was also from the US State Department and had been the ICFY Deputy Head of Mission before being moved to Sarajevo to meet up with Bildt. Earle had an excellent sense of humour and looked a bit like Saddam Hussein. He often joked around but had a razor sharp mind and I'm sure he deliberately used his antics to disarm opponents during negotiations. I hadn't known that Earle was now in Sarajevo and so it was somewhat comforting to learn that I wasn't the first person to have to make this particular trip after all. Likewise, it was reassuring to find out that I already knew one person in the OHR even though I hadn't got there yet. Working out what was supposed to happen after getting to the border was impossible. I had no idea how to legally get across it and the only thing I knew for certain was that someone would be there at some stage – hopefully around 12,00 o'clock – as someone had to bring

Earle to meet us. I couldn't find anything else out and so decided that it really wasn't worth worrying about it anymore.

I spent the rest of this last day with JW and Raimo, a Finn who had also been in Sector Charlie before being poached by the HQ to run logistics for the Mission. Whilst I was confirming my travel arrangements, the HQ had just received a fax from Carl Bildt which formally closed the Mission down. Raimo showed it to me; it was incredible to think that one piece of paper could mean so much. We all knew it was coming but we hadn't realised that it would be so soon. I felt remorse for those who I'd just left behind that morning and at the same time, gratitude that I'd departed before the official decision had been taken. Raimo was concerned about all the assets of the Mission and how to dispose of them. Technically Bildt was still in charge of ICFY as well as the new OHR and so the possibility of transferring the assets needed to be explored. Much of what we had in the Mission was donated by individual governments rather than bought with central (donated) funds and so the permission of the donors would have to be obtained before a transfer could be made. Nevertheless I needed to take all this into account once I'd arrived in Sarajevo and see what we could recycle before I purchased anything new.

The trip to Mali Zvornik the next day was uneventful. We called in at Sector Alpha on the way past and spoke to them about Bildt's fax, which they had also received the day before. It seemed that most people were in the same boat. A lucky few had jobs to go back to as customs or Police officers but the vast majority had nothing. Many talked about the prospects of the new UNTAES Mission in Croatia and almost everyone was keen to hear what I was up to, not that I knew a lot at that stage. We got to Mali Zvornik on time and called in at one of Sector Alpha's BCPs, which was situated on the FRY side of the River Drina. The BCP was manned by an American, Rick Bransford who had previously been in Sector Charlie and by Phill Figgins, the Royal Marine who had briefed me all that time ago in the Foreign Office before I started my Mission. Even in these remote parts it was incredible whom you kept bumping in to. Apart from the bridge crossing the Drina, there isn't much at 'Little' Zvornik at all. The town of Zvornik itself is several kilometres to the South and remains infamous as the site where the JNA crossed into Bosnia on behalf of the Bosnian Serbs and committed some of the most barbaric acts of ethnic cleansing during the early part of the war. The BCP was one of the new UN style containers and was situated next to the FRY Police and customs offices – also in containers. At the point where the road met the actual bridge and just in front of the cluster of containers, was an old Soviet 30mm anti-aircraft gun pointing horizontally and directly across the bridge towards the Bosnian Serb checkpoint one hundred and fifty metres away on the other side of the Drina. From this position one could easily see that the Bosnian Serbs had mounted a similar gun on their side of the bridge pointing directly at us. It was a surreal standoff between two opposing factions of supposedly the same people. Nevertheless, there was a lot of traffic freely crossing the bridge despite the guns pointing at each other. Behind the Bosnian Serb checkpoint, the ground rose steeply leading to an escarpment that dominated the whole area including the FRY side of the river. We had arrived early but after several hours there was still no sign of Earle and my transport to Sarajevo. By mid afternoon it was becoming really worrying but we had no means of checking what, if anything might have happened to them, we just had to sit it out. Finally we decided that we had no choice but to cross over on foot and see whether they were sitting there on the other side but for some reason were out of sight and unable to contact us. Clearly, I had to be the one that went and so I picked up my belongings and started to walk. My heart was thumping, I had no authority to travel, no documents save for my UK passport but no visa or anything and I was unarmed. The bridge reminded me of the Glieneker Bridge between East and West Berlin and my last job with military intelligence. The bridge was the one that had been used for spy exchanges during the Cold War as it linked the American Sector of West Berlin with Potsdam in the East. Now, some four years later, I was walking across a similar bridge, alone, under similar circumstances, with an anti-aircraft gun in my face and another pointing at my back. What on earth was I doing? To add to the theatrical drama and as if on cue in a scripted spy movie, two American attack helicopters popped up from behind the escarpment in front of me and hovered in 'hull-down' fire positions as they surveyed the area perhaps for the first time. I carried on walking slowly, my mind racing trying to figure out what to say when I got to the other side. Finally I got there and realised that there was no one there! Its difficult to bluff your way through a border without the proper documents under any circumstances, but its even worse when you are regarded with suspicion by a fully armed paramilitary Police force who have a total mistrust of the IC which had not long stopped bombing them. I'd picked up some Serbian language whilst in Montenegro, although not much, and so without the aid of an interpreter I just managed to persuade the Police to let me hang around and wait. I managed to keep the banter going on and off for about an hour before the customs officers decided that I wasn't going anywhere and so I'd better bugger off back to Serbia. I picked up my kit for the second time and started walking back across the bridge. I'd got less than half way across before the dulcet tones of Earle Scarlett, whose car had just drawn up alongside me, asked if I was going somewhere and whether I wanted a lift. God, was I glad to see him!

The problem now was that it was quite late and there was a lot of snow on the ground especially on the Bosnian side of the border where it was far more mountainous than the flat plains of Northwestern Serbia. My contact, Nick Haller, the recently acquired OHR transport manager (having been poached from the ECMM in Zenica) and a corporal in the TA with 10 PARA (one of my sister battalions) talked the situation over with me. The problem was compounded by the fact that Nick's car, a brand new OHR Land Rover Discovery, hadn't got insurance[67] or the correct papers to get in to Serbia and so it was stuck in 'no mans land' on the bridge. We had no choice but to turn round and try to reach Sarajevo that day. There was one other problem. There was only a couple of hours of day light left. At this stage in the game, travelling anywhere in Bosnia was a highly risky business but it was especially dangerous after dark. It was only about six weeks since the war had actually ended on the ground and Nick reckoned that we stood no chance of getting through once it got dark. Vehicle hi-jacking was prevalent and a nice new Discovery was rich pickings. Frankly, I didn't want to walk, neither did I savour the prospect of a bullet in the back of the head just over a set of car keys. Having loaded the vehicle with all my kit, we turned it around and set off back across the bridge. Since the Bosnian Serbs had just seen the vehicle cross out of Bosnia and had already seen me earlier, getting through the customs point was a mere formality of having to stop to show our British passports before being waved through. We turned South and headed for the main town of Zvornik following the line of the River Drina. Immediately the intensity of the war was quite evident. Wherever you looked, houses were destroyed – burnt out shells of what were once elegant buildings, peoples' homes. The architecture was like elsewhere in Yugoslavia, similar to the Southern German style. But these houses with their once white washed walls were now blackened and charred by fire, their roofs missing and their owners and contents long gone. As we continued South through the villages you were overwhelmed by the sense of destruction which simply lay evident everywhere. Whole settlements had been laid waste whilst even remote and isolated houses high up in the hills had not escaped the rape and destruction. It was as if nothing had been spared. The snow, ice and freezing cold added to the misery of the landscape. It was like a painting, a sinister picture devoid of any real colour, from which you were somehow removed, yet permitted to observe from the safety of your armchair. But here it was different. This was real. The destruction was real and one could only imagine the misery, pain and anguish that must surely have accompanied such wanton destruction of non– military targets. The other difference was that I wasn't sitting in the safety of an armchair, I was sitting in the passenger seat of a Land Rover Discovery trying my level best to map read whilst Nick negotiated the snow and ice which threatened to block our route to Sarajevo.

As we drove deeper and deeper in to the Bosnian Serb Republic, we came across the remnants of its Army. This Army was in tatters, it was dishevelled, cold, hungry, unpaid and starved of supplies thanks to ICFY and the UN blockade. NATO air forces had pounded it and now that the war had officially ended, it lacked direction. The Army had stopped fighting but it was still deployed in the field and its soldiers now lined the streets of countless villages that we passed through. It was a very sinister sight. In village after village there were thousands of soldiers milling around, fully armed with their weapons and ammunition bandoleers over their shoulders and their equipment strewn on the ground. There was no semblance of discipline, order or purpose, the Army was just standing still, lining the streets as if waiting for royalty to drive through the town on some sort of parade. But there was no parade; there was only Nick and I in our new Discovery. It was like running the gauntlet. Despite looking totally dishevelled and dejected, this Army had not been defeated. It had not lost the war. But neither had it won the peace. Peace had been imposed on it and the IC had imposed that peace. The Bosnian Serb Army didn't like that at all but they had no one to complain to, no one to take their anger out on; no one except Nick and I that is. In the dirty blackened drabness of the surroundings, we stuck out like a sore thumb! We pressed on, now heading Southwest away from the Drina towards Vlasenica and then on to the town of Han Pijesak, the location of the Bosnian Serb Army Headquarters and most probably where the already indicted General Ratko Mladic was hiding. The town was overflowing with soldiers and military equipment both on the streets and in the barracks that were off to the side of the road. Nick and I just looked at each other, we didn't need to speak – we knew the dangers of what we were doing all too well. As former paratroopers we both knew what these soldiers and their weapons were capable of. This was not a good place to be at this stage in the proceedings but we had no choice, there was no other way around, no side roads, no detour. To get to Sarajevo we had to drive through Han Pijesak and, as a consequence, through half the Bosnian Serb Army in to the bargain. It was a choice between driving too slowly and prompting some soldier to jump out and wave us down, and of driving too fast – attracting attention to ourselves and possibly having an accident as a result of the snow and ice. We decided that whatever happened we wouldn't stop, as we were in no position to negotiate on the finer points of diplomatic immunity with anybody, let alone with this Army. None of the traffic lights were working at the junctions and there were few other cars on the road and so we drove straight through assuming right of way and maintaining a constant speed, just fast enough to make somebody think twice before trying to jump out and flag us down. The trick worked although on several occasions soldiers did genuinely try to hitch a lift with us as they decided to de-mobilised themselves and set off walking back home to their families. We continued Southwest, through the town of Sokolac and over the mountains of central Bosnia. The scenery was spectacular and every bit as beautiful as in Montenegro. High up in the mountains, away from the villages and the destruction, the snow and pine trees gave the impression of being on some alpine road winding your way through the Swiss countryside. It was quite surreal, like many other things I had yet to experience in the Former Yugoslavia, one moment you witnessed abject misery and then the next, the quiet and beauty of the landscape. My reflections were soon shattered. As one approaches Sarajevo from the North you hit a main junction by a petrol station. If you turn left, you travel to the village of Pale, the wartime capital of the Bosnian Serb Republic and the seat of Radovan Karadzic's Government. If you turn right, you travel the last leg of the journey to Sarajevo, which lies some fifteen minutes along the mountain pass to the West. As we drove towards the junction a sea of humanity coming from the right met us. Bosnian Serbs were fleeing Sarajevo in their thousands. Some were on foot, many were in private cars but most were in trucks loaded to the gunnels with everything that they could salvage, their life's possessions piled high on roof racks, trailers or simply thrown in to the back of a truck. It was a pitiful sight yet at the same time one of great concern. Many of the trucks were military and at first we couldn't work out what was happening and consequently how we should deal with the problem. Our path was blocked. Everything was coming the other way and we were trying to go against the flow. We picked our way slowly through the on coming traffic and realised that the congestion was caused by vehicles trying to line up for the petrol pumps and the military presence was no more than the Army assisting its citizens to flee. There had been no real fighting for several months now and so this column of DPs did not reflect a mass exodus fleeing a war, but rather the fear in peoples' minds of what the future might hold. The IEBL was only a couple of kilometres to the West. Sarajevo lay firmly within Federation territory and as a result five whole districts of the city that had previously been held by Bosnian Serb forces would now find themselves within the Federation. These districts were almost totally populated by Bosnian Serbs, but Annex 1A of 'Dayton' required all three Armies to withdraw to their respective sides of the IEBL. In effect this meant that if the Bosnian Serb populations of these five districts wanted to say in their homes, then they would do so as part of the Federation and without the protection of the Bosnian Serb Army. They chose not to, and consequently the Peace Agreement which had heralded an end to ethnic cleansing, precipitated yet another round of mass ethnic migration as these five communities packed up their belongings and fled, leaving in their wake the smouldering ruins of their homes as they systematically torched what they couldn't carry. As we continued our way to Sarajevo, whole segments of the capital were on fire, and the burning was to continue for several weeks to come as the populations of one district after another fled to the other entity. To the casual observer it seemed that although the Bosnian Serbs had not lost the war, they had certainly lost the peace. But the problem wasn't just confined to Sarajevo. This cross entity movement was being repeated throughout Bosnia and in both directions, albeit not quite on the same scale as I was now witnessing as the day light finally began to fade.

Just before you hit the outskirts of Sarajevo you see a sign welcoming you to the 1984 Winter Olympics. Now, some twelve years later, the sign is rusted and peppered with the seemingly obligatory bullet holes. The road winds down the side of orange coloured hillsides which form a river gorge, and through a series of tunnels carved through the rock just like those I used to travel through in Montenegro on the way to the BCP at Scepan Polje. The difference here however, was that these tunnels had not been maintained and were full of deep potholes and fallen rocks which were lethal to the unwary. As you neared the city, the roadside started to sprout reinforced pillboxes and gun emplacements. Most of these looked as if they'd received a direct hit by some heavy piece of ordnance or other as they we're all in a bad state of repair and hardly functional as a fire position let alone a shelter. The road and verges were strewn with wooden ammunition crates and piles of brass 'empty cases' from spent small-arms ammunition. On the sky line one could see the back of the old Turkish Fort, which from its dominant position looks down over the city that lies to the South on the other side of the mountain. We reached the last tunnel and had to play 'chicken' with the oncoming vehicles since once you were inside it, it became passable only to single file traffic, as one whole side of the tunnel had been caged in to act as a hardened storage bunker. We emerged on the far side of the tunnel and past the last and almost obliterated bunker to begin our decent in to Sarajevo. It was almost dark by now and we were well pleased with ourselves for getting this far before the light faded. The road was covered in mud, snow and ice as well as the general debris of war. The view was both beautiful and shocking. As you enter the city from this direction you can see down the length of the River Miljacka and there is a wonderful view of small dwellings with red roofs set in to the hillside and several mosques with their minarets reaching up in to the sky. At the bottom of the hill is the National Library, previously one of the most beautiful buildings in Sarajevo and one that contained many historic and priceless documents of both national and international importance. The building was completely gutted and its contents long perished. The sacking of this building and its contents was without doubt a national tragedy and a war crime, which typified the nature of the Serb bombardment of the city throughout the war. The road bends to the right and follows a one-way circuit through Bascarsija, the old part of the city. Small timber framed buildings lined the dark street and tramlines marked the centre of the road, which remained largely uncleared of snow and ice. The buildings were peppered with bullet and shell holes and the road was cratered by artillery fire with huge 'splash' marks spreading out in all directions from the impact point. Few buildings had glass in them anymore and it seemed as if the whole city was held together with blue or orange plastic sheeting supplied by the UNHCR whose logo was written across each sheet. The odd pedestrian walked in the road partly to avoid the piles of snow that blocked the pavements and partly to avoid the debris, which frequently fell from the buildings in strong winds sometimes killing those who passed below. This custom was to continue for many years to come as old habits die hard, but with the increase in motor traffic that was to come with the influx of international aid agencies, it was to become a dangerous habit in itself. The road wound its way past the old 'Green' (fruit and vegetable) market where on 28th August 1995, thirty-seven people were killed outright and a further eighty-eight were wounded by a suspected Serb mortar shell which fell in to the crowded market place much to international condemnation, and then wound its way towards the Eternal Flame and in to Ulica Marshal Tito where it broadened into four lanes. Here the road straightened and passed tall imposing stone buildings that reminded me much of Berlin. The burnt out shells of several buses and tramcars littered the carriageway, surreal testaments to the bombardment that destroyed them, literally in their tracks. The odd car, perhaps only one or two, darted around the burnt out obstacles and mounds of snow, sending up a cloud of dirty soot in their wake as if they were rally cars on a dirt track. It was clear that the roads hadn't been cleaned for several years and the passing vehicles simply churned up the dirt, mixing it with the melting slush causing muck to fly in all directions. It was impossible to keep clean and even getting in and out of the cars made you filthy. The scene was quite disturbing. This was a capital city in the centre of Europe and it was almost totally devoid of life. Few people were out and about. The wartime nightly curfew of 11,00 pm remained in force and was to remain so for the rest of the year. In any case, there was no reason to be out, all the shops and bars were empty, there were no window displays, no advertising or lights of any description and the streetlights had long since failed. The city was falling to pieces and filthy dirty. Everything was black and white, or rather a dirty shade of grey. There was no colour, no lights, and no people. There was absolutely nothing to stimulate the senses, just destruction and destitution. I was completely shocked and an overwhelming sense of despair began to take hold of me. Sarajevo was miserable. It wasn't just that it looked bleak and terrible, the feeling was tangible and you could feel, almost touch the despair all around you. Over twelve thousand people had died in the city during the thousand-day siege; one thousand six hundred of them children and it was if the whole city was mourning their loss. As I pondered with trepidation just how on earth I was supposed to help this city, in fact the whole country to recover, I felt myself slip in to culture shock. Communism had failed in the long term to hold the three disparate ethnic groups together, nationalism had torn them apart and pitted them against each other in the bloodiest war Europe had seen since the Nazis, and now it was the turn of democracy to try and build a nation from the carnage and animosities.

Zetra: The main Olympic sports stadium in the centre of Sarajevo stands in ruin.

Nick Haller passed me across in to the capable hands of another ex-ICFY Brit Richard John, who had been in Sarajevo for several weeks attempting to sort out as much basic administrative and logistics matters as he could before returning to the UK at the end of his FCO contract. Richard had previously served with the British Army in the Royal Logistics Corps and had been loaned to OHR to help out where he could. It was now Wednesday night and he was leaving on Friday morning. Between now and then he had to brief me on as much as he could possible cram in to my head. I was emotionally drained, hungry, seriously tired and not at all receptive to the deluge of information pouring my way as we drove in his completely battered blue ICFY Nissan pick-up truck to his accommodation for the night. I told him the news about Bildt's fax and ICFY closing down, and so when we got to the tiny Muslim house at the end of a dark narrow street which was to become my first home, he threw me the keys to the Nissan saying, 'You might as well keep these as there's no one to give the car back to.' From now on he also wanted me to do all the driving as it was the quickest way to learn the layout of the city and time was not on our side. The house was small but clean and tidy, as were all the Muslim houses I was to live in over the next year or so. Unfortunately it was situated down such a narrow street in the old quarter of the city that it rarely saw any sunlight and soon became a main contributory factor to my increasing depression and overwhelming sense of loss since leaving all my friends and former colleagues in ICFY. However, the main irritation about renting accommodation within the local community, was that the landlords were never really absent. Unlike in the UK where when you rent a flat it becomes yours under the terms of the lease, here in Bosnia the owners merely move above, below or next door to you – if you were lucky. For the main they kept reappearing depriving you of any sense of privacy and they usually retained all their belongings just where they'd always been. This in effect meant that there was never enough space to hang up your clothes or put items away in drawers. Indeed, in the weeks to come, my new landlady took it upon herself to ensure that at no stage was I able to fully unpack and settle in. Every time I even moved an ornament in order to put my own things down, she would move everything back to exactly where it had been previously. Such idiosyncrasies were, after several months, to cause me to leave the house and move to different and brighter accommodation elsewhere in the city, which by then I had come to know well. To add to the initial discomfort of living in Sarajevo one had to put up with gas, electricity and water cuts. In effect this meant that it was always hit and miss whether you were able to cook a meal for yourself when you finally collapsed at home after leaving the office late at night. Further more, you could find yourself in complete darkness in a house that was easily colder than it was outside, and that was well below zero, and perhaps worst of all – there might not even be any water for up to twenty-four hours at a stretch. Water is central to life and in the West we simply regard this most precious of commodities as being freely and readily available. Yet in the developing world, millions of people have no access to safe drinking water at all. When so much of the West is contemptuously conspicuous by its over consumption, elsewhere in the world thousands die each day not just from drought in arid deserts but from water borne diseases as a result of drinking contaminated water. Before the war, the water supply in Sarajevo had been well maintained and was capable of meeting demand. But the years of bombardment and lack of maintenance had wrecked havoc with the distribution system. In order to maintain sufficient water pressure to survive the massive seepage, supplies could only be maintained to several parts of the city at a time and so suburbs received their water on a rotational basis. This had a nasty knock on effect. Whilst pipes stood empty in the cut-off parts of the city, the leakage continued albeit in reverse. Mud and contamination seeped in to the system through the holes in the pipes only to be flushed in to peoples' homes once 'normal' service was resumed. Drinking thus became a major problem, as did the niceties of washing and going to the toilet. The solution was to save water whenever one could in old plastic buckets and coke bottles for use when there was no mains supply.

The trip from Belgrade to Sarajevo marked one of the most significant milestones in my life. The journey was an event in itself, but it also marked the start of a new chapter in my life and one in which I would play a significant part in helping to rebuild the lives of four and a half million people. When Richard had finally stopped briefing me on that first night, I had crashed out on his living room sofa completely comatosed and oblivious to the outside world. With the next day, reality dawned – there was still nothing to eat. Richard got me to drive through the old narrow streets around Bascarsija, which looked as if they belonged to another age, and in to the centre of the city, which looked even worse in daylight. We grabbed a sandwich from a lone kiosk and then called in at the Fero-elektro building in 'Trg Oktobra' (October Square) at the end of Avenue Marshal Tito. The state run company had agreed to rent us two floors of their building for our offices and several diplomats had already moved in along with a contingent of the newly created UN Mission in Bosnia Hercegovina (UNMiBH). Nick Haller had managed to grab himself a small room as a 'transport' office, which at least had some windows in it to keep out the icy wind although it also served to keep in the acrid cigarette fumes from his team of local drivers. There were crates of Land Rover gearboxes and what was termed as '10% Spares Packs,' piled high in every corner. I doubted whether the floor was strong enough to support the weight. Richard continued to brief me all day and to introduce me to what few staff was already in place. A small military liaison office produced a rather surprised Hubert De La Porte, yet another ex ICFY member from Sector Charlie who was now wearing the rather splendid uniform of a French Army Colonel. We drove around the city with Richard attempting to orientate me as I negotiated the debris of war and bullet catchers[68] at every junction. We travelled out to the Western suburbs along the infamous 'snipers' alley past the PTT building and the Holiday Inn where UNPROFOR and the international press had remained throughout

*The twin **UNIS Towers** on 'Sniper Alley' almost completely gutted by Serb artillery.*

some of the fiercest fighting of the war. We reached the airport, which was now firmly under the control of the NATO led Implementation Force. The main road, which is perhaps two miles long at this point, runs South with the airport on the right hand side and a residential suburb on the left. The scene was horrific, not a single building, house, block of flats or dwelling remained intact. For the entire two miles absolutely everything without exception was obliterated, all sign of life extinguished by the mindless onslaught that had destroyed these properties with complete disregard for IHL. The whole tour of the city was numbing yet somehow I was supposed to be taking it all in as Richard was leaving the next morning. The airport was open to military traffic with the French Army taking responsibility for keeping it open. For OHR, it would become the only way I could obtain supplies to get our operation off the ground. Later I would be able to purchase equipment locally, but for the moment you couldn't even buy a pencil in Sarajevo. Just North of the airport lay the main tactical HQ of IFOR in the suburb of Ilidza. IFOR's land forces came from the newly formed Allied Rapid Reaction Corps normally stationed in Rheindahlen, Germany. The ARRC's HQ was deployed 'in the field' in a requisitioned hotel complex (Hotel Terne) just outside Ilidza. Richard showed

me where to go should I ever need to get in to see them and then we set off
back to the city. I seriously doubted that I could find Richard's flat again never
mind many of the places we had visited during the day. Our last place of call
was to pick up an IFOR ID Card from IFOR's main HQ located in the old
'Residency' building in the city centre. It was truly getting to be a small world
as the British Army woman corporal who issued it to me had previously been
under my command in Belfast when I was the Operations Officer with 1
PARA. And so ended my twenty-four hour 'hand-over/take-over' with
Richard. Early the next morning I drove him to the airport and saw him safely
on to the C130 Hercules, which was to fly him to Zagreb.

As I returned to my battered Nissan I felt totally alone and completely
daunted by the task ahead. I'd often been tasked with the seemingly impossible whilst serving in the Army, but in those days I'd had the benefit of
massive professional and logistical support such as the ARRC now had at its
disposal. Five years previously I'd been tasked to provide security for the
Queen during her first visit to Northern Ireland for fourteen years. I'd been
given six and a half thousand troops to play with and an area stretching from
Belfast to Lisbon to secure. I'd managed to exercise 'operational command'
of all air and land forces involved in the massive operation ensuring her
safety from all physical and electronic means of warfare. Now I thought of
what it would be like to be back in uniform with all that support and to be
a part of IFOR. For sure their role was critical in the overall scheme of
things and to be back in uniform was to be an integral part of a well-oiled
machine, something that I yearned for right now. In the years that followed,
many of my former military colleagues would be quick to criticise the
civilian element of the reconstruction process but they never really appreciated the complexities of what was involved. Neither did they appreciate the
difficulties of getting things done when you don't have an 'army' to support
you. Instead many viewed us with suspicion (how can you now work with
Russians?) and sadly with a tinge of jealousy. It became a cliché that all the
civilian component of the peace process ever did was to drive around the
city in nice new white four by fours[69] often with a pretty interpreter accompanying them, sit in café bars all day and retire to their nice private houses
in the evenings. For this we even got paid and far more than the average
soldier. The reality was actually quite the opposite. In all my operations with
the Army, and IFOR was no different, the military provided everything.
Soldiers had reasonable accommodation, which was free under field conditions and which included access to field bath units and showers with continuous hot running water supplied by engineers. They had constant power,
light and heating provided by portable generators. Their laundry was done
on a daily basis, postal-courier and telephone services were made available
via the Field Post Offices and all ranks were given access to satellite TV,
recreation and bar facilities. To top the lot, military chefs using supplies
flown in from Germany cooked them three square meals a day. Finally their
jobs were secure, they provided a pension and of primary importance under

current circumstances, they had access to excellent medical and heath care facilities. The thought of having running water – never mind hot water, some effective heating and to be able to sup a Guinness to wash down a plate of bacon and eggs or roast beef before calling home and speaking to my wife and children was simply a dream. In Montenegro I'd lived off beer, eggs, pizzas and pickled gherkins. Now if anything, the situation had got worse. Since leaving Belgrade two days previously I had only eaten a couple of sandwiches and I hadn't even sorted out my personal situation as I'd been using the limited time available with Richard to learn the ropes. And so with Richard gone and no army to support me, I spent the rest of that day in the Fero-elektro building getting to know some of the local staff who would help me put the OHR firmly on the map. That night after finishing work I decided to drive back to Ilidza and visit the IFOR camp if for no other reason than to see if I could get something to eat.

Under Dayton, the Serb populated suburb of Ilidza was to be handed over to the Muslim-Croat Federation and was not to remain within the new Bosnian Serb entity, Republika Srpska. The same migration that I had witnessed on the road in to Sarajevo two days before hand was now to be repeated in this suburb. As OHR had no security system, no way of disseminating information to its members and no voice communications system, I was completely oblivious to what was going on in the suburb as I set off down sniper alley hoping for some supper. As you reach the Eastern end of Ilidza the dual carriageway finishes and the road divides. One route takes you South towards Mostar in Hercegovina, the other takes you through the centre of Ilidza and across a bridge before approaching the IFOR HQ. As I neared the outskirts I could see that the sky was red, but it wasn't until I'd turned off the Mostar road and entered the built up area that I realised why. To my horror the Serbs were burning their own homes. Tall blocks of flats and once elegant Austro-Hungarian houses were on fire whilst hundreds of dejected people loaded their last belongings on to the backs of civilian and military trucks. What they couldn't carry, they burnt by the roadside in huge bonfires, their life's possessions going up in flames rather than leave anything to their old enemy. It was a pitiful sight and quite terrifying. I had no idea as to whether I should turn back perhaps drawing attention to myself in the process, or press on down the main street in my battered pickup and hope that I wouldn't suddenly become the focus of these people's attention. By the time I'd finished pondering the risk and my possible options, I'd already crossed the river and left the burning behind me. It had been like driving somehow in slow motion through a mini blitz albeit this time there had been no aircraft and no bombs, just people sacking their own homes. Whilst I'd been frightened it'd also been extremely sad to witness such action, people do not normally destroy their own homes and their livelihoods. Not for the first time and certainly not for the last, I questioned the sense of Dayton and its creation of two entities. How could you possibly rebuild one nation out of two entities, which the very terms of the peace agreement allow to polarise in to two opposing and hostile camps? I turned my attention to food and negotiated the armed sentries on the IFOR camp gate. I went to reception and not quite knowing how to go about things just asked to see any British Officer. As the Dutch military Police were pondering what to do with me I saw a British Major, Tom Mouat walking across the hallway. Tom and I had served together in Antwerp, Belgium several years before hand and his wife June, was God Mother to my son Thomas. I had no idea he was in Bosnia but he was completely dumb-struck to see me standing in front of him blocking his way. As far as Tom knew I'd left the Army two years previously and that was that. To see me working as a civilian in what the military describe, as a 'theatre of opera-tions' was too much for him. Needless to say Tom introduced me to several other old mates (and previous bosses) and then stuffed me full of food and plied me with several pints of Guinness as he and the others listened to me recount my recent exploits. It was a wonderful evening and slowly but surely the terrible feeling of trepidation and isolation began to lift. I no longer felt quite so alone and instead began to seriously consider how I was going to make this whole thing work. With a box of Danish military field rations tucked under my arm, I made my way home past the still smoulder-ing houses.

10

The Office of the High Representative

The Fero-elektro building was a rather nasty office block located at the Western end of Ulica Marshal Tito and was typical of the austere type of architecture that pervades all former Eastern block communist countries. Following years of war, the building, like most others in the city, was in a sorry state. There was little glass in any of the windows and most were now covered in plastic sheeting, much of the outside cladding and insulation had fallen off and there were holes in the actual walls where you could see right out in to the street. Inside it was much the same. The walls, cupboards and bookcases were peppered with shrapnel and bullet holes, there was no running water and the heating didn't work. In many of the offices the walls and ceilings had collapsed giving the appearance of a bombsite, which of course, it literally was. Power was intermittent but even if the supply could be maintained then the wiring was so old and had been patched or rather botched so often that it would never support the power requirements of a modern office. There were a couple of telephones wired rather dangerously in to 'sockets' – simply mere holes in the floor but there was no exchange or office-to-office communications whatsoever. Communications to and from the outside world was feasible via several CAPSATs and INMARSATs but phoning or faxing Bosnian Ministries down town was nigh on impossible. Just to add to the difficulties, most of the office furniture had been pilfered and the few desks and chairs that remained in the office all seemed to have only three legs. The walls were painted a horrid dark brown whilst the odd piece of grubby orange carpet that remained served only to trip the unwary. Within six months all this had changed, in fact so much so that you could easily believe that you were working in Bruxelles or any other European capital untouched by war. Yet new diplomats would arrive each month whinging and whining that things were not what they were used to back in their diplomatic service and how intolerable the conditions were. I often

The Office of the High Representative, Sarajevo: The Fero-electro building before renovation in early 1996.

wondered why these people did the work that they did and how their conscience demanded such luxurious standards when those around them were still subjected to immense hardship and suffering.

The 'High Representative' and former Swedish Prime Minister Carl Bildt, had already arrived in Sarajevo along with his 'Principal Deputy,' the German diplomat Michael Steiner. A few other diplomats, either ex-ICFY or US State Department officials, who had been involved in the negotiating process at Dayton, had also arrived. The US, who had after all brokered the Dayton Peace Agreement, had wanted and expected the first High Representative to be an American but had quite rightly lost out to the Europeans when Bildt had got the post no doubt in part due to the complete lack of American military ground support to UNPROFOR during the actual war.[70] With Steiner taking the second slot, the Americans were relegated to third position – 'Chief of Staff' (COS), a post taken by my immediate boss, Jock Covey. Covey wanted the 'Deputy Chief of Staff' (DCOS) also to be an American and had earmarked another former ICFY member, Soni Shaftnet who worked for MPRI to take the post.[71] The fact that the British Government had sent me to take that post was clearly an irritation in Covey's side as for one reason or another he was 'too busy' to even see me until the Saturday evening, some four days after my arrival. Covey was bright, intelligent and without doubt one of the most dedicated and hard working professionals I have ever worked with, but he was also too slow, over methodical and what can best be described as a minimalist. He also lacked vision, foresight and was a control freak. When Jock eventually decided to talk to me, he treated me as if I was a US Embassy 'General

Services Officer,' basically a gopher to be at his beck and call. Needless to say it required immense tact and self-control to work with him until things settled down during these first few months. At the end of the day one simply had to muck in as initially there was no alternative. However this was where our visions departed from each other. Jock never had a vision much beyond the immediate, whereas my vision was to establish something that would function properly and as soon as possible. Jock's reasoning came from his minimalist nature and his somewhat misplaced judgement that it would all be over within a year – perhaps a vision shared with the American tax payer and their historic isolationist nature. On the other hand, my vision was based upon following basic military practice and conducting a comprehensive analytical appreciation of the requirement and then producing a plan to meet it. Faced with the realities of everyday circumstances and life in Sarajevo, accomplishing anything would be very difficult but getting executive decisions out of Covey was to be one of the biggest obstacles to success I was to encounter. Indeed it often crossed my mind that his obstruction was deliberate and that I was often meant to fail. Such failure after all would look bad on the Europeans and not on the United States. By taking the main support roles and not the high profile leadership roles, the Americans could guarantee that they could influence the workings of the Mission but never had to stick their necks out in case something should go wrong. All in all, despite being a thoroughly nice guy, he was a nightmare to work with.

Having worked out my plan, I had a pretty good idea of what I wanted to achieve and how I was going to go about it. Essentially I had drawn up a rather hierarchical organisational diagram, which whilst not following the latest in-vogue management trend of de-layered multi-functional teams, did provide a basis for planning. The plan set out what the OHR was supposed to achieve and gave some semblance of structure by which it would attempt to achieve those aims. I had concentrated on how I might structure my own supporting side of the house but clearly I needed the whole overview if I was going to be able to allocate offices and structure local area computer networks and other hi-tech systems. My proposal to Covey involved establishing my administrative and logistic structure immediately since it is again a basic military principle of planning that the support elements are always first-in and last-out of any operation. Unfortunately minimalism won the day and for the moment I was forced to forgo my plans of creating an administrative and logistic structure which would have embraced key requirements such as transport, telecommunications, IT and finance to name but a few. Instead I had to divide these tasks amongst myself and six very young and inexperienced local members of staff (Amela, Dino, Ivica, Vesna, Keno and a newly pregnant Mookie). As work got underway in earnest, I made several calls back to London to appraise the FCO on Jock's minimalist attitude and his intention to appoint Soni as the Mission's Chief Administrative Officer (CAO). London responded by sending Peter Streams, a retired ambassador who had worked with the ECMM in Zagreb, to work along side Bildt and to act as a Mr Fix-it within the OHR. The whole episode was extremely tense as Covey clearly saw through the ruse and recognised the threat that Peter posed with yet another European muscling in on the act. Covey treated Peter far more disrespectfully than he had me and refused to discuss anything with him for a whole week. In the mean time Peter had to share an end of my three-legged desk and wait. This was not the way to treat one of Her Majesty's Ambassadors but Covey won the day, Streams was eventually sent packing and I was left to fend for myself.

Communications was a top priority as at present we were unable to communicate effectively with anyone including within our own office. My aim was to establish an Information and Communications Technology (ICT) Department and staff it with appropriately qualified staff who I envisioned would help establish and maintain all telephone, fax and satellite communications and all computers including a local area network within the office. Covey's idea was for me to continue to personally rewire telephones by putting my unqualified hands down the sockets in the floorboards. One has to remember that at the beginning of 1996, local area networks and even 'Windows 95' were pretty new concepts in the UK and few if anyone in Bosnia had come across such technology, indeed even email was almost a totally new concept. I was spending considerable time troubleshooting and fixing various wiring problems, and running back and forth to the Sarajevo PTT to buy in additional phone lines at over DEM 2,000 a time. The situation was untenable, as in no stretch of the imagination could I ever hope to support an office that was supposed to grow to several hundred staff, each with their own telephone, computer and internet requirements. Besides this, as I saw it ICT was only one of my many areas of responsibility. Thankfully OHR had established an office in Bruxelles, which was supposed to provide the link to various European institutions and the World Bank as well as resolve the division of assets that had belonged to the SFRY before Yugoslavia's disintegration.[72] The Bruxelles COS was a very bright and dynamic Norwegian woman named Laila Reffnes who had worked extensively with Bildt whilst he had been in Geneva. Laila was impatient with Covey's lack of progress and had hoped that I would get things moving, but she was also well aware of his step-by-step minimalist tendencies. She provided the support I needed and I was able to circumvent Covey on many administrative matters not least because at that stage of the game everything I required had to be purchased in Bruxelles and flown down to me on NATO military flights in to Sarajevo airport. Laila recruited my first technical expert Elaine Hopton, to be my ICT Manager in Sarajevo and to work under the guidance of the Bruxelles ICT Manager, Erik de Decker. Elaine had worked with Reuters for many years and was much admired throughout the media world as well as in the Balkans. Apart from a cat, her work was her life and she immediately set about holding the fort sorting out all the wiring problems whilst I discussed my plans with Laila. Bruxelles gave me their full support and so together we started to get the ball rolling at last. The Swedish telecomm giant, Ericsson donated and installed a new digital MD110 exchange and we found a local contractor to totally rewire the building installing proper telephone sockets in the walls rather than in the floor. Despite daily 'morning prayer' sessions, Covey provided no indication of staffing numbers, organisational structures or any other operational details, which one would normally expect to receive in order to plan future requirements. His style was to simply announce that a new member of staff had already arrived and then to ask why an office, desk, phone line, computer, email address and the like had not already been allocated; it was a nightmare. Computers and peripherals were flown in from Bruxelles as was all the necessary cabling and supplies to install a computer network within the building. After much searching we managed to find a local contractor to use these materials and install a Local Area Network (LAN). Our intention was then to expand the system to provide external Wide Area Networking (WAN) facilities to the rest of the world via the internet. All this was new to me and I had a steep learning curve to say the least. The solution to world wide access was to install a huge UNISERVE satellite dish on the roof and open a dedicated (twenty-four hours per day) 256 kbit bandwidth sat-link back to Bruxelles where a local Internet Service Provider (ISP) gave us access to the web and we were able to open our own OHR website.[73] Within two months of arriving, OHR had a largely paperless office environment with each member of staff able to communicate by phone, fax and email worldwide. This was a remarkable achievement that went largely unnoticed. People expected to be able to make calls whenever they wanted, but as I have already described, the state of the Bosnia PTT system and the official obstruction between the two entities made this almost impossible. When people from OHR called the Bosnian Serb leadership several kilometres away in Pale, they didn't realise that the call was not made via the PTT in the usual way. The Federation was not connected to Republika Srpska as the latter was on the Yugoslav, Belgrade switch. Nor could you dial Yugoslavia internationally as lines from Bosnia were blocked. Instead their call was made via the Ericsson switchboard to the UNISERVE system. From there it was transmitted via satellite to Bruxelles and then finally via international PTT from Belgium to Belgrade, Yugoslavia before crossing back in to Bosnia to complete its journey only some five KMs away from the originator. One other aspect of communications concerned me greatly and that was to do with security and the need for mobile communications. Much of the work of the office involved travelling around the country on roads that were extremely dangerous. The main threat to life was actually from simple road traffic accidents due to the dreadful state of repair that most roads were in and from winter driving conditions. However, one could not forget the mine threat or the new spate of vehicle hijackings that was on the increase. To my mind, it was critical that we had a mobile communications system of handheld and vehicle mounted radios which could be used for security purposes as well as for any other administrative or operational purpose that arose, and there were many. Covey's solution was for everyone to wait until Bosnia had set up a mobile phone system and then for us all to carry cellular phones. My investigations revealed that Sarajevo had a partial local cellular capability but that it did not extend beyond the city; neither had it ever done so. Clearly, it was extremely unlikely that the Federation and the RS would get together in the forthcoming weeks and agree upon a Bosnian wide cellular network, and besides creating one would take several years and not weeks. My memory of driving through Ilidza when the suburb was being burnt was fresh in my mind and as far as I was concerned the requirement for an immediate solution remained extant. As it happens, it was to take a further eighteen months to establish a cellular network in the Federation and almost four years to have an integrated Bosnian system of sorts. Despite objections from Covey, I entered in to negotiations with the American organisation, Darlington Communications and my old contacts Dane Kaiser, Bill Neff and Mike Cresswell who had supplied the communications system for ICFY and who I hoped would be able to release their equipment for use in Bosnia now that ICFY was closing down. My intention was to secure this equipment free as a donation from the American State Department rather than to use OHR funds, which were still unclear at that stage. American funding was certainly available for several months and Darlington was prepared to undertake the task of establishing a complete Bosnia-wide radio communications network. That is to say, to supply handheld and vehicle-mounted sets, base stations, spares and all the mountain top repeaters necessary to establish and maintain communications throughout the whole territory of Bosnia i Hercegovina. After an initial period, all the equipment would be leased to the OHR who would then have to employ a suitably qualified technician to independently maintain the network. This was an excellent offer but it required Covey to sign the Memorandum of Understanding (MOU) before the State Department would release the radios, which were currently sitting unused in the US Embassy in Belgrade. Finally albeit reluctantly and only after several weeks procrastination, he agreed to sign the MOU and the newly established Communications Office started to work along side Elaine and her ICT Department to complete the electronic coverage of Bosnia.

Although communications were a top priority, other matters still had to be address concurrently and so whilst I was still at the stage of ferreting down telephone sockets in the flooring, I also had to contend with many other issues. Sorting out the transport arrangements was one such priority although of course I had Nick Haller already working on the case. Nick was still in the phase of crisis management although I'm not quite sure he ever got beyond that phase in the year we were to work together. Nevertheless he held his small team of drivers together whilst they were at the beck and call of each and every department. Nick was operating with a small fleet of only six Land Rover Discoveries, which he had obtained via the UK. Jock considered that this was enough and that we only needed to better manage our assets in order to make do. He was right on one aspect, the department could always have done with being better managed as crisis management was no way to continue to do business, however he was way off mark regarding the size of the fleet. OHR was soon to expand, opening regional offices elsewhere in the country and each department had its own special needs, which continued to grow. Whilst Nick had his 10% spares packs loaded in wooden crates in his office, he had nowhere and no one to maintain the vehicles. Additionally both Carl Bildt and Michael Steiner now had possession of an armoured BMW and an armoured Mercedes whilst their French Special Forces Close Protection (CP) team had Toyota Land Cruisers. I of course had my trusty battered blue pick-up truck from ICFY and viewed my old mission as a source of additional free vehicles. I had discussed this concept with Raimo, ICFY's logistics officer in Belgrade before I crossed in to Bosnia. Essentially both OHR and ICFY were under Bildt's jurisdiction and so all that was required was to formally request the vehicles from ICFY so that Raimo could obtain authority from the original donors to transfer the assets between the two Missions. As the clock ticked away and other new Missions such as OSCE put their bids for vehicles in to HQ ICFY in Belgrade, Covey who ultimately had to allow me to make a bid, procrastinated and refused to accept that there was any need for additional vehicles. It is probably worth stating at this stage just how wrong he was. By the end of the year I had purchased neigh on one hundred additional vehicles, mostly expensive Land Rover Discoveries from the UK but also smaller VW Golfs and basic utility vehicles as well. I was never given authority to bid for the free assets from ICFY and simply had to watch as the OSCE and ICOM etc drove vehicles around Sarajevo that I physically recognised as previously belonging to ICFY. Belgrade, Bruxelles and London were furious and in the end a rather irate FCO Officer directed me to go to Belgrade and collect three Land Rover Defenders which had been donated to ICFY by the UK Government, and to accept them in to OHR regardless of what Covey wanted. I jumped at the chance to go back to Belgrade and arranged to take three other Brits with me in order to drive the Defenders back in convoy. Non of us had any visas anymore and so I wrote a rather pompous 'letter of authority' quoting that part of the DPA which stated that all signatories, including President Milosevic, had agreed to co-operate fully with the OHR and therefore should grant us freedom of movement. Adding a liberal application of official stamps for good measure, I hoped to bluff our way in to Serbia, spend an evening in Belgrade with Raimo, JW and Andrej before returning the next day with the British vehicles. To my surprise and great relief, the ruse worked and we reached Belgrade without incident only to be collared the next morning in the hotel lobby by a rather officious member of the MUP who demanded to know how and why we were in Belgrade. The policeman was refusing to return the passport of a hapless American businessman who for all I could see had done absolutely nothing wrong at all. Every time the American demanded to know when he would get his passport back, the policeman merely stated, 'It doesn't matter.' The American was getting nowhere fast in what was clearly a power play between the two which he was losing badly. Unfortunately my team needed to leave as soon as possible but the MUP officer was also clutching all our passports in his other hand. Since there was no other option, I took a deep breath and with an air of complete confidence and composure, cut in to their 'conversation' announcing to the policeman that, 'I've come for our passports.' Both the American and the Police officer looked shocked at the blatant interruption and the officer told me to, 'Wait.' I refused stating that, 'We've got to leave right now.' He wanted to know how we got in to the country without visas and again told me to, 'Wait.' Again refusing, I informed him that his President had given permission for OHR to be here and then as a token gesture showed him my IFOR ID which I kept firmly attached around my neck. The American was aghast that anyone could dare to stand up to the MUP. The policeman recovered slightly to demand, 'Where did you cross?' Clearly the customs post would soon be in for a right rollicking but as we still needed to get out, I simply snatched the passports right out of his hand and added, 'It doesn't matter' before beating a quick retreat to our vehicles.

As time progressed we had no other option but to buy in brand new vehicles, mostly additional Discoveries from the UK. We had a deliberate policy of buying light blue vehicles as we wanted to make a clear distinction between the OHR and both the UN, who drove white 4 x 4s, and the military who were in just about every conceivable variation of green. As the fleet grew we acquired four armoured Range Rovers which I was later to use to drive the Bosnian Serb President Momcilo Krajisnik, around Sarajevo.[74] But the size of the fleet caused both parking and maintenance problems. Jock wanted us to service the vehicles locally but no one had the capability to do this and Land Rover confirmed that they were not yet distributing spares to Bosnia. Within a year the Overseas Development Agency (ODA), later to become the Department for International Development (DFID) opened a Land Rover workshop near Ilidza but we needed something sooner rather than later and so Nick and I spent considerable time driving around the city trying to locate a piece of real estate big enough (and clear of mines) to create a depot and workshop for ourselves. Eventually we found a site across from the Holiday Inn and down from the National Museum, which we set about renovating. This was another major task that took several months to complete but when finished allowed us to service and maintain all our vehicles, and also to carry out quite significant body shop repairs as well as provide parking facilities in an increasingly crowded city.

Meanwhile the state of the Fero-elektro building had to be addressed. Two floors had been leased to OHR under the arrangement that we would eventually leave the building in a better state than when we had found it.

Clearly this was not going to be difficult since the building was in a terrible mess and so we had no choice but to repair and indeed, to enhance the infrastructure so that it could properly support our work. I have already mentioned that we set about installing a telephone exchange (PBX) and a computer LAN. The installation of the satellite on the roof in order to expand our voice and data communications presented a major challenge. UNISERVE staff were eventually involved in the installation but the original contract negotiated in Bruxelles just covered the purchase and delivery of the equipment and I had literally been presented with a set of blue prints on 'do it yourself' satellite installation. Whilst I was more than capable of setting up and operating a briefcase size INMARSAT or putting up a domestic satellite TV dish on the balcony of my flat, this was not what we were talking about here. This was a permanent dedicated satellite extension to both our Ericsson MD110 PBX and our computer LAN and the systems all had to be connected together and become interoperable. Getting the dish on to the roof required the loan of a huge crane from an Army engineer unit (once the engineers had finally decided that the roof, despite its shell damage, could probably support the additional weight). Thankfully Bruxelles renegotiated the contract with UNISERVE and together we got our communications working. This however presented another challenge, as the building was never designed to cope with all the new technology that we were installing as fast as the IFOR flights from Bruxelles could deliver it. Power became a major issue not just because the building couldn't cope with our growing demands, but because Sarajevo was still subjected to constant power cuts and had the nasty habit of producing periodic surges that could easily destroy a computer. I had decided from the outset to buy small UPS systems with each desktop on a one-to-one scale but we still had to protect the newly installed PBX and UNISERVE systems since if these crashed, then the computers were largely irrelevant. Also all the faxes and photocopiers, and the heating and lighting systems needed protection. To solve the problem we flew in a huge Perkins diesel generator which we then had to protect in a purpose built wire-mesh cage since it had to remain outside of the building and we had no secure compound to put it in. On the first floor of the office we installed a massive UPS system (again after engineer advice on whether the staircase could support the extra weight) and connected the two together and then both to the mains. In the event of a power cut, the UPS would immediately cut in taking on the whole load throughout the building. The generator would then also start automatically and maintain the UPS batteries. Whilst all this work was being undertaken, I set about negotiating contracts to repair and renovate the building with as many local businesses as possible. At this stage after the war, the means by which one could identify appropriate and competent contractors was severely limited and often done by word of mouth. I urgently needed to find builders, plasterers and carpenters; painters and decorators; plumbers and electricians, and then to find suppliers for every single fixture and fitting one could possibly imagine – desks, chairs, conference tables, coat and hat stands, waste paper baskets, window blinds, air-conditioning units, fire extinguishers, first aid boxes etc and finally to find suppliers for all the everyday consumables that a modern office needs such as ink and toner cartridges, paper, pencils and floppy discs etc. This was an incredibly time-consuming task and usually involved sending out my local staff to hunt around and then for me to go and view a short-list of options before making the final decisions on for example, which type and colour of carpet to buy and who to contract with etc. It was clear that more staff were needed to cope with the demands as both Elaine Hopton and Nick Haller were now heavily involved with their respective work which left me holding all the other balls in my own hands. What was also missing and what was needed from the outset were all the systems and procedures needed to run the office. Whereas the UN simply arrived in theatre bringing with them all the bureaucratic trappings necessary to run a major complex operation, the OHR had to start from scratch. Running around like a head-less chicken, whether sticking my hands down telephone sockets or even viewing carpets and desks, was not what I believed I should be doing. I needed to delegate these tasks as I had done with transport and ICT so that I could concentrate on addressing the structural and staffing needs of the organisation and set about designing and implementing the systems and procedure that were needed to run it. We were now recruiting more and more members of local staff but we did not have a clear guideline on career paths, employment categories, grades or salaries. We had no formal application form, neither did we interview in a particularly professional manner. Too much of what we had to do was open to abuse and therefore open to allegations of corruption. Everyone in Sarajevo had just been through a terrible war which had destroyed both lives and livelihoods and so it was only natural that those who could benefit from an income by what ever means, would try to do so whether that be by simple 'low-level' nepotism on employment issues or more serious financial abuses involving friends and relatives who knew someone – who knew someone else who would perhaps rent out their house to international members of staff or suddenly become painters and decorators. This is not to paint a sinister picture of wide spread abuse but simply to illustrate that systems and procedures, complete with checks and balances are necessary in any organisation. In the normal course of events these evolve over time but in OHR they had to be designed and implemented from scratch. Since OHR was open to audit, I saw it as my priority to get these systems up and running as soon as possible in order to have a professional and an equitable system for all. Slowly but surely I managed to get things organised and Jock finally relented on his demand for an American CAO rather sheepishly asking me to take on that role, one that I had in any case assumed by default from the first day! In addition to the drivers and mechanics, and the ICT and radio communications staff that we already had, I began to structure other administrative and support functions creating more departments and recruiting appropriately qualified staff. With a first year budget of ECU 19M (around £12M at 1996 exchange rates) we quickly recruited a finance officer and created a system of financial controls with budgetary expenditure codes that kept Price Waterhouse happy. We recruited security guards, receptionists and PBX operators, catering assistants, registry and distribution staff, diplomatic protocol staff and a set up a personnel department and a general services department that became responsible for all logistical and supply matters taking another weight off my shoulders. It was soon April Fools day and I had been working seven days a week since returning to ICFY after Christmas leave, working and living in dreadful conditions for almost three months without a single day off. I had got the ball rolling and now felt that I could at last take a break whilst my newly appointed staff got on with what was required. Feeling totally drained and somewhat relieved that I had somehow 'survived the first contact' to use a military expression, I clambered on the first of four flights that would eventually take me home to my wife and family.

11

Consolidation

The two weeks I spent at home with my family past far too quickly and I soon found myself making the trip back to the airport to catch the first of two flights that would take me back to Sarajevo. I always found it particularly hard to leave my family although both my wife Allison and my two children never really complained about what I did, although I know it hurt them too to see me leave. This was not something that I would be able to sustain indefinitely and as the years ticked by Allison was to comment that I was far more concerned with 'saving the world' rather than looking after my own family. She was of course right in what she said, it was the sense of doing something right, something to help the Bosnian people that sustained me during the dreadful months that I'd just endured and in the months that were to follow. In the end I would need to leave Bosnia and come home as the strain would become too much and we would all need to be together again living as a normal family. But for now I was going back, carrying as usual, one suitcase for me and one full of spare clothes and toys to distribute to local families who needed them. It was now late April and spring had arrived in England but within thirty minutes of departing Zagreb, the Greek C130 Hercules that I was travelling in had to divert from its flight to Sarajevo and land at the American airbase in Tuzla due to severe snow and ice problems at Sarajevo. It was a rude awakening.

Arriving back in Sarajevo was like entering another world, a somewhat surreal environment where time stood still or at least moved very slowly amid the destruction of war which still littered the largely uncleared streets. IFOR had completed its main task of ensuring that the entity armies had withdrawn to their respective sides of the IEBL and that the streets were no longer full of armed groups of demobilised soldiers or paramilitaries brandishing their weapons. Instead IFOR patrols dominated the ground, maintaining the tactical initiative and in the absence of a proper Bosnian Police force and a weak IPTF, keeping the peace. On the other hand, civilian peace implementation was painfully slow. By definition this was always going to be the reality since it is one thing to deploy an already existing and self sustaining military formation in to the field, and quite another to create an organisation from scratch and gather its component parts together in situ. Likewise, the tasks given to IFOR under Annex 1A, of the GFAP, were relatively straightforward and the only unknown variable was whether the respective armies would comply or not. As it happened they did and IFOR's task was made all the more simpler. On the other hand however, the remaining ten annexes of the GFAP related to civilian peace implementation. Clearly rebuilding a country physically (the reconstruction of the complete material infrastructure and industries) and restructuring it economically and politically following a sustained and ferocious war, was never going to be achieved as quickly as IFOR's tasks. Nevertheless, whether as a result of ignorance or simply pressure from the US Treasury to have a credible and quick 'exit strategy,' the American commander of IFOR Admiral Leighton-Smith, foolishly took it upon himself to openly criticise Bildt at a weekly 'Principals Meeting' stating that civilian peace implementation was far too slow. Having been more than pleased with what we had achieved over the last two and a half months, it was quite a shock to hear such criticism from someone who should have known better. Bildt on the other hand, was far from shocked – he was livid. Far from apologising for his implied sluggishness, he rounded on Leighton-Smith and proceeded to lecture him on the realities of post-war recovery in the Balkans and the allocation of resources. Bildt was enraged that Leighton-Smith could dare criticise his operation, which at that stage had still not received any of its pledged budget. Even if all the funds had arrived, Bildt told Smith that he was still expected to rebuild a complete country with less money than it would cost to buy a couple of Smith's Main Battle Tanks. Whilst the maths wasn't wholly accurate, the point was. Bildt was expected to achieve far more than Smith could comprehend and with a mere fraction of the resources. I for one was a case in point as my Foreign Office salary had long dried up and I hadn't been paid for the last two months.

But things were progressing and life in the city was slowly beginning to change. The city looked less haunting, much of the debris was slowly being cleared and dangerous segments of buildings were being pulled down before they fell on passers by. Shops were beginning to open as were many new café bars and restaurants – a staple industry in countries recovering from war where there is little other work available. Previously I had been forced by the lack of other options to eat in what was known as the 'UN Restaurant' (its proper name was Café Zeljo) located in Ulica Branislava Djurdjeva behind the OHR. During the war the UN troops had been able to eat here and so I guess the UN must have supplied the food at some stage. I had no idea what the arrangements were now following Dayton, but for several months it was about the only place where I could buy a decent meal each day albeit the restaurant was mostly full of IFOR troops and you needed an ID card to get in. An Internet Café also opened across from OHR in Ulica Pavle Gorania (now renamed Ulica Pruscakova) although this was later to move to bigger premises as the concept took off with the influx of internationals. All in all things were improving. Many of the mined areas were now

A residential area of Sarajevo rendered uninhabitable by the Serb bombardment. The area in the foreground is a badly marked mine field.

being cleared or at least properly cordoned off. Clearing the ground between the tramlines was given a high priority although I still considered it unsafe to cross sniper alley at any point other than at one of the main road intersections, as that at least meant that you could walk on tarmac. There were more cars on the road too. Many were from the steady influx of international aid agencies that were only now arriving in country. I met with a friend and former colleague from ICFY, Eamon O'Riordan from Ireland who was helping to establish ICOM in Sarajevo and then with Tim Stanning, who had been the Senior Operations Officer for ICFY in Belgrade and who was now the newly appointed COS of OSCE. As more and more aid agencies came in to the city, life began to appear more normal as people once more began to go about their normal daily business. But much of the improvements were a cosmetic illusion that lay only on the surface. Deep down there had been little improvement for the ordinary citizen. It was far too early for that and OHR had barely begun to attack the main problems that were still prevalent within the country and which had been largely responsible for taking the country to war in the first instance. Whilst IFOR began to get out their cameras and behave like war tourists, and the IC to congregate in their own café bars and restaurants, I preferred to mingle with local people and to learn their ways and culture, and to listen to their stories of what really happened in Sarajevo during the war. For me, too many of the IC, especially some of the more senior diplomats, behaved like they belonged to a colonial power, keeping their distance from their subjects. I wanted to stay and talk with local families, to eat their food – Cevapcici, Sagan Dolma, and Pavlaka, and to drink Turkish coffee with them in their bars. For me, this was the only way to really find out what was happening and one that would stand me in good stead for my next job with ECMM.

Life in the office was also beginning to take shape. As some semblance of structure evolved, the recruitment of staff continued and so the division of responsibility became more equitable and in the end people got far more done since they could concentrate on what they should be doing and not on crisis managing something else. In the main, local staff were Bosniaks, that is to say Bosnian Muslims if for no other reason than the other two ethnic groups were no longer properly represented in Sarajevo having themselves either been ethnically cleansed or fled voluntarily after Dayton. I sought to redress this imbalance by actively recruiting Bosnian Croats and Bosnian Serbs on to the OHR staff. I wanted to do this deliberately, not least because the current imbalance was unfair, but because OHR was about rebuilding Bosnia and not about rebuilding just one third of it. Imagine how it would look to an outsider if the employment statistics were analysed and OHR was seen to employ only Muslims. Further more, there was the purely practical side of things. None of the existing interpreters were keen to travel with OHR staff to Pale or to any other Serb area. They had good reason as they were scarred, but increasingly more often we were not just attending conferences in and around Sarajevo but making trips away for several days. The prospect of over-nighting in another's entity was not going down too well at all. I therefore set out to actively recruit local staff from the other two ethnic groups. Actually, this was far harder than it seemed and in the end I only managed to put a small dent in the problem but to some extent the problem was largely to go away once OHR established a regional presence throughout Bosnia. However, at this stage I had no idea what the future would have in store.

By the beginning of May I had managed to reduce the working week to six days per week with the Saturday finishing time being at 2,00 pm. This was done formally on the basis of the contracts for locally employed staff and limited their working hours to 40 hours per week. The international staff was still expected to work as and when required and I for one still made brief visits to the office on Sundays to check if things were still running smoothly. As more vehicles were available we were able to take advantage of them and to leave the city to explore the rest of the country and to get an idea of what it was like outside Sarajevo. I had previously got to know every inch of Montenegro because of all my patrolling there, but apart from the trip to Belgrade, I hadn't yet seen much of Bosnia at all and so I jumped at the chance to visit places at the weekends. Initially we visited Gorazda where the British, unlike their Dutch counterparts, had fought the Bosnian Serbs to defend the UN Safe Haven albeit finally being overrun with the loss of several Special Air Service (SAS) lives.[75] We also visited Visegrad, the subject of Ivo Andric's novel 'The Bridge over the Drina,' and then Pale, Mount Igman, Tuzla, Niksic, Mostar with Tom Mouat from IFOR and

Mostar: *A view of the old part of the city. You can just see the wire bridge that has been erected across the river where the old medieval bridge had been.*

finally as summer arrived – the Adriatic coast of Croatia. But one aspect of work hadn't changed, Covey was still not really confiding in me despite our continuing morning prayer sessions. I was still being hit by new arrivals, new office requirements indeed the complete reallocation of office space to accommodate new establishments etc without any prior warning. The effect was to keep my departments constantly on their nerves as they battled to extend the LAN and connect new users to a system that had been changed so frequently that it now began to look as if it hadn't ever been planned in the first place. With each change, Jock's extremely efficient secretary Lynn, would smile at me with a sickly grin that simply reinforced my view that

Jock never wanted anything in OHR to work and that his whole style was a deliberate attempt at sabotaging the European effort. But despite all these hot potatoes, nothing had prepared me for the conference that I was called to at the end of April.

The GFAP had called for the establishment of JCCs and JMCs which were to be set up at the regional level throughout the country. Covey had never once discussed with me any of the implications of this requirement yet it was clear that he had always been aware of the intention not simply to establish these Commissions on paper and to meet on a regular basis, but for OHR to create a permanent regional presence throughout Bosnia i Hercegovina by opening up new offices at strategic locations in both entities. Lynn called me to tell me that I was required in a planning meeting that Bildt was chairing down in the conference room. When I arrived, the meeting was already well underway and Covey beckoned me to sit down next to him where there was a spare chair. My first indication of any require- ment to open any further offices was when Bildt looked up at me and asked, 'When you installed the satellite link to Bruxelles, did you take in to account the need to patch in to our new office in Banja Luka?' A million questions raced through my head like, 'What new office?' but these were immediate- ly overtaken by a burning desire to expose Covey's childish behaviour for what it really was. Nevertheless loyalty and a desire not to look completely stupid got the better of me and I simply answered that the UNISERVE contract did not at present include further expansion but that it was techni- cally feasible to extend the satellite network to the new office in Banja Luka. That seemed to suffice since Bildt then went on to announce to the confer- ence that the new OHR Regional Office would be opening on Monday 6th May with a formal cocktail party for all local dignitaries, civic and political leaders and members of IFOR's British led 'Multi-National Division Southwest' (MND) which was moving its HQ from Vitez to Banja Luka at the same time. Since it was now Thursday 25 April, that left me with only just over a week to repeat up in Banja Luka, everything that I had done so far in Sarajevo during the last three months! I was completely 'gob- smacked' and serious considered walking out then and there. Further more I was furious with Covey for not forewarning me weeks ago as he surely knew that the requirement existed even if he hadn't then known all of the details. The wretched satellite was quite frankly, the last of my concerns. The first was to find and acquire a suitable building to use as an office, then to think about recruiting a stop-gap skeleton staff, then to supply at least some basic equipment so that it could at least function of sorts until such time as the cocktail party was over. And of course there was the issue of communi- cations both voice and data and last but not least finding a venue for the cocktail party, organising the catering, sorting out the hosting and finding out just who to invite without missing someone off the list and causing a diplomatic incident. All this had to be done with proper regard to diplomat- ic protocol. Just printing the invitations would be difficult enough let alone setting up an office in the mean time. To add to the problems, not only was there no system of communications between Sarajevo and Banja Luka (which would make liaison over the next six days neigh on impossible), but there was no method of transferring money between the two entities and so yet again everything would have to be done using the proverbial suitcase full of cash.[76] If proof was ever needed that Covey had long since known about the requirement, he called me in to his office and informed me that, 'The British Foreign and Commonwealth Office are supplying the new Head of Office, Tim Clifton and he'll sort things out when he arrives.' Covey asked for my plan knowing full well that I couldn't possibly have one only two minutes after the meeting had ended. Both he and Lynn had that satisfied smirk across their faces as I left for the sanity of my own office upstairs.

Determined not to be beaten by the US State Department, I immediately sent out a 'Warning Order' to all my Heads of Departments, instructing them to drop whatever they were doing and to attend a brain storming session straight after lunch. I gave out as much details about the requirement as I possibly could in order that they had something to dwell on over their lunch. I then busied myself conducting an 'appreciation' of the requirement, detailing all the factors and headings I'd need to address in order to come up with a credible plan and operations order. I also called back to the FCO in London to check on Tim Clifton and see just when he was planning to arrive in theatre to help out. Naturally London had no real idea and so I called Tim at home since he was on 'gardening leave' in the countryside. Tim was nonplussed and in no hurry to go anywhere. He'd been negotiating with Bruxelles about a contract for some time now but had got nowhere. When I confided in him and told him that I had yet to be paid even once by Bruxelles, he basically sacked the whole idea, which then left me totally in the lurch. The plan that emerged after lunch during discussions with my staff, was to send up an advance party to Banja Luka tasked with reconnoitring a shortlist of three possible office venues (having enlisted the help of the local Mayor and political leader of the Democratic Patriotic Party – Predrag Radic), then to attempt to open a bank account and preferably to enact a bank transfer between the two entities, to establish voice and data communications whether by PTT, laptop remote dial-up networking or even by satellite, and finally to start to address the protocol issues surrounding the cocktail party. I sent four small teams, one for each main area of responsibility, headed up by my General Services Officer, an American CIMIC[77] officer named Vanessa Ortiz, to crack on with the tasks before calling me up in two or three days time in order to pull all the component parts together. The teams worked well doing all if not more than was required of them. I arrived In Banja Luka on the following Wednesday to assess progress and to view the options before making my decision on where the office should be. Vanessa had done her job well and we chose an excellent site in a medical faculty in the centre of the town, which also offered parking facilities. Indeed, the décor of the building and the facilities it offered far exceeded those in the main office in Sarajevo and most importantly, there was room for expansion should the need arise later. I left Vanessa to draw up a contract to lease the necessary office space and we then negotiated agreement to hold our cocktail party downstairs in the main reception area of the office block and in the adjacent canteen. With that settled we could now seriously address the issue of protocol. Angelika Hamilton, the German wife of a British IFOR officer was working on the case and she, like the others had established a temporary office in a vacant shopping booth behind the lobby area of the main hotel in Banja Luka where we were all staying. Pantelija Damljanovic, the Vice President of the Serb Radical Party owned the hotel and was being particularly helpful. Angelika did a magnificent job of determining who was who and in arranging the whole party. Meanwhile Elaine had sorted out rudimentary communications and we were all set to go. On Thursday, Bildt turned up to survey the preparations and to meet with Bosnian Serb officials. His off duty French bodyguards decided that it would be a good idea to unwind and together all of us decided to head for the local night club, 'Portorico.' We were all exhausted and in need of some relaxation but none of us really knew quite what to expect, indeed I was the only one who had actually had any experience of the Serbs before, from my time in ICFY. Whereas West European towns are littered with 'No Smoking' signs, Banja Luka was littered with 'No Guns' signs. These were of exactly the same design as the 'No Smoking' signs but with the picture of a cigarette replaced by a picture of a pistol. As about ten of us went to enter the club, we were stopped and asked whether we had any guns. The scene was totally bizarre as one by one the French obediently emptied their holsters of all their weapons which ranged from 9mm pistols, through 9mm Heckler Koch MP5 machine pistols to a 66mm light anti-tank missile! The 'bouncer' didn't even bat an eyelid as he simply dropped the weapons behind his seat and issued a rather grubby looking receipt.

We had done the seemingly impossible and everything was ready on time. For sure it would take several more weeks, in fact months before the office could be described as a fully functioning part of the peace process, but to all intents and purposes it was ready and at least able to host a proper cocktail party to celebrate its official opening. My staff had pulled out all the stops and really excelled themselves. Whilst there was no need for any of them to remain in Banja Luka any longer, I invited them all to stay and to take part in the official OHR opening as well as to attend another cocktail party to mark the opening of the new British IFOR HQ in Ramici just outside Banja Luka. The British General was Major General Mike Jackson MBE. Jacko or POD (standing for the Prince of Darkness) as he was known to his fellow officers in the Parachute Regiment, had been the CO of 1 PARA back in 1985, and I had served as his Adjutant at the time. I had last seen him in Belfast during 1991 when he was commanding 39 Infantry Brigade and I had been 1 PARA's Operations Officer. To meet him again in Banja Luka was a tremendous stroke of luck and he was equally shocked to see me out of uniform, wearing a suit and attending his cocktail party. I met many other old military friends that evening and thoroughly enjoyed myself watching the Red Devils Parachute Display Team jump in to the car park knowing that another of Jock's hot potatoes had successfully been put to bed.

Having done it once before, we were now all expecting the next official opening of a regional office. What we didn't know however, was where and when. At the beginning of July, I got the information I needed. The next office was to be opened in Tuzla, in the Federation, which at least meant that there wouldn't be any of the previous currency and communications difficulties like we had experienced in Banja Luka. Further more the office was to be little more than a small 'cell' and would employ only one or two international political staff with a couple of local support staff. In fact this time Jock was quite helpful. There was no immediate rush, no big cocktail party to arrange and Jock even suggested that I liaise with the ECCM HQ in the town who would undoubtedly be in a position to suggest possibilities. This time we intended to take an initial look just spending a day up in Tuzla returning as and when necessary to sort things out. I took a small planning team up with me to ensure that all the proper questions were covered by the experts and called in at ECMM first. ECMM were located in the main hotel in Tuzla, named after the town, and had several rooms that they had converted in to offices just as we had done back in Hotel Onogost in Niksic. Unbelievably the Head of Office was yet another Brit Ian McCleod who I knew very well indeed. Ian had been in ICFY Sector Charlie before I had arrived but everyone had talked about him and so I knew he had been there. I had also seen his signature in the British Embassy's visitors' book when I first arrived in Yugoslavia and so knew he was in theatre. But my knowledge of Ian steamed back even further than that of General Jackson. Ian had been one of my first COs when I had newly joined 1 PARA back in 1979 as a young subaltern. When I had last seen him in 1989, he had been a Brigadier commanding a TA Brigade in Lancashire and now we were sat drinking Turkish coffee together in Tuzla; the world was getting smaller each day. The arrangements that Ian had made were perfectly suitable for our needs too, and so over the next few weeks we set about negotiating a suitable contract and arranging to purchase and deliver all the necessary office and communications equipment. The new Head of Office was to be an American on secondment from the US State Department which had certainly got its act together better than the FCO had with the Tim Clifton saga. Paul Hacker had quite simply one of the best minds I'd ever met. He knew everything there was to know on the Balkans and spoke upwards of ten languages fluently. Not only could he speak Serbo-Croat like a native speaker, he could write Serbian in Cyrillic script as fast as he could in English. There was one over riding problem however. Like many people with brilliant minds, Hacker was clueless about everyday life, he was simply not of this planet and something as mundane as a radio scarred the living daylights out of him. Essentially, whilst he could be left alone to rebuild the whole country single-handedly, he could not be entrusted to even fill his own car up with petrol – he needed both a minder and a gopher. Covey's solution was yet again to engage American CIMIC officers on the task.[78] Apart from the fact that I didn't trust the State Department's motives in furtively secreting their military throughout all major international organisations, and that I wanted no part of their grand strategy whatever that might have been, the CIMIC team in Tuzla rapidly became useless – that is if it was ever really operational in the first place. American CIMIC staff in Sarajevo were under the watchful eye of their HQ but they operated within the French Sector. Likewise, the team in Banja Luka operated within the British Sector. This meant that American rules and regulations were not so strictly adhered to as they were within their own Sector in and around Tuzla. The main problem was the American 'Force Protection' rules. These were political constraints put on all American troops that simply stated that any casualties, however small were unacceptable back home and therefore unsustainable. From this premise came a whole plethora of restrictions that governed all aspects of American military operations. Fore example, 'Force Protection' was the overriding concern of all commanders from General Nash downwards. This was and remains an unprincipled criterion since regrettably armies do take casualties from time to time. This is part and parcel with military duty and the military ethics of self-sacrifice, although clearly this is not so within American military culture. Secondly it remains unprincipled since the whole purpose of IFOR, SFOR and indeed KFOR that followed, was to first protect the beneficiaries of the Peace Accord, namely the Bosnians, from themselves. The second purpose in providing framework security was to provide a peaceful and stable environment within which the IC could go about its business of relief, rehabilitation, reconstruction and development. Nowhere was it ever envisioned that to protect oneself would become the first and overriding principle of any element of IFOR. If America wanted its troops to be safe and to put this additional requirement above the first two, then it should have kept its troops safe at home in their barracks where surely they would have been safest. Instead, American troops had to drive around in convoys comprising of at least four fully armed vehicles regardless of the nature, length or purpose of the journey. This intimidated local people, creating both a sense of hostility towards the Americans and a sense of 'siege mentality' amongst their troops who really thought that they were back in the Wild West. As a consequence, many American troops committed suicide under the self-induced pressure that they imagined themselves to be under. Notwithstanding these criticisms, from a purely military point of view, in both my opinion and that of Louise Arbour, the Chief Prosecutor for the International War Crimes Tribunal in The Hague, these restrictions rendered the mighty American military completely non-effective in Bosnia.[79] In the Banja Luka office, the CIMIC team continued to wear suffocating flak jackets and helmets inside the office until I ordered them to take them off since they were an affront to a diplomatic mission.

Nevertheless in Tuzla it was a different story. Even inside the protection of their own massive 'Eagle Base' surrounding Tuzla airfield, American soldier had to carry their weapons, wear their heavy body armour, helmets and webbing belts at all times. This even involved trips to the showers wearing PT shorts. The team that had been attached to OHR was no different and despite being commanded by a Colonel, was too frightened to even stretch any of their Force Protection rules. I was now faced with a CIMIC team which was supposed to be supporting Paul Hacker but which was not capable of even delivering a letter to a local politician or municipal representative in town without first calling for a four-vehicle back-up convoy to escort them. Even trying to put it politely, as it was hardly their own fault, they were completely non-operational and of bugger all use to anyone! After several head-to-heads with Jock in which I insisted that the team be removed immediately, Jock finally relented and agreed to speak with General Nash to find a solution to the impasse. Several days later Jock called me in to his office to discuss the implementation of his and Nash's agreement. The crux of the 'agreement' was that Nash had (despite very strong advice from his lawyers) agreed (at great personal and professional risk to his career) to relax the Force Protection rules so long as the OHR met certain criteria (demands). Jock was at pains to patiently explain to me the background of the Force Protection Policy and to explain just why it was of paramount importance to ensure that not one single American died on this Mission, stating that, 'We can't afford to loose a single American on this Mission,' and that, 'It is your duty to ensure that this never happens.' He then read out Nash's criteria cum wish list which consisted of buying in two additional armoured Land Rover Discoveries which were to be equipped with inter-vehicle radios and satellite communications. … I stopped listening! I had never been so insulted before in such a smug and sincere manner. Here was a guy telling me to spend perhaps $100,000 from the OHR budget needlessly protecting four American officers who I didn't need on my staff in the first place, and that American lives mattered more than any other nation's and that of course included my own life I presumed! As the French General and former UN Commander General Philippe Morillon put it, 'What sort of soldier is it, who wants to kill without the risk of being killed?'[80] Within the week I had sacked Nash's CIMIC team and hired an American civilian Chris Fey, to take on the task of supporting Paul Hacker.

12

Post-war Recovery: The Initial Steps

Although each Annex of the GFAP had assigned individual responsibility for certain aspects of the peace process to separate organisations, such as security to IFOR under Annex 1A, regional stabilisation and elections to the OSCE under Annexes 1B and 3 respectively, the OHR had been charged with overall responsibility for the co-ordination and progress of all civilian aspects of the post-war recovery process. Accordingly, Bildt divided his office in to several small departments each with specific responsibility for a particular area of interest such as human rights, economic reconstruction, legal matters and political affairs. Apart from my own supporting empire, there were also other supporting functions such as Public Information and Media Affairs. Each of the major departments were usually headed up by an Ambassador seconded from a donor country who then held the position of 'Deputy' (High Representative) within OHR with Michael Steiner being the 'Principal Deputy' High Representative to Carl Bildt. Each of these departments faced differing challenges but from the very outset, progress was stifled by the continued presence of those Bosnian political leaders who had by and large been responsible for taking the country to war in the first place.

The GFAP made it illegal for those persons indicted for war crimes to hold public office. At this stage in the proceedings the ICTY was openly publishing its indictments and brown coloured 'wanted' posters listing indictees and showing their mug-shots were commonly available rather like in the old Hollywood western films. Later on, the ICTY was to respond to criticism about its methods and issue 'sealed indictments' so as not to compromise the intelligence and security operations which preceded any armed intervention to arrest those indicted.[81] Yet despite this clear and uncompromising position that OHR would not deal with Persons Indicted for War Crimes (PIFWC) as they were not entitled to hold office, many continued to do so. In the case of Republika Srpska, the wartime leader Radovan Karadzic, continued to hold the office of RS President. With the first elections not scheduled until September 1996, it raised the possibility that little progress would be made in the RS for almost the whole of the first year unless Karadzic could be removed. The resulting stalemate that ensued meant that as aid came pouring in to the Muslim-Croat Federation, only a fraction – some two per cent in the first year, was entering the RS. Karadzic knew that he had to stand down and although the Bosnian Serbs had not represented themselves at Dayton (as Karadzic had already been indicted at that stage), they had delegated their negotiating rights to Milosevic who had signed the agreement on their behalf. As such, the decision was binding and Karadzic's insistence to remain in post was illegal and at the same time, was economically crippling his country and suffocating its prospects of recovery. Despite growing disparities between the two entities, the Bosnian Serbs continued to hold the IC responsible for their plight largely because they didn't know any better since their leadership still controlled all aspects of the media. Karadzic and his cronies continued to exploit their own people, run import-export smuggling rackets and by retaining power, to starve their people of urgently needed humanitarian assistance whilst blaming the IC for waging a vendetta against the Serb peoples. Such propaganda was of course reinforced by the American led policy of 'conditionality' which played directly in to the hands of the nationalist hard-liners who were then able to justify their claims that the IC was against them.[82] The removal of Karadzic from political life and preferably his arrest and deportation to The Hague, therefore became a top priority. Bildt kept up the pressure on Pale and during the G7/G8 Summit in Lyon on 28-29 June, the IC reiterated its demands for Karadzic's resignation. On the 18th July, some seven months after the GFAP was signed in Paris and some two months before the first 'free and fair' elections were scheduled to take place, Karadzic bowed to international pressure, completed the final version of his resignation letter and faxed it through to OHR. Karadzic's departure left a vacuum in the civilian leadership of the entity. As Bosnia wide elections had not yet taken place, the three-person Bosnian Presidency envisioned by Dayton did not yet exist and now the RS entity had just lost its own President. The position had to be filled and so as an interim measure Biljana Plavsic, a biologist and another hard-liner from the war-time 'Serb Democratic Party' (SDS) ruling caucus, became the acting President of the RS until September. Plavsic was eventually to turn away from those around her whom she saw as profiteering from the misery of their own people and to attempt to reform the SDS leadership. In this she was later to fail and instead she was to form her own party, the 'Serb People's Alliance-Biljana Plavsic' (SNS-BP), dissolve the RS Parliament and move it from Pale to Banja Luka where it remains today. These revolutionary events were not to take place for another year and when they did, I was to witness them first hand playing a vital role in the battle to reform and reject nationalist politics within the RS. In the mean time IFOR continued with its security mandate which including the provision, '... to arrest PIFWCs as and when they were encountered in the course of their normal duties.' Such a loose provision permitted IFOR to argue the case that they rarely if ever came across PIFWCs in 'the course of their normal duties' and also that there was therefore no requirement for them to take the lead and go and look for them. Quite who else was supposed to take on this particular responsibility remains a mystery even today. What was clear, however, was that IFOR was not at all interested in escalating the stakes in what was after all, still a rather fragile peace. Neither was it inclined to assume a role that it saw as an additional, rather than an integral requirement of its mission. In American military parlance, this phenomenon is termed 'Mission Creep' and in this instance the term was used to legally justify just what their troops could, or put more succinctly, what their troops could not do. The Americans were paranoid about Mission Creep and about being sucked in to the morass of the Balkans and in to what they still saw as basically a European problem. Doing anything outside of what their legal advisers saw as the letter of the law, was an impossibility for their commanders and so whilst Karadzic had resigned, both he and his most trusted General – Ratko Mladic, remained at large and untouched by IFOR. Of course turning a blind eye is not always as easy as one might assume and both Karadzic and Mladic were believed to be in hiding somewhere in Han Pijesak, which lay within the American military sector. Ever since the Americans had taken over their AoR in the North of Bosnia, they had been trying to gain access to parts of the RS Army – Vojska Republika Srpska (VRS) – barracks in Han Pijesak, the same barracks that I had driven past when I first arrived in Bosnia and driven to Sarajevo with Nick Haller. On several occasions, American military patrols had been denied access to a secure bunker within the complex in direct violation of the terms of the peace agreement. They were rightly getting sick of this and so Commander ARRC – British Lieutenant General Sir Michael Walker, KCB. CBE, came up with a contingency plan based on a formal 'graduated response' to the non-compliance. At the initial end of the scale, continued non-compliance would result in the Serbs being warned that military action would be taken against them to force their compliance. To demonstrate IFOR's resolve, the first move would involve withdrawing all IFOR military liaison officers from the VRS thus removing the possibility of hostage taking, a problem that had beset NATO and the UN back in 1995. Next in line would be the withdrawal of all other personnel from Republika Srpska, a clear indication that IFOR was preparing to fight.[83] At the more drastic end of the scale were the actual battle plans, which had been drawn up in case IFOR actually needed to carry out its threats. These plans involved various measures such as the use of the American Multi-Launch Rocket System (MLRS) used so devastatingly in the Gulf War and the use of the US Airforce (USAF) Strategic Bomber Command's B52 bomber fleet. Walker's graduated response followed standard NATO doctrine and allowed for a gradual escalation over a period of about two-weeks. The Americans tried once again to gain access to the facility but were denied. The stakes had now been raised and Walker sent in Brigadier Charlton Weedie, the 'Chief – Faction Liaison' in another attempt to gain access. Weedie was also rebuffed and Walker consulted the newly appointed COMDIFOR, Admiral Joseph Lopez for authority to escalate a rung. What happened next remains clouded in secrecy but what was clear to any observer at the time, was that there was to be a rapid and almost incomprehensible escalation of the 'conflict.' The Americans believed that they had been denied access because both Karadzic and Mladic were inside the barracks being hidden and protected by the VRS. Whether this was the case or not, I never found out but to say that the proverbial shit had hit the fan was to over use the English custom of playing down events. Lopez and Walker consulted with NATO's Supreme Commander in Europe (SACEUR), the five star American General – George Joulwan based at Supreme HQ Allied Powers Europe (SHAPE) in Bruxelles. Joulwan told Walker, 'I am fully prepared to support you in any action you take so long as you bomb them within twenty four hours.' With Walker's two-week graduated response plan torn in to shreds, Lopez acting independently of Bildt, 'ordered' the immediate overnight evacuation of all members of the IC from all areas of Republika Srpska. American MLRS batteries and the USAF B52 bomber fleet were put on full alert, presumably with the intention of raising the whole of Han Pijesak to the ground. The enormity of the consequences of such a rash, brazen and wholly inappropriate reaction beggars belief. When Bildt learnt what had happened overnight he was furious with Lopez and frantically tried to deal with the problem before the bombers left their bases in the United States to strike their targets. In any democracy the military are always subordinate to the civil power. Clearly this fundamental principle of the military's role in civil society had been lost on both the American officers as neither Lopez nor Joulwan had consulted with Bildt at any stage. Meanwhile Walker, who had previously established a Crisis Management Group with the entity leaders, had the composure to call President Plavsic in Pale and warn her of the impending military action. Walker then drove to Pale, collected Plavsic and together they flew to Han Pijesak in a small reconnaissance helicopter. They landed inside the barracks and, under the continuous close surveillance from an orbiting NATO 'Predator' remotely piloted vehicle (RPV) that had been 'locked' on to Walker to follow his every movement and beam real-time pictures back to Ilidza, gained access to the installation 'proving' that there was not a restriction of movement on IFOR personnel. This personal intervention by General Sir Michael Walker and President Plavsic was sufficient to advert a catastrophe that might have led to a further outbreak of war and that arguably would have set the peace process back immeasurably. In the end the bombers never took off but we were all left wondering just what planet the Americans came from. The incident gave my friend Major Tom Mouat, who was still working in HQ ARRC in Ilidza, plenty of material for his comic strip that he continued to produce anonymously each day throughout his

whole tour of duty. Tom's comic strip characters were know as Second
Lieutenant Styreen Foame and Private Richard Paarts and they (or rather he)
delighted in taking the piss out of the Americans at every opportunity, not
least because they all seemed to be devoid of any sense of humour or personality. Tom would stick up copies of his comic strip each night whilst the
Americans did their level best to tear them down as soon as they appeared.
After the bombing incident, 2Lt Foame and Pte Paarts were to be found discussing music, various bands and pop concerts and bemoaning the fact that
the UNHCR concert with the 'B52s in Han Pijesak' had been cancelled
because it would have been too noisy. Following this fiasco, there were to be
no further attempts to arrest PIFWCs for another year until July 1997, when
the British SAS (in part successfully) raided Prijedor in the Northwest RS, in
an action that again paid scant attention to the political consequences at that
specific time.

The status of Brcko in the strategically vital Posavina corridor in
Northeast Republika Srpska had not been resolved at the negotiating table
in Dayton. As such, the decision on its final status had been deferred for one
year when the international arbitrator Roberts Owen, and three nominated
arbitrators from the entities were supposed to announce whether the town
would become part of the Federation or part of Republika Srpska, or of
course whether they had any other solution in mind. Meanwhile the governments of both entities were busy preparing and submitting their arguments
as to why the town should belong to them. Geographically the town
provided access to the River Sava, a strategic waterway that passed through
Croatia and Serbia to link with the mighty Danube and hence Europe and
the Black Sea. From an economic point of view both sides considered the
town to be economically vital but the Serbs also claimed that to loose the
town to the Federation would cut the RS entity in half. For this reason they
argued that the town was vital to their security. In this, they had a convincing argument but of course these were not the only factors that Owen had
to consider. One of the main factors was the pre-war ethnic balance in the
town and not just what the population was now. The Serbs might well have
been the majority ethnic group in the town after the war, but this was
because they had taken it by military force and the other ethnic groups had
fled. For Owens to ignore this fact would be to reward ethnic cleansing,
something that would be impossible for the arbitration to do. Deliberation
was not a simple process and although not technically a core function of the
OHR, the office did support the work of the arbitration panel throughout.
As the first anniversary of Dayton approached, the panel announced on 8th
December that there would be a two-month extension to the arbitration
process, until 15th February 1997. But the delay did little to quell fears and
as the new deadline approached, both sides were to tentatively rattle their
cages and begin preparations for war.[84]

Whilst the status of Brcko remained in dispute throughout the whole of
that first year, other military and security issues were resolved rather sooner.

One of the first consequences of Dayton was the transfer from one entity to another of areas specified in the GFAP, notably specific areas in and around Sarajevo and in the 'Anvil' around Mrkonjic Grad. A further requirement of the GFAP was that no entity was permitted to have a military presence in another entity and so with the transfer of territorial areas from one entity to another came the need to move each of the three ethnic armies back to their own entity. The BSA now known as the VRS was withdrawn from all Federation territory and re-deployed within the RS behind the IEBL. Likewise, both the HVO and the ABiH were withdrawn from RS territory to behind the IEBL within the Federation. Either side of the IEBL the ZOS extended for two KMs in either direction and it was illegal for any entity army to have any presence whatsoever within the Zone. Throughout 1996, IFOR deployed its ground forces to ensure that this narrow separation of forces was maintained. Technically the whole exercise was actually about the transfer of territory and it was not about the movements of armies or peoples. However whilst the transfer of areas went according to the agreement and the re-deployment of military forces went smoothly, the political rhetoric that accompanied the moves precipitated the migration of thousands of people throughout Bosnia who thought it safer to move with their armies rather than risk remaining within a former enemy's entity. For example, before the war approximately two hundred and twenty-five thousand Serbs had been living in the ten municipalities that made up greater Sarajevo. During February and March 1996, one hundred and fifty-five thousand Serbs left the city mainly from the areas of Ilidza, Hadzici, Grbavica, Vosgosca and Ilijas as these areas were to become part of the Muslim-Croat Federation. The SDS, the ruling Bosnian Serb political party, ensured that both power and water supplied were cut to these areas and then physically removed much of the industrial infrastructure as possible to the RS whilst encouraging their own people to flee. I had witnessed the tragic plight of many of these Serbs leaving these areas during my first few days in Sarajevo and have already criticised Dayton for causing a further round of ethnic cleansing after the fighting had finished. But the role of the ruling nationalist parties must not be overlooked either. It is difficult for an outsider to imagine why a political party that is supposed to stand for the very protection of its nation, should engage in activities that result in such misery for its own people. But all three ruling nationalist parties were to frequently engage in such activity in order to maintain power. In this instance, the SDS needed to ensure it had direct control of its ethnic group, as this was its electorate and power-base. Likewise in the future, whilst Bosniaks were often keen to return to their pre-war homes in the RS, Bosnian Serbs were discouraged by their government from ever returning to the Federation. The reasons are complex and revolve around the need to retain a manpower base for military conscription and other external factors such as the plight of the Krajina Serbs that had fled Croatia in 1995.[85] The transfer of areas took place within the given time frame (D+45 i.e. 3rd February 1996)[86] and the transfer of Police and civil authority in the final suburbs of Sarajevo was completed by 18th March following the burning down of Grbavica, the last Bosnian Serb suburb to be handed over. IFOR then set about providing framework security throughout Bosnia dividing the country up in to three MND AoRs. Each MND was based on the military HQ of one of the three lead nations. The British, initially in Vitez and then in Banja Luka, commanded MND Southwest; MND Southeast was commanded by the Americans in Tuzla and MND South by the French based in Mostar. In order to maintain links between IFOR and the OHR, and also with the Bosnian and entity defence ministries, the OHR opened a small Military Liaison Cell which was initially run by General McAlistair, late RTR, and then successively by Air Vice Marshal John Thompson RAF, and Admiral Ian Forbes RN. In addition, the French had their most senior General permanently attached to the office, General Bertrand de la Presle from the Foreign Legion. Meanwhile IFOR also changed as the British led HQ ARRC was replaced by the German led HQ LANDCENT and overall command changed from Admiral Joseph Lopez to General William Crouch on 7th November. Throughout this period, the military – security situation remained stable thanks to the dedication and professionalism of IFOR. There was one other significant development however, which depending upon your personal opinion served either to promote or to undermine security throughout the region. The US had entered in to negotiations with a number of Islamic states such as Turkey and Saudi Arabia, to supply and train the new Federation Army.

The resulting programme was known as 'The Train and Equip Program' and it set out to totally modernise the remnants of the HVO and ABiH through the provision of specialist training to be conducted by MPRI contractors, and the supply of main armaments including main battle tanks, self-propelled artillery and armoured personnel carriers. The training was to start first and a number of Americans who had worked in ICFY soon arrived in Sarajevo to get things started. Tragically Jim Moran, one of the first people I had met as I got off the aircraft in Podgorica nearly a year ago when I first entered Montenegro, died of a heart attack whilst out running as part of his training schedule. Despite this sad loss, I could not reconcile my feelings that the Train & Equip programme would radically alter the balance of forces in the region. The OSCE had responsibility for this issue and each nation in the region had made commitments at Dayton and earlier under the Cold-war era – Conventional Forces in Europe (CFE) negotiations, to maintain their military forces at agreed levels and in specified proportions to each other. I have no doubt that the Americans were extremely careful to ensure that non of their actions were in contravention to the CFE Agreement, however their actions did alter the balance of forces, of that I have no doubt. Firstly, the HVO and ABiH were not up to scale and new weapon systems could be delivered without breaking any existing agreements. Secondly, old and obsolete equipment was easily done away with in order to make room for far more capable modern Western weapon systems.

The first delivery of equipment arrived in the Croatian Free Port of Ploce on 21st November and the tanks were brought in to the Federation via the newly repaired and reopened railway that runs from the Adriatic through Mostar and up to Sarajevo. Despite the undoubted legality of this delivery in statistical terms, one could not ignore that it clearly went against the spirit of Dayton since the HVO and ABiH at that stage had no intention whatsoever of co-operating with each other let alone becoming a single military institution. The Croats were still hankering for the creation of a third entity, which they had in effect established anyway in the CRHB despite this being banned and the formal deadline for its dissolution, the 31st August passing without any action from the IC whatsoever. Nevertheless, the Americans went ahead and supplied both the HVO and the ABiH despite protests from the Bosnian Serbs who were still staved of humanitarian, let alone economic or military aid.

On the economic side of the house, OHR established an Economic Reconstruction Department headed up by Ambassador Victor Massena from France. Dayton acknowledged that economic revival and the long term rebuilding of the economy were major preconditions for both peace and political stability in Bosnia i Hercegovina. OHR's role therefore was to assist the various world-wide economic implementation agencies such as the World Bank, the EC, the European Bank for Reconstruction and Development (EBRD), the International Monetary Fund (IMF) and the International Management Group (IMG) as well as bilateral donors, with their efforts to generate reforms aimed at generating economic recovery and easing Bosnia i Hercegovina's transition to a market economy. OHR's main priorities were to revive the country's basic infrastructure; to generate employment opportunities and to restart the means of production; to strengthen local institutions and government departments and agencies at all levels; and finally to promote the social sector and provide support to vulnerable groups and refugees.[88] To achieve these tasks, OHR established and led an Economic Task Force to discuss and plan courses of action, and to co-ordinate the political and operational aspects of economic reconstruction as well as policy recommendations that were being made to the State (BiH) and both entity authorities. Whilst under normal circumstances one might expect a beneficiary country to be pleased to receive such huge amounts of aid as was being poured into Bosnia, nothing in the country was normal. Entity, indeed tri-ethnic politics continuously interfered with the essential reforms needed to restructure the Bosnian economy and which were the prerequisite for progress. It was not acceptable to OHR, neither was it to the donor community, to simply rebuild what had gone before, that is to say – a communist command economy in which company directors were appointed by the ruling party and then came rich from fat salaries and in many cases from substantial pilfering. The whole system needed to be reformed including the wholesale privatisation of state industries and the system of social housing that came with the job. To precipitate progress,

OHR worked with the JCCs and their Working Groups at both the national and regional level to remove such political obstacles and to force through progress. This was a painfully slow procedure with very few significant achievements in the first year. In deed, in 1996, industrial output in Bosnia i Hercegovina was about five per cent of output in 1990, and the annual per capita income was around US$500 compared to about US$1,900 in 1990. Not until 1997-98, did things start to improve with some progress being made with privatisation for example, and with OHR pushing through measures to counter economic and political obstruction such as by introducing a common currency and proscribing the use of the Yugoslavian Dinar and the Croatian Kuna.[89] In the mean time OHR continued to battle on in order to improve the lot of the Bosnian people and met with some success in various sectoral areas ensuring the restoration of public utilities such as water, electric power, gas, telecommunications and road and rail links. Without the restoration of these sectors, especially road and rail links, and telecommunications links between the two entities, it was impossible for them to even contemplate reopening trade with each other – a critical aspect of building a united Bosnia i Hercegovina. Sectoral Task Forces were established with the World Bank and the EU in these and in other areas such as housing, the health sector and education. In all, some $5.1 billion was to be poured in to the 'BiH Priority Reconstruction Programme' for the years 1996 - 1999. The overall aim remained as stated at the outset, but the long-term objective was never in doubt. Such aid was to provide the driving force behind Bosnia's transition to a market economy allowing the country to wean itself off its dependence on foreign aid.[90] By the end of 1996 however, Bosnia remained almost wholly dependent upon such aid and the OHR had simply begun preparations for the next stage of the recovery process, namely the preparation of a package of laws which if adopted by the Bosnian Parliament, would provide the legislative framework to enable Bosnia's transition to a market economy. This 'Quick Start Package' as it became known, consisted of major pieces of legislation such as foreign trade and investment laws, customs tariff laws and the law on the Central Bank. Getting these adopted was to be the next problem

Another priority for the OHR was to address the human rights situation in the country. The war was synonymous with some of the worst violations of human rights and IHL witnessed in Europe for nearly half a century and so it was inconceivable that these or similar abuses be allowed to continue during the peace. Human rights is a vast area covering not just imprisonment and torture as many people imagine but also the right to life, to assembly, to property and the right to freedom of movement (FoM) to name just several of the main areas of concern. Violations of human rights were associated with each of these areas throughout Bosnia and in many cases they were interconnected. The right to property could not be enforced without the right of thousands of refugees and DPs to return home. This they would never contemplate as their most basic of all human rights, namely the right to life could not yet be guaranteed and in any case there was no real FoM to even travel to their homes in the first place. Many of these abuses were symptomatic with the nature of the State and were actually being conducted by State institutions such as the entity Police forces as a matter of course. The priority was to establish the Rule of Law within the whole territory of Bosnia i Hercegovina and at the same time to gather together and to co-ordinate the efforts of a broad forum of agencies and international human rights organisations that worked in this field. The IPTF was responsible for ensuring that the Rule of Law was established whilst OHR would co-ordinate not only their efforts but those of the UN Centre for Human Rights (UNCHR),[91] the UN Special Rapporteur, the UN Expert on Missing Persons, the UNMiBH (which included UN Civil Affairs and the UN IPTF), the Office of the Ombudsperson, the OSCE, the ECMM, the Council of Europe, the UNHCR, the ICRC, the International Criminal Tribunal for the Former Yugoslavia (ICTY) and the EC as well as other international and national NGOs. These organisations met under the auspices of the Human Rights Task Force (HRTF) which was established by the High Representative to discuss the co-ordination of human rights implementation. Within OHR itself, Bildt established a Human Rights Co-ordination Centre (HRCC) on 14th March headed up by an American, Peggy Hicks. The HRCC was to act as the central registry for human rights reporting in Bosnia i Hercegovina, identifying any gaps in monitoring and protection efforts and suggesting methods to resolve any such problems. As a general rule, the HRCC did not intervene directly in human rights cases, but channelled cases of particular concern to the appropriate implementing organisations. Regarding the Rule of Law, the IPTF under its first Commissioner, Peter Fitzgerald set about trying to reform the entity Police forces with no greater power than the threat of issuing a 'Non Compliance Notice' on the offending officer or commander. The IPTF were an unarmed international Police force and their role was essentially one of monitoring, albeit later on they were to take a far more proactive role in training and reforming the indigenous Police forces. Initially however, they simply had to contend with trying to convince the local Police to follow the Rule of Law especially in relation to the arrest, detention and interrogation of suspects, and in relation to the almost continuous harassment of anyone from another ethnic group. Such harassment was most evident when it concerned the FoM of people by road, not least since each ethnic group had during the war, established a different type of vehicle licence plate. The Bosnian Serbs used a plate displaying the four Cyrillic 'C's (latin 'S') that spelt out their slogan 'Samo Sloga Srbina Spasava,' – 'Only Unity Saves the Serbs.' The Bosnian Croat's plate displayed their chequered flag – the Sahovnica, whilst the Muslim – Bosniak flag cleverly displayed the fleur-de-lis shield with 'BiH' written underneath.[92] With such a system it was completely obvious to any Police checkpoint, whether the approaching car belonged to a different ethnic group. The effect was that the Police deliberately targeted different ethnic groups routinely enforcing dubious financial penalties or even arresting and physically assaulting the occupants. As the IEBL cut across the main trunk roads that connected different parts of the country, the effect was to almost totally put a stop to travel from one region to another. For example, to travel from Bihac to Jaice, both in the Federation required one to cross the 'Anvil' an area under Serb control. Throughout 1996, it was almost impossible for Bosniaks to complete this journey safely and as late as February 1997 I was involved in multi ethnic negotiations with both the mayors and the Police forces of Mrkonjic Grad, Bosanski Petrovac and Kljuc in an attempt to resolve this very issue. Initially OHR set up working groups to address this issue but these were soon replaced by weekly meetings with OHR, IPTF and the entity Interior Ministers. OHR continued to stress the importance of FoM as it was not only an obligation under the GFAP but was a central prerequisite to the return of DPs and refugees to their homes, to the conduct of the forthcoming political elections and to the restoration of trade between the entities.

13

The Political Landscape

The 'initial steps' taken on the road to post-war recovery mentioned in the last chapter were undertaken by OHR concurrently with what was probably its main focus of activity, namely to reform the political landscape. As with economic reconstruction, it was not acceptable to the IC to simply rebuild what had gone before. Bosnia had never known democracy and so all the institutions and trappings of such a society had to be created from scratch within the framework laid down at Dayton. Bildt and his principal deputy, Michael Steiner led this process with the aid of a political department within OHR itself. Additionally, the OHR continually hosted visiting foreign dignitaries who came and went to briefly observe progress and give their penny's worth of advice. The most frequent visitors came from NATO and the United States. General George Joulwan and Xavier Solana were repeatedly calling in to the office during their frequent trips to IFOR HQ in Sarajevo, and both Warren Christopher and Richard Holbrooke frequently met with Bildt to discuss high-level policy matters. Bildt's starting point for all political reform, and one could argue, for all the post-war recovery processes, was the Constitution of Bosnia i Hercegovina. As Bildt himself remarked,[93]

> 'The Constitution ... is one of the most complicated constitutional documents blessed by the international community in recent times. It represents a decentralised model of how to organise a state, giving important governmental functions and powers to the two entities ... but also reserving to the common institutions those powers vital to the functioning of the modern state.'

The Constitution of Bosnia i Hercegovina, which constitutes Annex 4, of the GFAP, provided for six common institutions, namely the Presidency, the

Council of Ministers, the Parliamentary Assembly, the Constitutional Court, the Central Bank, and the Standing Committee on Military Matters. Additionally each entity had its own entity level Parliament and municipal level local parliaments, and in the Federation – cantonal level parliaments as well. All of these institutions, whether common or unique to each entity had to be establish and the prerequisite for this in terms of the various parliaments, was the staging of free and fair elections. Under Annex 3, of the peace agreement, the OSCE had been given responsibility for organising and staging elections throughout Bosnia and under the direction of its Head of Mission (HOM), Ambassador Frowick, had planned to hold them for all parliaments on 14th September.

The process of staging free and fair elections in a country devastated by war is bewildering complicated and sadly misunderstood by many commentators. Far too often, the OSCE was criticised for failing in some aspect of its responsibilities, but more often than not such criticism was from people such as senior British military officers who simply did not comprehend the complexities of what was involved. For starters, who was able to vote, where were they currently residing, how could they identify themselves, where could they physically go to vote and where (which constituency) could they actually vote for? Taking each of these in turn, the last census in Bosnia had been conducted in 1991, and records of births, deaths and marriages if maintained at all, were secured in municipal buildings up and down the country, which could easily now be under the control of an 'opposing' ethnic group. Municipal authorities effectively blocked the release of any information that would enable voters from a different ethnic group to register. In the same way, obtaining identity documents – another prerequisite for registration, was equally difficult. Before the war Bosnia was not an independent state but an integral part of the Socialist Federal Republic of Yugoslavia and many people carried old SFRY identity documents. During the war, each entity had issued some form of ID or another although these were not universally carried, as many hadn't needed to renew their old documents as they hadn't expired. To complicate maters further, many people were of mixed marriages and it was now technically possible for one partner to carry what was now deemed as a foreign ID. There was also the all too often forgotten case of the Krajina Serbs. Bosnia didn't just see an exodus of refugees, it witnessed an influx too. Part of the legal definition of a refugee requires that an individual has crossed an international border. If a person has fled persecution but remains within their own country then they are deemed to be 'displaced' and not a refugee. In Bosnia, those who crossed to another entity were classed as DPs whilst those who fled to other countries in Europe and beyond were classed as refugees. However, the Krajina Serbs came to Bosnia from Croatia after President Tudjman launched his two offensives, 'Storm' and 'Flash' in 1995. This ethnic Serb refugee population now living in Northwest Bosnia was of Croatian nationality. They were born and raised there and all held Croatian passports and not Bosnian ones. As such, non-of them were entitled to vote in the Bosnian elections. As a point of interest, these people were unable to vote in Croatian elections either and, at the time of writing, remain effectively disenfranchised. Firstly, the reality on the ground was that they could not safely return to register or vote inside Croatia. Secondly, they were not physically able to travel or register there even if they had decided to take the risk. Tudjman had changed the Croatian passport and the old documents held by these (Krajina Serb) Croats were no longer valid. In effect, none of them could physically cross the border to return to their own country although the Croatian government kept up the pretence that it was simply a matter for these people to post off their applications to renew their passports and that these would be processed. It was not until the Croats opened a small consulate office in the OHR building in Banja Luka almost two years later, that the Krajina Serbs were finally able to submit applications for new documents to enable them to return home. But documentation was only one of OSCE's problems. Approximately half of Bosnia's population had been displaced by war and so this was a huge problem and in effect the complete re-registration of the entire population was necessary before one could even consider staging elections. This raised the next problem of where people were now living. In addition to the hundreds of thousands who had been internally displaced within Bosnia, thousands more had fled as refugees and still remained outside of the country. All of these people had to be given the ability to register and vote regardless of where they now resided. But ethnic cleansing had destroyed the multi ethnic structure of society and people were now living in areas where they had fled and not where they came from. Many wanted to return to their homes, many more didn't and of these some wanted to stay put where they were currently residing whilst many others wanted to move on again to start a new life in a third location perhaps with relatives. The OSCE decided that people could 'physically vote at' a polling station where they had either currently settled or alternatively where they had come from (should they be brave enough to travel back to an area no doubt now within the control of a different entity). But in trying to resolve where people could 'vote for,' the OSCE made a critical mistake which led to widespread political manipulation of the electorate by the nationalist parties and finally forced Frowick, on 27th August to cancel all municipal level elections for a further year. OSCE decided that all non displaced and all internally displaced (i.e. DP) voters could vote for the electoral district where they were currently living thus expressing the reality that many DPs wanted to remain where they had fled. They also decided that DP and 'Out of Country' –refugee voters must be allowed the alternative choice to vote for the electoral district from where they had fled thus annulling the effects of ethnic cleansing. With hind sight, the decision that caused all the problems was the decision to allow these same DP and refugee voters a further option of voting for a third location, one where they envisioned that they would set up a new life but was not where they had come from nor was where they currently resided. The OSCE stipulated strict criteria regarding the choice of this third location. Any DP or refugee wanting to exercise this option had to prove their connection to that area by showing that they owned property or had family and relatives there, or that they had employment there. In reality, thousands of DPs were manipulated by their own nationalist political parties in to falsely and fraudulently registering their desire to live in highly sensitive and disputed areas such as Brcko and Srebrenica reinforcing the previous ethnic cleansing in that region. It was if the whole population of London suddenly wanted to live in the small border town of John O'Groats and as a result the registration of voters for municipal elections became untenable.

The second problem the OSCE faced, was to establish who the electorate would vote for? To establish this it was necessary for all the political parties, coalitions and independent candidates to register their intention to run in the election. In 1996, the three nationalist parties still dominated the political scene and sadly there were few other serious contenders for political office.[94] This process of registration went on until 14th June whilst voter registration continued until 8th August for Out of Country voters. The third problem, which the OSCE had to resolve, was how to actually conduct the election; that is to say, what laws would be followed? As there were currently no parliaments in existence, the OSCE had to draw up the provisional election laws which were codified in what became known as the 'Rules and Regulations' (R&R).[95] These R&Rs were constantly updated and a year later were even used to attempt to redress gender inequalities within the political system by stipulating the number of women that must be listed as candidates within a party list. Responsibility for enforcing these R&Rs was delegated to the Provisional Election Commission (PEC) which was established on 1st January 1996, was chaired by the OSCE HOM, and consisted of representatives from each ethnic group in Bosnia. Below this, working at a local level were the Local Election Commissions (LEC) which were formed on 24th May with the responsibility for ensuring that the elections were facilitated smoothly within municipalities.

Last but not least, the OSCE had to arrange for the actual conduct of the election. This was no doubt the only part that SFOR officers got to see and to base their criticisms on, but quite frankly this part was the easy bit albeit still a logistics nightmare. In a corrupt system controlled by ruling elites, the media throughout Bosnia was firmly in the pockets of the nationalist parties. Political campaigning by opposition parties was almost impossible and where conducted, their rallies and meetings received almost no media coverage whatsoever. The OSCE attempted to reverse this practice by stipulating regulations for an equitable access to airtime on TV and radio, demanding accurate reporting in newspapers, punishing those who incited anti Dayton or anti IC sentiments, and even by providing funds to support election media campaigns and party promotional materials. On top of all this, the OSCE had to monitor all political party activities and media coverage throughout the whole of Bosnia to ensure compliance with their R&Rs. Next were the actually preparations for the election itself. Once all the voters had registered and once all the political parties, coalitions and independent candidates had also registered, the OSCE printed an official registers of voters which was then checked and amended prior to the production of the Final Voters Register. Likewise once the parties were known, the OSCE could print appropriate ballots with party, coalition and independent candidate details on. Polling stations then had to be found and earmarked for use over the election period. Each location had to be visited and checked to see whether the buildings still had roofs on, whether there were phones inside or whether radio communications was possible back to the OSCE Field Offices. Many were destroyed, inaccessible in winter conditions, lacked basic provisions or were simply unsuitable for a whole host of reasons and so LECs were instructed to locate alternative sites. Once these were known and confirmed, both the Federation and the Republika Srpska's interior ministers, Avdo Hebib and Dragan Kijac respectively, had to agree on special 'voters' routes' down which the OSCE were able to bus (in protected armed convoys) DP voters from one entity who had chosen to return to their original municipality in order to vote. Nineteen such voters' routes were agreed upon and both sides undertook to guarantee the safety of voters on these routes. Finally, IFOR was involved in helping to print off maps showing these routes and in physically providing the framework security to forcefully back up the interior ministers' pledges. Prior to the election, polling station committees had to be nominated to staff each polling station and then these committees along with the LECs had to be trained in the conduct of the election and how to manage their stations and to conduct the count of ballots. International supervisors were also required in huge numbers as each and every polling station had to be supervised by a member of the IC. This entailed the selection of appropriately qualified and willing personnel from around the world, their deployment in to theatre, their training and their deployment to their respective areas of responsibility suitably trained and equipped with a car, driver, interpreter and communications. When one considers that the OSCE, like the OHR, had only arrived in Bosnia at the beginning of the year and that all this had to be up and running by September, then I consider their achievements to be outstanding, not least because at almost every turn they, unlike charities simply donating aid, had to contend with mindless obstruction by the very people that they were trying to help.

By comparison, events during the election were almost an anti climax. For sure they were numerous incidents throughout the whole length and breadth of the country but all the hard work had been done previously and the plan worked well when all was said and done. I had busied myself during this period by ensuring that OHR was able to fully support the OSCE and helping to organise the deployment of over half of the office staff in to the field to monitor events. I had deployed all our transport and communications resources and had even had to hire vehicles to make ends meet. We'd also set up and staffed a mini operations room to provide the communications link between the field and Sarajevo and then back to the OSCE as required. It was a busy period all round but I still managed (between shifts) to attend the funeral of our chief interpreter's father who was buried in Zenica on Election Day. For OHR however, the real hard work started after the election. The OSCE and the PEC confirmed the election results on 29th September revealing that all three nationalist parties had been returned to power and that Alija Izetbegovic, Kresimir Zubak and Momcilo Krajisnik would form the three member presidency of Bosnia with Izetbegovic (the one with the most votes) serving as the first 'chair.' OHR now had to ensure that the newly elected parliamentary bodies were properly formed and constituted and that they then met and functioned. In Bosnia, simply holding an election and announcing the results did not mean that anyone would comply with the results nor settle down to the affairs of state and govern the country. On the contrary, if anything the election had given the nationalists a further mandate to continue their policies of ethnic conflict albeit now by political means. Nevertheless, the elections were deemed to have been 'free and fair' and in response to this declaration by the OSCE, the UN Security Council passed Resolution 1074 on 1st October which lifted all the remaining sanctions imposed on the FRY. Back in Bosnia, OHR's first task was to get the three-member presidency to meet with each other. This was not easy as none of them were overly keen to talk to the others. Whilst Izetbegovic and Zubak had occasionally been meeting with each other recently, neither had met with Krajisnik since before the war broke out in 1992. In fact, no Bosnian Serb leader had set foot in Sarajevo proper since the start of the war and to my knowledge none had even ventured in to Federation territory since the peace agreement had been signed in the previous year. Understandably Krajisnik feared for his life and the idea of driving in to Sarajevo was inconceivable to him. Yet, if Dayton was to work, then these three men had to meet otherwise the election would have been a completely pointless exercise. Krajisnik reached a compromise with Steiner and agreed to meet with the two Federation members of the presidency in a small hotel on the Northeast outskirts of Sarajevo. Hotel Saraj was located just after the last tunnel on the road from Pale but before the destroyed National Library where I had first entered the city several months earlier. I was given a day to organise everything for the meeting including security, protocol arrangements, VIP transport and administrative and logistic matters such as computers, printers, office fixtures, refreshments and interpreters etc. By now my international heads of departments were well versed in dropping everything to pull off the seemingly impossible and they all sprang in to action stripping computers out of offices, rescheduling interpreters and drivers itineraries and they even pinched my own circular conference table for the Presidents to use rather like King Arthur had his round table to ensured that no knight was more important than another. The meeting went ahead as planned and agreement was reached to schedule the Inaugural Ceremony of the three-member Bosnian Presidency and of the House of Representatives of the Parliamentary Assembly of Bosnia for Saturday 5th October.

Yet again I had been given less than a week's notice to prepare for a major event, however this time, it would be an event that would undoubtedly attract the attention of the world's press and media and would involve the presence of the IC's entire diplomatic corps. The inaugural ceremony would be the first time since the war began that the collective leadership of the Serb, Croat and Muslim peoples of Bosnia would meet in central Sarajevo and it was intended that they would all pledge their allegiance to a single-united Bosnia. Sarajevo's National Theatre was chosen as the venue for the ceremony and not only had the building to be prepared but so too did all the security and protocol arrangements for the ceremony. Whilst Steiner and to a lesser extent Bildt, shuttled back and forth to Pale to ensure that everything would go smoothly, I set my department heads to work organising everything from music to flowers but it wasn't easy. Invitations, seating plans, security passes, metal detectors and secure temporary storage facilities for guns, radio nets and an operations room etc all had to be prepared and in a way sensitive to ethnic sensitivities. Flowers could be anything so long as they weren't Lilies and there couldn't be too much green as both were associated with Muslims. The Serbo-Croat language overnight became three different languages instead of one as Croats substituted an odd word or two in a different dialect and even then there were still two official alphabets, one in Latin for Croats and Muslims and the other in Cyrillic for the Serbs. The Serbs then objected to Beethoven being played and insisted in signing the oath in Cyrillic. There were problems with oaths, flags, anthems and speeches. Every imaginable accommodation was made to get the three sides together since this was to be the crowning moment, the most significant achievement in the whole peace process to date and one that marked the first step towards a truly united and reconciled multi-ethnic Bosnia. The whole of the IC's diplomatic corps had been invited and were being treated to cocktails in the chandeliered splendour of the Austro-Hungarian theatre whilst the state orchestra played Dvorak and others. In the basement however, all was not calm. I had set up a small operations room with computers to accommodate any last minute changes that always seemed to be inevitable these days, and with several briefcase size INMARSAT satellite phones and UHF radios. The Police had sealed off practically the whole of down town Sarajevo in an effort to reassure the Serbs that they were safe to travel in to the city and their efforts had been backed up by a huge IFOR operation involving tanks and helicopters. Nick Haller was in Pale awaiting President Krajisnik and the Serb delegation but nothing was happening. Pale was not the easiest place to talk to by radio due to there being a mountain range in the way and so we were trying to establish a satellite link to him (since the normal phone lines from Federation territory to the RS still remained cut). We eventually established a connection and Nick simply informed us that the Serbs weren't going to play! By this time everyone upstairs was beginning to start ticking and since the Serb delegation was clearly already late, rumours were starting to circulate. Steiner took charge desperately trying to convince Krajisnik and his delegation to come to Sarajevo but it was an impossible task on the Satphone and so he sped off to Pale in his car for some personal intervention. Upstairs we rescheduled the opening ceremony delaying it for an hour hoping against all odds that Steiner would pull it off. As the hour passed without any visible sign of progress, tempers started to fray and several diplomats walked out and others demanded that we re-arrange their flights out of Sarajevo. Everyone was fidgeting and we now had to face the question of what to do next? It was a terrible moment, it seemed as if the whole peace process was hung in the balance, to have got so far and to simply give up now would have been such a tragedy. Bildt decided to wait for Steiner and then make a decision. The theatre's auditorium began to empty as more and more people got up to leave or to simply stretch their legs and so we had no choice but to ask all the Croat and Muslim deputies to leave their seats as well. For a further hour, I personally kept all forty-two of them locked up in a back room of the theatre to ensure that non of them, unlike their international diplomatic guests, left the building as it was critical that all the deputies were present for the signing of their oaths and it would have been a disaster for any of them to have left whilst there was even a slim chance that the Serbs might still turn up. Finally Steiner reappeared. He was alone and had failed to get the Serb delegation to come to the ceremony blaming the unseen hand of Radovan Karadzic as being behind it all. After a quick briefing in the basement Ops Room, Bildt decided to go with what we had and so after a three-hour delay, the Inaugural Ceremony went ahead without President Krajisnik or any of the Serbs. With as much pomp and circumstance as could be mustered under the circumstances, all the Croat and Muslim deputies took their oaths to a united Bosnia and then Presidents Izetbegovic and Zubak gave their speeches. Neither President had anticipated the events of the preceding three hours and neither of them had taken action to rewrite their speeches. Instead, both chose to deliver their original texts in full without amendment. Both singularly praised Krajisnik and the Bosnia Serbs for their brave initiative in coming to Sarajevo to take their oaths.

With the disastrous Inaugural Ceremony behind us, the OHR and other diplomatic missions, not least that of the United States, set about rebuilding bridges and putting pressure on Krajisnik to get him to come to the inaugural session of the presidency scheduled for the 22 October, at which it was envisioned that he could then take the solemn oath. Presidency meetings were planned to take place in Sarajevo and in the neighbouring Serb suburb of Lukavica in order to provide balance between the three ethnic groups and two entities. In Sarajevo, the National Museum was chosen as the venue, the third different location to date. At least this time my departments had just over two weeks to organise the venue, a task that consisted of renovating parts of the building, providing office fixtures and fittings including communications and computer facilities. Each member of the Presidency required separate accommodation as they only met together at the conference table, adjourning at regular intervals to withdraw to the privacy of their own delegations and specialist advisers. To watch them at work was so frustrating as the whole process was so slow and ponderous and at the end of the day it was always my staff who had to pick up the pieces. For example, it was my always translators who had to transcribe their agreed text from Bosnian in to Croatian, which to the rest of the world was still the same language. Whilst the diplomats worked at ensuring that Krajisnik would turn up this time, my staff had ample time to sort the administrative arrangements out. There was one thing however, that we were going to do differently this time. Rather than wait for Krajisnik, we planned to go to Pale with a fleet of armoured Range Rovers and physically collect and deliver him and the Serbs to the negotiating table in the centre of Sarajevo. If we pulled it off, then we would have made history as success would mark not only the first occasion that this had happened since the start of the war in 1992, but would signify that the peace process was back on track. Krajisnik however, still needed convincing and so entered the Americans. The US Ambassador, John Menzies and the US Assistant Secretary of State for European and Canadian Affairs, John Kornblum had arranged to meet President Krajisnik and warm him of the continued dangers of following Karadzic's lead and continuing to boycott the three-member presidency. To make the point, Kornblum had insisted that Krajisnik come to the American Embassy in the centre of Sarajevo for the meeting and OHR was to take responsibility for getting him there. On the morning of Monday 21st October, Nick Haller and I gathered together with members of IFOR and the IPTF in Jack Kern's office for a final briefing on the pick up. Jack was Jock Covey's assistant and like a lot of others in OHR, was yet another American CIMIC officer in disguise. Fortunately he was well placed to co-ordinate a joint civil-military operation, which was precisely what this trip was going to be after all. Equally fortunate was the fact that both Nick and myself were former paratroopers well acquainted with convoy and anti-ambush drills although we both hoped that we wouldn't need those particular skills on this trip. Jack produced a standard Operations Order (Op Order) following the usual NATO format setting out everybody's role in the overall plan. My role was to act as the overall Convoy Commander and also to ensure that the proper protocol was followed once in the Serb capital of Pale. Nick and I were to take two armoured Range Rovers and a further four non-armoured Discoveries for Krajisnik and his advisers. The IPTF were to co-ordinate the civil Police from the Federation and to provide a lead Police car to 'front up' the convoy and identify it to the Police securing the route. IFOR was to provide framework security along the whole route and in the air. In an attempt at deception (and options were severely limited) we were to use the top road in to Sarajevo, Mladih Musilmana, passing by the Jewish Synagogue, dropping down in to Grbavica, doubling back on ourselves to cross the Vrbanja Bridge where the first casualty of the war had been shot dead and finally to head North up Alipasina to the Embassy itself. The trip to Pale went without incident despite the uncleared snow and ice that made driving conditions treacherous for the heavy Range Rovers. Pale was located about thirty minutes drive from Sarajevo and was little more than a village. Nevertheless it was the self-proclaimed capital of the Bosnian Serb Republic – Republika Srpska. The seat of government was centred on a rather nice looking chalet style hotel called Hotel Panorama. As Nick rearranged and lined up the convoy in the small car park outside, I met with Gospodin Vukovic, President Krajisnik's chief of security to discuss the move in and out of Sarajevo and to share a small glass of Rakija together. It was a tense half-hour as Krajisnik had still not appeared although his aides kept reassuring me that he would indeed turn up this time. Nick kept Jack Kern fully briefed by radio and eventually Krajisnik turned up with his delegation and then, perhaps for Dutch courage, we all took another Rakija together before finally taking the plunge stepping outside to face the news cameras. It was now 1,30 pm and it was freezing cold with clear skies. The journey was quite surreal albeit without incident. It was like I was back in Belfast inside an armoured patrol vehicle or APV as the macralon Land Rovers were known, wondering where the next shot or improvised anti-armour grenade would come from. IFOR were everywhere, tanks and armoured fighting vehicles were on every junction and helicopters followed us every inch of the way. Far from reassuring me, all this security merely emphasised what a lovely target we were and what a superb prize it would be for any Muslim to kill Krajisnik now. As we drove along Mladih Musilmana we had a perfect view of the city below us on our right hand-side and could clearly see some of the worst effects of the fighting, as it was from this very area that the Serbs had sustained their merciless bombardment of the city below. I tried to gage the Serbs' feelings but it was impossible to tell and in any case I was too busy calling out the 'code words' that we had assigned to numerous 'report lines' we'd established on the map. Having dropped down in to Grbavica the streets were all cleared and at a standstill except at the bottom of Alipasina itself where the Federation Police had not stopped the traffic. This was probably one of the busiest junctions in the whole city but I had no intention of stopping since if we had done so, then the convoy would certainly be split up in to small vulnerable packets. I radioed for the IPTF car to keep going but it hesitated. Both the armoured Range Rovers had blue lights in the radiator grills, which Nick and I had already turned on, but we also had Police sirens which we now put on to full effect. Several drivers coming the opposite way had seen the convoy about to cross their right of way and had decided that discretion was the better part of valour and stopped. Others followed suit and we were able to drive straight across the junction, picking up the IPTF on the way past, and finish our last leg up to the Embassy, which was crawling with security guards and in any case already resembled Fort Knox. The meeting inside lasted an hour by which time we had reversed the convoy and were ready to return to Pale. We followed the same route back, if for no other reason than this was not normal practice, arriving in Pale around 4 pm when IFOR was stood-down and we were left to our own devices to get back to Sarajevo. The meeting had been a success for the peace process and Krajisnik had assured Kornblum that he would indeed turn up at tomorrow's inaugural session at the Museum. For our part, the journey had past without incident and had been a significant milestone in Bosnia's post-war recovery efforts marking as it did, the first occasion that the Bosnian Serb leadership had visited Sarajevo since before the war had begun. Now all that remained to be done was to repeat the whole process the next day so that Krajisnik could take the oath and get down to the real business of governing the country.

The next morning we held another meeting with Jack to go through the Op Order for the move. Essentially the task was the same, get President Krajisnik and the Serb delegation in and out of Sarajevo. What was different this time was all the timings, the venue, the number of vehicles involved and of our own making, the route. Our first problem was that Krajisnik delayed the move by two hours and so both Zubak's and Izetbegovic's delegations had to be informed of the alternations. Once new timings had been established, arrangements were much the same as the previous day with Nick and I going up to Pale to collect everybody and drive them in to town. As he left Hotel Panorama, Krajisnik looked pensive but determined having clearly made up his mind previously about whether to go through with it all this time. We delivered him to the Museum safe and sound at 3 pm, ten minutes after Zubak and five minutes before Izetbegovic. Once inside, the fun and games started again. We were supposed to take Krajisnik back to Pale at 5,30 pm but instead we waited on tender hooks for an additional two and a half-hours whilst he delayed signing the solemn declaration. Finally the break-through came and the press and selected guests were invited to a small ceremony in the Southern part of the building. In the mean time we had all been freezing cold, as there was no heating in our part of the Museum, waiting around for news of any developments. Few if any of us had eaten and I had made the decision hours previously to stand-down Nick's cars and drivers albeit they were only a few hundred metres away in a holding position by their now renovated transport office and workshop. Jack Kern, on one of his few trips out of the office, was ticking like a budgie and so to placate him I called the transport forward and had it lined up ready to move about an hour before it was actually needed. Eventually Vukovic, ignoring Kern, came out to speak with me and check our preparedness to leave. Nick and I moved the cars up to the steps of the Museum with doors open, armed bodyguards covering the left and right flanks and the Holiday Inn across the road, collected our delegation and had departed within less than a minute. It looked and indeed was, incredibly professional despite the paranoia of Kern.

Once back in Pale, the Serbs relaxed and you could feel the tensions lift from their shoulders. They had taken a huge step forward and although none would openly admit it, had clearly and understandably been worried about their own security. I released the convoy, which returned back to Sarajevo, and at Krajisnik's invitation stayed behind with my Montenegrin interpreter for a celebratory drink with them all in Hotel Panorama.

Two days after toasting the peace process with President Krajisnik and the Bosnian Serb leadership in Hotel Panorama, I was aboard a plane to the OHR office in Bruxelles to see Laila Reffnes. A day later I was travelling on the Eurostar to Ashford on my way home for a well-deserved spell of leave with my family. It was great to see everybody again but painful to think that it wouldn't be for long. The separations were getting harder to bear each time not least because the work in OHR was becoming less and less enjoyable. As more and more new faces arrived, they demanded more and more. Many of those arriving now would never have survived the initial months, as they simply couldn't cope without their every whim being taken care of. Running around after many of them now seemed to be an exercise in placating a classroom of spoilt children rather than the challenge of establishing the principal organisation charged with the overall responsibility for rebuilding the country. I felt that it was time to play a more active role in that reconstruction process rather than merely support others in their efforts. I wasn't a career diplomat, but I had already absorbed a fantastic amount of information about what was going on in the country, and I had an enormous wealth of operational in-theatre experience and a good understanding of many grass-roots cross-cultural issues that the diplomats were dealing with. Although very bright and capable, many of the seconded diplomats arriving in OHR had little knowledge of the Balkans and I felt that if they could succeed, then I too could put my knowledge and experience to better use. Jock had asked all of the international administrative staff to review their options as all our contracts were due to expire at Christmas. This was because when OHR was originally conceptualised at Dayton, the thinking was that the mission would only last a year. This was clearly not going to be the case and so my staff and I had to think about what we wanted to do next. The staffing situation was always fluid with people coming and going all the time, but to my mind Angelika Hamilton had got it right when she had moved a few weeks previously from administration to Humanitarian Affairs where she was now taking a far more active role out on the ground. The other consideration that I had to take in to account was one that exists in any office the world over; namely the forming of power cliques. When one is working away from home and in a potentially hostile environment, where you are constantly subjected to enormous levels of stress not just at work but in everyday life where food, water and heating etc are hard to come by, and where the people you are working with are from different cultures and have different political and religious beliefs not to mention work ethics, then it is inevitable that some friction will occur. OHR was no exception to this and it was becoming increasingly more difficult to play the role of boss, decision-making, motivator and arbitrator one moment, and then friend and colleague the next. As the immediate post-war imperative of simply getting things done was being replaced by less exciting and less challenging rules, regulations and procedures, many of my staff who had been there right at the beginning began to question what they were doing and with time on their hands, began to form in to several little cliques. With the same thing happening with many of the local staff, my open door policy was costing me a lot of time and effort listening and sorting out peoples' problems. I decided that the time was right for a change; I had lost interest in all the squabbles and could no longer motivate myself to continue to provide management support to an office that had never once thanked me or any other member of my staff for their efforts. On returning from leave I approached several departments within OHR to tentatively enquire about moving across to them. My main choice was to get involved with humanitarian affairs just like Angelika had managed previously. But whereas she had agreed to take a lower 'local-rate' salary as her husband was also in Sarajevo working with IFOR, I needed to retain an international salary as I was sending most of this home to keep a roof over my family's head and feed them. This proved to be the stumbling block as the OHR budget would not support a diplomatic post as these had to be filled by seconded personnel. Only the administrative posts, such as my current one, could be funded by the operational budget. Since I had overall responsibility for finance I knew this of course, but it was my intention to get the Foreign Office to fund the position if at all possible. I spoke on several occasions to the same senior FCO Officer in EAD who had been responsible for managing the ICFY Mission and who had engineered my OHR appointment in the first place, but little happened as I think he thought that I was calling his bluff and would eventually decide to stay put. The FCO had vivid memories of what had happened to Ambassador Peter Streams at the beginning of the year and was taking my bemoaning as par for the course. Finally in mid December as crunch time was fast approaching, I informed Jock that I'd had enough and made one last call back to the UK to tell the FCO that since they weren't about to help out, that I was going to end my mission with OHR. The next day was spent commuting President Krajisnik to and from Pale again, as this was now becoming a routine operation for us during the frequent sessions of the three-member presidency. I returned to the office late that evening having dropped the President off and to my surprise the FCO called. There was still no way that they were going to second me to OHR, but what they wanted to know was whether I was interested in working for the ECMM. I immediately said yes, as this was an option that would surely give me the opportunity I was looking for, the ability to work in the field and influence what was really happening out there rather than be at someone else's beck and call. All they wanted to know was when I could start and so I told them straight after Christmas. We set the Start of Mission date for 7th January

1997, the same start date as Brian Jupp, a good friend and old ICFY colleague of mine. And that was that.

Leaving OHR was simplicity in itself. I had several days leave owing and
so I worked backwards from 31 December and booked an appropriate flight
home. I had collected far too much personal effects over the last year and a
half and there was no way that I could take all these home with me and so I
boxed them up and took them across to the ECMM HQ in Sarajevo where
another former ICFY colleague, Ken Lindsey had arranged for them to be
secured until the new year when I could collect them again once I knew my
posting details with ECMM. Saying good-bye was difficult and in some cases
quite traumatic, as I had known several of my colleagues for the whole
eighteen months that I had been in the Former Yugoslavia. Officially
however, nothing was organised and neither Bildt, Steiner nor Covey made
any attempt at a speech, presentation or even a formal thank you. Not that
there was a precedent for such ceremonies as people were generally far too
busy for such social occasions. One or two people had thrown small drinks
parties in the office but these weren't too well attended and in most cases
they had been planned well in advance. My decision to leave and join ECMM
was made at the last minute and it left little time for me to say my personal
goodbyes and so office drinks went by the way side. Nevertheless it was still
sad to think back at what I'd achieved over the last year and to think that I
was simply going to walk out of the office one morning soon and end it all
without so much as a thank you from anyone that mattered. It was especially sad when you consider the efforts Urpo and I went to in Niksic to ensure
that every time someone left, that we held a party and small ceremony in 501.
Nevertheless that's precisely what happened. On the last morning, I came in
to work, said as many goodbyes as I could to those who were around and
then loaded up my bags and departed for Belgrade airport. Although I'd be
returning in the New Year, I was leaving behind me a Bosnia that was now
one year in to the peace process, and I had been the person responsible for
getting the organisation that was in charge of that process up and running. I
remembered my arrival at the beginning of the year, it seemed so long ago
with the deserted streets littered with the debris of war, the burnt out tram
cars and the gutted buildings with UNHCR plastic sheeting for roofs and
windows. My first impressions of the battered Fero-elektro building; the
bullet holes in all the walls, collapsed office roofs, shattered window frames
and the archaic state of the water and power supplies and the telephone
system. The office now had over two hundred people working for it and
there were regional offices in both Banja Luka and Tuzla. I'd spent the last
month negotiating with the European Union Administrative Mission
(EUAM) in Mostar, which was headed up by the former Royal Marine
General, Sir Martin Garrod, in order to take over their operation and assets
in the New Year. OHR was now big business and with elections and inaugu-
rations behind us, things were really starting to move forward. There was still
much to achieve however. In Republika Srpska, vital humanitarian aid was

still being withheld due to the leadership's hard line political attitudes and corruption. In the Federation there was little sign of the harmony envisioned by Washington[96] or Dayton between the Muslims and Croats. In deed, the Croats were actively calling for the creation of a third entity. There had been little to no progress whatsoever regarding the return of DPs and refugees, and sadly harassment and human rights abuses by entity Police forces were still prolific if not a way of life. All these things and many more would be addressed in the years to come. Not only had I already made that possible by putting the OHR firmly on the map and equipping it with the tools it needed to address such issues, but with my move to ECMM, I was now going to take a far more active role in ensuring that the IC overcame the obstruction and corruption so prevalent within Bosnian culture, and effectively implement all aspects of the Peace Agreement.

OHR Staff: *Members of OHR's staff join the High Representative, Carl Bildt and the Principal Deputy High Representative, Michael Steiner for a group photograph towards the end of 1996.*

PART THREE

THE EUROPEAN COMMUNITY
MONITOR MISSION
JANUARY 1997 - JULY 1998

14

The Men in White

The European Community Monitor Mission (ECMM) to the Former Yugoslavia was established even before ICFY on the 7th July 1991, as a result of what was known as the Brioni Agreement. Initially the concept of having a monitoring presence within the rapidly disintegrating Socialist Federal Republic of Yugoslavia (SFRY) was conceived in Prague within the framework of the then Conference for Security and Co-operation in Europe (CSCE).[97] The European Community[98] then took up the idea and reached agreement with representatives from the six republics of the Former Yugoslavia for a combined EC and CSCE mission to be established. Unlike normal practice, the new mission's mandate had no fixed expiry date although it could be terminated at any stage with fifteen days notice by either side. Member EC states (except Luxembourg) along with the CSCE states of Poland, Norway, the Czech Republic and Slovakia all contributed personnel and resources to the mission with the intention of stabilising the situation on the ground, supporting the peace process and of containing the crisis within the region. The mission's initial role was to help stabilise the confrontation line in Slovenia where the first war had broken out, to clear roads ensuring Freedom of Movement, to exchange prisoners and bodies, and finally to monitor the withdrawal of the JNA from Slovenia and subsequently from Croatia when that second war had started. In order to ensure that these conflicts were contained within the region, the ECMM reinforced its mandate by signing various Memorandum of Understanding (MOU) with neighbouring countries such as Bulgaria in September 1992, and then with Hungary and Albania in December 1992. The mission then maintained an operational presence in all these countries with a total strength of around three hundred and fifty monitors, of which around twenty at any one time were British. This contribution cost the British taxpayer around £4M per annum in personnel, transport, communications and logistic costs. In return, HMG policy objectives of containment and regional stabilisation were achieved. Put bluntly, it was far cheaper to try and keep the conflict at an arm's length and contained within the Balkan region than to risk having to fight another full-scale war in Europe. And that was precisely what was feared at the time. Many will now ask why we were involved, why did we spend this money and why did our soldiers have to put on their blue helmets and support the UN forces in the region? Many lost their lives and so it is a poignant question but the answer reflects the reality that had we not done so, then we might now be living in a completely different world than we do today and one devastated by conflict with destruction on an unprecedented scale. We simply could not afford for the conflict to spill over or for Russia to take the sides of their Orthodox allies – the Serbs, or the Islamic world to intervene within NATO's sphere of influence on behalf of the Muslims, or for NATO and the EU to fragment perhaps with the Germans and Austrians siding with the Croats. Too much was at risk and so Britain committed her troops to the UN Protection Forces (UNPROFOR) and twenty or so unarmed monitors to the front line with the ECMM. Dressed from head to foot in white clothing in order to identify themselves as unarmed

The Men in White: The author in ECMM whites and EU armband.

and under a sign of truce, monitors carried out these tasks throughout the fighting with only minimal loss of life.[99] Now that the fighting in Bosnia had ended, ECMM was slowly adapting to a new set of demands. The EU's contribution to Dayton included maintaining the ECMM. The Mission continued to monitor the military and security situation but now also provided the

OSCE with its eyes and ears on the ground reporting on the prevailing social and political situation prior to the elections. Additionally it began looking at humanitarian relief and reconstruction efforts as well as human rights and socio-economic issues within Bosnia on behalf of the EU and the OHR whilst at the same time downsizing its earlier commitment in surrounding countries such as Hungary and Bulgaria. ECMM's role remained essentially the same, namely to promote a long-term peaceful solution to the conflict in the Former Yugoslavia and it achieved this by monitoring its areas of interest, reporting on them and where possible by establishing confidence building measures between the former warring factions acting as a neutral third party.

During the war in Bosnia, both the UN and the ECMM had established their HQs in the Croatian capital, Zagreb where it had been far safer and operationally more viable to do so. In January 1997, Dayton was already over a year old and whilst I had spent the whole of 1996 establishing the OHR in Sarajevo and the UN had also moved to the city, the ECMM HQ remained in 'Hotel I' in Zagreb. The excuse for this misnomer was that ECMM still had a presence in neighbouring countries other than just in Bosnia. Whilst this was true the argument belied the fact that the missions in Hungary and Bulgaria were closing and that the ECMM presence in Belgrade, Montenegro and Albania consisted of no more than a small handful of monitors. Only Croatia and Bosnia had significantly sized missions and by far the largest was in Bosnia, which in any case, was where the main centre of gravity was supposed to have been for the last year. Nevertheless ECMM had not moved and both the mission hierarchy and the enormously ponderous 'national delegations' maintained their sinecures and remained in the luxury of the hotel until July 1997, some eighteen months after the peace agreement. Because of its overly hierarchical structure, the missions inside Bosnia and Croatia needed HQs of their own. These HQs were called 'Regional Centres' (RC) and ECMM had maintained an effective HQ in Bosnia throughout 1996 known as 'RC-BiH,' which was also where I had left all my personal kit over Christmas. The RC directed five smaller HQs known as 'Co-ordination Centres' (CC), which were located throughout Bosnia in the towns of Tuzla (CC-Tango), Zenica (CC-Zulu), Mostar (CC-Mike), Sokolac (CC-Papa) and in Banja Luka (CC-Bravo). Each of these five CCs in turn directed between three and four field based monitoring teams consisting of two or three monitors whom together provided complete coverage of Bosnia. Monitors were assigned to a location anywhere within the mission depending upon what their delegations decided and could 'win' from the 'presidency.' Unlike ICFY, ECMM was not a meritocracy and new mission members did not start on the bottom rung and work their way up the promotion ladder, neither did they compete openly and transparently at interview for more senior posts. There were two reasons for this; one was political and the other military. Both were inextricably connected with the way the mission had been established and staffed from its inception and when combined were to become the mission's Achilles heal and weakest link although few recognised it as such. At the highest level, the HOM was appointed by the EU state that held the rotating presidency of the EU. That meant in practice that the HOM changed every six months with the rotation of the presidency. Key decisions were supposed to be taken by a Troika consisting of the previous, the current and the next presidency state but in essence the state with the current presidency dominated the decision making process. Worse still, it was normal practice for the new HOM to bring with them a completely new 'administration' rather like the American system of government. That meant that most of the senior jobs in the Mission HQ in Zagreb and the Heads of the regional and co-ordinating centres (HRC and HCC) as well as those field posts deemed by the incoming presidency to be of 'national interest' were allocated to new people en masse every six months. In ICFY there were no national delegations as everyone worked as a team. In ECMM however, national delegations were deemed essential in order to 'contest' posts and ensure 'influence' within the system. This was a tragic waste of money as a small empire of rear echelon diplomats perpetuated their existence and drew fat salaries with nothing to do other than to 'fight their national corner' adding no value to the mission whatsoever. It was a very lucrative sinecure not least for the three semi-retired British diplomats who took it in turn to act as the UK Head of Delegation (HOD). Second fiddle to all this was whether any of the incoming team was actually competent or not. Usually it was a 'numbers game' played out over the short term with senior diplomatic posts going to inappropriate and unqualified short-termers whose only 'assets' were their seniority in their normal careers – usually the military. This led to the second problem; namely that of the military. If the situation wasn't bad enough, it was made worse by the fact that most nations simply seconded personnel to ECMM from their own military forces. As ex-military myself, I could see the merits of military training which could easily come in handy when trying to cross cease fire lines or when negotiating the exchange of prisoners and bodies between the various warring fractions. But time had not stood still, we were one year in to the peace process and many of the 'soldiers' being 'posted' to ECMM were not capable of getting amongst Bosnian civil society and finding out what was really happening on the ground. Many lacked the individuality and resourcefulness to act independently, had little understanding of the context in which they were operating and the complexities of the situation in the Balkans and worse still, didn't want to be in the mission in the first place. None of them were experts in humanitarian affairs, human rights, political systems or any other appropriate area that might have proved useful. Professional soldiers are renowned for their flexibility but to forcefully take one away from their home and family, to put them in a foreign country, to expect them to operate away from their military unit and to ruthlessly question and examine what they saw and were being told by their interlocutors whilst also being sensitive to complex cross-cultural issues, was far too much to expect. Many rose to the challenge and did extremely good jobs, but the history and culture of the Balkans is too complex to grasp in six months and by the time a monitor was ready to leave the mission, many were only just becoming tuned to the vagaries of the situation that they were operating in. There were a few exceptions to this generalisation. The German delegation employed mostly retired career diplomats who were able to remain for longer periods on open contracts. Likewise the Norwegian government employed monitors from the NRC on indefinite contracts. The British contracts were the same as in ICFY. There were no serving military personnel in the delegation whatsoever albeit most, although not all of us were retired officers. We were employed on short-term renewable contracts but in practice we all had a wealth of experience in the Balkans having been around the area in some guise or another for several years. This experience provided the backbone of the ECMM as without the UK Delegation there would have been very limited continuity and almost no institutional memory whatsoever. But twenty people was never enough to make a real difference and so by early 1997, ECMM was in great difficulty although few would admit it. The mission lacked true direction and substance. It had been supplanted by and subordinated to the OHR and the OSCE, had little to offer its interlocutors, was suffering from a system that replaced its leadership every July and January and was mostly staffed in the field by short-term soldiers with little enthusiasm for the job and who constantly rotated in and out of the mission. All in all there wasn't much going for the mission although at this stage in the proceedings I was not fully aware of how these issues would affect operations. For sure I knew many of the problems and within days of arriving in Zagreb in early January, it was readily apparent that the mission was top heavy and that the national delegations had nothing to do but to bicker with each other and to dine out in expensive restaurants down town. On my first evening in Hotel I, the Belgians handed over responsibility for the mission to the incoming Dutch presidency. It was a very pleasant evening washed down with liberal quantities of fine Belgium beer. Three former colleagues from ICFY; Lena Larssen from Sweden, Mike Austin from the UK and 'Mother' Olga from Belgrade, had also come to visit me from Ilok where they were now based with UNTAES some eight hours drive away on the far side of Croatia. It was great to see them all again and it really lifted my spirits to see some people I knew. Not that that was really a problem. I met Erik De Deker, my OHR IT manager from Bruxelles, at breakfast and already knew several ECMM personnel having stayed at Hotel I on several occasions previously when flying to and from the UK when on leave from OHR. The hand over of the presidency to the Dutch typified the lack of continuity that plagued the mission. I was new to the mission but I had already been in theatre for eighteen months whereas for most of the new Dutch hierarchy taking up their senior positions in Zagreb and in the RCs and CCs throughout the mission, this was their first taste of the Balkans. I was joined by another British newcomer, Brian Jupp who had been with me in ICFY albeit in another Sector. We remained in Zagreb until Friday completing the standard ECMM training package along with all the other newcomers and then departed on a shuttle ride to hell. Those of us who were being posted to RC-BiH needed to travel to Sarajevo to complete our training in theatre. Under normal transport arrangements the journey would have taken me about four and a half hours driving via Slavonski Brod, Doboj, Maglaj and Zenica. However ECMM transport moved in bounds. There was no central transport system and instead one had to get on a shuttle provided by one CC and move to the next area of responsibility where you swapped vehicles and joined one provided by the next CC. At each stage in the proceedings you would have to wait for the connection to arrive and then cross load vehicles. It was yet another freezing Balkan winter with the temperature well below zero, the vehicles were freezing and the journey down to Sarajevo took nearly twelve hours. By the time we arrived and were dumped in a rather horrid transit block for overnight accommodation, none of us were too keen to venture out. Nevertheless most of us did pop in to town for a short look around at the grim spectacle that was Sarajevo in winter. It was a rather strange feeling for me. Three weeks previously I had been living and working in this city, I had had my own flat, a vehicle and a good set of friends and colleagues. Now I was starting all over again. We had driven past my old flat and I was now standing outside my old office, but non-of it was part of my life anymore. The city was cold and covered in snow, it looked as bleak as the day I had arrived a year previously and I felt somewhat saddened by the thought that I had given so much of my life to helping the people of this city and yet it seemed as if nothing had changed. Walking aimlessly around the city streets in the freezing cold didn't do anything for me and so I called in to see some old Serb friends of mine who were still living close by in order to celebrate orthodox Christmas and New Year with them. Saturday and Sunday was spent training and then finally on Sunday afternoon we were all told our actual postings by the RC. I had been told that I was being posted to CC-Bravo in Banja Luka but at this stage I did not know which team they would send me to. Indeed, all I knew was that on Monday I had to contend with yet another shuttle trip back up the very same route I had just been down on Friday, and that was something I wasn't looking forward to. In the mean time I had to arrange for all my boxed possessions to be unlocked and made available for my departure early on Monday morning. Getting everything in to the bus was to be another problem.

Monday was another freezing cold day. Several of us who were going back up the route towards Zagreb loaded our possessions in to the back of the mini bus ready for the off. Over the last eighteen months I had accumulated a whole host of kit including such luxuries as my own TV satellite dish and decoder. Getting all my paraphernalia in to the bus simply wasn't an option, not least because I had been issued with several additional items of equipment by my delegation in Zagreb including a white helmet and an extremely heavy bullet proof vest cum flax jacket. There was no other option but for me to leave half of my personal kit behind and ask Ken Lindsey to forward it up to me next week with the next shuttle run. The journey was another nightmare. As we passed numerous towns on our way North, we dropped off monitors returning to their posts from leave until eventually we crossed back in to Croatia, crossing over the River Sava at Slavonski Brod once again. This was a ludicrously long way around to get to Banja Luka but that was how it was done. Finally we swapped buses again and headed back up the same motorway due West towards Zagreb before stopping off at a motorway exit just South of Okucani. After travelling for some ten hours, we were now only about one to two hours away from Zagreb where we had departed from only on the previous Friday, and still about an hour North of Banja Luka, and what's more, we were still in another country. Thankfully the shuttle from CC-Bravo was waiting for us at the junction and I was able to cross load my kit for the last time and head off South on the last leg of my journey back in to Bosnia.

Banja Luka was the largest city in Republika Srpska although not the seat of government as that remained in Pale where Krajisnik still ran the show and presumably where Karadzic was still in hiding. The city was much smaller than Sarajevo, and so it had a lovely 'human sized' quality about it. Furthermore, apart from the mindless and wanton destruction of the main Ferhadia Mosque[100] in the city centre, it had not been ravaged by war, a factor that had undoubtedly contributed to the need for the Serbs to negotiate a rapid peace at Dayton before Dudakovic's 5th Corps and Alagic's 7th Corps reached the city. The ECMM HQ, CC-Bravo, was housed in a small motel cum restaurant-café bar called the Golden Card, which was located just on the Northern outskirts of the city. I had visited there once before when we were trying to open the OHR office in the city and had called in at the Golden Card to ask the ECMM for their advice on where we might find suitable office space. Little had changed in the intervening year and their whole set-up looked as dirty and unprofessional as it had all that time ago. The mission had rented three rooms on the first floor of the motel for use as office space for the CC. One room, on the rear of the building housed admin and finance functions and also served as the radio room (if and when one could hear oneself think), a multi-purpose storage facility for years of accumulated junk, and as the main location for all the files and reports that the ECMM generated as its core function. How anyone could work in such an environment remains a mystery to me to this day but needless to say people made do. A second room, situated on the front of the motel and overlooking the courtyard and a huge gravelled parking area used extensively at night by truck and bus drivers as they availed themselves of the services of the local prostitutes who were the motel's other main source of income, was used solely by the newly appointed Dutch HCC, his French deputy and long serving British Operations Officer. On the face of it this office looked a little better managed however the allusion was only skin deep. The walls were covered in maps giving a professional impression but I was later to learn that they were no more than a façade hiding a disorganised HQ, one that had been neglected by frequently changing HCCs, incompetent French DHCCs and which was held together by the institutional memory of the Operations Officer who for the most part kept it all in his head and did little to share his accumulated expertise with anyone else. The final room was also on the back of the motel and was used solely as a recreation room. In previous years the international monitors had also lived in the motel, not something to be recommended by any standards, and there had been need of a rest room for them to relax in after hours, watch TV and perhaps cook some snacks. As such, the room had several easy chairs and a huge orange sofa placed around a small glass coffee table. At one end of the room there was a TV and at the other end behind a small wall was a tiny kitchen. The room stank of stale cigarettes and was filthy. All the furniture was broken, the chairs and sofa had long lost their support and the glass table was shattered and stuck together with sellotape. There was left over food on plates both in the kitchen and in the main part of the room and the thought of actually using any of the utensils turned my stomach. To think that the ECMM ought to be briefing visiting EU diplomatic delegations, ambassadors, ministers or even members of its own staff in such an environment was appalling yet no one was bothered. In the end it had always been like this and so no one saw fit to tackle the problem. Everyone now lived-out in the city and there was no real need for a rest room as such. The TV was a useless hangover that merely attracted waiting drivers and interpreters in to the rest room where they smoked all day watching TV disturbing the work of the Ops Officer. What was needed was a briefing or conference room, indeed a massive reorganisation of the whole CC. All this was obvious to me within minutes of entering the motel but of course the workings of the CC was, at least for the moment, none of my business. I was met by the HCC and then one of the interpreters helped me to get a room for the night. I unloaded everything from the transport and reported back up to the Ops Room for an in-briefing. It was Monday 13th January and New Year's Eve in the Orthodox calendar. Banja Luka would be in a festive mood tonight and it would be good to get in to town and join in the festivities. David, the Operations Officer had been in the UK Delegation for several years already and was without doubt a leading authority on events in the Banja Luka area, indeed in the whole of Northwest Bosnia since he had operational control of teams that reported back to him from as far a field as Bihac in the West and Prnjavor in the East. As one might reasonably expect, David had got to know an awful lot of people during the past few years and so was also looking forward to celebrating the Orthodox New Year with some friends in the city. Clearly the thought of having to brief yet another newcomer was one irritation too many for him and so consequently he managed to finish the whole spiel on the political, socio-economic situation of the whole of NW Bosnia in under ten minutes before taking the keys to a vehicle and speeding off down town leaving me with only myself and the wretched TV for company. I wanted to follow but as the traditional celebratory shooting had already started and I couldn't really rely on my memory of a year ago to find my way around a strange Serb city in the dark, I reluctantly opted to stay put and curse my fellow Brit and HCC for their lack of basic hospitality. I'd been in the mission for exactly a week and so far I had seen little to be impressed with. Tomorrow I was going to travel to Sanski Most in the Muslim-Croat Federation in order to join Team Bravo-2 which was headed up by an old Austrian Colonel called Max. Little did I know but the fun and games had only just begun!

15

Sanski Most

The trip from Banja Luka to Sanski Most should have taken around two hours considering the dreadful winter conditions, had we driven South from Prijedor that is. Instead we continued to drive Northwest towards Novi Grad on my third successive trip to hell. To make matters worse, we were driving in an armoured Land Rover, which like all such vehicles made by the UK's best and finest, had no heating that actually worked and in our case had broken windscreen wipers to boot. To the layman, driving through the snow and ice in a Land Rover would probably seem to be the best that one could hope for, but the armoured variant of the Land Rover Defender was an unwieldy and top heavy beast at the best of times and in the snow and ice it was practically lethal. When one considered that we couldn't see where we were going either, one begins to imagine just how ECMM was looking from my perspective, a complete world away from the surreal luxury of the HQ back in Zagreb. The temperature was well below zero and my driver, a Greek called Andreas, and myself were dressed from head to foot in all the foul weather gear that we owned right down to the thermal underwear. The idea was to show me a bit of the AoR before being dropped off in Sanski Most. To that end, the plan was to drive via Prijedor to meet team Bravo-1, and then to go on to Bihac to meet team Bravo-4. The fourth and last remaining team within the CC was team Bravo-3 at Prnjavor, a small town Northeast of Banja Luka and completely in the wrong direction to Sanski Most (not that Bihac was on the way either). Prnjavor would have to wait for another day but as we drove further towards Bihac, I wished that Bravo-4 could wait as well. The road was treacherous and Andreas was hard pressed to keep the armoured fridge on the road. Once past Bihac it began to snow heavily and our lack of wipers on the outside started to become as serious a problem as the freezing mist on the inside of the windscreen. The problem was that the motor didn't have enough oomph to complete the upward swing of its sweep. Now that there was some serious snow to contend with as well, there was no chance that the wipers would work. We kept stopping to climb on to the bonnet and clear the screen by hand but were having to do so about every hundred metres or so now. In the end we found a solution and tied an elastic bungee around the top of the large HF radio antenna which was mounted on top of the roof, and tied the other end to Andreas's wiper blade. The effect was that the elastic pulled the blade upwards due to the force of the antenna trying to right itself, whilst the motor managed to pull it back downwards again. Our wipers worked – for the time being at least – and we managed to arrive in Sanski Most in one piece, albeit frozen and over eight hours after leaving Banja Luka. Sanski Most may have been a nice place before the war although I doubt it. Now it was really terrible. There was no life to it whatsoever. Much had been destroyed as the town fell to successive sides as the fighting ebbed back and forth northwards towards the Serb town of Prijedor and then southwards again towards the Muslim town of Kljuc. In Serbo-Croat, 'Most' means Bridge. 'Sanski Most' refers to the bridge that crosses the River Sana at the place that gave the name to the town. Apart from the bridge and the local hotel, aptly named Hotel Sana, there wasn't much else in the town, at least not from first impressions. If my aim had been to unwind from the hectic rat race and pressures of OHR, then Sanski Most was probably the backwater that I should have been dreaming of. But if my first impressions were right, then this was going to be too much of a backwater and as we drove up to the house that served as both the team accommodation and office, I started to worry about what one did in such a place. The team in the CC had warned me about Max, my new team leader, but had neglected to tell me why I should be on my guard. They had simply assured me that whilst others hadn't managed to stay the course with him that I would be different as I had years of experience to fall back on where the others hadn't. As we pulled up the drive, the door to the accommodation opened and out stepped Max looking just like the archetypal Austrian Colonel Blimp that I had imagined, complete with glass monocle and thinning grey hair contrasting against a blush red face. Max was approaching sixty years old, or at least he looked it and like most senior officers of that era, was completely set in his ways. After all, Max's ways had served him well for nearly six decades so who was to tell him any different now? What's more, who was going to tell a Colonel anything anyway, surely not a young English civilian who had once been a lowly Major? Not wanting to stereotype or jump to rash conclusions, I greeted Max in the best German I could muster for the occasion and put the CC's warning behind me. Max was polite and correct in his manner, ushering us both inside and in to the warmth of the building whilst taking the 'post' from Andreas's outstretched hands. Once inside we were immediately instructed to take our shoes off, although this was actually quite a normal courtesy in a Muslim house despite our feet being frozen from the journey. Max then pointed to an A4 sheet of paper that he had stuck on the wall, it was entitled 'House Rules' and contained a list of dos and don'ts that Max had made up for, 'The well being of all.' Still with my coat and gloves on, and still standing shivering in the entrance hall, Max then proceeded to go through the daily routine of the team (the team consisting of just the two of us plus an interpreter who lived in her own home). Max first explained that, 'Reveille is at 7,00 am.' He continued to tell me that he would, '... then listen for several minutes to the BBC World Service' on his radio to catch the news headlines and then, '... at precisely 7,03 am' he would, '... take a shower. At precisely 7,20 am, I shall finish my shower and shave and at precisely 7,25 am, you can (taken to mean must) take a shower and shave.' Whilst I was showering, Max would boil the kettle for tea (which I would have with lemon) and boil us both two eggs which would be ready, 'At precisely 7,45 am.' Whilst I very much appreciated some kindly old soul boiling me up some eggs in the morning and putting the kettle on for a pot of tea, the thought of the whole thing being so regimented scarred the living daylights out of me and so far I hadn't even got past the entrance hall yet! I knew instantly that this wasn't going to work. What if I didn't want eggs, what if I wanted toast, Cornflakes or even sausages? What if I wanted fried eggs instead? I have a mischievous streak and so no matter how well meaning and intentioned someone is, there was no way that for the foreseeable future I was going to get up at 'precisely' the same time each morning and follow the exact same regime. The mornings are for waking up and not for some bazaar parade and so I knew that if we were going to live, eat, work and sleep in the same building for perhaps the next year, that I would need some space of my own and a life away from Max. This was why the 'others' that the CC team had spoken about had cracked. There was no escape and living with Max was too claustrophobic for them and they had demanded to be moved to other teams. The problem was that the field teams unlike the CCs and RCs, had to stay together in a designated house rented by the mission (for which you in turn paid rent to the ECMM) and equipped by them with computer and communications equipment. Teams were required to live and work together in these houses and in many instances, the local interpreters also lived-in as well. It was not an option to live-out and so I was stuck with Max and just had to make do hopefully lasting longer than my predecessors. The sad thing was that Max was blissfully unaware of all the problems that he left in his wake. In his mind he was perfectly well behaved and the very epitome of an excellent monitor and team leader. At a later stage he even remarked to me that he resented the CC always taking new monitors off his hands. In his mind, no sooner than he had finished invested all his time and effort in to 'training them,' monitors would be removed and sent to other teams. He believed that was being used by the CC as a trainer and although his ego liked the idea of being so well thought of that he had been entrusted with such a task, he also resented having new people around the whole time. What he couldn't comprehend was that these monitors had all asked to be moved for their own sanity and that it was not a great conspiracy by the CC to have him train all their new monitors. And so it was with quite some trepidation that I settled down to my first night with Max.

Sanski Most was positioned at one end of a strategic fault line created by Dayton. At the other end of the fault line, some twenty minutes to the North by vehicle lay the notorious Serb town of Prijedor. Prijedor had been the place where the Serbs had run three concentration/extermination camps during the war and was still regarded as the most hard-line Serb stronghold in the whole of Republika Srpska.[101] Consequently the ECMM did not send new monitors to the town but only those whom they thought were experienced enough to handle the political and security situation there. For the time being then, Prijedor was not my concern although I had to learn all about the history and politics of the area if only to understand the Muslim perspective at the other end of the fault line in Sanski Most. The connection between the two towns was now inextricably linked as many thousands of Prijedor's pre-war Muslim population had fled South and were now living in the neighbourhood of Sanski Most. These DPs were concentrated in and around the small settlement of Lusci Palanka some thirty minutes away to the West on the main route past the British SFOR base at Kammengrad. Of course the population movement had been in two directions with Serbs from Sanski Most also fleeing the war and the advancing Muslim forces, and settling in and around Prijedor in the now vacated Muslim suburbs such as Kozarac. These Serb movements attracted little attention within the IC as most commentators and observers were content to concentrate on only the plight of the Muslims ignoring any reciprocal injustices done to the Serbs. There were a number of reasons for this. One was simply that most aid agencies dealing with DPs viewed the Serbs as the bad guys and as being responsible for starting the war. On the face of it, there was more than a grain of truth in this analogy but I was never one to subscribe to the view that the IC should now punish the whole of the Serb people for the injustices perpetrated by some of their kind and their political leaders. The second reason was that in this particular area, Prijedor had such a bad name due to the presence of the concentration camps that few if any members of the IC really cared about the Serbs. Finally, the Muslim DPs had several renowned public figures on their side who were to prove highly successful in winning the hearts and minds of the IC in their campaign to win support for their cause, sadly at the expense of the Serbs whose plight continued to be ignored in what was a highly complex issue. The renowned figures in question were both former soldiers. One, Mehmed Alagic was formerly the commander of the ABiH 7th Corps and held the rank of Brigadier General. During the war, Alagic had led the Muslim forces along with Dudakovic's 5th Corps in the breakout of the Bihac pocket and had directed his assault against the Serbs in a drive eastwards towards Banja Luka. He had retaken Sanski Most and was well on the way to taking Prijedor, which remained the last Serb town between him and his goal at Banja Luka. The peace agreement had stopped him achieving his aim and his Army had been brought to a halt half way between Sanski Most and Prijedor where the IEBL now stood. Alagic had been 'defeated' by the peace but was now the Mayor of Sanski Most and in a close analogy to the military philosopher Carl Von Clausewitz, had vowed to take Prijedor 'by other means.' To achieve this, he like many of the war-lords that littered the Balkans in the immediate aftermath of the war, had removed his uniform and put on a suit. Likewise he had 'disbanded' his former military Staff Officers and appointed them as his municipal officers within the local authority that he now controlled as his own fiefdom. To help him achieve his final goal he had a trusted lieutenant, the second renowned figure in the area and one of his former officers, Sead Cirkin. Cirkin had been a Captain in the ABiH's Special Forces and was now the highly vocal spokesman of the Muslim DPs assembled in Lusci Palanka. From the very outset Cirkin vowed to return all the Muslim DPs to Prijedor with the use of force if necessary. Within days of my arrival in Sanski Most, he threatened to march around twenty thousand DPs northwards and to camp them in tents on the outskirts of Prijedor until such time as they were properly housed. Such claims may seem totally justifiable but they sent the IC in to blind panic. Firstly, SFOR would never have been able to protect the DPs and there would certainly have been armed resistance by the Serbs to any such move by the Muslims. The Serbs were paranoid of Cerkin and were convinced that any movement of DPs across the IEBL would be accompanied by a covert armed infiltration by Cerkin's Special Forces concealed amongst the returnees. These fears were well founded and without doubt would have led to a Serb police intervention if not a military one to stop the mass movement of DPs. SFOR knew this and since it was their responsibility to ensure that the entity armies remained behind the IEBL and did not confront each other, any threat by Cirkin to cross the IEBL was viewed as extremely dangerous and destabilising. Had twenty thousand DPs attempted to cross the IEBL it would not have been unimaginable for full-scale war to have broken out again, such were the stakes that were being played in this dangerous game of bluff. Secondly, UNHRC, who were responsible for DPs as well as for refugees, would not have been capable of feeding or of providing shelter for the DPs. Aid agencies including the Red Cross and the Muslim organisation 'Merhamet' were already hard pressed to meet the basic humanitarian needs of these people in Lusci Palanka and would have found it neigh on impossible to stretch their aid to cover an additional site in Prijedor. Even if the logistics of such a move had been feasible, to support the DPs had they moved to Prijedor would have brought into question the neutrality of these agencies. Whilst SFOR was not a neutral force, it was the instrument of its political masters and nation states, aid agencies rely on their impartiality and neutrality in order to operate and maintain their freedom of movement. This may seem to the lay observer to be crass stupidity and to often lead to situations where agencies sit back and do nothing because they have 'no authority' to work. But aid agencies have no guns and one should note that in conflict situations the military actually only operate within the areas that they 'control' perhaps from time to time taking armed action to extend that area or to defend it from attack. Aid agencies however, always venture across cease-fire lines, indeed across confrontation and front lines without consideration for which side they are on. The 'humanitarian imperative' calls for aid agencies to help all those in need and not to become partisan in their efforts. Had UNHCR for example, decided to support Cerkin's threat to move twenty thousand DPs to Prijedor without the consent of that town's municipal authorities, then their action would rightly be seen as partisan. They would also have laid themselves open to accusations of supporting and encouraging further displacements since one would have to consider the question of where these Muslims were going to live? Perhaps in houses now occupied by Serbs who had similarly fled the fighting but in this case from Sanski Most, or as was the reality, from the Serb Krajina in Tudjman's unrepentant Croatia. Any influx of Muslims would force an exodus of Serbs to make room for them, but to where?

The job of ECMM was to get amongst the population, its civic leaders and industrialists and to find out what was really going on and then to report back on one's findings adding analysis and comments wherever possible. To do this the team, complete with our interpreter Sahsa, would make appointments to visit and meet with individuals during the course of the day, usually in the mornings or around mid day and then scoot back to our accommodation to 'write up' the report before sending it off to Banja Luka for onwards transmission to Sarajevo where it was cut and pasted with many others to compile the Regional Report which was sent to Zagreb and then on to Bruxelles and other European capitals. It was quite satisfying to think that our reports, or at least excerpts of them, were read each morning at the 9,00 am Situations Briefing in the Foreign & Commonwealth Office following on from the daily MI6 update. I had been taken around the elegant and newly restored briefing room one morning when I was back in London on a debriefing, and shown where our reports were discussed each morning, and although impressed with the splendour of the setting, I wondered how anyone sitting there reading our edited reports could ever be expected to grasp the complexities of the real situation on the ground. Nevertheless, from Monday to Friday we met with our interlocutors to conduct our meetings and make our reports. Depending upon where we had to travel to and the time the journey would take, we would schedule one, two and occasionally perhaps even three meetings each day. I use the term meeting rather than interview since as was quite often the case, I would have a subject that I wanted to interview the interlocutor about but they would want to discuss something else. When this happened is was quite usual to find that what the interlocutor had to say was far more relevant and up-to-date than what you had intended to discuss although you always had to be on your guard that you weren't simply being thrown off track by someone trying to deflect one's original questions. Adapting one's approach to each different meeting required a high degree of flexibility and also an extremely good understanding of the current situation, not just in the local area but of that in the entity and in Bosnia as a whole and quite often in neighbouring countries as well. Many of the ECMM monitors that I worked with didn't have this knowledge and so when an interlocutor changed the subject they could often find themselves floundering to respond to a particular statement that might well have been of great significance but the point was lost on them. To guard against this eventuality, most monitors went in to meetings with a series of around ten questions to ask their interlocutor and they deviated from these at their peril. These questions were usually prepared the night before and quite often had been 'suggested' by the RC in Sarajevo. Max relied heavily on this method and would repeatedly compile a set of bland questions such as 'what is your political platform?' or 'will you join in any coalitions with other political parties?' Such rigidity led to senseless-ly boring meetings where little rapport was ever built between monitors and their interlocutors and worse still, to mindless reports that more or less all said the same thing. Of course the reason for RC Sarajevo suggesting such a line of questioning was not just to help out floundering monitors in the field, but to make it easy for the short-term, non-expert, current presiden-cy-nominated Staff Officer in the HQ who was compiling the composite report. So long as all the field-based teams supplied the answers to these simple stereotyped questions, then the task of collating them all in to a single report was so much easier. I hated this approach as it generated stale lifeless information, which as a former military intelligence officer was an anathema to my background and training. Unfortunately Max always set the agenda and so each evening was spent first writing the report (since Max was not of the computer generation) and secondly dreaming up ten questions for the next hapless interlocutor.

Meetings were nearly always the same wherever you were in Bosnia, indeed throughout the whole of the Balkans. The more senior an interlocu-tor, the more of a show they put on. It seemed as if every office in the county had been built and equipped exactly the same regardless of its function. Traditionally one might expect to enter an office to find the tables and chairs arranged in a 'T' shape with the interlocutor sat at the head of the 'T.' We, the visitors would always sit either side of the stem of the 'T' looking up towards our host. Usually Max and I would sit opposite each other and whoever was actually going to take the lead in the meeting would place Sahsa behind their shoulder so that she could translate from behind whilst we maintained eye contact with the interlocutor. Each meeting started with introductions and then the host would always offer a drink. For the most part this was either coffee or orange juice but occasionally some form of Rakija or Slivovitz was offered. At 9,00 o'clock in the morning this was never a good idea but often it proved difficult to refuse and of course it always caused extreme offence to refuse too much. Fortunately as Slivovitz was also an Austrian drink, Max would drink our host's health whilst I pretended to do so, drinking under sufferance, as I much preferred beer to spirits. I spent two months with Max driving around the AoR meeting with a whole host of interlocutors, conducting our meetings and writing our reports. Despite the inadequacies of the system we built up a pretty good picture of what was going on in our back yard but Max and I never got to meet General Alagic together. Every time we entered the municipal building in Sanski Most, Alagic would make an excuse and cancel the meeting. Alagic knew Max and had met with him previously, so perhaps that was why we were getting nowhere fast! Max certainly had a knack for alienating people despite his ever so formal and correct etiquette. What was quite amusing was that he could actually claim to be a Yugoslav, – well as much as anyone else could these days. Max had been born at the start of the Second World War in Maribor in Styria, an area formally within the old Habsburg Empire and heavily populated with German speaking peoples (Austrians). Following the First World War however, Styria was ceded to the newly formed Kingdom of Yugoslavia where it remained until Yugoslavia's partition in 1943. Max was from an old noble Habsburg family, which somehow had managed to retain their family seat in Maribor despite Versailles. Max, the archetypal monocled Austrian colonel, had therefore found himself born in 1941 in Yugoslavia albeit once the country was partition in 1943, the city again found itself under Austrian control. Following Austria's defeat by the Allies in 1945, Maribor once again found itself a part of Yugoslavia, this time as part of Tito's SFRY and within the constituent republic, and now independent state, of Slovenia where it remains to this day. After four weeks with Max it was time for him to take some well-earned leave. Well earned for both of us that is. Max was showing the strain of working under such dreadful conditions and needed to pamper himself in some of the small luxuries of life which were sadly missing in Bosnia whilst I just needed a break from him. Max was slowly driving me mad what with his morning routine – from which he had never once deviated and with his incessant moaning and groaning. There were two things he hated most about Bosnia, apart from the fact that no one ever kept the time properly that is. One was that in every café-bar we went in to, they always played loud music, which he despised, and secondly that he couldn't find any paper napkins anywhere. He was simply obsessed with paper napkins. On every journey back from a meeting we would stop off on the way and he would go and search for some napkins and every time he would come back empty handed. He just couldn't accept that people didn't use them and that the shops didn't stock them. Finally, after more than a month of his incessant cursing I eventually lost my rag as he exclaimed in front of Sahsa 'What sort of bloody people are these that don't have napkins?'

'People who don't have bloody roofs on their houses, whose walls have been blown away, people who are dying from exposure, people who are starving to death eating one bloody meal a day if they're lucky, that's who.'

I exploded pointing to the nearest set of destroyed houses, mere burnt out shells without roofs and with missing walls yet still inhabited by families huddled around open fires burning on the floor of what was once their living room attempting to gain some warmth against the bitter arctic temperature and the snow that lay all around. Life was hard for us but nowhere as bad as it was for many of the locals and Max needed to regain his sense of proportion. Under normal circumstances no monitor would ever be left on their own in a team whilst their partner was away on leave. Usually there was a whole host of visitors and new arrivals who could move around and plug gaps at will to cover any leave periods. With Max away on leave during mid February and with no stand-in available, I was instructed by the CC to carry on with meetings on my own. This was highly unusual but the alternative was to close down, something that I didn't want to do and besides, I was determined to meet with Alagic even if Max had failed. On Valentine's day I succeeded and together with Sahsa we went to see the General in his office in the municipal building after I had used the satellite phone to call back to the local flower shop in Eastbourne and order a bunch of flowers to be sent around to Allison. Alagic was quite an imposing figure even if somewhat slight in stature. He had built a huge reputation for himself as a General during the war and like many fighters throughout Eastern Europe and Africa, had failed to relinquish his power as a war-lord once the peace had arrived. Instead he capitalised upon his status as a warrior in order to promote his civilian status, power and income during the peace. At this stage in Bosnia's post-war recovery, few members of the IC would openly state what Alagic really was, pretending instead to believe that he was a true hero and was dedicated to rebuilding a multi-ethnic country. Such naivety belied the fact that Alagic wanted to reassert Muslim domination of the area and that his views had nothing to do with equality and reconciliation and everything to do with personal power. I listened to Alagic for almost two hours, a very long meeting by any standards, and noted all his rhetoric and his vision for the future. He cleverly shrugged off any connection with Cerkin and openly invited all Serb DPs who were originally from Sanski Most to return whilst knowing full well that such a 'return' would never materialise. For this was the start of a game of grand strategy to win the support of the IC, and it was a game that he played very well. Most of the IC and especially the German government (listening to their Balkan Representative, Schwarz-Schilling) were taken in by this and similar offers calling for the Serbs to return failing to understand the intricacies of what was being played out in front of them.[102] In deed this was where the ECMM had the advantage over many others. We were not an aid agency and so all we had to do was to meet with people and build up a picture. When ever an interlocutor made a statement or a claim about anything, all we had to do to check it out was to arrange further meetings with third parties who would be affected by the claim and ask them to comment on what we'd been told. It was like investigative journalism and we had a free hand to go and speak with whom we wanted to. In the case of Alagic's claims that the Serbs could return, it was simply a matter of informing our fellow team in Prijedor and then waiting for the feedback from them on what the Serb reaction to the invitation was. In this way, teams co-operated with each other and fulfilled a useful function as an intermediary, a function that was still vitally important since other forms of contact such as the telephone were still not working between the entities. Conversely, the fact that ECMM wasn't delivering aid often hindered our work. By 1997, there were now many agencies operating inside Bosnia and each and everyone of them met with the limited number of civil dignitaries to decide upon their own priorities for the aid they offered. It wasn't long before these civic leaders became tired of all these meetings with the IC and ECMM was beginning to draw the short straw. Many interlocutors now demanded to know what you could offer them as a prerequisite for granting a meeting. Meetings with ECMM were essentially a one-way process as we were the ones gathering the information so that we could maintain 'regional stability' and 'contain the crisis.' These aims were seen to be of benefit to Europeans and not to Bosnians and so many interlocutors now asked why they should meet with us, what was the purpose and what was in it for them and their community? Responding was becoming more and more tricky as one had to explain the benefits of informing the EU so that it could make informed policy decisions on wider strategic issues, for example how to allocate Billions of ECUs of aid to the country as a whole rather than a small aid project to replace a school roof. Usually it worked but it was getting increasingly more difficult as time progressed.

To compound the routine difficulties that we were now experiencing in obtaining our meetings, there was increasing hostility across the board towards the actual Dayton Peace Agreement. Saturday 15th February, the day after my meeting with Alagic, was decision day on the final status of Brcko. The decision by the international arbitrator, Roberts Owen had already been delayed from December and as we moved in to February the situation was becoming more and more tense. Both sides began threatening each other and began moves to enhance their preparedness for war. This was getting serious especially as each side altered its military posture first cancelling all military leave, then recalling reservists to the colours and then even calling for an entity-wide effort to donate blood in case of actual war. SFOR was seriously worried and so was I. Max was away which left me on my own in Sanski Most and worse still there was good reason to believe that if the ABiH and VRS were to take each other on in another war, that one of the main trusts of any offensive would be down the Sanski Most – Prijedor fault line. As was so often the case, I was yet again in the wrong place at the wrong time. On 11th February an extraordinary meeting of the JMC placed a ban on all military training and exercises confining both militaries to their respective barracks. I rechecked my evacuation orders and drove the route to the SFOR base at Kammengrad, which would have been my first port of call, had the bullets started to fly again. In the event, such measures were not needed and on the 15th Roberts Owen announced the conclusions of the arbitration panel, '... providing for the interim international supervision of Dayton implementation in the Brcko area for not less than one year.'[103] The decision meant that the arbitration panel had failed to find an acceptable final solution to the problem of Brcko and that for at least the next year the IC were to be responsible for ensuring that the GFAP was complied with within the area of Brcko. To achieve this, the panel called upon the OHR to establish an office in the town, which was to be headed up by a Deputy High Representative who would hold the appointment of the 'Brcko Supervisor.' On 7th March, the first Supervisor, US diplomat Bill Farrand was appointed to run Brcko and my former boss, colleague and now friend Ian McCleod; ex 1 PARA, ex ICFY, ex ECMM and now OHR was later appointed to be his deputy.

With Max back from his leave and the Brcko crisis put on hold for another year, we set about conducting our routine meetings trying to get a real feel for what was happening in our area. Although based in the town of Sanski Most, our AoR was quite large and covered an area that extended northwards half way to Prijedor where our boundary with team Bravo-1 was at the IEBL, southwards as far as the major town and municipality of Kljuc and westwards almost but not quite as far as Bihac which was run by our other team, Bravo-4, and to its South, Drvar which was controlled from Mostar of all places. Apart from Kljuc, the area included the municipality of

The High Representative: *Carl Bildt visits the municipality of Kljuc during his tenure as the High Representative.*

Bosanski Petrovac and the unfortunate Serb municipality of Ribnik. I say unfortunate since Ribnik was the only Serb area within our AoR and was almost completely landlocked by Muslim controlled municipalities. At first glance on a map (which was no doubt how the diplomats in Dayton had come to create this anomaly) Ribnik was situated adjacent to the Serb dominated area of Mrkonjic Grad and with it formed part of the notorious 'Anvil.' But what the diplomats had missed was that within the municipality of Ribnik was the small Serb settlement of Drinic which was only reachable by road or track, via Kljuc. This gave the Mayor of Kljuc, Amir Avdic, another former ABiH ranking officer now in civilian guise, and his police the power to extract revenge on the people of Drinic for any restrictions of movement (RoM) enforced by their Serb counterparts in Mrkonjic Grad. Travelling from Bihac to Jajce thus became impossible in a tit-for-tat war of RoM played out by the authorities of both municipalities stifling trade, reconstruction efforts and any hopes of reconciliation. In Drinic itself, where the population was not actively involved in the misdemeanours played out by their brother Serbs from Mrkonjic Grad, life in the sub-zero temperatures had already become unbearable with little or no food supplies, humanitarian aid, or means of heating reaching them. During the war, the Muslims had stolen all the farm equipment from Drinic (the Serbs had also stolen all the logging trucks from Kljuc's sawmill) and so now it was impossible for the Serbs to even feed themselves properly. We visited the settlement several times and then highlighted their needs to all the other aid agencies working in the area at the regular Monday morning 'inter-agency' meetings that we attended in the Hotel Sana each week. We managed to secure the immediate delivery of food and hygiene packs and also the subsequent delivery of 'sporets,' a 'range' style wood burning cooker cum heating stove that most houses in the outlying settlements and villages used to heat their homes and cook their food. The next problem was to tackle the issue of the RoM on the main road through Kljuc. The UNHCR office at Bihac was taking the overall 'regional' lead on this one and they wanted to gather together representatives from all the municipalities involved. We had met with Dmitrovic, the Deputy Mayor of Ribnik and Amir Avdic, the Mayor of Kljuc several times to address this issue and had actually managed to get them together for the first time in five years to talk with each other in a small motel on the Eastern end of Kljuc called the Hotel Lovac (hunter). We had had to personally collect and deliver Dmitrovic to and from these meetings in order to guarantee his safety otherwise he would never have taken such a bold step and come. But it was worth it as Avdic agreed to control his police and ensure the FoM for the people of Ribnik so long as he received a reciprocal guarantee from the police in Mrkonjic Grad. To achieve that we had to go outside of our ECMM AoR, something that was not allowed. In deed we had already overstepped the line because our remit was only to report, something that I was beginning to find rather abhorrent when one was witnessing such suffering on a daily basis. I felt that ECMM needed to evolve further and use its local knowledge to help guide and direct other aid agencies such as we had done with Ribnik and also to actively get involved with the population and to mediate where necessary such as we were proposing to do now. But our remit was only to observe and report, that's what 'monitors' did and that was what we were, monitors. I felt that we were missing an opportunity to develop and that had we taken a more proactive role that our problems securing quality meetings would have disappeared. Unfortunately the mission didn't evolve in this direction and officially we had to content ourselves with the belief that our reports were doing some good by influencing the decision-makers within the EU corridors of power. Sadly I never had such misconceptions and I remain of the opinion to this day that most of what I wrote, my analysis and recommendations, never so much as tweaked an eyelid in Bruxelles or London. Instead I was to continue for the next eighteen months to overstep the mark and to use my authority and position as the EU's representative on the ground, to speak up and influence what was happening around me rather than to remain the passive onlooker. I am sure that I was not alone in such a stance as many monitors, especially those British ones who had the knowledge and experience of the region, did far more than simply observe. But sadly such people were in a minority and far too often the ECMM kept its reports and opinions to its self, adding little value to the overall peace process. Nevertheless Max and I decided to play with the UNHCR and we made all the necessary arrangements to get both Avdic (who was now the one crossing in to 'enemy' territory) and Dmitrovic to a round table meeting in Mrkonjic Grad. I acted as secretary to the meeting, which lasted all day in a freezing cold room in a hotel just above the town. The discussions were for the most part totally mindless and off the point with speaker after speaker banging on about the injustices and crimes inflicted upon them during the war. No one wanted to move forward, just to relive the past in order to justify their current stance. It took a lot of effort by all the IC present especially the UNHCR and IPTF representatives but eventually an agreement was reached to guarantee the FoM through the Anvil and therefore also through Kljuc for the people of Ribnik and Drinic.

Bosanski Petrovac was a major DP settlement. Most of the Muslim DPs who had settled there had come from Prnjavor to the Northeast of Banja Luka, where team Bravo-3 was located. In addition to its own Mayor Gospodin Hidic, the municipality of Bosanski Petrovac also boasted a Mayor of 'Prnjavor in-exile.' This was the traditional way that the DP populations organised themselves, complete with their own municipal authorities 'in-exile.' Whilst Prnjavor was renowned for its pre-war shoe industry, the main industry in and around Bosanski Petrovac was connected with timber. In the town itself, there was a huge sawmill. Indeed there were sawmills in Kljuc and the burnt out remnants of an excellent furniture factory in Ribnik both testament to what was once a thriving timber industry in the region. Nowadays things were not quite so rosy although the mills were still operational – of sorts. In Bosnia timber, which was an ample natural resource, was also a commodity controlled by the black market along with coffee, petrol and tobacco. Most of the timber used to supply the sawmills of Kljuc and Bosanski Pertovac came from the vast nearby forests that paralleled the country's border with Croatia and more specifically from the area of Ostreli just North of Drvar. Despite the American belief that the idea of a Muslim-Croat entity was a going concern, the Federation in this neck of the woods was looking decidedly un-Federal. The Bosnian Croats controlled the whole area paralleling their 'mother country' – Croatia, and had continued to deploy their own Army, the HVO in the area. The HVO and the ABiH weren't supposed to exist anymore as they were supposed to have been joined together to form a Federation Army, hence the American Train and Equip Programme. But despite the American dream, the reality on the ground was totally different. The HVO had a main garrison located in Drvar and from here had deployed troops forward to Ostreli to stop the Muslims from Bosanski Petrovac from felling timber in the area. We reported the situation back to ECMM but no one took any notice. For the Staff Officer in the RC it was just yet another report from a team in the field. Although the significance of what was going on here was explained to them, they failed to understand the severity of the issue. Here was a concrete example of where the Federation wasn't working and further more an example of where the HVO was being used independently to support the economy of the Bosnian Croats. This was not what Dayton was about and something should have been done about it at the highest level to remove the HVO threat and sanction the Bosnian Croats for their infringements of the GFAP, but of course nothing was. 'Conditionality' it seemed, only applied to the Serbs. But this was not where the issue stopped. The Bosnian Croat stronghold of Drvar was a nationalist hotbed that also depended upon timber for its livelihood. There was also a huge sawmill in Drvar and the mill provided the town with its main source of employment. Drvar, like Mrkonjic Grad was outside of our AoR and so we couldn't get in to the town but it didn't take long to dig around elsewhere to find out what was happening there. Drvar was at the centre of an international scam centred on Croatia proper with the strings being pulled by President Tudjman himself. When the Croatian Army (HV) launched its attack to rid the Krajina of its ethnic Serbs in Operation Oluja (Storm) on 4th August 1995, it had temporarily crossed in to this area of Bosnia aided by the Armija's 5th Corps under General Dudakovic sweeping South from Bihac towards Knin. The Serbs had fled and towns such as Bosanski Grahovo had been raised to the ground. With the HV back on Croatian soil and the ABiH withdrawn to fight towards Mrkonjic Grad and Sanski Most, the HVO filled the vacuum on the ground although Croatian control of the area remained extant. The Croatian leadership needed its black market revenue and Drvar was a profitable source of income that they were not going to let go of. This control was exercised through the auspices of the main Croatian and also Bosnian

Croat – nationalist political party, the HDZ. The municipal authority in Drvar was controlled by the HDZ and as was always the case in Bosnia, the ruling party appointed its own directors to run the principal industries in the municipality. In this way, the sawmill in Drvar was run by a set of HDZ cronies all of whom personally benefited from the arrangement. The actual director however was non other that the then current Croatian Minister of Defence, Susak. By exercising control of the Hv and the HVO, Susak ensured that only the Bosnian Croats felled the local timber and that all the timber went to his mill for processing. The Muslims were being squeezed out and the profits from the organisation not to mention a lot of the timber, was going directly to Croatia (without being declared to the Bosnian authorities and the due payment of customs tariffs) and in to the waiting hands of Susak and his boss, Tudjman. What I found most disturbing however, was not the fact that such a scam was being perpetrated at the highest levels of government, but that my own HQ did little or nothing with the information which I was feeding them. For the most part, my reports were being ignored or simply filed and at best they were being edited with small excerpts being cut and pasted into a composite regional level report. Moreover, it wasn't a forgone conclusion that what was used to compile the composite reports was necessarily the most relevant piece of information. We tried everything to ensure that we got our message across including the official solutions which were firstly; to flag up the important parts of a report with bulleted headlines, rather like a newspaper headline, which we placed at the top of each report; and secondly to write separate detailed 'Special Reports' on specific matters of interest. Finally and perhaps the most depressing, was the realisation that even if we did see a detailed composite regional report, at the end of the day we still had to ask ourselves, what was going to be done with it? We never ever had any feedback, no one ever said we've passed this on to the High Representative or to the OSCE HOM or to a specific government for example. Ringing up to find out was pointless as we were always fobbed off and besides we were supposed to channel such requests for information through our own CC in Banja Luka and not to call Sarajevo direct. Unfortunately the CC rarely got anywhere either. It was a most depressing situation as I began to realise that the job was totally thankless as the hierarchy in Sarajevo and Zagreb simply wanted to move paper up the chain of command and not to get involved with actioning anything themselves. They really didn't want clever arses in the field digging up all sorts of issues that half of them hadn't the knowledge to appreciate let alone to deal with. If I was going to continue to dig deep, uncover the reality of the situation in my area of Bosnia and to write detailed analysis of what was going on calling for action by the higher level and appropriate bodies, then all I was going to do was to earn myself a reputation as a pain in the arse. What ECMM wanted was someone who just went out each day, did one or two interviews with anybody – who cared actually who? – and filed a short concise report that didn't overload the staff in the

HQ. So, in part to ease my conscience and in part to spite the hand that fed me, I decided to continue to be a pain in the arse. In the CC in Banja Luka however, my efforts were appreciated and as reward for sticking it out with Max for two months with only one or two incidents of note between us, I was asked by the Dutch HCC, Marinus, whether I would take on the challenge of becoming the next team leader in the notorious hard-line Serb stronghold of Prijedor. Naturally I jumped at the challenge.

16

Prijedor

I had packed my bags again and left them in the team accommodation in Sanski Most where Max and the new Spanish monitor replacing me looked after them until I returned from my fortnight's leave back with Allison and the children in the UK. I had missed Harriet's birthday by one day but had been lucky enough to be there for Allison's. Nevertheless by the first day of spring I was back in Banja Luka and was being briefed by Philip Bailey, the new (British) Operations Officer who had taken over from David. I could have stayed the night in Banja Luka but had still not forgotten the last time that I had stayed there on New Year's Eve and so chose to continue on to Prijedor and meet my new team as soon as possible. The team had been through quite a few changes lately. The original plan had envisioned that when Roberto, the Spanish team leader had left, that Richard, the second team member, would move up on promotion and become the new team leader. An Austrian monitor had already been sent to the team to take Richard's place as the second team member and he had already been in place several weeks by the time I arrived. To add to the numbers of 'Men in White,' there was also a team driver, a Slovak named Roman. With my arrival there would have been five monitors in white and so Peter the Austrian was moved to a new permanent slot in Bihac leaving me two weeks to learn the ropes from Roberto before his final departure. Technically speaking of course, Richard should have moved up to take the team leader slot but under the new plan this was not going to be the case. Richard, a very amiable French Army Officer who I really liked and respected, took the whole thing in his stride and gave me his total support in my efforts to learn the ropes. In addition to Richard, Roman, and me, the team's interpreter Dijana also lived in the accommodation as she did not have any family in Prijedor to live with. Dijana was a Krajina Serb, originally from Zagreb and although she was regarded as ethnically Serb, she was born and bred in Zagreb and still held a

Croatian passport despite the fact that it was now worthless. She and her family were now stateless and living as official refugees inside Bosnia where they had fled to during the mass flight of the Krajina Serbs during the Croatian Army's 'Operation Flash' in 1995. Dijana and her family had been just one family amongst that sea of thousands riding on their red tractors that I had personally witnessed clogging up the Zagreb – Belgrade motorway during the winter of '95. Now her family had settled in Novi Grad, the nearest point to Zagreb in the whole of Bosnia. Neither parent had yet managed to obtain work, and so Dijana's sister worked as a dental assistant whilst Dijana brought in most of the family's income courtesy of her ECMM salary. I had already met the team on many occasions and so I quickly dumped off my belongings from the flight in Prijedor and then set off imme-diately to Sanski Most to collect my other possessions. Moving in was like a breath of fresh air. Far from being worried and intimidated by the fierce rep-utation of the town, I welcomed the change of scenery and the far more relaxed atmosphere that surrounded the team. The accommodation was well sited too as it was located at the start of a small cul-de-sac which also con-tained a small restaurant and also both the SFOR CIMIC[104] house and the OSCE Field Office. This made for a very sociable and tight knit community of internationals all of whom were able to work well together. It was really an ideal situation. The town of Prijedor itself had not suffered in the war and there was little to no evidence of any destruction whatsoever. This however could not be said of the surrounding suburbs. Two main suburbs, Kozarac to

Kozarc: Once a prosperous Muslim area, this town was almost totally destroyed and ethnically cleansed. Those Muslims who managed to escape the three camps fled mainly to Sanski Most where they remain in the surrounding areas awaiting an opportunity to return.

Kozarc: The ruins of the main Mosque.

the East and Hamberine to the West had been largely Muslim settlements before the war and here the Serbs had done their worst. Both settlements had been completely destroyed and every house burnt, looted and then totally gutted of every fixture and fitting right down to the electric wiring and window frames, in a deliberate and systematic act of ethnic cleansing. This ethnic cleansing was not as many people and politicians believed, a manifestation of a brutal and primitive war, but was a deliberate policy and military strategy to achieve the political and ideological objective of creating a united and ethnically pure homeland for the Serbs. That had been Milosevic's aim from the outset when he engineered the 'oppression of the Serbs' in Knin where it had all started back in 1991. Now both of these settlements remained abandoned and devoid of life testament to his policy of driving out non-Serbs to make way for the Greater Serbia he desired so much. Not satisfied that their destruction had been total the first time around, the Serbs had gone back to Hamberine on the first anniversary of Dayton and planted landmines in the corners of each gutted structure. Over ninety detonations had brought the reinforced concrete tumbling down, further reducing these gutted and destroyed homes to mere piles of rubble about one metre high. Regardless of whatever progress the politicians were making around their negotiating tables, the message from the people of Prijedor was clear, they did not want the Muslims back, ever. In contrast, the centre of town was untouched by war and just like Banja Luka was another human-sized place, although slightly smaller than Banja Luka with a pre-war population of about one hundred thousand. And unlike Sanski Most, the place was awash with small café bars and restaurants and even boasted an excellent night club, the Pacific, a small cinema, a museum and a theatre. There was a definite café culture about the place which suited me fine as café bars were always an excellent source of low level information and a great place to get to grips with and to understand the politics and cross cultural issues of the area. All in all, despite the very real security threat and its infamous nature, Prijedor seemed a much nicer place to life and work, so long as you stayed alert and knew what you were doing that is.

Sadly the ethnic cleansing and destruction of the two suburbs of Kozarc and Hamberine were not Prijedor's greatest crimes. What happened to the Muslim populations that had once populated these suburbs far exceeded any of the horrors of the war seen elsewhere. As early as 1992, the Serbs had started rounded up the civilian Muslim population in the areas that they controlled and, in complete contravention to IHL, had interned them in a number of concentration camps in Northwest Bosnia. Three of these camps were located in and around Prijedor. The closest to the town was in a small ceramics factory located within the city limits on the main road out to Banja Luka at a place called Keretern. The brick walls of the factory and its ovens

Keretern: The ceramics factory on the Eastern edge of Prijedor town; one of three concentration camps highlighted by Roy Gutman

had the same sinister connotations as the last Nazi extermination camp that I had visited a few years previously in Oranienburg just North of Berlin. The second camp was located in a small school building in an outlying settlement called Trnopolje, which lay to the Southeast of the town and on the main East-West railway track that past through Prijedor. It was here that Roy Gutman working for the American magazine Newsweek and an ITN

television crew had first stumbled across evidence that the Serbs were com-
mitting atrocities and beamed back their pictures of bare-chested emaciated
prisoners standing behind barbed wire fences. But it was the third and final
camp that was the most notorious. The camp was located in the village of
Omarska, again Southeast of Prijedor on the same railway line as Trnopolje
but nearer to Banja Luka. Omarska was the site of a large iron ore mine and
part of the principal industry of the area, which was the state-controlled
Ljubija Mining Company. It was here that most of the prisoners ended up
and many of them were beaten, tortured, raped and finally killed, their
bodies supposedly being dumped in to the mine excavations. It was a dirty,
dark and sinister place to drive around even now several years after these
events had taken place. But we were not the only ones showing an interest
in what had gone on here in the past. Investigators from the ICTY War
Crimes Tribunal in The Hague were literally digging and diving around in
the water filled pits in an attempt to recover any bodies as evidence of these
crimes. And, even more quietly, certain members of SFOR were now beginning to take a more active interest in these crimes as well.

The problem with Prijedor was that its café bar society typified the Serbs
as a whole. The people were obsessed with their own suffering and really did
believe that the whole world was against them. Sadly the action of the IC to
date with only two per cent of the aid reaching the RS, seemed merely to
reinforce this belief and did little to break the mould. As such, all the prominent Serbs we met with continued to cite examples of their own suffering
without any hint of self-criticism. For what it mattered to them, Keretern,
Trnopolje and Omarska might never have existed, since all any of my new
interlocutors were concerned with, was the historic and continued suffering
of the Serb people as victims of other peoples' misdemeanours. Whilst you
could find evidence of regret for the wasted years of the war and the
economic collapse that the war had brought, there was never any evidence of
any remorse or guilt for their own crimes, simply justification. Of course
there were differences between the different interlocutors we met, not
everyone we met in Prijedor was a hard-liner and I think this was the genuine
difference between them and the Muslims and Croats I had met with previously, the Serbs did not sing with one voice. The Serbs were essentially
honest even if they were bloodthirsty. It might not be any consolation, but if
a Serb was going to shoot you, then you would certainly know about it
because he would have told you so to your face. That was not what I had
found to be the case with the other ethnic groups, they were far more street
wise, saying one thing, namely what you wanted to here like 'DP and refugee
returns are welcome,' and then going off and doing the complete opposite. If
you were going to be stabbed by a Muslim and especially a Croat, then I felt
that it would be in your back. This was a strange discovery for me since most
of the IC in the early days preferred to work in the Federation, presumably
because the Muslims and Croats were seemingly far more co-operative and
amenable. But it was also because the IC was genuinely afraid of the Serbs

who for most of the war had been portrayed in the Western media as the bad guys. Of course the reality was that there were always going to be good guys and bad guys on both sides. The Serbs of course represented the largest single group and had the ways, means and opportunities to commit the most crimes. Statistically therefore, it was inevitable that in such a brutal war the Serbs committed the most crimes. Nevertheless I now preferred to work with them since if I had to deal with someone particularly nasty, then at least I knew about it in advance. That said of course, Prijedor was still full of bad guys. On Monday 7th April, after a two-week handover from Roberto who had left that morning on his end-of-mission, I had asked Dijana to set up a meeting for the next day with the Mayor and the Executive Board of the Municipality in order to introduce myself to the town's leaders. This was to be my first meeting as team leader and so I was quite nervous. I instructed Richard to open the meeting from our side and then to introduce me to the assembly. I would then contrive with some form of introduction about myself and round off with some spiel about how I hoped that the co-operation between the municipal authorities and ECMM would continue, not that there had been much of that to date. Prijedor's Mayor was a small, dark, squat and slightly balding man named Miomir Stakic. I have been in the presence of some very high powered – commanding people with dominating personalities and quick tempers before, but I had never before felt the huge sense of unease as I did when I met Stakic for the first time. Stakic radiated more than just power, in my mind he personified evil. He had piercing dark eyes and a penetrating icy stare that could see right inside you and his presence dominated the boardroom creating an aura of tense unease that permeated his own staff and not just the team. Looking back in to his eyes and meeting his icy glare was like looking in to a body without a soul. It was if I had come face to face with evil and I remember a cold shudder passing through my body as I forced myself to remember that I was a diplomat and regardless of what murky past lay concealed behind those eyes, I had to deal with this man as the 'lawful' representative of the town. Stakic welcomed us in the traditional manner and ordered coffee, and then Richard introduced me and I gave my prepared spiel all the time thinking that I just wanted to get out of there. There were about ten other officials in the room, all members of the Executive Board or Municipal Assembly and when I'd finished, the President of the Municipal Executive Board, Gospodin Malic asked me, 'You have been in this country of ours for eighteen months now and have met many people and worked in high places, so tell us, why is the world against the Serbs? The question reflected the Serb mindset and their genuine belief that this was indeed the case. To simply say that such a notion wasn't true would firstly have been stretching the truth a bit too far since most of the world did and probably still does see the Serbs as the bad guys. Secondly, to reply that the answer to their question lay at the doors of Omarska, Trnopolje and Keretern and that they only had themselves to blame was hardly a diplomatic way to further professional co-operation between the municipality and the EU whom I represented. But to try and suck up to them and placate their fears perhaps attempting to show that my team and I were 'on their side' was inherently wrong and fraught with dangers too. For sure, in the short term it might have made my life easier and far safer to say that we were fully behind them. But ECMM was neutral with a deliberate policy of mixing team nationalities for this very reason and to say anything of this nature would have been grossly unprofessional and would have condoned the genocide that had been conducted by several of Prijedor's leading dignitaries. I knew enough about the Serb mentality of truthfulness and frankness to use the same cultural mindset on them now. I told Malic, 'You are your own worst enemy. You bring it on yourself so don't blame others because it's all your own fault.' I could see the faces beginning to redden and Dijana's looks of exasperation as she couldn't believe the insult she had just translated. I continued to tell the truth as I knew, or rather had gambled that in the end, the truth however unpalatable would win me their respect. I told them, 'You are too honest, it is in your nature to tell the truth. If you don't like me or what I'm saying, you'll tell me so, politely but you'll tell me. This is your downfall. In negotiations you argue in front of the cameras, why – because you want a deal that you can sign, one that will work, one that you can and will implement. You're stupid. The others will smile and sign in front of the cameras and look the good guys but when the cameras have gone, then they argue even though they've previously signed and agreed to everything. Then they don't implement what they've signed, who cares, what does the IC do about it? Nothing of course!' I cited the 'returns process' as a concrete example and how the Serbs were seen as obstructing (which they were of course) and yet for example, the Federation had agreed for Serbs to return to Sarajevo. The reality on the ground however, was that none of the measure to ensure that Serbs could register their intent to reoccupy their properties in Sarajevo or measures for the authorities to evict illegal tenants, had ever been put in place. Malic and the rest of the Board had been shocked by my frankness. I had managed to criticise both sides for delays and obstructions albeit the Serbs for obstructing before reaching an agreement and the Muslims and Croats for obstructing afterwards. The effect was still the same of course, namely obstruction, but I had answered Malic's question and I had earned their respect, which was everything. The rest of the meeting went smoothly with Stakic informing us of his fears about Cerkin and Dudakovics' latest statements about returning to Prijedor and Banja Luka respectively.

Although we lived and worked in Prijedor, the municipality was in fact only one of five local municipalities that were within my AoR, the other four being Novi Grad, Srpski Kostajnica, Dubica and Bosanski Gradiska. As spring arrived, the team settled down in to a pretty slick routine of meetings throughout our whole AoR. I would pick a theme based on what was happening at the time, whether this be an event in the RS, the Federation or even in Croatia or Serbia. In this way I could challenge and question the local politicians, civic leaders and industrialists with matters and issues that would affect them gauging their reaction to national or international events. It was fascinating work made more so by the fact that you had to be 'diplomatic' throughout. It was one thing for an investigative journalist to criticise an interviewee's remarks perhaps stating that their idea was pure fiction and wouldn't work, and quite another for us to do so. In short we couldn't and never did criticise no matter what rubbish we were being fed. Instead you had to learn ways of saying that you thought something was rubbish without actually saying it. For example, I was once told by Drase Stojancic, the Director of the Ljubija Mine that, 'The mine will soon be fully functioning and will then start selling ore to its previous customers,' something which I knew to be simply bollocks. So instead of commenting as such, I asked him, 'Of course I know you won't be selling your ore to Zenica because the foundry there (in the Federation) isn't functioning yet, so that means that you must be selling it to Smederavo?' Smederavo being the only other pre-war customer that the Ljubija mine had, and which unfortunately for them was located South of Belgrade in Serbia proper. As was so often the case with many interlocutors, his answer to such a leading question was, 'Yes.' I continued the game, playing within the rules and bounds of politeness with my next question, 'As there's no direct road links and the quantities of ore in question would be far too much to transport by road anyway, I presume that you've going to transport the ore either by rail or barge?' Again, his answer was 'Yes, of course.' Finally, albeit still with the utmost courtesy of course, I went in for the kill, 'Of course the River Sava (the only waterway route that he could possibly use) isn't yet navigable to barges as it hasn't been dredged for six years and now it's littered with floating mines. But I suppose you sorted that issue out with the Croats when you got their agreement for your trains to cross in to Croatia and use the (only) rail line in to Serbia?' 'Well actually we plan to speak to the Croats very soon and open negotiations about the railways' came the reply from the rather embarrassed director who knew he'd been caught out but had somehow managed to retain a token amount of his dignity. Having made my point I'd move on and change my line of questioning. Whilst I enjoyed playing this game it actually entailed a lot of homework and preparation before each meeting. One could either except an interlocutor's remarks or one could try and verify them and doing the latter required an awful lot of knowledge about what was going on around the place, and as the previous example serves to illustrate, at least a basic knowledge of the politics, geography and industries of neighbouring countries too. But my main area of interest was not socio-economic and neither was it specifically connected to war crimes, human rights or the security situation albeit I did pay these careful attention. My main interest was to research and investigate the political situation and to uncover and highlight any injustices or any obstruction to Dayton. Prijedor and its surrounding municipalities provided me with ample material for my interests. Whilst industrialists were busy telling me that they were essentially European in outlook and culture and not at all like their 'peasant' brethren in Hercegovina

and in the Southeast of the RS, their politicians were preaching an unrepentant message of hard-line rhetoric aimed against both the Federation and the
IC, and not necessarily in that order! By far the biggest and most influential
political party in the area was the Serb nationalist party of Karadzic, Krajisnik
and Plavsic; namely the SDS. Close behind the SDS were firstly the extreme
left wing 'Socialist Party of Republika Srpska' (SPRS) which was the Bosnian
off-shoot of Milosevic's own Socialist Party of Serbia (SPS), and secondly the
extreme right wing 'Serb Radical Party' (SRS) led by its charismatic president
Nikola Poplasen. What was encouraging however was that unlike in the
Federation at the time, there were also a whole plethora of other smaller
parties offering a less xenophobic range of policies. As spring progressed I had
my team repeatedly tour the AoR visiting all these parties, small and large in
each of the five municipalities to learn about their political platforms and
agendas, and their commitment to Dayton. The period coincided with the
time when all political parties, independent candidates and coalitions had to
reregister their intent to contest the next elections and so these meetings
proved to be an invaluable source of information about the politics of the
moment. On 6th March, the OSCE announced that the municipal elections
were to be postponed again and confirmed that the new date for these elections would be over the weekend 13-14 September, one year after they should
have originally taken place. By late April all the parties, independent candidates and coalitions had registered and on 2nd May the OSCE announced that
in Bosnia as a whole, ninety-three political parties had applied to run in the
elections, forty-five of them registering for the first time. Four days later the
PEC fully approved eighty-two of these and conditionally approved a further
five. Between 5th May and 16th June the electorate again registered themselves although this time the error that had caused the initial postponement –
that of being able to vote in a third location, had been rectified. On 12th June,
just before the deadline, the OSCE announced that the period of voter registration would be extended until 28th June in a bid to encourage the many
thousands who had not yet registered, to do so.

A prerequisite for 'free and fair' elections was the freedom of movement
of all voters so that they could travel safely to and from the polling stations
and cast their votes. This was essential for those wishing to return to their
original municipalities to cast their votes in person rather than to tender an
absentee ballot where they now lived as DPs. Although Max and I had made
progress ensuring the FoM across the Anvil and through Kljuc, RoM was
still widespread across Bosnia. Perhaps the single largest cause of RoM
remained the entity Police forces who continued to stop and search vehicles
at will, just as their colleagues had been doing in the Anvil and in Kljuc. In
an attempt to curtail the Police practice of stopping vehicles of a different
ethnic group (and the physical assaults and random fines that accompanied
this practice) the OHR directed that the entity Police forces must now
register all their checkpoints in advance with the IPTF. The IPTF would
then 'authorise' those it deemed necessary and also randomly supervise

them on the ground. This measure slowly began to lead to progress but all three Police forces still continued to operate illegal checkpoints despite the IPTF issuing non-compliance certificates on the respective Police chiefs. In the early days, one of the main excuses offered up by Police chiefs defending their illegal checkpoints was that they were searching for war-criminals and that many of those dragged from their vehicles, arrested and beaten were in fact guilty of war crimes. Nevertheless, this 'excuse' was not legal justification for the continued abuse of human rights that was going on despite the best efforts of the IPTF. The situation was brought to a head with the illegal arrest by the Federation Police in Bihac of a prominent Serb politician, Milo Marceta for alleged war crimes. Marceta was not a war criminal, but he was a thorn in the sides of the local Croats in the Drvar region where he had been a respected municipal figure. His arrest and continued detention despite the best efforts of the OHR to have him released were an affront to the IC and so the IC decided to raise the stakes. During the 'Rome' meeting of the 'Contact Group,' the PIC decreed that entity Police forces were not permitted to arrest anyone suspected of war crimes. The decree, known as the 'Rules of the Road' even prohibited entity Police forces from arresting persons indicted for war crimes unless that indictment had been issued by the ICTY in The Hague. This in effect stopped entity courts acting in tandem with their Police to issue trumped up indictments in order to justify false arrests. From now on, the IPTF checkpoint policy would be rigorously enforced. Only duly authorise checkpoints would be permitted and these could only arrest suspected war criminals if their indictment had been issued by the Hague which was where they would then have to stand trial. To reinforce the IC's determination to overcome continued Police intransigence, the IPTF and SFOR commenced joint patrols on 26th May and forcefully removed all illegal checkpoints they came across.

Continued RoM did not just affect peoples' ability to vote, it affected their ability to return to their pre-war homes and livelihoods. In and around Prijedor and Sanski Most, a cynical game was being enacted by the politicians, which affected the return of both DPs and refugees from all ethnic groups. The game was complex and few understood what was really happening. Some manifestations were clear to see although visual progress was not a sure indicator that all was well as perhaps too many believed. For example, in Kozarac many houses were being repaired and there was evidence of humanitarian aid finally trickling through to the RS as more and more gutted houses began to spring new roofs. This apparent success however, hid much of the reality. All the aid organisations knew that to be successful, the returns process had to be 'sustainable.' In practice, this meant that to only rebuild homes was insufficient as livelihoods had also to be rebuilt. In Prijedor the main employer had been the Ljubija mine and despite the optimistic claims of its Director, it wasn't about to reopen and provide for full employment, at least not for another five years or so at any rate. Those promoting a quick and speedy returns process to Prijedor thus conveniently overlooked livelihoods.

There were perhaps two reasons for this. One was that to the IC and especially the American engineers of Dayton, success was measurable by two factors, one being successful democratic elections at all costs regardless of whether the country was ready for them. The other being successful returns. Both premises are sadly and wholly wrong and worse still can in fact engender further conflict if forced through too soon driven by an outside nation's desire for a quick exit strategy. The second reason was that many nations simply wanted to get rid of their 'temporary refugee' populations at home and especially in the case of the German Government, just wanted to back load these people as soon as there was a roof to put over their heads. Visually then, Prijedor's suburb of Kozarac was slowly being rebuilt but no one was addressing the employment prospects of these Muslim returnees, in fact no one was addressing the employment prospects of the Serbs who lived there either. This in itself caused a second problem as the Serbs from Prijedor watched humanitarian aid finally reaching the RS, after over a year without receiving any of significance, only to see it now spent totally on the Muslims. This without doubt renewed hostility between the ethnic groups and did nothing whatsoever towards reconciliation. Many shrugged off such a criticism stating that it was Muslim houses in Kozarac that were destroyed and so why should any effort be put in to rebuilding Serb livelihoods? This position of course ignores the fact that many of the Serbs living in Prijedor at the time were themselves DPs from parts of the Federation and uniquely, were also Refugees from Croatia and in neither of these places were Serb homes being rebuilt for their return. But animosity was not just limited to between Serbs and Muslims. Muslims themselves were aggrieved with each other. Many of those who had survived the horrors of Omarska or perhaps had lost family members and friends during the war were now returning to their homes struggling with what little 'in-country' aid was available. This contrasted sharply with many of their neighbours who as refugees had fled the war to Europe and beyond and had suffered little by comparison except the loss of their property. Neither had these people fought during the war yet now they were returning to Kozarac unharmed and armed with the trappings of the decadent West. Many refugees drove back to Kozarac from Germany in their second hand Mercedes that they had bought after years of living in the West. Many more had satellite dishes, so many in fact that they began to sprout up like mushrooms almost before the roofs were complete. And all came with a wallet full of DEMs – a last cash bonus from a grateful German Government given to those that were leaving voluntarily and before they started to expel those who didn't want to leave. To those who had stayed in Bosnia and who had fought and lost everything, these refugees returning from Europe with their flash cars, satellite dishes and bulging wallets represented a different face of Bosnia and one that was bitterly resented. Thus, whilst things looked like they were progressing, there was much maligned beneath the surface. But perhaps the greatest misconception about the whole process wasn't to do with the distribution of humanitarian aid or the rebuilding of houses and livelihoods. It was a political issue concerned with why the goal of a 'two-way returns'[105] process wasn't achievable in and around Prijedor. To understand this and the game that Alagic and Stakic were playing, you had to step back and understand both the Muslim and the Bosnian Serbs political strategy as well as Prijedor's pre-war history. The Muslims had fought the war to maintain a single united multi-cultural and supposedly multi-ethnic Bosnia. To them, the wholesale return of Muslims to their pre-war homes in the RS was vital in achieving this goal. In theory, the return of Serb DPs from the RS to their pre-war homes in the Federation was also desirable if there was to be a single unified Bosnia i Hercegovina. Conversely, the Bosnian Serb war aim had been to create an ethnically pure state uniting the Serbian areas of Croatia and Bosnia to Serbia proper – the notion of Pan-Serb unity. Following Dayton, the Serbs attempted to maintain this aim by actively seeking to dissuade Serbs from returning to their pre-war homes in the Federation. Likewise, and perhaps far more difficult to achieve, they also wanted to stop Muslims returning to the RS and diluting their ethnically pure entity. This then was the actual political position that both sides represented. In reality however, the Muslim claim to want to encourage Serb returnees was not at this stage being facilitated on the ground but then neither did the Serbs admit to a policy aimed at hindering their own people leaving and stopping the Muslims from arriving. Added to this backdrop one also had to consider the unique role of the Krajina Serbs. These people, like Dijana my interpreter, had fled from Croatia where they had been born and bred as Croatian citizens and were now taking asylum in Bosnia as official refugees. There were perhaps one hundred thousand of them in and around Northwest Bosnia, all in the RS and mostly in the area close to the Croatian border known as the Posavina. Tens of thousands had settled in and around Prijedor and along with the thousands of Bosnian Serbs DPs that had also settled there, the town – despite the numbers of Muslims that had fled to the Federation – now supported a bigger post-war population than pre-war. With a burgeoning population, two destroyed suburbs and a wrecked economy, Prijedor was in a sorry state. Only with all these pieces in place could one begin to understand the game that was being played out. Alagic wanted investment and to get it he convinced the IC that he fully supported the two-way returns process. It was fairly easy for him to do so since the population of Sanski Most was roughly the same as it had been during the war. It was just that it was made up differently now, since Muslims that had fled southwards had replaced its Serb population, which had fled northwards to Prijedor during the war. Alagic was happy to support the cause of those DPs in Sanski Most who wanted to return to Prijedor. It fitted in with the pre-war aim of a single nation and it would relieve his municipality of the burden of supporting these people. Further more he knew that the process would never be two-way since he was well aware that the Serbs were discouraging their own kind from ever leaving the RS. Alagic knew that the population of Sanski Most could only shrink whereas the already swollen

population of Prijedor stood only to grow further. With no risk to his municipality, Alagic proclaimed his 'open city' status duping the IC and obtaining
his funds. On the other hand the mayor of Prijedor could make no such
claims. Prijedor's population was now bigger than it had been before the war
but only some of this influx had come from the Federation. It wasn't about
simply swapping two populations, it was about swapping three because the
Krajina Serbs also had to be brought in to the equation. This population had
to move back to Croatia in order to make way for any returning DPs but no
one from the IC was interested in their plight, indeed even OHR wasn't
interested since its mandate was in Bosnia and one had to deal with Tudjman
and Croatia to get any movement on the Krajina Serbs. Faced with these
refugees remaining in situ for the foreseeable future and the reluctance of the
Bosnian Serb DPs from the Federation to leave the RS, it was little wonder
that Prijedor's mayors refused to entertain the idea of the mass return of
Muslim DPs to the municipality. There was simply nowhere to put them and
no hope of any livelihood to sustain them. Nevertheless, whilst turning a
blind eye to Tudjman's intransigence, the IC continued to pressurise and
penalise Prijedor's authorities for not evicting Serbs from Muslim homes and
thus facilitating the so-called, two-way returns process.

17

The Drive for Reform

As Prijedor was situated in the Northwest corner of Bosnia, it was relatively close to the ECMM HQ in Zagreb and the relative delights and luxuries, which that city afforded. On some weekends we worked but thankfully most were now becoming relatively free and it was therefore quite normal to take a trip up to Zagreb once in a while in order to call in on one's delegation, find the Irish Bar down town in order to partake in a smooth Guinness and to call in at the American PX at the UN base, Camp Pleso, which was situated close to the international airport. On my first such trip, I had gone with the whole team from Prijedor including Dijana and we had taken the shortest and most direct route there via Novi Grad and through the Krajina. On subsequent trips we mostly took the longer but quicker route via Banja Luka and Gradiska up to Okucani and along the motorway, the opposite of the route that I had taken (cutting out the Sarajevo leg) when I had first arrived, back in early January. But the first trip had been by far the most interesting. At the time there had still been snow and ice on the ground that had added to the surreal eeriness of what we witnessed. Having crossed the bridge at Novi Grad[106] and entered Croatia, we soon passed through the now divided town of Kostajnica, half in Republika Srpska and half across the River Sana in Croatia, and within minutes had left all signs of life behind us. This area had not been fought over during the war, instead the Croatian Serbs living here had simply fled in front of 'their own' advancing Army. Two hundred thousand ethnic Serbs had fled the Krajina leaving behind them their homes, their livelihoods, their traditions and their history; indeed everything that couldn't be loaded on to the back of a tractor and trailer. Historically, these ethnic Serbs had settled along the Croatian border with Bosnia in order to fight for the Austro-Hungarian Empire defending it against attack from the mighty Ottoman Empire that had already claimed Bosnia. In Serbo-Croat, 'Kraj' means 'end' and in this instance is used to signify the end of the Empire or its frontier. It was these warrior-peasants who had 'defended Christendom against the Turks' throughout the centuries and without them the Habsburg Empire would not have lasted as long as it had. Croatia had been an integral part of that empire and owed its existence to these ethnic Serbs who had long been granted full Croatian citizenship. But the break up of the Former Yugoslavia also broke these ties. Milosevic had tried to unite these Krajina Serbs with the Bosnian Serbs to forge a united Pan-Serbian state. Tudjman had not forgotten the Serb uprisings that Milosevic inspired although he had conveniently forgotten his own oppression, and so in 1995, with the secret backing of the Americans who had used MPRI contractors (including my old friend and ex-ICFY Operations Officer, Bob Freeman) to help train and prepare his Army, he launched two offensives – 'Storm' and 'Flash', to drive out the remaining Serbs and ethnically cleanse the Krajina. Attacking a wholly civilian population, Tudjman's Army met with complete success as the Serbs fled in front of his advancing forces. The Krajina Serbs, unlike the Bosnian Serbs did not have an Army of their own with which to counter the Croatian onslaught and so could offer no resistance.[107] The effect was dramatic. For over an hour we drove through village after village, all devoid of life yet completely intact. Unlike in Bosnia, there was no destruction. The houses were beautiful, not the normal modern German-style whitewashed chalets that littered the Balkans, but old traditional Swiss-style wooden farmhouses with hand painted gables and window shutters. But they were all empty. There was no one in the street, no cars, no signs of life whatsoever. The whole region was abandoned as if they had all woken up in the middle of the night and had left en masse. It wasn't so much a ghost town, but a whole ghost region and the fact that it was all perfectly preserved and looked to all intent and purposes like Switzerland, made it all the more surreal and something that I will never be able to forget.

By late June, ECMM had finally made sufficient preparations to enable itself to step in to line with all the other missions in the Balkans, that is to say, it was ready to move its HQ from Zagreb to Sarajevo. To mark the occasion, the HQ had planned a non-stop 'marathon run' between the two capitals with pairs of runners running in relays. The whole thing was well organised but as with most pleasurable events organised by ECMM, mainly involved HQ personnel as nobody else could really be spared. Such division was always a real bone of contention between the field and HQ staff. Practically every time I'd been to Zagreb whether at the weekend or when flying in or out from leave, I had seen flyers stuck up on notice boards in Hotel-I, canvassing for day or weekend trips to Hungary or Slovenia for example. These were never, never put out to monitors in the field despite the ability for many of us to take part in these activities had we known about them in advance. Keeping with tradition, my team had been tasked to work rather than partake and we were thus made responsible for facilitating the smooth crossing of the border at Novi Grad. Actually this was quite a simple task although it involved a lot of running around speaking to Police and customs officials not just in Novi Grad but also in the Croatian part of Kostajnica. Life was fairly difficult for several days since the Dutch Staff Officers in the HQ still insisted on receiving full daily reports from meetings with 'proper' interlocutors and refused to accept that driving to and from Kostajnica, holding meetings with the Police and then the customs, actually took up most of the day. Likewise, we were all 'invited' to attend an official ECMM reception in Sarajevo on the Friday to mark the grand opening of the new HQ. For once, we had been invited to something but no one knew where the new HQ was, not even me and I'd lived in Sarajevo for a year! The UK Delegation weren't interested in faxing us a map and worse still the Dutch again insisted that we had to file a report on the very same day as the reception. So on Thursday 26th June, my team and I dutifully sat on the Croatian side of the border at Novi Grad to await the runners and help smooth their way across. They arrived just before mid-day, just enough time for us to drive back to Prijedor and file an actual report, albeit one from a meeting held the previous week and kept 'in the bank' for just such an occasion. The next day, we repeated the farce. Not wanting to be totally screwed up by the Dutch who still insisted on a report from all the field teams, and with the traditional lack of support, sympathy or even interest in our situation from the UK Delegation, we filed another report from 'the bank' and set off on the four hour drive to Sarajevo hoping to find the HQ and arrive before the runners did at mid-day. Fortunately we arrived in time and had the opportunity to enjoy a few beers whilst waiting for the runners to arrive. The HQ itself was very plush and much nicer than the OHR office that I had created eighteen months ago, although it was situated quite some distance out of town. To be honest, the building was too plush and having poked my head inside, it was quite sickening to see the completely new and networked computer equipment when one compared it with the struggling 386DX – Windows 3.11 machines that we were using in the field. The occasion also marked the end of the Dutch Presidency which had had its ups and downs but had certainly achieved something, what with the move of the HQ. The next Presidency fell to Luxembourg who sadly were not represented in the mission and so the Dutch simply continued the motion on their behalf. There were a few changes as the 'six-monthers' all went home but many of the Dutch including the HOM stayed on to serve for twelve. In Banja Luka however, the HCC – Marinus, was replaced by a new Dutchman – Hans Koks. Koks was a Colonel in the Dutch Special Forces and thought that he was still serving with them rather than leading a civilian diplomatic mission comprised of many different nationalities and cultures. As such he was a particular difficult person to work for and one with whom I was later to have a seriously clash of personalities.

Back in Prijedor the team continued with its tasks monitoring the post-war recovery process and meeting with civil society. The team had changed again as Richard had departed and been replaced by a less amenable French

Captain named Alan. Alan, like me was a paratrooper but he was one of those who lived and breathed the role. He was not terribly sociable and initially found it hard to fit in to the small tight knit international community in Prijedor. Over time he found his feet and once he'd re-found his sense of humour, went on to do an excellent job as team leader in Sanski Most following his promotion and move there. A Major from the Dutch transport corps named Henk also joined the team. Henk was huge and quietly spoken for most of the time although he was quick to warm up after a few beers. He was also excellent at keeping Roman in check and ensuring that he properly maintained the team's Land Rover, something that he could not be completely relied upon to do on his own. Whilst the new team was bedding itself in, the political situation in the RS was fast developing. Krajisnik and his cronies in Pale were still not playing ball with the IC nor playing a full part in Bosnia's fledgling 'Joint Institutions.' In deed, although Dayton permitted each entity to establish and maintain relationships with neighbouring countries, such external relations were supposed to be secondary to internal, inter-entity relations. But Krajisnik wasn't interested in building relationships with the Muslim-Croat Federation and instead he looked eastwards towards Serbia to establish 'Special Parallel Relations' with Milosevic's regime. On 28th February, Krajisnik had met with Milosevic in Belgrade and signed an agreement linking the RS to the FRY. The Serb agreement was similar to that signed between Croatia and the Federation back in December 1995, however in April 1996, Bildt had voiced his concerns over that agreement to the UN Secretary General.[108] Of concern with this new agreement was that the RS and FRY were negotiating a joint customs union between themselves, something that the RS as an 'entity' and not a sovereign state, had no right to do. Secondly, the fact that the agreement had been signed by Krajisnik who was the RS Member of the Bosnian three-member Presidency, was considered unconstitutional since any agreement between the RS and the FRY should have been signed by Biljana Plavsic, the RS President. A customs union with the FRY would have linked the RS to Yugoslavia forever and would have been the death of a unified Bosnia i Hercegovina. Bildt warned Krajisnik that the agreement on Special Parallel Relationships between the RS and the FRY was, as it stood, unconstitutional and if not revoked would result in, '... a severe reduction in planned economic aid and an increase in social turmoil which would, ultimately, be to their own disadvantage and that of the people that they purport to represent.'[109] As part of the war time ruling SDS caucus, the RS President, Biljana Plavsic wasn't totally innocent of war crimes as a result of her activities when she had been Karadzic's trusted lieutenant and she was therefore well aware of what was happening in Pale.[110] Despite being the RS President, her power base remained weak. Nevertheless she identified more with her people than she did with the hard-line rhetoric of Krajisnik, who was still becoming rich from his import-export scams at the expense of his hard-pressed population. With Bildt's threat of even worse to come, she decided to force the issue. If Krajisnik and the SDS wouldn't listen to her reasoning and comply with Dayton, then perhaps they'd listen to the people, if only the people knew what was really happening that is. The problem she faced of course, was that the people had no idea what was really happening, just what the SDS was telling them, and that was that their misery was all the fault of the IC and that the Serbs had to stay united if they were to be saved – 'Samo Sloga Srbina Spasava.' Plavsic had already moved her Presidential office to Banja Luka leaving both her own Parliament and Krajisnik in Pale, although he arguably was best placed there since he was the Serb representative to the Bosnian Presidency which was located in Sarajevo. The fact that the RS National Assembly (RSNA) remained in Pale was a misnomer that shut Plavsic off from her own government. Plavsic first wanted to reform it and then to move it to Banja Luka, a city she viewed as being a far more appropriate seat of government. Banja Luka also represented a far more respectable side of the RS. Pale was tainted as the war time location of the Bosnian Serb Republic from where Karadzic and Mladic had conducted the war. Banja Luka on the other hand was seen as far more respectable and closer to Europe. The only thorn in the side of this argument however, remained the town of Prijedor, which had been tainted by the three concentration camps and remained a hard-line SDS strong hold. In part, the reason that Prijedor had remained so intransigent and belligerent in the face of changing attitudes and opinions, was that the war-time leadership had not been replaced since municipal elections had still not yet taken place and were not scheduled to do so until mid-September. Most sinisterly, two of the commanders of the Omarska concentration camp not only remained at large, but remained in public office. Dr Milan Kovacevic had been part of Prijedor's Municipal Assembly during the war and had run Omarska along with Simo Drjaca who had been the town's powerful and brutal Chief of Police. Kovacevic was now practising as a doctor and was the 'respected' director of Prijedor's hospital. Drljaca on the other hand had become involved in an incident with IFOR back on 16th September 1996, and had been removed from his post. One of my friends, known simply to us all as 'H' and who was now working at the OSCE Field Office just down the road from my own accommodation, had been serving in IFOR at the time and had been part of that incident. 'H' was a junior NCO in 21 SAS[111] and had been attached to a small unit known as AMIB.[112] Originally AMIB had been made up wholly from British JCOs[113] all of whom had been SAS. It was a hang over from the days when General Sir Michael Rose had commanded UNPROFOR (Rose had previously commanded 22 SAS) and used the SAS as his personal eyes and ears on the ground rather than trust the UN. Now AMIB and the JCOs were separate organisations and both had 'internationalised.' In '96, 'H' and his team had been outside the Police station in Prijedor when Drljaca had appeared with his close protection team all sporting long-barrelled weapons, something explicitly forbidden under Dayton. What ensued can best be described as a Mexican Stand-off with

'H's' patrol demanding that Drljaca's men hand over their weapons, Drljaca refusing, 'H's' team making 'ready,' Police reinforcements from the station surrounding 'H's' team and 'H' then radioing for some armoured fighting vehicles to back him up and show precisely who had the most fire power. Drljaca had backed down in the end and had consequently been relieved of his command. That said, no one in Prijedor including the IPTF, were in any doubt as to who remained in charge of the Police in the town; Drljaca.

In April, as things were beginning to hot up, I had gone to celebrate Easter in the Orthodox Church in town and found myself standing next to Drljaca. It was a coincidence that we ended up together, but at the same time others were beginning to take a deliberate interest in his and several of his associates' activities. Throughout the following months I had no idea that Drljaca was in fact the centre of attention. Indeed I thought all the interest was in Stakic who I'd long suspected of being on the ICTY 'Wanted-List.' Members of AMIB kept offering to buy me beers in town only to rather amateurishly sneak in a question about his daily routine. To be truthful I didn't really have much to do with Stakic and so I was never of much help although I certainly appreciated the Ministry of Defence buying the beers. In Belfast I'd spent many hours sat up in a reconnaissance helicopter as it hung stationary in the air above the city. I'm sure that to most people, such activity was inconsequential but in reality it was an essential part of the intelligence war against the terrorist. Small as they might seem, these helicopters were bristling with electronics and optical devises that permitted us to see, record and even relay in 'real-time' (live), what was happening on the ground, day and night. With gyroscopically stabilised binoculars, image intensifiers, thermal imagers and powerful video cameras, the British Army was capable of maintaining a high altitude 'stand-off' position overlooking a target area and conducting detailed surveillance for hours without alerting the target. I had never seen such activity in Bosnia before but during May and June, the Army Air Corps was active off to the South of Prijedor almost every day. The 'combat indicator' was obvious to those who knew what to look for and who knew what to deduce when they'd seen it. Something was brewing. I didn't know what, but I knew enough to keep my mouth firmly shut.

In June, the war of words between Presidents Plavsic and Krajisnik started to really hot up. Plavsic wasn't getting anywhere in her attempts to reform the leadership of the SDS who remained intransigent to her pleas to cease their corrupt activities and to start to govern the people fairly. Plavsic decided that she had no other option but to go public with her plea and enlist the help of the people she was trying to help. In a public campaign aimed at discrediting her political opponents and winning the support of the IC, who remained her only ally, she branded the SDS leadership traitors accusing them of, '... getting rich whilst our sons died [in the war].' The response was swift and decisive. Krajisnik and his cronies banned the President from talking to the media and denied her access to Serb Radio

Television (SRT), the state controlled TV channel of the RS. Plavsic counter attacked trying to gain access to independent newspapers and TV channels where she could, but the SDS leadership had effectively closed down the elected President of the RS. Plavsic responded in two ways. Firstly she took to the streets and staged a series of open air, public political rallies in towns across the whole of Republika Srpska. Secondly she attempted to enlist the help of the IC, help that should have been rapidly available to exploit this one off opportunity to reform the RS leadership from within their own ranks, something that if successful, would have been acceptable to the Serb mindset, which mistrusted anything foreign. Instead, the IC missed this politically strategic opportunity and blew it demonstrating once again just how ignorant of the Serbs we had remained despite years of dealing with them. Plavsic's own Interior Minister, Dragan Kijac, was obstructing her at every turn. On 27th June she suspended him from his duties and embarked on a presidential trip to London to seek the support of the British Government. Throughout this period, the British Government had direct access to the ECMM reports coming out of CC Banja Luka being written by Philip, the UK Operations Officer, and to my own reports coming out of Prijedor. Yet despite the information at their fingertips, the British Government were the ones who would eventually take action that very nearly succeeded in driving a final nail in to Biljana Plavsic's coffin and her efforts to reform the Serb entity.

On 29th June, Plavsic departed London on the return stage of her trip. As neither Sarajevo nor Banja Luka airports were functioning, Plavsic flew to Belgrade where it was planned for her to be collected in her official cars and driven back to the RS. Both Milosevic and Krajisnik knew that they couldn't just kill her, those days had long past, now that the IC was taking an active role in Balkan politics. But they needed to put a stop to her activities as she was harming their lucrative 'business' activities and eroding their power base. Milosevic had Plavsic arrested at the airport and detained her just long enough to amply demonstrate that she was indeed powerless to protect herself should he decide to remove her from the political scene. When she was released, all was not over. She drove back to the RS in her official motorcade and crossed the FRY-RS border at Bijeljina where her own Police acting under the orders of the suspended Kijac promptly arrested her for a second time. She was powerless, or so Kijac and Krajisnik thought. She was again released and this time flew the last leg back to Banja Luka in a VRS helicopter and not an SFOR one as was later reported on the SRT News in an attempt to further discredit her in the eyes of her own people. But Krajisnik and kijac had miscalculated Plavsic's resolve and far from putting an end to her campaign, her arrest sparked nothing short of a constitutional crisis in the RS.

The following day, Monday 30th June and only three days after the move of ECMM's HQ to Sarajevo, all hell erupted in the RS as both sides slung accusations at each other. Krajisnik denied that Plavsic had been detained and then accused her of being a stooge of the IC and taunted her for running to SFOR for help and flying back to Banja Luka in one of their helicopters. SRT media fell firmly behind the SDS leadership in Pale despite one of its two editorial offices being located in Banja Luka, in fact in 'Banski Dvor,' the same building as Biljana Plavsic's own offices. On 1st July the SDS demanded that she leave Banja Luka altogether and return to Pale. Two days later Plavsic trumped them all and on 3rd July she issued a Presidential Decree ordering the dissolution of the RSNA and called for new parliamentary elections. The RS was in chaos and the IC left struggling to keep abreast of developments as the constitutional crisis grew each day. The OSCE had been preparing to stage the municipal elections that had been postponed from the year before and now it was facing a situation where the only elections it had managed to conduct; namely those in 1996, had just been declared null and void throughout half of the country. On the face of it, it was a disaster. But actually it wasn't anything of the sort, it was a fight over democracy, accountability and moreover about freedoms; freedom of information, of assembly and of speech. Plavsic had attacked the old corrupt order and exposed it for what it really was. When it wouldn't bend to her demands she had sacked it. Now all she had to do was to get her message across to the people so that they could see the old guard for what they really were and vote in new leaders to replace those that she had sacked. But achieving this was never going to be easy. The SDS still controlled the media and despite the RSNA being dissolved, the Deputies and Ministers continued to wield power and hold the nation's purse strings. On 4th July, the RSNA sat in session in Pale in complete defiance of Plavsic's orders and continued to conduct business as if nothing had happened.

Plavsic took to the streets once again and staged rallies in the Western RS. In Bijeljina, SRT provided coverage of her rally but showed pictures of the crowd well before the event incorrectly stating that, 'Few if anyone had turned up to listen to her and her discredited stories.' On the ground the truth was quite the opposite, her campaign was gathering momentum and the SDS were running scared as more and more people wanted answers to her accusations of corruption against the ruling caucus. The SDS smug with their hold over the state's institutions, put the matter to the Constitution Court to decide whether Plavsic had the authority to disband the RSNA. As the Court sat, Plavsic moved to consolidate her political power in the Northwest RS and announced that she would stage a rally in the heartland of the hard-line SDS. At 7,00 pm on Tuesday 8th July, Plavsic intended to stage a rally in Prijedor.

The atmosphere in Prijedor was electric and when I informed the CC that Plavsic was going to come to the town, they instructed me to evacuate. The very idea appalled me but to be on the cautious side I made the decision to attend the rally in civilian clothes and not in our customary white ice cream suits. Team Bravo-2 in Sanski Most also sensed the occasion and asked my permission to come up for the night, off-duty of course. I agreed. To ensure that we were gauging everything as correctly as possible, I was spending as much time as possible out on the streets and in the local café bars talking to as many people as possible. Official interlocutors only tell you so much and usually what they thought you wanted to hear. Now it was critical that I knew the truth however unpalatable that might be. As events began to unfold the team had been meeting with the Police and the municipal authorities quite frequently but on the morning of the 8th, I decided to go one stage further and meet with a liaison officer from the local VRS 5th Brigade ominously based in Omarska. I wanted to sniff around and check out whether they intended to get involved in the proceedings at any stage. I didn't expect a direct answer to any of my questions on the subject but what I was able to do was to look around the barracks and see what was happening there for myself. Fortunately, all was quiet.

By late afternoon Prijedor was ablaze, literally. Hundreds of rubber tyres had been positioned around the streets and set on fire filling the air with dark acrid smoke. It looked quite sinister and might have put us off attending the rally if it wasn't for the fact that the actual people on the streets were in a carnival mood. It began to rain fine persistent drizzle and so we took our umbrellas as we ventured out in to the town. The place was packed with expectant people including families with small children – a reassuring sign if you were half expecting trouble. Plavsic never stood a chance of denting the SDS's support in the Southeast of the country as the rural peasants that lived there had long believed the SDS rhetoric. It was vital therefore that she won over Prijedor first, as it was the only municipality in the whole of the Northwest that stood in her way. In military parlance, Prijedor was 'Vital Ground.' If Prijedor fell to Plavsic then she would hold the reins in the Northwest, an area covering approximately one third of the RS but containing two thirds of its population and almost all of its wealth and industry. Once politically secure here, the Southeast would slowly fall in a domino effect or at least it would be out-voted. The concept should not have been lost on the military as it smacked of cold-war doctrine but sadly the American CIMIC team situated right next door to my own accommodation hadn't been doing its job properly. In fact because AMIB and the JCOs had all been running around falling over each other in an attempt to gain some useful intelligence on Stakic and the other PIFWCs, the CIMIC team had been sidelined and had been solely occupied in running small scale humanitarian 'projects' instead of getting to grips with what was really happening on the ground and how that might interface with the military.[114] Consequently the British military, to whom the CIMIC reported, would deal Plavsic and the peace process an almost fatal blow in her most crucial hour.

Amid tight security from the local and military Police, the rally, dubbed 'The Rally of Truth', opened at 7,00 pm with a local poet, whom I recognised from the town's theatre group, reciting some poetry (another apparent contradiction in the Serb psyche – a cultural obsession with poets such as

Njegos and more recently Ivan Ducic, yet brutal in their outlook on life). By now the crowd was huge, almost as big as it had been when the VRS had recently celebrated 'Army Day' in Prijedor's main football stadium. Dudurovic, Radic and Lazarevic, the leaders of some of the main opposition parties spoke first and then Plavsic took the stand to a tumultuous applause and told the crowd that the SDS had been robbing and cheating them

President Biljana Plavsic: *Biljana Plavsic, the President of Republika Srpska, in Prijedor's main sports stadium during the Bosnian Serb Army's celebrations on 'Army Day.'*

throughout the war. That Karadzic, Krajisnik, Klickovic, Kalanic and Kijac had been lining their own pockets whist their sons had indeed died on the front line. She asked them, 'Is this what your sons died for? Did your sons lose their limbs for these criminals?' and she told them that, 'The greediness for money undermines them like a sickness ... the Serb people have been fighting for freedom, they have not been fighting for one narrow circle of men who are ripping the skin off their peoples' backs.'

To most gathered there on that cold wet summer's night, it was the first time that they had ever heard a politician making such accusations. The crowd was truly shocked by what they'd heard. Plavsic had got her message across and some difficult questions were now being asked of Krajisnik and his cronies.

I spent the next day writing up a detailed report of what had happened at the rally and gave my analysis of the events of the previous night. Without doubt, it had been a turning point in Bosnian history. Plavsic had raised the stakes and taken the game to the SDS. It was crucial that she succeed if Bosnia was ever to be truly united and the nationalists defeated. I wanted to gauge the reaction of the local SDS but they wouldn't agree to meet me. The local party President, Savanovic refused my calls and even Marko Pavic, a leading SDS member and the director of the local PTT with whom I had a good working relationship, was not available. The SDS were on the run and were working out their future strategy. By the end of the day, Plavsic's lead over the SDS was reinforced by the Constitutional Court in a fudged ruling that found in her favour. The Court stated that, 'Until such time as the Court can come to a final judgement on the constitutionality of the President's decision to dissolve the RSNA, all enactments by state organs are suspended.' That meant in practice that even if the RSNA continued to sit in defiance of the President, any laws that it passed would not be considered legal. Plavsic was well on the road to victory and with it to reforming Bosnian Serb politics forever. She had spoken to the people throughout the RS and they had wanted to listen. Even in Prijedor the people had turned out in their thousands (despite what was broadcast on SRT) and had come to learn the truth. They were prepared to listen and not to blindly follow the nationalist rhetoric. But the nationalists had several unlikely allies, ones that Plavsic could never have predicted; General Angus Ramsey, 22 SAS and the British Government!

18

10 July 1997

The small recce helicopter had done its job well. Targets had been designated, intelligence had been collected, collated and analysed. Small teams of SAS had been deployed from Hereford and had been given their final briefings in theatre before the strike went ahead. I had seen the preparations but had kept quiet. I trusted implicitly in my own side, in the forces that I had been a part of for fifteen years of my life. I believed that the military was subordinate to the civil power and that no military action would ever take place without first considering the civilian consequences. I believed that my reports were being read in London, that somewhere someone was taking an interest in what I was saying. I was wrong. I was risking my life being in Bosnia gathering human intelligence (Humint) and in the end no one was taking a blind bit of notice. So why the hell were they paying me? At 9,30 am, in a brilliantly well executed and co-ordinated military operation, teams from 22 SAS simultaneously struck at two targets, Milan Kovacevic who was on duty in the hospital, and Simo Drljaca who was out fishing with his son by a lake just Southeast of the town. In what may have been an on-the-spur decision by one of the soldiers rather than a deliberate act of policy, the unit taking Kovacevic used a Red Cross parcel to bluff their way in to the hospital and reach him. In doing so they broke International Humanitarian Law through the improper use of the Red Cross Emblem; it was like using a white flag of truce to trick your enemy in to falsely believing that you had surrendered. To many it appeared trivial and compared to what had happened at Omarska it was, but technically it was still nevertheless a war crime and it laid SFOR open to unrelenting accusations of unlawful arrest. Within minutes of the strike, Kovacevic was whisked away in an unmarked white Nissan and taken to the American camp 'Eagle Base' in Tuzla from where he was flown in a C130 Hercules to The Hague. SFOR had successfully arrested its first ever PIFWC. Drljaca wasn't so lucky. At the same time as Kovacevic was being seized at the hospital, five helicopters and several Armoured Personnel Carriers swooped-in on him and his son whilst they were out fishing in a river close to the village of Gradina just outside Prijedor. Both he and his son had been armed, as was expected, and had drawn their weapons on the SAS team that attempted to arrest him, firing and hitting one soldier. It was typical Serb bravado and a fatal mistake. Drljaca was instantly shot dead. His son was seized and taken all the way back to The Hague before finally being released and returned to his family. SFOR was delighted with their two successes, but there may well have been another target that morning. At exactly the same time as the other two teams were striking at Kovacevic and Drljaca, a third so called JCO Team arrived at the main offices of the Municipality without an appointment asking to see the Mayor, Stakic. For some reason, Stakic wasn't there that morning and the JCOs left without waiting. Stakic remained in the municipality for several days, refusing interviews with the IC although he continued to take telephone calls. He immediately convened an emergency session of Prijedor's 'Council for Civil Defence' and made several statements on local TV and Radio placing the blame for what had happened on 'outside elements of the IC and SFOR.' Stakic called for the people of Prijedor not to trust the IC although rather interestingly he also told them not to retaliate against the IC in Prijedor as we, '...had not been part of the operation.' What then happened was that Stakic, clearly fearful for his own safety and believing his name to be on the list of sealed indictments, fled the town. Stakic was never again seen in Prijedor and it was widely rumoured that he had most probably fled to the relative safety of Greece, which interestingly was both a member of NATO and SFOR.[115]

No one outside of the British SFOR HQ at Ramici on the outskirts of Banja Luka, had been informed about SFOR's intention to arrest two, perhaps three PIFWCs, and only those military personnel actually involved in the operation would have had any idea of what was going on. Restricting the amount of information available prior to an operation is quite normal under such circumstances and normal military units that would have usually patrolled the area, in our case a Czech paratroop battalion, would simply have been told to 'stay out' of specific areas until told otherwise. The civilian components of the peace process, that is to say the international diplomatic missions such as ECMM and OSCE as well as the UN and all the small NGOs and charities that were working in the area, usually referred to by the military as 'tree huggers' would have been regarded with total suspicion. SFOR could never have told us about their intentions because we would have all reacted differently to the information and ultimately compromised the operation and endangered the lives of the soldiers involved. Sadly however, and as is all too often the case with aid workers, no one seamed to care about endangering our lives. The SAS had arrived, done their business and departed within minutes. They were fully armed and as was the case with Drljaca, had used their weapons to defend themselves. SFOR should now have been concerned with ensuring our safety but instead were more concerned with their own (force protection) and any resulting backlash that might come their way. Quite what they envisioned I really don't know, perhaps they thought everyone from Prijedor would get in their private cars and drive to Ramici to attack the barracks there. Needless to say that never happened, instead the people of Prijedor took their protests on to the streets. More specifically, my street.

Such was the secrecy surrounding the operation, and of more concern, the total lack of communication after it, that we were still unaware of events as late as mid-day. In fact, we never received any official notification or account of events until such time as we met with General Angus Ramsey to vent our frustrations eleven days later, and that was already far too late from a personal security point of view and because we, as representatives of those who had carried out the action, had already been called to account by the town's authorities to explain what had happened and why. The first I knew that something had happened was when I came out of my scheduled meeting with the SPRS, the RS branch of Milosevic's own Socialist Party of Serbia. I had arranged to meet a local Serbian girl from Omarska called Mirjana in one of Prijedor's bars at mid-day on a 'blind-date.' One of my old employees, a Muslim girl called Amra from OHR in Sarajevo, had asked me several months previously to try and find an old school friend of hers. Before the war, both Amra and Mirjana had lived as next-door neighbours in Omarska but thankfully Amra and her family had left there before the war and moved to Sarajevo. I had thought it quite nice that Amra still wanted to trace Mirjana after all this time and despite the reputation that Omarska and its Serb population now had. Using 1991 census records and the updated voter registration records that were loaded on to several of the OSCE laptops, I managed to trace nearly four hundred Serb families throughout the region with Mirjana's family name, Beric. After much narrowing down of options I managed to find the right family and confirm that she was in deed Amra's long lost friend. We had arranged to meet as a matter of courtesy and so that I could update Mirjana on Amra's whereabouts and the like. Just before the meeting, Mirjana called the accommodation and cancelled. She was very nervous and said that it was too much for her to risk being seen with any 'internationals' right now. I asked her what she meant and it was only then, from a Serbian girl in Omarska who had seen the helicopters fly over her house and had heard the shooting take place, did I learn what had happened that morning.

The paratrooper in me was delighted that 'two-two' had got in there and produced the goods first. That really was something and yet again showed the world just how good the British Army really was.[116] On the other hand the political analyst in me was screaming blue murder. What on earth did Ramsey think he was up to? Was he stupid or did he simply not have the correct intelligence assessments and comprehend that his actions might wreck all the political achievements that Biljana Plavsic had realised so far and risked so much to achieve? I couldn't believe that the military had con-sulted the new High Representative, Carlos Westendorp before carrying out the raid, as I knew that Bildt would never have allowed the operation to go ahead at such a delicately balanced point in time.[117] Plavsic had the SDS on the run and the people were falling in behind her but now the British, the very people she had travelled to London to see and gain their support, had stabbed her in the back. What SFOR had inadvertently done was to rein-force the Serb mindset. The Serb belief that only their unity would save them was dramatically reinforced and graphically illustrated by Drljaca's death, which played straight in to the hands of the SDS. Here was ample proof that the whole world was against the Serbs and was not to be trusted. Plavsic's reform campaign was instantly discredited, as one that wanted to ally itself with the IC and take the RS in a direction away from the ideal of Pan-Serb unity. Plavsic had risked her own professional career and her own personal safety in an attempt to take on the hard-liners. She had circumvent-ed their obstruction, ignored their threats, bypassed the SRT blockade, taken to the streets and even dismissed her own Government. After months of campaigning she had won the tentative support of the Constitutional Court and had won the hearts and minds of the people of Prijedor, the town that held the key to denying the hard-liners their remaining support in the Northwest. Within thirty-eight hours of her rally in Prijedor, Ramsey had literally taken the ground from beneath her feet. News was starting to come in and I phoned the OSCE Field Office and spoke to the Head of Office, a Dutch girl named Jolanda Van Dyke. Jolanda had also just heard and was equally shocked. Those of us who lived and worked in Prijedor were not taken in by the headline success that this action would undoubtedly generate; we knew what the reality was. We had been working in and amongst the town's Serb civil-society for months trying to bring about the changes that would lead to reconciliation and lasting peace. We knew that bringing war criminals to justice was an integral part of that process, but what we didn't understand was why now, and why here of all places? After all, SFOR and IFOR before them had taken no action against PIFWCs for the previous eighteen months apart from the Han Pijesak incident that is. If SFOR was supposed to support Dayton, then I couldn't think of a worse thing to have done. It was all wrong – the place, the timing, everything. The best chance Dayton had of succeeding in the RS at the moment lay with Plavsic and her reforms. She might well have been responsible for war crimes and corruption during her time in Pale during the war but now she was the best hope that the IC had of getting rid of the Serb nationalists in Pale that were obstructing Dayton at every turn. Regardless of the military imperative to arrest some PIFWCs, it was politically expedient at present to support Plavsic and that is what we should have been doing and not under-mining her. I took my team across the street to Restaurant Mont, and was joined by Jolanda and several of her office colleagues and also by Nita, the local UN Civil Affairs officer who worked along side the IPTF giving them their political advice and analysis. We all managed to fill in the gaps between our stories and a fairly good picture of the morning's events emerged. There were two immediate concerns that bothered us though. The first was wondering what the security implications were going to be; after all we knew that the Serbs were not going to attack Ramici but that they might attack us. Secondly we were concerned over the political fall out both in terms of the local politics in Prijedor and in terms of national politics and Plavsic's reform campaign. Far from rejoicing, we were seriously concerned but there was also one other aspect that complicated matters. 'H' and I were the only Brits in Prijedor and both of us had military backgrounds, 'H' as a TA soldier with 21 SAS and me with the regular Army as a paratroop Major. It was quite possible that the two of us would be singled out for retaliation because of our nationality, a prospect which was made more probable in the days ahead when the British press started to print pieces on the raid stating that 'for several months, undercover SAS troopers have been spying on their [Kovacevic and Drljaca's] movements working out their daily routine and planning the operation.' We were the only Brits in town and many already suspected both of us as being more than just ECMM and OSCE monitors, an unfounded assumption. We left the restaurant having decided to report in to our respective HQs and then to keep each other regularly informed of events. We did not yet want to evacuate but the prospect of rapidly needing to do so in the near future was not far from our minds.

After lunch, I instructed my team to start to pack all their surplus kit away in their bags and to have an escape pack ready just in case we needed to 'bug-out' in a hurry. As I reported in by phone to Philip at the CC in Banja Luka I got Henk and Alan to look at the coax cable that went from the INMARSAT up to the satellite antenna on the first floor balcony. All the communications cabling had been put in professionally by the ECMM support staff but leaving in a hurry was not something they'd considered at the time. Consequently there was now a jungle of wires all firmly pinned down to the window frames and to the outside of the building that would have taken hours to untangle and pull free if the need had arisen. If we had to bug out in a hurry, then we would have to leave things behind by necessity but I was determined that the Satphone was not going to be one of them. Ten minutes in to their task, Henk and Alan came back in. They looked pretty nervous as Henk told me, 'I think you'd better have a look at this!'

He directed me to look out the front window and not to come out the door, which was just as well. It was now only some five hours since Kovacevic had been snatched and Drljaca killed but a mass demonstration had already been organised and had marched through the town picking up people on its way. Its destination was our accommodation and by the time that it arrived there, there were several hundred demonstrators in the procession. Packed in to the small street between our front garden and Restaurant Mont, a hundred plus people look quite formidable especially when it's you they're shouting at. As we'd been doing admin tasks and climbing around the outside of the building, none of us were in our 'whites' anymore but instead were wearing tracksuits and sports clothes. Dijana was upstairs in her room and so I sent Alan to get her. Philip in Banja Luka was still holding on the phone and so I picked it back up and told him, 'Philip, just listen. I've got an angry mob outside the house, maybe several hundred or so. I'm bugging out the back and I'll call you if I can but I'm leaving everything.'

'OK, catch you later,' replied Philip just before I put the phone down on him.

Djana had arrived downstairs and was looking very nervous, as were Henk and Alan. None of them had been through anything like this before and both my fellow monitors were still relatively new to Bosnia. This was like their worst nightmare coming true, after all, hadn't all their briefings about Prijedor and the Serbs been about how bloodthirsty they were and how dangerous it was?

I looked at them all and said, 'We can't get out the front and worse still we've got nowhere to go. The car's blocked in and there's no way I'm going to try and get in it and drive through them, it'll just make matters worse.'

They all looked even worse than when I'd started but I continued, 'We're going to have to stay put but I'm not staying in the house. If they want to smash it up or burn it down then I'm not about to be inside it when that happens so we're going to get out the back now before anymore of them come and surround us. When we're out, lock the door, keep the key, jump through two or three of the next door gardens and then move out on to the street and join the rear of the crowd. Nobody speak, nobody say nothing, just mingle in the crowd and watch what happens. Stick close. If they burn the house down, fine, don't do anything, just keep quiet and stay on the street in the crowd. If someone tries to speak to you just pretend you're drunk or something and move away, OK?'

This was becoming unreal, we were preparing to pack our kit and prepare the Satphone for just such an eventuality but all the evacuation plans required us to drive to predetermined assembly points. Now we didn't have access to our vehicle and if we didn't hurry we stood a good chance of being held hostage inside our own accommodation and God knows what might have happened then. I took another peep out the front window; it was actually quite terrifying. The crowd had grown in size and was continuing to shout their abuses in our direction. I felt a cold shudder as I realised first hand what it was like to be cornered and boxed in, surrounded by an enemy with no escape route.

I turned to my team as it was now or never, 'You ready?'

Three nods of the head.

'OK, let's go and remember, mingle in with the crowd, its our only chance.'

Next door in the American CIMIC centre, the troops didn't have the option of changing clothes and bugging out the back door. In fact, their presence put a whole different angle on the situation. Inside, the Americans had gone on to full combat alert, donned their helmets and body armour and were preparing to defend their position with rifles and machineguns. Had the crowd decided to attack that house then I was in no doubt that there would have been a bloodbath and the irony of me being shot by an American bullet as I stood at the back of the crowd wasn't lost on me. The American Major in charge had come out the front of the house with a couple of his soldiers to meet with the demonstrators. It was quite a courageous thing to do under the circumstances and my respect for him immediately went up. I caught his eye and it was evident that he was surprised to see me standing there but he obviously realised that we were 'safe' and that was one less thing for him to have to worry about. By now the crowd had stretched itself along the whole length of the street and was also outside the OSCE office hurling abuse at Jolanda and her staff. It was interesting to be in amongst the crowd as I felt quite safe and knew that unless someone spotted me for what I really was, that I'd remain so. In all we must have stayed standing outside for about half an hour before the crowd started to peter out. They had done their bit, made their token protest and had now decided either to move on elsewhere or to go home, I wasn't sure which. I signalled to my team to follow some of them around the block and only then to double back on ourselves and slip back inside the accommodation. I didn't want anyone to see us just leaving the crowd and walking up the path and in through the front door as that might have added insult to injury. Once inside I called Philip and brought him up to speed on the situation and then we all sat down and each sank a cold beer. Jolanda came across as she and several of her international staff were concerned about what to do next. It was my opinion that we were relatively safe at present as the crowd could have turned nasty if it had wanted to but hadn't. All the OSCE staff lived away from their office in various private houses dotted around the town and were therefore feeling quite vulnerable to individual attack and so I agreed to Jolanda's request for all of them to kip down for the night on our floor so at least we would all be together should anything else happen.

Apart from receiving a telephone call which simply played a traditional Serb nationalist song, 'Prepare yourselves Chekniks, there will be a great fight,' that first night passed without further incident but the next morning it was the turn of the doctors and hospital staff to demonstrate. This time there were perhaps five hundred demonstrators all protesting about Kovacevic's arrest and subsequent detention in The Hague. They had had a day to prepare for this protest and many came with banners and placards protesting against the ICTY, SFOR and the IC in general. This time our information was good and we'd learnt about the protest just before it arrived in the street. We had tried to meet the local branch President of the Serb Patriotic Party (SPAS) but he like everyone else in the town was now refusing to meet with us. My team had been reluctant to venture out, almost to the point of refusing to leave the accommodation. Although both Henk and Alan were serving military, I couldn't and would never have dreamt of ordering them to do anything they didn't want to. I was a diplomat and although technically their team leader I actually had no authority to order anything. Instead I reasoned with them and with Dijana. My argument was relatively simple. The average person on the street was now caught between the reality of what Plavsic had told them and the reality of the SDS and local Police who were undoubtedly pressuring them to turn out and were orchestrating the protests. I believed that their hearts weren't really in it but as patriotic Serbs they had to show that they mourned the loss of these two war criminals. I knew that it could be dangerous for us in Prijedor over the next few days but I genuinely believed that the threat came from individual hard-liners and the Police, and not from the population at large. To make the point I argued that to drive around Prijedor in our Land Rover might well be seen as provocative right now but equally to stay hull-down hidden inside our accommodation was about as worthwhile as evacuating. We would loose credibility amongst those reformers and early tentative Plavsic supporters who now looked to us for support even more than before, and we would find it almost impossible to return to work 'as if nothing had happened,' if we had run away scarred in the mean time.

I called my team's bluff, 'Look, I'm going to this meeting and if I can't see him I'm going to see if I can find Stakic. Further more I'm going to walk there, we're leaving the car behind because even ordinary people will through rocks at a car but it takes a special kind of person to throw rocks at an unarmed person in the street. We'll be much safer on foot.'

Dijana looked horrified but she knew I'd got the mentality right and gauged the situation correctly. She said she'd come which was just as well because although I was more than prepared to leave the other two behind, I would have been as much use as an ashtray on a motorbike without an interpreter. My fears were done away with as suitably motivated, both Henk and Alan agreed to come for the walk.

In the street we attracted a lot of attention and I can't think of any other time when I wished I could have simply disappeared in to a hole in the ground. It was dreadful in our whites as we were so conspicuous. No one from SPAS would see us and so we walked to the town centre to try and locate Stakic since at that stage we didn't yet know that he was permanently 'missing.' On several occasions irate locals stopped us in the street to berate us. The need for an interpreter however, creates artificial gaps in anyone's spiel and thus affords the immediate opportunity at the start of someone's protest to stretch out your hand and offer to shake-hands with them before their vitriolic attack is translated. The ploy is both simple and effective as it almost always disarms an attacker and usually they will be more prepared to discuss rather than simply berate. What's more, at the end of such conversations, people nearly always shook your hand to say thank you for listening. We eventually got to the Town Hall and met Malic, the President of the Municipal Executive Board, who was coming out the front entrance. Malic was deeply offended and hostile towards us. He wouldn't stop to speak properly as he would have brought shame on himself had he done so. Instead I quickly offered enough of a sympathetic word to briefly get his attention without seemingly siding with either Kovacevic or Drljaca, something that would have been all too easy but morally quite wrong.

'I'm sorry about what happened yesterday, it wasn't very good timing and perhaps it could have been done differently – but in the end they had to face trial.' I let Dijana translate and then continued, 'To my knowledge Drljaca was armed and tried to kill the soldiers, he brought it upon himself. Please be assured that none of us who are living and working here were in anyway involved in what happened and neither have we misplaced your trust and respect that you've shown us by spying on you.' I again let Dijana translate and then added, 'I appreciate that you can't see us now but I'd like your assurance that we can meet in a few days time. We need to work this thing through and that means we need to talk.'

Malic paused for several moments looking deep in to my eyes before replying, 'Thank you for taking the risk to come and see me and I accept what you have said but you should not be here now as it's not safe and we shouldn't be seen together. We can speak later, but not now. Be careful, there's another demonstration at your house this morning.' And with that he left.

We got back to the house in time to warn both the CIMIC and the OSCE to expect the demonstrators from the hospital at any moment. In fact it turned out to be a well-organised event, led by the deputy director of the hospital and several senior doctors supported by nurses and ancillary staff mostly sporting white coats. In total there were about five hundred demonstrators in the procession. It was an opportunity too good to miss and so I grabbed Dijana and still dressed in white, unobtrusively joined the procession as it marched down our street. It turned out to be quite bizarre as I walked at the head of the demonstration attempting to interview a senior consultant from the hospital on his views about Kovacevic and what had happened. I felt that feelings were not running that high and although most were angered about the use of the Red Cross parcel as a trick and were genuinely saddened for Kovacevic's family, few were really upset that he had gone. As far as Drljaca was concerned, no one from the hospital that I managed to talk to wanted to talk about him. It was as if the IC had done Prijedor a favour and ridden the community of one of its notorious gangsters. It was his hold on power and his physical influence that was making the people weep crocodile tears in his memory. We walked with the crowd for about half an hour and then broke off as unobtrusively as we had joined.

The team again had lunch with the OSCE in the Mont, and Jolanda told us that she'd learnt that there was to be a candle light vigil that night in the town with several thousand demonstrators expected to turn out. The parade would start in the town centre, march down our street yet again and then end up back at the Town Hall. So far no one had tried to attack our accommodations but we were still nervous that it could happen at any stage and especially at night, which was to be a new development with this procession. I instructed my team to check that their personal kit was still packed in case we needed to escape in a hurry. We had a discussion about what to do next and all agreed that we didn't want to sit in the house like lame ducks and wait for something to happen. We all decided it was better to be proactive and take the initiative and so later that night we set off into town to see what was happening. There were probably about two, to three thousand people taking part in the vigil most of whom were carrying candles. It looked like a peace-protest except in our minds there weren't advocating for peace and reconciliation but bereaving the death of a war criminal and the arrest of another. As the head of the procession past, I saw Malic walking with several other civic leaders and so quickly got the team to jump in behind them and followed for a while before breaking off again. It was long enough for him to know that we were there and to force his recognition but short enough so as not to embarrass or compromise him. We met up with him again at the end of the evening and he had the manners to come across and speak with me and thank the team for attending the rally. He promised to co-operate with us and offered us the chance to meet with him the following week. This had been the third protest in two days and it was still only some thirty-six hours since SFOR's action. So far apart from having our car's tyres slashed and a door damaged during the evening whilst we were out attending the demonstration, nothing untoward had happened to any of us. But what we didn't know was that the Police were planning a rude awakening. On orders from Kijac, the bombing started.

The first to be hit were the International Police. The IPTF worked in a suite of offices located in Hotel Prijedor and like the OSCE staff, all lived-out within the local community. They too were vulnerable to attack when off duty and it was at them that the first bombs were targeted. In total several attacks were launched against IPFT personnel in the town although usually there was little real attempt to kill anyone. Two bombs went off outside the front of officers' accommodation and on one occasion a device was placed under a car. All exploded without injury to anyone although of course people could easily have been killed had they been passing by or in the car in question when the devices had gone off. The IPFT reacted by moving all their personnel in to the Hotel until further notice where ironically the local Police (who had previously been bombing them) placed a guard to protect them. Apart from the IPTF, only the OSCE and my own ECMM team were left in Prijedor as everyone else had left at the first opportunity. People in the town were still relatively hostile to us but on the whole I still felt relatively safe. I was trying to gather as much information as I possibly could about what the general feeling towards us was in the town and so I had to continue to go out and speak to people. Official inter-locutors were still refusing to see us but 'RC Sarajevo' was still screaming at us for information and routine reports. The problem was that there was nothing routine to report. I decided to go out in to the café bars and snoop around for information and try to gauge what peoples' views were. It was inherently dangerous, as people didn't want us in their bars let alone to talk to us. Henk and Alan both thought that this was a bridge too far and well beyond the call of duty and so I went out with Dijana and Sinisa, an interpreter from the OSCE Field Office, and canvassed opinions in the many café bars in the town. It was an uncomfortable feeling as I wasn't welcome at all although interestingly enough, I was always served. In order not to compromise the bar staff, most of whom I knew by now, I only stayed for one drink in each bar and then moved on to the next. In that way I showed them that I wasn't going to go away and that I was here to stay whilst at the same time giving them the space to distance themselves from me. The ploy worked and after a few days I was able to build up a picture that basically said that the people of Prijedor were ready for change. No one had liked Drljaca who despite being sacked as Chief of Police the previous year, had continued to exert a hold over the town. By and large people were upset about Kovacevic but not surprised that he had been taken and no one could care less about Stakic. What they feared most was to be isolated by the IC and left to the devices of their own hard-liners and corrupt politicians. They actually wanted us to stay put but felt powerless to do anything to assist us. This was an interesting development but one that would get nowhere unless it had the backing of less corrupt and most importantly, powerful politicians. I needed to gauge the political mood and so it was vital that I met with the town's political leaders as soon as possible, the blockade had gone on long enough.

Fixing up a meeting with anyone who mattered was still a formidable task. No one of any consequence would speak to us although all the smaller parties were falling over themselves to get airtime with us. The problem was that although our meetings with these smaller parties gave us good background information, they didn't tackle the central issue; namely whether President Plavsic would ever recover her lost ground or would the hard-liners and their SDS henchmen win the day thus delivering a further blow to the peace process? On Thursday 17th July, one week after the SFOR action, I got the breakthrough I wanted, Marko Pavic, a senior and much respected figure in the SDS leadership in Prijedor and the director of the PTT, would meet with us the next day. Pavic was a big figure of a man who had an imposing personality however his eyes betrayed a softer side and even a good sense of humour. He was a professional, but above all else he was a realist and knew what was at stake. What was interesting however was that it was Pavic who had asked me for the meeting and so I knew that something fundamentally important was about to be raised and that I was going to have an important part to play in it.

On Friday 18th July, I took my team to the PTT offices in the centre of town and met with Pavic. I knew Pavic to be a staunch member of the SDS and I suspected that his appointment as director of the PTT had been handed to him by the party, as was normal practice throughout Bosnia. After all the recent events in Prijedor I knew this meeting wasn't going to be about his efforts to unite the two entity PTT systems and open up cross IEBL phone lines, there were far more important matters to discuss. Getting started and broaching the subject was an extremely delicate matter and particularly tricky. We kicked off talking about telecommunications and soon moved on to politics once our nerves had settled. Pavic told us that, 'The RS President had the right to dismiss the NA' and that 'The leadership of the municipality would not organise anything against the IC, IOs or SFOR and they condemned the individual reprisals which had taken place as they benefited no one.' This was our first indication that he wanted to support Plavsic against the SDS hard-liners but was clearly frightened to make the first move. The SDS had ordered the Police to start bombing the IC and had previously arrested Plavsic in Bijeljina and so they could easily have 'removed' Pavic if they wanted to. As our conversation continued it became clear that he had approached several other SDS members in Prijedor and that there was a small caucus of reformers who would put their support behind the President if the circumstances were right. The problem was that nobody was prepared to make the first move and expose themselves especially as the President's own future was now in question and the hard-liners had resorted to violence on the streets. What Pavic wanted to know was whether President Plavsic and any SDS reformers that joined her, would have the support of the IC. This was not a question to be taken lightly. If the reformers were to be expelled from the party by the SDS, then not only did they risk loosing their livelihoods but they risked loosing their lives too. I very nearly panicked as I really needed to pass this question up the chain of command but Pavic expected and wanted an answer straight away. All I could think of was a bunch of short-term, bored and uninterested Dutch Staff Officers back at ECMM HQ sitting out their six months tour of duty all of whom totally oblivious to the significance of what was on offer here. I didn't have the authority to commit the EU let alone the whole of the IC to a particular course of action but I was the EU's representative in Northwest Bosnia and Pavic was waiting for an answer. I regained my composure and as convincingly as possible told him that I spoke for the EU and not for the whole of the IC, but that, 'It is my firm belief that the IC would support any move you made to reform the SDS.' My answer even shocked myself as I had in effect given him the green light to go ahead with whatever he had in mind. I pressed him for details and learnt little more other than he wanted to speak with the party's Prijedor branch members and get them to turn their backs on Pale. That was a tall order in itself as not everyone would want to join him in switching their allegiance to Plavsic. It was clear that Pavic needed my help. First and foremost he needed help to sound out the SDS and secondly he needed help to sound out the Municipal Assembly. He asked me to arrange meetings with them both and raise the matter of reform to see if they'd listen to reason and determine who might go along with him or not. I agreed but told him that I had been trying to meet with them anyway for precisely that purpose in order to report my findings to ECMM. He said he'd speak with both organisations and see if he could get them to agree to meet us. As we concluded the meeting I turned to him and remarked, 'You have to stop the bombing.'

Pavic looked at me and said, 'I know, I'm trying. Believe me we're all trying. We know who it is, just leave it with us but it'll take time.'

HQ ECMM had finally woken up and eleven days after Plavsic's open air rally in the town and nine days after the SAS strike, Ambassador Dann Everts, the Dutch HOM turned up in Banja Luka to see what was happening for himself. Koks, our new HCC, had called me in to the CC to brief the HOM's delegation and to escort him around the area. It was Saturday 19th, the day after my meeting with Pavic and everything was a bit of a rush. I decided to leave my team behind in Prijedor to prepare for the HOM's arrival and travel to Banja Luka on my own in the team's Land Rover which I had been instructed to swap for the armoured version that I had used on my initial trip to Sanski Most. The HOM was accompanied by the HRC from Sarajevo and a Dutch TV crew from their equivalent programme to the British 'Newsnight.' It was all or nothing. One moment no one was listening to what I was saying and the next the whole world was. I rose to the occasion and a presented a succinct overview of events and my analysis of where it was all going, or at least the options depending upon whether the IC fell behind Plavsic or allowed her to fail. The point was well taken and the HOM asked me to join him in Banski Dvor[118] where he'd arranged to meet with her. The President's office was on the third floor of Banski Dvor and on arrival we were all promptly escorted to an office where we awaited her. The meeting itself was congenial enough although conducted along formal diplomatic lines. It was clear from the outset that the HOM was out of his depth regarding any of the substantive issues at stake, although to his credit he did manage to keep the discussions going. Philip, the Operations Officer had also come along to the meeting and from time to time we simply looked at each other and cringed. It would have been far better for us to have led the discussions although we both knew that only the HOM had the authority to sign up to any deals that might be put on the table. In the end neither Philip nor I learnt anything new although the HOM was clearly enlightened and Plavsic happy that finally someone had come to listen to her. Most of the stuff that the HOM had discussed was old hat and had been reported by the CC on many previous occasions. The fact that he had to keep going over old ground and consequently missed the opportunity to explore 'future intentions,' merely reinforced Philip's and my own views that the whole of the Sarajevo 'Head-Shed' didn't know what we were doing up here in Banja Luka. I was none too impressed with what had been a wasted opportunity and wanted to escape back off to Prijedor for lunch but I couldn't as I still had the TV crew to take around. Back at the CC, Koks instructed me to take the crew back to Prijedor with me and spend the rest of the day helping them in anyway I could. The ECMM Press Officer who was accompanying them gave me permission to go on camera if I was asked and to take part in the film they were making. Then, as I was about to leave, the HOM invigorated by his discussions with the President, asked me if I thought it safe for him to come to Prijedor too. Although the bombing was still ongoing, I thought it would still be safe for him to visit and I also considered it an excellent opportunity for a senior diplomat to see events first hand rather than rely simply on written reports and the incessant prejudice that was forever flying around. Just to be safe however, I drove the ambassador in my newly acquired armoured Land Rover with the HRC, Press Officer and TV crew following behind in their own vehicles.

It was a sunny Saturday afternoon in Prijedor when the HOM arrived and down by the River Sana they had just opened a new café bar that had been precariously built on wooden planking laid across sixteen metal military assault boats. To celebrate the occasion, a small fairground had been set up on the nearby bank and families and children had turned out in their hundreds to have a go on the Ferris Wheel and other amusements. The contradiction between the reality that awaited the visitors and their expectations couldn't have been so marked. Here was a normal town at play in the summer sunshine and it was in complete contrast to the visions conjured up by the horror stories of Omarska. The TV crew was the most amazed and I went on film to explain the reality of what was happening here. Prijedor had been stigmatised, rightly so. But now most of its population wanted to throw off the shackles of hard-line nationalist politics and get on with rebuilding their lives. The bombing campaign against the IC was being orchestrated in Pale by SDS hard-liners who were desperate to hold on to power. I said the IC should support the reformers and not do anything to upset this process and although I was clear in my support, I nevertheless cited the SAS action as being insensitive to this political reform process and badly timed. I concluded that the situation was, as a consequence, now delicately balanced and risked failure and that the IC should do everything in its power to ensure success.

I was due to go on leave the following week and it was strange to think that a week from now I'd be sat at home with my children. I was actually finding it harder and harder to adjust each time I went home as I had little in common with people who had nothing better to do with their lives than to busy themselves looking for something to moan at. My neighbourhood was full of retired people who always found something to complain about like lighting a bonfire in the garden. These things were insignificant compared to what I'd just been through since taking over the job as team leader in Prijedor. I had no time for such people but sadly it seemed to me that we'd bred a nation of people who got excited about the most irrelevant things, and in the main it was the older generation that were the worst. Anyway, I was looking forward to going home and was actually quite worried about my views as it wasn't healthy to identify too closely with what was going on in the RS. There was a term for what I was beginning to experience and I didn't want to succumb to it, and that was 'going native.' With that in mind, I still had one mater to sort out before I went home to my family. If I still couldn't get to see the SDS or the Municipal Authority, I wanted to speak to General Ramsey and find out just what had been going on in his mind when he authorised the SAS strike. I wasn't alone in that either, both Jolanda and Nita wanted to speak with him and on the following Monday we all managed to get together in the CIMIC house to attend a meeting he'd arranged with the Americans. Ramsey was in jubilant mood and quite defiant of any criticism. Put simply he had come to bolster up the moral of his troops, all of whom were feeling quite vulnerable stuck out in the civil community outside of the protection of the military wire at Ramici. It was clear from the outset that he had little time for us civilians. From his pompous and condescending attitude it was clear that he had naïvely expected to come to Prijedor and listen to our security fears and then perhaps graciously grant us some extra protection. In fact, he had already done that as we already had a platoon of Czech paratroops permanently based in our street and my team's front garden. We were of course grateful for such support but none of us had gathered in the CIMIC Centre to ask for extra security or to listen to him revel in the success of the military operation. What we all wanted to know was who had authorised the operation and why he hadn't taken account of the political situation before giving the green light for the strike? Ramsey was offended, not just because the line of questioning had completely disarmed him but because he wasn't used to being held to account by those he considered inferior and were certainly his junior – in age if nothing else. In response we got some inane nonsense about needing to bring PIFWCs to account but nothing that answered our specific questions although he did confirm that SFOR's Ammunition Technical Officers had traced the grenades used in the attacks on the IPTF back to the Serb Police. It was clear that Ramsey was not aware of the infighting within the SDS or even the real significance of Plavsic's rally in Prijedor and I believe that he was genuinely shocked to find that his action had met with such hostility from ourselves. Presumably he thought that we should be congratulating him.

To finalise the proceedings, I asked him direct, 'Did you get authority from the High Rep' to stage this operation?'

Whether Ramsey knew that I was once a Major, I don't know for sure but he gave me a really evil stare and simply replied that, 'The operation was properly authorised.' An answer that I took to mean 'no,' and which raised an interesting question for future military doctrine, that although the operation would certainly have been sanctioned by Tony Blair, was that enough in what was essentially an international protectorate? Which 'civil authority' should the British Army have been subordinated to under these circumstances? The UK Parliament, as was clearly the case here, or the High Representative? Had it been the latter, as might reasonably be expected in an international setting such as Bosnia, then I remain quite sure that Westendorp would not have sanctioned the operation at that point in time.

After work on Thursday, I started to pack my bags for my flight home the next morning. I was tired as things were still very tense in the town and I needed a break. It was about 5,pm and I'd just popped out in to the back garden when all hell broke loose around the front of the house. I jumped over the wire fence just in time to see several paratroopers drag an armed Policeman in uniform and another man in plain clothes out of a blue Mercedes that they had stopped just short of the CIMIC house and blocked in with their Armoured Personnel Carrier. Apparently the officer had driven up and down the adjacent road several times during the day already, attempting to run down one of the Czechs soldiers and had just done it again for the third time. I left them to it and went back in to the house for another beer; it was definitely time for some leave.

19

Decision Time

It was Tuesday 12th August 1997, and after two weeks at home in the UK spent camping in Snowdonia with my family, I again found myself flying back to Zagreb. For some unknown reason I was flying Austrian Airlines and so had to go via Vienna and change flights for the last leg to the Croatian capital. I spent the night in Hotel-I, and was collected the next morning by a driver from the CC to take me back to Banja Luka. The CC had long since binned the idea of catching the regular shuttle service, as the route was just so ridiculous. It was stinking hot in Banja Luka and although I had enjoyed my two weeks of Welsh summer, I much preferred the dry heat of the Balkan summer and this was already my third one in a row. I stopped for some lunch with the members of the CC and to await my own team's arrival as I had arranged with them before I'd left on leave, to pick me up in Banja Luka. The wait provided an opportunity to talk with Koks, the HCC and with Philip, the Operations Officer. It was good to catch up slowly on all that had happened whilst I'd been away. Prijedor was still tense and the threat of violence continued to be high. My team had done well in my absence but sadly, although not unexpectedly, had not yet managed to speak with any of the SDS or the Municipal Assembly and so that was definitely going to be top of my agenda as from tomorrow.

I arrived back in Prijedor during the late afternoon. It was still a lovely warm summer's day and it was good to be back with Henk, Alan and Dijana and to catch up on what had been happening whilst I was away as they had all done a really good job. Henk and Alan wanted to do some training and so Dijana and I went off for a walk to 'Kims,' a local café bar just behind the OSCE Field Office. On the way we met Nita, the UN Civil Affairs officer attached to the IPTF, who was sitting across the street in 'Marco Polo,' another of Prijedor's many café bars. Nita briefly filled me in with a summary of things that had happened over the past fortnight and her assessment of where it was all going. She was exceptionally good at her job and her views were invaluable, but sadly it was impossible to talk with her about anything else and so after a while you felt that you needed to escape from her clutches. Fortunately for me Suzana, a barmaid from Kims who I always mixed up with her twin sister Svjetlana, who was a waitress at the Aeroclub restaurant which had been owned by Drljaca before his death at the hands of 'Two-Two,' called me across. Sinisa joined us and we spent the rest of the late afternoon catching up with each others' stories and drinking cold beer.

That evening after we had all eaten, something that we always did together as a team, we spent the rest of the night back at Kims having a few more beers. Several of the OSCE staff joined us and it was a good atmosphere that helped to take my mind off my family that I had only just left behind that same morning. When I had gone on leave a fortnight previously, Henk and Alan hadn't wanted to join me out in town as it was still too dangerous. I'm not sure that they had been out much if at all in the intervening period, but at least now they both felt relaxed enough to join me. That wasn't to say that it was safe, just that we had to get on with our jobs and weren't about to be put off by the Police bombing campaign. We left the bar just before 11,00 pm and walked the short distance back to our accommodation which was still being guarded twenty-four hours a day by Czech paratroopers. Despite all the overt security surrounding the house, I had a rule, which was a personal hangover from my own days in the military and my concerns over the IRA. When I'd joined the Army eighteen years previously, I had been taught never to turn a light on inside a house at night unless the curtains (or blinds) were shut. I still followed that rule despite having left the Army over three years previously and now made my team follow that precaution too. By now it had become a simple drill that we all carried out without being told. Once in the house we'd ensure that the blinds were down before turning on the lights. Often, we'd put them down before going out since Dijana would frequently forget or simply not bother and turn the lights on without thinking. Fortunately on this occasion, Dijana went straight upstairs to her room and Henk and Alan sorted out the blinds in the downstairs living room. A message had come in on the fax machine in the far corner of the living room. I left Henk and Alan to read it as it concerned the work they had been doing whilst I was on leave and I didn't want to butt in on that now that I was back as it might have seemed insulting. I said goodnight and at exactly five past eleven climbed the stairs up to my room.

The explosion was deafening and bloody close. In fact, it hadn't been close, it had been a direct hit. I had barely made it to my room when the grenade had gone off and fortunately was still dressed. Dijana was already in bed as I burst in to her room and instructed her, 'Quickly get up and dressed as fast as you can. Stay low – on the floor, away from the windows and keep the bloody lights off. Don't come downstairs until I tell you.'

I ran down the first flight of stairs to the bend on the landing, which meant that I could see the downstairs hall but was not in 'line-of-sight' with the front door. I didn't want to get in the way of any rounds that might end up coming through the front door and so I remained there and shouted down to Henk and Alan, 'Are you two OK, what's happened?'

By the sound of Henk's voice he was clearly shaken, 'We're OK but the living room's hit.'

I was relieved, at least we were all OK, at least for the moment. I was also confused, I had heard an explosion but had not heard any shooting. Light from the outside street lamp was pouring in through the solid wooden front door which looked as if it had been peppered with bullet holes but it couldn't have been. Also, I didn't understand why there had been no return fire from the Czechs. Henk had also said that it was an explosion and not a shot – I shouted down to him, 'The front door's full of bullet or shrapnel holes. I didn't hear any firing, what about you?'

Henk shouted back, 'We didn't hear any shooting.'

'OK, stay on the floor and keep the lights off. I'm coming down.' I was worried about the state of the front door because if anything else had gone off, it wouldn't have provided any protection and I had to run past it. I was also worried about the Czechs, either they hadn't been on guard where they should have been, although we had just walked past them not two minutes ago, or they'd been hit by the bomb. I leapt down the remaining stairs and joined Henk and Alan who were still on the floor by the fax machine. They were lucky as the whole of the front part of the living room was a mess and they had been shielded by a small dividing partition between the living room and what was previously the dining room and now our office. Light was streaming in through what had once been the windows. The whole place was covered in shattered glass, the wooded blinds on the outside of the windows were in tatters and there were chucks of the ceiling missing from where the grenade shrapnel had pierced the plaster. Henk and Alan owed their lives to two things. Firstly, the small partition which they had been standing behind reading the fax as it had shielded them from the flying debris and shrapnel, and secondly the fact that we had put the blinds down before doing anything else. Less than a minute had passed by since the explosion and the three of us were still lying on the floor in the dark. I told Henk, 'Get Dijana down here and keep her calm. I'm calling the CC and sending a 'Contact Report.'[119] To Alan I added, 'See if you can see what's happening outside but don't go out there just yet.'

I picked up the phone dragging it on to the floor beside where I was lying and thought 'This isn't going to work.' Supposedly HQ ECMM had a Duty Officer system but I had tried to use it before and it rarely worked as it depended upon a bleeper and no one ever got back to you for ages. The radio wasn't being monitored at this time of night so that only left me the option of phoning the CC and everyone lived out. Fortunately I had Philip's home number although I knew that the actual phone was downstairs with his landlord and not in Philip's apartment. As Dijana still hadn't turned up, this was going to be a good test of my Serbian language skills. I called the

number and thankfully the call was answered. Sure enough it was his
landlord and so in my best Serbo-Croat introduced myself, apologised for
the lateness of the call and asked to speak to Philip immediately. Philip had
been in bed but knew that something must have been amiss for me to call
and was suitably responsive when he answered.

I instinctively rattled off a formal 'initial contact report' to him, 'Philip,
its Ian. Contact – two minutes ago – my house – bombing – no ECMM
casualties. The downstairs living room's taken a direct hit, it's a fucking
mess. Don't know about the SFOR guys outside but there was no return fire
so I reckon they might have been hit.'

Philip was calm and reassuring, 'OK, no worries, can you see outside?'

I wasn't able to see and had deliberately told Alan not to go outside just
yet. 'No, we're all lying on the floor in the dark in a pile of broken glass. I
don't know what went off. If it was a grenade then whoever threw it will
have buggered off by now but if it was a bomb then I'm not going to go
outside for a while in case there's a secondary device.' The planting of a
second bomb a short distance from the first and timed to detonate minutes
later as the security forces arrive at the first incident was normal practice for
the IRA, and so I really wanted to know what had gone off before I
ventured outside.

'OK' said Philip, 'when you can, find out what the score is outside. I'm
going to go in to the CC and open up the Operations Room and call the RC.
When you can, call me there.'

Good, things were actually moving and it was still only a matter of a few
minutes since the bomb had gone off. 'Listen' I told Philip, 'once you're in
the CC, you call me first so I know you're there and I don't waste time
trying to get through to you, there's enough to sort out here as it is. If we
don't answer, it's because we're outside so don't panic just leave a message
on the answering machine then I'll know to call you back.'

With that we hung up. Dijana had joined us on the floor and we all lay
still for a few seconds listening for any movement outside. It was unerringly silent and it shouldn't have been as the Americans should have followed
up on the incident even if the Czechs had been taken out. There wasn't
much else we could do, we had to take a look ourselves. I left Henk inside
with Dijana and Alan and I went out through the back door and came
around the side of the house to peer around at the front street. There were
several Czech paratroopers in the street looking at a hole in our front
garden. What had happened was that someone, unseen, had thrown a hand
grenade in to the street. The sentry had seen the grenade land and had taken
cover before it went off but had not seen anyone throw it, as who ever had
done so, did it from behind a tall hedge in our neighbour's garden. As such,
the attack had been made blind and the attacker would not have really
known what he was going to hit, if anything. The Czech paratrooper might
have been killed but it was unlikely that he was the specific target. Likewise,
almost all of the damage done was to our accommodation but I considered

it unlikely that ECMM was the specific target either. Instead, I believed that it was another general attack made against the IC in Prijedor on the orders of the SDS in Pale. Whoever had thrown the grenade had simply tried to get it as far down the street as possible and he hadn't really cared who he killed in the process.

The next morning we were all out surveying the damage not least our landlady who was furious. The grenade had landed several feet in front of our living room window just on the side of our front path where there was small hedge, perhaps a foot high. There was now a small crater in the path, a large gap in the hedge and blast marks across the narrow garden leading up to the front wall. Shrapnel from the grenade and flying pieces of concrete from the torn up path, had penetrated our front window blinds making a right mess of the living room beyond. Even our ceiling was peppered with holes. The outside of the house and the front door were similarly peppered with small holes and craters as were the walls of the CIMIC house and the Mont restaurant, albeit to a lessor extent. Even our armoured Land Rover had been hit by several pieces of shrapnel along one side although thankfully none had penetrated the armour. Interestingly enough however, the fuel tank on the vehicle was not armoured and was left very exposed on the underside of the chassis. One piece of shrapnel had missed the tank by only several inches and now lay embedded the metal frame beside it. A few inches to the right and that really would have been a big explosion.

All of a sudden Prijedor was in the limelight again. I even got a phone call from the FCO in London, as they wanted to check that I was all right. Both the CC and the RC gave me permission to evacuate immediately if I wasn't already doing so. SFOR were out in force and another huge armoured fighting vehicle joined the paratroopers on guard. Even Ramsey turned up again and sneered at us as if to say, 'And these are the people you're trying to work with.' Well, he had a point I guess but I remained convinced that if they – the Police that is, wanted us dead, then they had ample opportunity to kill us. Instead they simply wanted us to run away scarred, something which would bring discredit upon ourselves. I was determined not to give them that satisfaction and told the rest of the team that I was staying put. Again I had to convince them of my reasoning but my belief that this last attack had been 'against the street' and not against ECMM won the day and they, to their credit, agreed to stay with me yet again.

It was now more critical than ever that I spoke with Malic and members of the Executive Board of the Municipal Assembly, if not all of the elected Deputies. Getting a meeting arranged took another week but on Wednesday 20th August I finally got in to see them. Malic had assembled about ten members of the Executive Board to meet our team in the main Boardroom of the Municipal building in the town centre. The atmosphere in the room was very tense, as the Serb delegation knew what was at stake. Put frankly, it was decision time. Either they broke with Pale and put a stop to the bombings or they would become increasingly more isolated and margin-

alised by the IC and suffer the humanitarian, economic and political consequences. It was their choice and I intended to tell them so in no uncertain
terms. I too was nervous, these were all hard-liners and, unless they'd seen
reason and changed their allegiances, were either staunch SDS or SRS
members. I knew that Malic was a moderate and Pavic had given me an indication that he and others were ready to join the reformers but I didn't know
how many would openly do so.

I asked Malic, 'Where is Gospodin Stakic these days?'

We all knew by now that Stakic had fled but the question served to point
out that the municipality was effectively leaderless and would remain so
until the municipal elections scheduled for mid-September. Here was an
opportunity to change direction if they wanted to take it but the window of
opportunity would only remain for another month. Malic wanted to be con-
ciliatory and apologised for the bombing of our house, asked if we were all
right and gave us his assurances that everything was being done to put a stop
to it all. This gave me the opening I wanted.

I told him, 'If it continues for much longer then you will have succeeded
in driving out all of the IC and then you will have no friends left here.'

I continued, 'If we all leave then the hard-liners will have won and
Prijedor will suffer. You won't get any more aid since no one will want to
come here anymore. You got only two per cent of the total international aid
coming in to Bosnia last year because of the anti-Dayton policies of
Karadzic, Krajisnik and the SDS. Ninety-eight per cent went to the
Federation. If we leave, you'll get none and it's your people who will suffer
and they will have you to thank for it!'

Even the hard-liners were beginning to take it all in, slowly but surely. I
reinforced the point, 'If we go and if SFOR go, which is what I think Pale
want, then there's nothing between you and the Armija. 7th Corps is twenty
minutes away and it's been trained and re-equipped by the Americans for
the last year. You wouldn't stand a chance. If there's another war Prijedor
will fall to the Muslims. Alagic, Cirkin, they're both dying to retake this
town and as soon as we've gone – they'll try.'

The Board had no way of verifying what I was saying as they would
never consider driving across the IEBL to take a look for themselves so they
had to take it from me. The atmosphere was electric, small whispered conversations had broken out between the deputies as they discussed what I'd
told them and their possible options.

Malic asked, 'What shall we do?' The room went quiet.

I paused for a while and then answered him – addressing them all, 'It's
your choice gentlemen. You have to decide. You can follow the orders of
your parties in Pale, in which case the bombing will continue, we and the
few others that remain will evacuate and then the fighting will start. Either
between SFOR – as they take on your Police, or with the Armija. Whatever
happens, your people will suffer and you won't get any more aid.'

I paused again allowing time for Dijana to translate and for my words to sink in before continuing, 'Or, you can reject Pale and join the President's attempts to reform the SDS, help the people and support Dayton.' Another pause before concluding, 'My team will stay here for a while longer but not forever. If the violence continues, we'll leave, so you have to make your choice – now.'

The room was quiet and it was clear that no more needed to be said, and that the deputies now needed time alone to discuss their game plan amongst themselves. Malic thanked me for my frankness and support, and asked that we stay in Prijedor and give them a chance to sort things out. On behalf of my team, I agreed and then we all left.

I had given Prijedor's Executive Board an ultimatum and a choice of two visions of the future. Now they had to decide which one to take. Following Plavsic and her reforms wouldn't be easy, her campaign had been knocked back in to the Stone Age by Ramsey and meanwhile the SDS were still after her blood and the Executive Board knew it too. A lot had happened in the RS in the month or so since the SAS strike in Prijedor. On 19th July, the same day as the HOM and I were having our meeting with the President, the Main Board of the SDS in Pale had expelled her from the party. She was technically out in the cold and all alone although two days after that, on 22nd July, the RS Supreme Court, in a show of support for the President, had dismissed the RSNA's petition against disbanding the National Parliament. The crisis in the RS had already become a tit-for-tat political battle sharply dividing opinion between the Northwest and the Southeast. By late July, her hopes of reforming the party had been no more than a pipe dream. With the OSCE deadline for the registration of political parties, independent candidates and coalitions long since past and only one month to go before the municipal elections, the concept of unilaterally declaring her independence from the SDS seemed somewhat pointless. If she split from the ruling party to form her own party of reformers, it wouldn't be allowed to stand in the forthcoming September elections and so she resisted the temptation to do so for as long as she could. Then, on the 15th August the RS Constitutional Court found against her and the Supreme Court's earlier ruling, and controversially ruled that her decision on 3rd July, to dissolve the RSNA and call for new elections, was unconstitutional. She had finally had enough and so on the same day decided to split from the SDS forever. In a statement to the press in Banja Luka, she announced that she was forming her own political party which she named, the 'Serb People's Alliance-Biljana Plavsic' (SNS-BP). Her counter attack continued and on 17th August she made public various allegations that her own Police in Banja Luka were involved in human rights abuses, action of an undemocratic nature and had placed her under illegal surveillance. That same day, the IPTF supported by SFOR tanks raided the city's Public Security Centre and confiscated several illegal weapons. Their investigations later revealed that they had, '… unequivocal evidence of serious criminal activity being conducted in the main Banja Luka Police station, which includes the bugging of the President's communications.' On the 18th, Plavsic rejected the Constitutional Court's ruling on the RSNA on the grounds that its judges had been physically threatened with their lives and announced that the RSNA remained dissolved. So, by the time of my meeting with Prijedor's Executive Board on the 20th, battle lines had long been drawn and it was little wonder that the atmosphere had been so tense.

I gave them two days to think things through and then on Friday 22nd August went back to see Marko Pavic. This was to be my last working day in Prijedor as the HCC, Hans Koks had asked me to move to Banja Luka and take Philip's place as Operations Officer. I had agreed, it was after all a promotion and although Prijedor had certainly been the centre of gravity in the RS over the last few months, I felt that the battle was being taken to Banja Luka and that was where I wanted to be. Pavic was in a coy mood and pleased to see us.

I asked him whether he thought the IC should stay in Prijedor and he told me that, 'you shouldn't always think to leave the area each time an incident occurs,' and then suggested that if we had any ideas to improve security then we, 'Shouldn't hesitate to tell me and I will implement it.'

It was as if he was speaking with some form of higher authority and the whole tone of the meeting was completely different from our previous one just before my leave. He was no longer frightened nor undecided as he had been then and I wanted to know why and on which side he and the others had come down on. I couldn't simply ask him directly whether he was going to 'reform,' as that would have been insulting if he was going to stay with the hard-liners as it would imply that I thought that the SDS needed to be reformed. Instead I asked him whether he would take up his seat on the RSNA at its next (illegal) meeting. Pavic knew what I was about and commented that, 'The decision of the Constitutional Court started the whole crisis,' and then added that, 'The decision by the SDS to dismiss the President from the party was too hasty, immature and was not to the benefit of those who took it.'

I pressed him about the SDS and he said that, 'There are only two ways that voters can make the distinction between the hard-line SDS and the new SNS-BP moderates and that was for them [the deputies] either to resign from the existing SDS individually ... or for the Municipal Board as a whole to say that we are on the other side.' He also said that he thought that, 'The number of defections to the SNS would increase after the next elections.'

Pavic never gave me a direct answer to whether the whole municipal board would realign itself with the pro-Plavsic camp, but nevertheless he gave us all the clear impression that they would. We left my very last meeting in Prijedor as team leader convinced that the town was no longer a hard-line pro-Pale strong hold and reported the assessment to the CC in Banja Luka. The next day, Saturday 23rd August, my interpretation of our meeting was proved correct. It was clear that Prijedor's Executive Board had listened to my warning and that several of the key figures on the Board including Marko Pavic had finally struck up their new colours and joined the SNS-BP. Whilst the Bosnian Serb Government announced its decision to sever its relations with their President, Marko Pavic accepted the post of RS Interior Minister from Biljana Plavsic. He'd known about the appointment during our meeting the day before but had kept quiet, which was why he had been in such a playful mood. But now the situation was far from playful, for now there were two Interior Ministers in Republika Srpska, the Presidential appointee, Marko Pavic, and the supposedly sacked hard-liner in Pale, Dragan Kijac.

20

Banja Luka, Republika Srpska
Serb - versus - Serb
On the Verge of Civil War

As each side attacked and counter attacked the other, control of the media was fast becoming a vital ingredient in the battle to win power. Pale had long since banned Plavsic from access to the 'state' run TV station, SRT and had continuously been miss-reporting her campaign and main arguments at every opportunity. In an attempt to get her message across she had embarked on a series of public rallies throughout the RS such as the one in Prijedor thirty-six hours before the SAS strike, but these rallies were never going to be effective enough for her to win her campaign. She needed access to the media and now that she had formed her own party, it was more crucial than ever. Krajisnik's control of the media was in flagrant violation of Dayton, which had called for a free and independent media and so on the same day as my last meeting with Marko Pavic, the High Representative Carlos Westendorp, wrote to Krajisnik and warned him that, 'The continual instances of deliberate misinformation, inflammatory commentary, insulting language and highly biased reportage ...' had to stop. On Sunday 24th August, the SRT studios in Banja Luka that were located next to the President's offices in Banski Dvor, started to broadcast independent programmes through a transmitter station located on the top of the Kozara Mountain to the East of Prijedor. At the same time, the studio severely limited the amount of broadcasts to the region being made by the studio in Pale. In effect, SRT had also divided in to two components; one working for President Plavsic in Banja Luka, and the other for President Krajisnik in Pale. Krajisnik however, was not about to stand idly by and watch Plavsic take control of SRT piece by piece and so on Monday 25th August he ordered the employees of SRT Banja Luka to regain editorial control of the studio and to remove its director. By coincidence, Krajisnik's instructions coincided with my very first meeting as a member of the CC. That afternoon I joined Philip on a hastily arranged meeting with the director of SRT Banja Luka in the main studio in Banski Dvor. We knew that the studio had started broadcasting alternative programmes the day before and wanted to find out exactly what was happening. As we attempted to conduct our meeting in the director's office, we were continually interrupted by frantic members of staff running in and out to appraise him of the latest developments and inform him of whether or not his staff would back him or bow to the pressures from Pale and remove him from his directorship. The whole meeting was quite bizarre as person after person rushed in and out in a blind state of panic. Meanwhile the director stoically refused to panic and simply issued instructions before returning to our discussions as if the whole episode was quite normal. Needless to say he carried the day and officials from the SDS office on the ground floor were left in no doubt what they could do with Krajisnik's instructions.

Not deterred by his failure to retake control of the main studio in Banja Luka, Krajisnik ordered the seizure of all SRT's transmitter and repeater stations across the RS. Serb Police and gangs of armed militia moved to physically take control and defend many of the sites prompting an SFOR patrol on 27th August, to fire warning shots at the Serb Police who had surrounded the Doboj transmitter station. The next day Serb demonstrators 're-took' the station forcing SFOR to arrest seven militiamen as they again intervened to defend the SRT employees from armed intimidation. On 29th, NATO formally authorised its troops in SFOR, '... to use force to shut down media that incite the population to use violence.' But they weren't the only ones prepared to use force. That same day the bombing campaign arrived in Banja Luka with a vengeance killing one person and injuring another two. Two days later Krajisnik moved to call SFOR's bluff. Around two hundred and fifty people surrounded the Udrigovo transmitter and threatened the SFOR guard. On this occasion bloodshed was averted as the crowd was dispersed by SFOR's use of CS tear gas. Seemingly enough was enough, and OHR's Principal Deputy High Representative Jaques Klein, and the new Comd SFOR General Erik Shinseki, successfully reached an agreement with Krajisnik in his capacity as Chairman of the SRT Board of Directors to curb inflammatory reporting against the IC, including SFOR. To all intents and purposes it seemed as if Krajisnik had been put back in his box but in reality he was not to be taken so lightly. Little was to change regarding SRT's broadcasts until the end of the month when Krajisnik had used and lost his trump card. But for now, he had one more trick up his sleeve.

On Monday 8th September, Krajisnik planned to stage a massive political rally of hard-line SDS supporters and he intended this rally to take place on the streets of Banja Luka. But this wasn't going to be an ordinary rally, this was to be a serious attempt to bring to heal the rebel President and her supporters. It was to be a physical attack striking right at the very heart of her political power base and in effect, an attempted coup d'etat and an armed one at that. Philip and I were usually in work by about 7,30 am each morning and our first two tasks were always to check for messages and to put the coffee percolator on. This Monday our priorities were very different. We had both got word of the impending rally and so immediately drafted a special report about what little we knew and sent it off to Sarajevo as a warning of what might come later. At that stage all we knew for sure was that the SDS planned to stage their rally in front of Banski Dvor at 6,00 pm that evening and that both President Krajisnik and the SDS party President Alexsi Buha, were expected to attend. We also knew that the RS newspapers were carrying notices announcing the availability of free buses from all over the RS for those who wanted to join the rally. Finally, having checked with the local RS (Banja Luka) Police, we knew that it was their intention to ban the rally. What was clear to both of us was that the conflicting elements within the RS were intent on a head to head, that it would be violent and that it would happen in Banja Luka tonight. We briefed Koks, the HCC when he came in and the rest of the team when they arrived, not that they would take any active role in helping out during the day, as they never did. Philip and I began to check in with as many organisations as we could and also got our interpreters to recheck with the local Police. By 10,00 am we had learnt from the IPTF that the local Police had set up a series of heavily armed road blocks around Banja Luka to intercept the hundreds of buses that were expected and from SFOR that they had reinforced these positions with armoured units including the British artillery battery of 155mm self-propelled guns from Kamengrad near Sanski Most. The UN had started to withdraw all of its personnel and was making arrangements for all of them to sleep over in their secure compound that night. We sent another report to Sarajevo, again without eliciting any response. Whilst the UN was setting about ensuring the safety of its personnel, Philip and I decided to take a trip in to town to see what if anything was happening. Dressed in our whites we felt completely conspicuous. Normally it just didn't matter at all but now it was completely different. Thousands of demonstrators were being bussed in to the city, mostly from the Southeast of the RS and all of them were coming to voice their disapproval of Plavsic and her cosy relations with the IC who they all saw as the reason for their current impoverishment. It was still early, only late morning but already gangs of men were aimlessly walking the streets drinking from bottles, passing offensive comments at the two of us and taking the occasional pee against the side of a building. This wasn't normal for Banja Luka but it got a lot worse as we walked up towards the Presidential Palace. Banski Dvor was being defended by the VRS who had put up a defensive perimeter around the building. Two armoured personnel carriers sporting heavy machine guns were parked threateningly blocking the main access road to the building. Anti-terrorist Police in paramilitary uniforms were everywhere acting as close protection for the President and her quarters. In the surrounding streets, local Police were stopping and questioning men, asking for their IDs. With over seven hours to go before the rally, the situation in

Banja Luka was already quite tense. We left Banski Dvor and walked across the main North-South tree-lined boulevard that divides the city in to two and walked towards the main hotel, Hotel Bosna. The Deputy President of the hard-line, right wing Serb Radical Party, Pantelj Damljanovic, owed the hotel. I had already got to know Damljanovic and the SRS President Nikola Poplasen, and knew that they were both 'in bed' with the SDS. Damljanovic had made the hotel available for Krajisnik and his delegation and as Philip and I walked towards the entrance we saw the sacked interior minister Dragan Kijac, pacing up and down in front of the hotel with about fifteen plain-clothes bodyguards and uniformed Police from Pale. The anti terror-ist unit standing outside Banski Dvor had also seen him and they rapidly deployed across the street to take up positions blocking Kijac from moving anywhere. We watched the armed standoff for about ten minutes before Kijac backed down and went back inside the Bosna. It was time to report back again.

Throughout the afternoon the Banja Luka Police reinforced by SFOR intercepted as many buses as possible before they reached the city. Weapons were confiscated by the crate full, not just knives and batons but pistols, assault rifles and hand grenades. Things were getting ugly and God knows what might have happened if all this hardware had got through. That said of course, some of it must have done. At 5,00 pm most of the CC predictably went home. Koks stayed behind to monitor the radio and phones, and Philip and I went back in to the city centre. We had both changed out of our whites and had each taken a hand-held Motorola with us. I was dressed in a scruffy pair of jeans, a baggy T-shirt and training shoes in an attempt to look as much like a local Serb as possible, something that never really ever worked but at least we had to try. Somewhat ironically, I had made arrange-ments several days before the rally was public knowledge, to meet up with Mirjana again in order to give her a letter from Amra who had sent it up with the ECMM post as there was still no postal service between the two entities within Bosnia. I was due to meet her inside Hotel Bosna of all places at 6,00 pm that night and despite my frantic efforts, I had not managed to get hold of her to cancel. Philip thought I was completely stark raving mad even to contemplate going inside the Bosna as it was literally surrounded by plain-clothes bodyguards and armed Police from Pale. Once inside the building it was probably just as dangerous since if Krajisnik was there, then he would also have his close protection staff with him. On the other hand, we both wanted to know who had turned up for the rally. We'd seen Kijac that morning but as of yet no one had reported seeing either Krajisnik or Buha and there was only one-way to find out. I put Amra's letter inside an envelope and wrote 'Mirjana Beric' on it in thick black felt pen in Cyrillic letters. I told Philip I was going inside, turned the envelope round to show the Cyrillic lettering and walked straight towards the main doors of the hotel. The doors were blocked by two armed bodyguards, I approached confidently and simply slid between them uttering, 'Molim vas. Samo malo' as I passed. My next problem was to get upstairs to the main bar and that required me to walk through the reception area which was packed with people, half of them dressed in suits and the other half in denim jeans and black leather jackets. I kept going, making it safely to the spiral stairs that led up to the bar and immediately bumped in Vukovic, the Chief of Krajisnik's personal security who I knew from when I'd driven the President in and out of Sarajevo the previous year. Of all the people to meet, it had to be him. I had no idea how he'd react, as it was obvious that all of the security personnel were extremely nervous, but at least now I had a pretty good indication that Krajisnik was indeed in the building. Vukovic recognised me but couldn't place me. I wasn't about to give him chance either and so when I met his eyes, I simply nodded, smiled and said, 'Dobar dan,' and carried on going. The ruse worked and a few seconds later I made it in to the main bar. Mirjana was sitting facing the entrance with her boyfriend and her sister, Mija. She saw me and her face dropped, clearly I hadn't been expected and now that I'd turned up she quite rightly thought that any connection with an international would put her safety at risk. She looked horrified as I walked towards her and started to glance nervously around the room. When I got to where they were all sitting, they stood up and we quietly greeted each other. I gave Mirjana the envelope saying, 'Ja cu nazovete kasnija,' (I'll call you later) and then immediately turned and much to her relief, left the same way as I'd come in.

I rejoined Philip outside and we made our way South, down towards the main 'Boska' shopping centre where a band had started to play in prepara- tion for the rally. I told him that I thought Krajisnik was inside and that it looked as if they were all preparing themselves to come out on to the street after all. There was no platform at Boska as the Banja Luka Police had stopped one being erected, neither was there any PA system and so if Krajisnik did turn up, he'd have fun trying to make himself heard. By 6,00 pm it was quite apparent that the road blocks had worked and that the buses found to contain weapons had successfully been turned back. Only about two hundred SDS supporters had gathered in the square. These consisted of about fifty 'heavies,' another fifty drunken youths and around one hundred elderly peasants from the Southeast. Around three hundred Banja Luka onlookers were slowly encircling them and occasionally bombarding the inner circle of SDS supporters with bottles, sticks and small pieces of wood. After about half an hour, the heavies decided they'd had enough and tried to charge the not so passive onlookers. The move was quietly stopped by the intervention of the local Police and the heavies then drifted off back up the road towards the hotel. At 7,00 pm they returned, this time with a large number of armed bodyguards and with Krajisnik in tow. Krajisnik took the floor and attempted to address the crowd but he couldn't make himself heard over the whistling and jeering of the pro-Plavsic crowd. At this stage I couldn't hear or see anything either and so I crossed over the road and made my way slowly through the crowd of SDS supporters until I was physically stood right next to the President. Sticks were raining down quite a bit now and Vukovic and his team of bodyguards looked decidedly unhappy to say the least. They'd all closed in around their principal and were concentrating on ensuring that non-of the flying objects struck him. Krajisnik looked decidedly small and fearful. He was clearly rattled and unnerved by what was going on and it was obvious that he really hadn't anticipated the kind of reception he was now getting. He was fighting to retain his composure and his dignity and he wasn't doing very well. An SRT camera crew jumped me as I watched Krajisnik fumble along. The crowd was jostling around quite violently now as more and more people were getting hit by the assorted flying debris. Krajisnik couldn't be heard over the noise and the last thing I needed right now, standing no more than two feet from him, was for a TV crew to launch in to a interview with me not least because my Serbo-Croat wouldn't have stood the test and my cover would have been blown. I ducked from a flying object and pushed the camera and microphone aside shouting, 'Od jebi,' which thankfully they did.

After about half an hour, Vukovic pulled the plug on his boss, physically grabbed him and together with his security team, started to bundle their President off along the main pedestrian shopping street. Some of the Plavsic supporters followed and continued to harass him whilst others made their way up the main boulevard towards Hotel Bosna where they intended to cut off his escape route. I went with this second group, as I had to rejoin Philip who was waiting by the side of the main street. We hung back slightly and briefed each other on what we'd seen and then followed on behind the crowd, which had already got to the Hotel long before Krajisnik could reach it. Vukovic had miss calculated his escape route and now the President was trapped on the street with a group of demonstrators behind him and another group between him and the relative safety of the hotel. Both groups of supporters were now in full view of Plavsic's Presidential Palace and its full complement of VRS and anti-terrorist Police who were nervously flexing their trigger fingers. Unable to get at Krajisnik, who to their professional credit was now actually being protected by the local Banja Luka civil Police, the demonstrators by the hotel turned their pent up aggression on Damljanovic and more specifically on his BMW, which they systematically started to demolish by hand. Philip and I watched the proceedings for about ten minutes until the remainder of Krajisnik's Police from within the hotel mustered enough courage to baton charge the crowd. Caught up in the ensuing chaos, we barely managed to extract ourselves without getting hurt. Vukovic seized the moment and with the help of the local Police and the Pale Police, managed to force a way through to the hotel with a severely shocked President in tow. Krajisnik had survived the rally although both his own and his party's reputation in Banja Luka was now in tatters. But it was not all over yet, Krajisnik and the whole of his delegation were effectively trapped inside Hotel Bosna and there was no way that the hostile crowd of Plavsic supporters were going to let them go free.

The siege had settled down to a stalemate and so Philip and I had left town and headed back up to the CC where Koks was waiting. Together we supped several of the local Nektar beers and filed our last report of the day at 11,00 pm. The next morning we went back in to town and took another look at the hotel and with the aid of an interpreter found out as much as we could from the remnants of the crowd and the local Police. Plavsic had offered Krajisnik safe passage but he had declined the offer and stayed put with his entourage. Both he and Kijac with around fifty heavily armed security guards remained in the hotel along with about two hundred hapless guests who were also temporarily trapped inside. The Banja Luka Police now wanted to question Kijac and disarm the bodyguards up to a 'normal and acceptable level' but much to their annoyance, no one was playing ball. As we stood watching and speaking with the Police, the crowd outside grew sizeably bigger until around five hundred demonstrators surrounded the building. The mob was being led by a man named Braco Zemic, the owner of the local disco bar 'Music Hall' which was located across the river over looking the city's Castle. Zemic promptly announced that unless Kijac and all the weapons were handed over to the Banja Luka Police within thirty minutes, then he and the crowd would storm the hotel. In the meantime, OHR's PDHR Jaques Klein had been inside the hotel in negotiation with Krajisnik in an attempt to find a peaceful solution to the unfolding crisis. Klein called General Ramsey to join him in the negotiations and at around 2,30 pm two British armoured fighting vehicles arrived at the front of the hotel. It was so bizarre to stand and watch Krajisnik's thugs leave the hotel under British Army protection, surrender their weapons and climb in to the back of the British vehicles. The crowd cheered the soldiers and whistled at Krajisnik's thugs as all but the President and around twelve of his professional close protection team, left the building. Philip and I continued to monitor developments throughout the rest of the afternoon as SFOR, the IPTF and Gospodin Lukac, the head of the Banja Luka anti-terrorist Police, all went back and forth to discuss a face saving solution for Krajisnik who finally slipped away quietly during the early evening. It had been an interesting two days and a frantic start to my tour in Banja Luka. Krajisnik had gambled that he could defeat Plavsic on her home turf but had miscalculated badly and lost. Neither him nor the SDS had been defeated however, as both retained their control of the Southeast, but they were severely damaged and had all but lost their credibility in the Northwest. The RS had been on the verge of civil war but thankfully that had been averted, at least for now. Sadly the entity remained divided but in four days time its people would take to the polls to voice their own verdict on events in the first set of municipal level elections since the end of the war. Plavsic's new party couldn't contest these elections as she hadn't formed it early enough to register it, but she had also disbanded the National Assembly and so for the moment the entity remained ungoverned. She had yet to announce the date of that second election but when she did, her party would be ready and able to stand.

CC Banja Luka didn't really have a monitoring team of its own. It should have done and certainly was big enough. The HCC was supposed to be the main person leading the CC's meetings with interlocutors assisted by the Deputy HCC. In this way, our Daily Report should have included at least two major items of information each day. For some reason however, the DHCC who was always appointed by the French delegation, never ever went out to conduct a meeting and instead busied himself with administrative tasks all day long. Even some months later, after many complaints to the HRC, when we finally got an admin NCO to do these tasks, the DHCC still refused to go out and conduct meetings. This meant that the Operations Officer (Philip) had to do the DHCC's tasks along with his own duties such as checking, validating and often rewriting the four field team reports before submitting them to Sarajevo. Both Philip and I were in fact quite happy to get out of the Ops Room and conduct meetings but on top of this we would also have to accompany the HCC on his meetings (without being allowed to speak) just so that we could write up his report for him. To add to this unfair burden, the HCC task of writing Special Reports and compiling the Weekly Assessment Report also fell to the Operations Officer. Philip had managed to do all this and for the most part, retain a decent sense of humour but he was completely burnt out. Hardly anyone else in the CC lifted a finger to help him and in the end he had asked to be moved. Instead of keeping abreast of what sterling work Philip had almost single-handedly been doing and looking after his welfare, the Head of UK Delegation considered Philip's badgering for a move to be 'making waves' and so Philip unjustifiably earned himself a bad reputation. It was a lesson in British politics that I didn't learn from Philip and a bad mistake on his part, which sadly I would repeat to my own cost within three months of taking over from him. The CC's accommodation in Motel Golden Card was both filthy and inappropriate. No one seemed to care either, but as I prepared to take over from Philip I decided that it had to be sorted out. Two things urgently needed doing, we had to get more and properly equipped office space, and we had to sort out the archives. The French DHCC should have sorted out the appropriate furniture scales etc but despite not going out to conduct interviews, he had not sorting anything else out either even though things were simply screaming out to be done. I got Koks's permission to bypass the DHCC and went to Drago, the Mafia boss owner of the Golden Card. I liked Drago and had known him since 1996 when I'd first come to Banja Luka with OHR. At risk of loosing our custom, I got him to agree to let us another two rooms and to totally revamp all the offices with proper lighting and office furniture, and to completely redecorate and re-carpet the place. I spent several days touring Banja Luka in his S-Class Mercedes and managed to spend over DEM 18,000 of his money, an almost incomprehensible amount of money in the RS at that time. On my insistence we even turned the disgusting recreation room and kitchen in to an elegant conference and briefing room complete with mock leather chairs in which I instigated morning briefings complete with coffee in the hope that even the uninterested admin wallahs would be drawn in to the machinations of the CC and ideally begin to feel a part of it all. The only aspect that I wasn't able to address was the constant power cuts that affected the city. Drago was unable to help with this either and in any case it was ECMM's responsibility to provide what we needed to operate and he had already done more that he needed to. I had to rely on the DHCC to get hold of small UPS systems for each of our computers. These did eventually arrive before I finally ended my mission almost a whole year later, but they were still not the complete solution. With the power cuts, everything failed and whilst the computers would keep running off the UPS batteries, there was no power to run any lighting and so half the time I couldn't even see my notes when I was trying to write up all the reports. Since no one else wrote reports, it was always me and Rutger the signaller (an excellent Dutch communications Sergeant who aspired to be a Royal Nederlands Commando and who had to wait for me to finish the reports before he could transmit them to Sarajevo) who had to deal with these problems. During a power cut we would have to venture out and start the petrol generator in order get some power in to the building via miles of interconnecting and dangerously overloaded extension leads. In the mean time, the HCC, DHCC, admin NCO and driver would all sit with the three interpreters and do nothing. I pressed the DHCC for months to sort out a proper office wide UPS system like the one I'd had installed in OHR Sarajevo but it never materialised. The archiving problem was far more easily solved, it just needed some effort but sadly again only Rutger offered any help. Since the whole raison d'etre of ECMM was to research, analyse and report, it went without saying that the proper archiving of our own product; namely our reports, was a core activity. Sadly I was in a majority of one but I couldn't just forget about it as we were often unable to locate even the simplest of documents when requested to comment on an area of concern or worse still, to brief a visiting ambassador or European politician. In all, it took Rutger and I around four days to completely re-label and re-file everything in a coherent manner but it was well worth the effort as more and more high level European delegations visited Banja Luka demanding to be briefed by 'their monitors.' Sadly though, although my efforts brought about a quantum improvement to our working environment, Koks would later dismiss my efforts as inconsequential.

The weekend following Krajisnik's ill-fated attempt to quash Biljana Plavsic's reform process saw the staging of municipal elections across Bosnia and also Cantonal level elections in the Federation.[120] The build up to the elections had been tremendous as many observers thought that there might be serious trouble. Following their postponement the year before, the country had continued to be run at the local level by its war-time leadership and so these elections represented the first opportunity for the people to chose an alternative to nationalism at community level. They also marked a significant milestone on Bosnia's road to recovery. People would be able to vote for where they now lived or for where they originally came from and in theory they would be able to travel freely to and from the polling stations. But a possible consequence of such free and fair elections, if enough people voted for their original constituencies, was that the election might produce results that reflected the original ethnic balance of the municipalities, something that did not now mirror the reality on the ground. Indeed, this was an intention of the election – to redress ethnic cleansing by giving DPs and refugees the ability to vote for candidates of their own ethnic group in the municipalities they had fled from. The intention of course, was to facilitate their eventual return leading to the re-composition of multi-ethnic municipalities and the demise of 'Municipal Authorities in Exile.' And so with this grand aim in mind, the country went to the polls over the weekend 13-14 September. According to the OSCE, over two and a half million people had registered to vote and so to cope with the supervision and observation of the whole process, hundreds of international supervisors had been recruited, flown in to the country and trained to ensure that everything went smoothly. I had briefed and helped train many of the long-term observers in Prijedor and did the same for the short-term observers in Banja Luka. Our own role within ECMM was to assist in the general observation of the elections, not just at the polls like the OSCE observers and supervisors, but in the wider area and along the designated voter routes. I had our four field teams out and about through-out both days and I collated their periodic reports and forwarded a composite email to Sarajevo every couple of hours. We also provided support to the OSCE Office of Democratic Institutions and Human Rights[121] and had been instructed to fax through their hand written reports to Sarajevo. A few tele-phone links between the Federation and the RS had been established on 5th August, but these only worked if the call was instigated from the Federation, it was still physically impossible for us to call the HQ from the RS. A limited number of lines were eventually established both ways but not until after the election on 19th September, although clearly the senior Dutch Army officer acting as the Head of Communications at ECMM HQ had absolutely no concept of this difficulty. I had told Koks that we couldn't use the fax (as we couldn't instigate a cross-IEBL call) and he had subsequently been told to use the Mini-M, a small INMARSAT satellite phone to which we could link our normal fax machine. The problem was that the Mini-M worked extremely slowly, taking about five minutes to fax a page of A4 paper and the ODIHR teams reporting in to us had around four hundred pages between them that needed to be faxed through. The cost of satellite communications is largely prohibitive and I calculated that to comply with the ill informed instruction would have cost at least several thousand US Dollars and in any case would have taken someone continuously sat at the fax machine over thirty-three hours to fax it all through thus negating the value of what was being reported. I refused to use the Mini-M and sent all the material to Sarajevo by car, a road journey of no more that three and a half hours, at a fraction of the cost. Koks and his Dutch counterpart in Communications were decidedly irritated.

The election itself passed by without any major incidents in our area and in this respect was quite dull in comparison to expectations and all the hype. It was the post-election implementation of the results that was to become the most crucial aspect of the whole process and sadly the most misunderstood aspect at that. These elections had been in preparation for a year and once they were over the IC breathed a huge collective sigh of relief. But staging the elections was only ever the beginning of the process and many in HQ ECMM simply failed to appreciate that the election meant nothing unless those who had won could formally take their seats and where necessary, exercise appropriate power. This was to be OSCE's greatest challenge yet, and to help them ECMM monitor teams joined newly created 'Election Results Implementation Committees' (ERIC) located at OSCE Field Office level and the five ECMM CCs in Bosnia each joined a 'Regional Election Results Implementation Committee' (RERIC) located at OSCE Regional Centres. As the Operations Officer in Banja Luka, my remit was to oversee the observations of my four field teams and to represent their views along with my own observations from Banja Luka, at monthly RERICs. A caucus consisting of the OSCE Director and his Elections Officer, myself, an OHR representative and a UN Civil Affairs representative, would review events in each municipality and decide whether the authorities were behaving correctly or not. What was at stake was each municipality's legal status since the OSCE national level 'NERIC' had to decide whether or not to grant 'Final Certification' to each and every municipality. Final Certification would only be granted if there had been a fair and equitable hand-over of power between the old war-time leadership and those newly elected. Without Final Certification an authority was deemed to be illegitimate. On the face of it, this was a simple issue yet it was incredibly difficult to police and I was to continue to work on the Banja Luka RERIC right up until the day I left in the following July. In effect that meant that in several municipalities, we were still trying to get those elected, in to office nearly nine months after 'free and fair' elections had taken place. All ethnic groups played the same game and all were guilty to some degree or other of gross obstruction, intransigence, intimidation and even violence towards each other. The reasons behind their action and the methods employed to achieve their aims were as complex as the country's history and consequently most of the ECMM HQ Staff Officers did not understand what was happening nor did they really care. Part of the problem was the short-tour syndrome and the fact that the election itself had been so hyped up that all that followed was deemed unimportant. But it was also a problem connected with the EU Presidency. When the British took over from the Dutch-Luxembourg Presidency on 1st January 1998, we all had high hopes that matters within the HQ would improve. Sadly if anything, things got worse and as far as election matters were concerned, the incoming UK Presidency simply wasn't interested in something that had happened over three months previously. Elections were dead and as the months passed by, I was repeatedly told that my reports were too detailed and unimportant. Sadly, such an attitude permitted General Alagic to be returned to power in Sanski Most when both my team there led by Alan, and my own reports were detailing his manipulation of the results and the Municipal Assembly, and strongly recommending that he should be struck off the electoral list. Even a frantic call to Harry Quirk, the delightful Irish DHRC, pleading for him to take up our case at the NERIC in Sarajevo fell on deaf ears.[122] Intellectually it was far too much for him to comprehend and sadly a miscarriage of justice was committed by letting Alagic retake office.

The obstruction of the results implementation process had many facets. To start with, the war-time leadership in a municipality might simply dispute the figures and refuse to honour the official election results. The system of voting was extremely simple and in effect voters merely voted for a party and not a personality unless they were voting for an independent candidate. Each party had a list of candidates in ranking order and depending upon the proportion of votes cast for the party, would take a proportionate amount of seats on the assembly filling them from the top of their list and working downwards. In effect this meant that all parties with votes above a threshold would win seats, but rather than allow the Muslims and Croats to take seats in RS municipalities, the various Serbian parties would club together and claim that they had the overwhelming majority and so were entitled to all the seats. In the Federation, Muslim and Croats would say the same to keep out the Serbs. ECMM and OSCE teams would attend municipal assembly meeting and closely follow the proceedings and report on such obstruction. The ERICs would then raise the matter with the RERIC where we would decide how to tackle the issue. Once one issue was resolved, possibly through the threat of sanctions, then another circumvention of the regulations would surface. For example, having forced the Serbs in Prnjavor to allocate seats to Muslim DP candidates currently living in exile in Bosanski Pertovac, the Serbs would again club together to deny the Muslim Deputies positions on the Executive Board. Once they had been forced to allocate positions on the Board, they would only offer minor appointments. Occasionally, a municipality might relent and offer a senior position such as Vice President only to have the Muslim party turn it down, as they secretly wanted a more junior yet more influential and critical position such as 'housing,' a post that would give them control over the means to return. To extract advantage over the other and favour with the IC, all sides would submit claim and counter claim. Even after all the seats had been properly allocated amongst all ethnic groups according to the results, Muslims often refused to attend inaugural meetings in the RS claiming that the solemn oath pledged loyalty to the RS or that the RS flag was flying. Likewise once that had been resolved they still wouldn't attend assembly meetings because the official record of proceedings were being made in the Cyrillic script, or they hadn't been notified in sufficient time to get there, or that they felt it wasn't safe to travel. In some cases their complaints were wholly justifiable, as the Serbs simply wanted to keep the other ethnic groups out. In other cases their claims were simply lies and attempts to discredit a legitimately elected authority in which they had lost. With each new scam, ECMM and OSCE had to investigate and get to the bottom of the issue to resolve it. And with each resolution came a new scam. After security issues came transport issues, then over night accommodation and then finally when Deputies were expected to have moved back to their former homes in order to receive their returning DP communities, the issue of permanent housing and even privileged jobs and company directorships surfaced. The whole issue of results implementation was a constant battle against corrupt politicians who still associated politics with personal power and wealth and not with service and leadership of their community. I have no doubt to this day that had we not forced many of these politicians to work together, then they and their communities would still be at each others' throats. Faced with such strong domestic resistance to reconciliation and reconstruction at almost every turn, the IC working throughout Bosnia gave their all and in several cases even their lives trying to forward the peace process. On 17th September, just three days after the elections and long before the implementations process had even begun, a UN Mi8 'Hip' helicopter carrying twelve members of the IC crashed into a hill side in Bugojno killing all the passengers on board. Five members of OHR including the new Deputy High Representative Ambassador Wagner and Leah Melnik from the HR Office were killed. With Jim Moran's earlier death, I had now lost a total of six former colleagues killed in the service of the Bosnian people. Sadly these were not to be the last.

21

Consolidation

With municipal elections over and the battle to implement the results underway, Plavsic and Krajisnik still had to sort out the matter of the RSNA. In actual fact, President Plavsic's dissolution of Republika Srpska's Government had nothing whatsoever to do with Krajisnik, who as the Serb member of the Bosnian three-person Presidency should have been involving himself instead with matters of state and not of one entity. In reality however, Krajisnik was inexplicably linked with whatever went on in the RS and even after his humiliating defeat on the streets of Banja Luka, continued to influence decisions that should have been taken either by Plavsic or by the RSNA had there been one. Likewise and perhaps more ominously, as he was the head of state of a totally different country, the hand of Milosevic was still often at play directly influencing events within Republika Srpska. On 24th September, both Plavsic and Krajisnik met with Milosevic in Belgrade and discussed when they should hold the next set of elections. Their original decision was that elections for the RSNA, to be supervised by the OSCE, would be held on 15th November, and that elections for the Serb member of the three-person Presidency would be held on 7th December. What was of interest was the fact that no one had previously intended or announced that Krajisnik had to step down and re-stand for election. Indeed, both his and Plavsic's Presidency were not in dispute, only the RS Parliament. The fact that Krajisnik in discussions with Milosevic had decided that he should reconfirm his mandate as one of Bosnia's three Presidents smacked of intrigue and it took a while before I realised what their game plan was. Krajisnik was gambling that he would be returned to office and that his move would force Plavsic also to reconfirm her own mandate, something both he and Milosevic thought wasn't so secure. They wanted her to step-down so that they could ensure either by hook or by crook that she wasn't re-elected. But

Plavsic was shrewd enough not to fall for their ruse and in the end she had some strange allies come to her aid. On the face of it even an expert observer might reasonably have expected both Izetbegovic and Zubak, the Muslim and Croat members of the three-person Presidency, to have welcomed Krajisnik's decision to stand for re-election in the hope that he fail. After all, Krajisnik was obstructing the Presidency at every opportunity. Yet it was precisely these two who objected to any form of re-election for the Serb seat demanding that Krajisnik sit out his whole term of office. Again it took me a while to figure it out but Balkan politics are never straightforward. In simple terms, it suited the interests of both Izetbegovic and Zubak for Krajisnik to forever obstruct, stall and wreck the workings of the Presidency and the Joint Institutions since they too had no desire to see these functions of government work. They like Krajisnik were non-too happy with a two-entity Bosnia where its three ethnic groups were forced by the IC to live and work together in harmony. So long as Krajisnik was around, he would take the blame for the failings of the Presidency whilst both their slates remained clean and so both of them refused to allow Krajisnik to stage any further elections for his post leaving just the elections for the RSNA to take care of as originally intended.

Krajisnik had not kept his 2nd September agreement with Jaques Klein and General Shinseki to tone down the hostile nature of SRT broadcasts, instead he had attempted to retake the Banja Luka studio and then to topple Plavsic but failed on both counts. As a result of his failure to re-exert control over SRT, Plavsic, Krajisnik and Milosevic also reached an agreement in Belgrade on how SRT would be managed in the future. The agreement, which was kept, permitted SRT Banja Luka and SRT Pale to broadcast throughout the RS on alternative days. What clearly wasn't covered however, was the editorial content of the programmes put out by each side. As a result, the distortion of facts and events put out by SRT Pale continued unabated and on 28th September a press conference by the Chief Prosecutor for The Hague Tribunal Louis Arbour, was totally distorted by Pale. On the same day, Krajisnik's supporters renewed their terror tactics against the free media, this time blowing up the offices of an opposition newspaper, the 'Alternative,' in Doboj. On 1st October, Carlos Westerndorp requested NATO's Secretary General to authorise SFOR to physically seize and control four SRT transmitters in the East and Southeast of the RS at Udrigovo, Duge Njive, Trebevic and Leotar thus effectively closing down Krajisnik's means of fighting a propaganda war against Plavsic and the IC. A week later Westerndorp issued a series of criteria to Krajisnik demanding the restructuring of SRT but on the 18th October, an unreformed STR Pale came back on the air in complete defiance of the international ban. Two days later the key pro-Banja Luka SRT transmitter site near Han Pijesak at Veliki Zep was sabotaged forcing the United States Airforce to fly electronic warfare flights broadcasting an SRT 'test card' explaining what had happened. On the 20th, the Bijeljina transmitter was also destroyed by a powerful blast leaving SRT Banja Luka no other means than to use a satellite link to restore its pictures in the Eastern part of the RS by the end of the month. Although the SRT Banja Luka studio announced at the beginning of November that it would comply with full restructuring in accordance with the High Representative's demands, this tit-for-tat battle for control of the media would last for another five and a half months. It was not until 13th April in the following year that SFOR finally withdrew its troops from the five transmitter sites it had by then occupied.

On 30th October, the PEC announced that the elections for the RSNA would take place over the weekend 22-23 November. The lead up to the election coincided with an RS wide poster campaign by the SDS supporting the cause of their previous President and ousted former war-time leader and PIFWC, Radovan Karadzic. Posters of Karadzic were being pinned up just about everywhere one could imagine and it was physically impossible to ignore them. In Banja Luka the locals tore many down but enough were put up to inspire the OSCE Election Appeals Sub-Commission to disqualify three SDS candidates from their party list prior to the election. In the CC, things were moving along as before although if anything, the work load continued to grow as more and more agencies, visiting delegations, European MEPs and ambassadors began to take a far keener interest in events in the RS and demand that we brief them on current events. I was already working at full capacity and it was rare for Rutger and I to leave the office much before 9,00 pm each evening. But things were to get far busier following the elections as it was Plavsic's intention not just to simply re-elect the parliament, but to move it lock stock and barrel from Pale to Banja Luka. As had been the case with the previous month's municipal elections, these parliamentary elections passed smoothly and without incident in our area. But again, it was what would happen afterwards that would be crucial to the reform process and in this case the fun and games started on 7th December when the OSCE announced the provisional results.

As had been expected, the SDS won the biggest number of seats, twenty-four in total. A multi-ethnic coalition, the 'Coalition for a Single and Democratic Bosnia' (Koalicija) came second with sixteen seats. Then came both Poplasen's Serb Radical Party and Plavsic's newly formed Serb Peoples' Alliance with fifteen seats apiece. Zivko Radisic's Socialist Party of the RS got nine seats and Milorad Dodik's Party of Independent Social Democrats (SNSD) got two seats, bringing the total number of Deputies in the new RS National Assembly to eighty-one. From these results it soon became clear that the Muslim-Croat Koalicija held the key to power in the new RSNA. The SDS could always count on the support of the SRS giving the hard-liners a combined total of thirty-nine seats. Plavsic's party, under the leadership of its Vice President, Ostoja Knezevic, needed the support of almost all of the remaining deputies if it was ever going to achieve any of its reforms. The problem was two fold. Firstly, Plavsic could not necessarily count on Radisic's support, after all his SPRS was the sister party of

Milosevic's own SPS. Secondly, she could not assume that all of the minority groups within the Koalicija would support her either, and even if they did, it might be counter productive for both of them to be seen to be supporting each other. Although Plavsic badly needed their support, she knew that in order to secure it that she would have to offer them something in return. Whilst this was straightforward enough, she knew that any deal between a Serb party and the Muslim-Croat Koalicija would be exploited by the SDS to the full and even risked alienating her own supporters, yet she simply had to deal with them for her own political survival. Whilst all the deals were being knocked out behind the scenes, another battle was being fought in the open. Plavsic insisted that the Assembly move to Banja Luka where it would sit in the concert hall within Banski Dvor. At first Krajisnik and the SDS refused to move but he no longer had absolute control of the Parliament anymore and so half of the deputies accepted the move despite his objections. Initially Krajisnik responded by suggesting that the Inaugural Session take place mid-way between Pale and Banja Luka in Bijelina but again he simple didn't have the backing to carry it off. Instead, the session was held in Banja Luka on 27th December whilst I was back in the UK on leave. At the session, Plavsic proposed an economics professor who had spent considerable time in the UK studying at the University of Glasgow and who was not tainted by the war or by inter-party divisions, to be the next Prime Minister. Mladen Ivanic was seen by all sides as a neutral choice and had he accepted the position, would undoubtedly have been a unifying force in the RS.

Back and suitably refreshed from leave, I rejoined the CC and quickly settled in to a hectic schedule under the leadership of the new HCC, Robin Seaword who had thankfully replaced Hans Koks. Robin was also a retired Major from the British Army and had joined the UK Delegation of ECMM having been recruited by the FCO just before Christmas. Like many of the new intake of Brits, recruited to bolster our numbers whilst the UK held the EU Presidency, Robin had considerable Bosnian experience having served in Bosnia during the war and, as an intelligence expert, had commanded the Defence Debriefing Team back in the UK. He was a breath of fresh air, knew precisely what he was about and was keen to get stuck in as I was. In fact, if it weren't for Robin I would never have lasted the course as I was exhausted from working for Koks and was rapidly beginning to think that the whole mission was pointless and had long decided that it was thankless. Robin's arrival injected new life in to the CC and the timing of his arrival came at a critical point when our workload was about to triple due to the arrival of the RS Government in Banja Luka. We worked together brilliantly and complemented one another filling in the gaps and covering for each other's weaknesses so that together we were quite a formidable team. I immediately started to enjoy going out on meetings again and we would spend hours afterwards going through all the nuances of what was said to determine the progress of Republika Srpska's nascent democracy. After all the excitement of Prijedor and the early days in Banja Luka, it was a long period of calm albeit an exciting time if you really delved into and immersed yourself in the everyday events around you. It was a time of thinking, for being proactive and for investigating rather than reacting to rapidly unfolding events and violent attacks. Our reports no longer captured the headlines but instead covered the detailed machinations of a Government and entity grinding through the slow and tortuous pains of reform. What ECMM needed now was monitors who understood the intricacies of what was really going on behind all the rhetoric and who had the mental dexterity to stick with it. But Robin and I were never going to be able to cover everything on our own and so after much quibbling, Robin managed to secure another two monitors out of the new HRC in Sarajevo and we were able set up our own monitoring team within the CC. In practice, the two new comers did not form a team of their own, instead Robin and I each took one under our wing so that we continued to field two full teams but with an expert in each. Both the new comers were excellent men; John Durnin a Commandant[123] from the Irish Army who would later take over from me as the CC's Operations Officer and Jon Strandeness, an excellent Norwegian seconded from the Norwegian Refugee Council who sadly asked to be moved out of Bosnia[124] in protest at the ridiculous tasking being sent to us from the British Presidency. Jon's departure was a sad loss as he needn't have been driven away. The UK Presidency attempted to give the CCs more direction in their work and to give some long awaited feedback. In practice, tasks allocated to CCB distracted from our mainstream efforts and the feedback was limited to an unwanted critique on our reports (they were always too long) rather than telling us what we wanted to know; namely what was being done as a result of them. As such, the Feedback given to us totally missed the point. Jon's feelings, and ours, was that many new tasks were poorly formulated and had already been answered previously, something that the HQ should have known had they bothered to look. The final straw had been when I was tasked to compile a Special Report entitled, 'The Barriers to Trade' and directed to answer specific questions such as, 'Do the customs checkpoints either side of the IEBL have documentation in each others' languages?' Firstly, even the reader will now realise that the IEBL is an internal boundary rather like the one between Devon and Cornwall and that there aren't any customs post either side of it. Secondly, even if there had been, the Muslims, Croats and Serbs of Bosnia all speak the same language; namely Serbo-Croat albeit with slightly different dialects. Even if one really wanted to find an excuse for the lack of basic knowledge shown by the British Staff Officer drafting the ridiculous question and interpret it as a question on external borders, one still arrives at the same answer. Bosnia only borders former Yugoslav republics, Croatia to the North, Serbia to the East and Montenegro to the Southeast. They still all speak the same language! As Operations Officer I protested at this and similar tasks only to be firmly told off and told to get on with it. Relations within ECMM between the HQ and the field had never been good but now under the disastrous British leadership they were rapidly disintegrating.

Robin and I took it in shifts to attend the second session of the RSNA on 12th January and to observe the political infighting as Deputy after Deputy took to the floor and issued proposal and counter-proposal in order to elect the President and Vice-Presidents of the Assembly. In the end, the SDS stalwart and former Prime Minister, Dragan Kalinic was re-elected to the top position whilst the Vice-President slots went to Nikola Poplasen of the SRS, Jovan Mitrovic and following much behind the scenes dealing, to Savet Bico, the Muslim SDA leader of the Koalicija. Ivanic, whilst retaining the position of mandator, had still not accepted the post of Prime Minister and was secretly having personal doubts as to whether the time was right for him, as a reformer, to assume the mantel of trying to reform the RS when there was still so much apparent opposition to it within the country. The session ended without Ivanic's appointment and behind the scenes negotiations continued at breakneck speed to find a candidate suitable to all sides. Robin and I embarked on a series of meetings with all the main parties, meeting their presidents and trying to find out what was likely to happen. On Friday 16th January we'd arranged to meet with Milorad Dodik, the leader of the SNSD, in the small spa town of Laktasi, in his constituency just North of Banja Luka. We met him in the restaurant of Hotel-Laktasi and sat down with him to have coffee whilst swapping pleasantries. There was a buzz about the place and on several occasions we were interrupted by aids bringing Dodik news. We knew that Ivanic had gone to Belgrade to meet with Milosevic, who despite everything, still continued to dictate what would and would not happen in the RS. Robin knew Ivanic from Glasgow where he had met with him several times whilst with the DDT and didn't think that he'd take the job as Prime Minister. We both agreed that it was potential suicide for him not least because he didn't have the support of a party of his own to fall back on. Dodik on the other hand was seen by many to be neutral, a man of integrity and a businessman whom the IC could deal with. He was also a good friend of Milosevic although not necessarily in his pocket. We also knew that if Ivanic turned down the post, that Dodik was probably the next on Plavsic's list of possible candidates. As such, we wanted to speak with him to see what, if anything he would tell us. Dodik was being very coy and did not give much away at first. After about half an hour we were again interrupted and this time Dodik left us briefly. When he returned he announced that he had just spoken with Ivanic and Milosevic in Belgrade, that Ivanic had turned down the job of Prime Minister and that he had accepted it instead. It was excellent news as we were literally the first to know, Dodik hadn't even called President Plavsic to inform her that he'd accepted the position of mandator. We ordered drinks and toasted his appointment managing to squeeze in a few more questions before he departed for Banski Dvor to inform the President of his decision and to schedule the next meeting of the RS National Assembly for the next day.

Dodik's first test as mandator was to form a new government and that wasn't going to be easy for him as his own party had won only two seats in the new parliament and one of those was his own. On the 17th January the RSNA reconvened and confirmed Dodik's appointment as Prime Minister. Slowly but surely the SDS were loosing their hold over the Parliament and as Dodik set about appointing his Government of reformers all they could do was to try and discredit him by playing the nationalist card once more. The SDS needed to prove that Dodik was not a patriotic Serb and had sold-out the Serb people in a secret deal with Bico and the Koalicija. When the voting to confirm the appointment of his Government ministers started, the SDS and SRS group sitting on the left of the Assembly demanded that the SPRS, SNS-BP, SNSD and the ethnic minority parties vote first, indeed the hard-liners were threatening to boycott the vote if they didn't. One by one, Plavsic's Deputies, the Independent Democrats and the sixteen Koalicija Deputies got up and cast their vote in a so-called secret ballot. Robin and I were sitting in the Assembly watching the SDS in silence as each of the Deputies placed their ballot papers in the 'sealed' box on the front left of the stage. When the Koalicija had finished it was then the turn of the SDS to vote but they remained firmly in their seats demanding a count right then and there. The Muslims refused having realised what was happening far quicker than Robin and I who were left wondering what was going on for a few minutes longer. Suddenly all hell broke out and it was chaos as numerous Deputies left their seats shouting and trying to force the issue. It was then that it dawned on the both of us what they were up to. If the SDS and SRS didn't vote and a count was made now, one would easily be able to tell whether the Koalicija Deputies had voted for Dodik's proposals or not. It was a simple matter of adding up the votes and then seeing whether Dodik had won or not. If he had, then he must have done a deal with the Muslims and Croats, something that the SDS would be sure to expose for all its worth. The Koalicija realised the scam before the two of us and as Robin and I moved to the front of the hall to get a better look at what was going on amidst all the chaos, Rusic the charismatic leader of the HDZ, the Croatian (nationalist) Democratic Union, unseen by all but us, leapt forward and grabbed the ballot box. Whilst the black metal box had been sealed with a padlock on the top, the bottom of the box didn't have a base at all and so as Rusic lifted it off the table, all the ballots fell out on the floor of the Assembly Hall. We watched in disbelief as he grabbed a hand full of secret ballots and stuffed them down the inside of his jacket and into his pockets before turning to make his escape. I caught his eye and he winked before rapidly disappearing out the back of the hall. The session had been a farce but at least the SDS could not now expose any secret deal between Dodik's fragile fledgling Government and the ethnic minority party.

In the months that followed, Dodik slowly managed to move the Government ministries up to Banja Luka from Pale and Robin and I busied ourselves going around meeting with each new Minister as and when they arrived. Dodik's task was harder than one might have thought. Most of the new Ministers already lived in and around Banja Luka but many had to move to the city with their families from Pale. The real issue however, was moving the actual Ministries and not the Ministers! Krajisnik again tried to block the move and he and his SDS cronies refused to relinquish power without a fight. All the existing Government departments had their offices in Pale. That meant that staff, computers, records – indeed all the bureaucratic paraphernalia of state were in the village. Dodik had to either move all the civil servants or find and employ new ones in Banja Luka loyal to the new regime or preferably, apolitical. He had also to move all the government files, records, and office equipment in to new premises. Not only was he short of new staff and appropriate office space in Banja Luka, he also had to contend with the departing hard-liners who not only stole all of the computers and the Government's fleet of official cars including Audis, Mercedes and BMWs, but froze and tried to steal the entire Government's financial resources from Bank accounts over which they had direct control. To begin with the new Ministers started to conduct their Government duties whilst remaining in their old jobs. Marko Pavic was appointed to be the new Minister of Transport and Communications and in order to meet with him I had to go back to Prijedor and interview him in his old offices in the PTT building. The procedure was repeated at almost every meeting but slowly things started to improve. It was quite bizarre at first, going to meet a Minister whose ministry consisted of nothing more that a newly appointed secretary and a telephone/fax machine. They didn't have any staff, computers, a budget or even a car yet they had been elected to reform and rebuild a country destroyed not just by war, but by two years of peace – and neglect. Almost all were without any direct experience of government and none really knew what democracy meant or what was really expected from them by their electorate and the IC. Meeting with them required all the diplomatic skills I possessed as their situation was both laughable and at the same time, deadly serious. They all lacked experience but made up for it with determination and an eagerness to learn. But what they now needed most of all, was rapid support and advice from the IC to reinforce their victory against the hard-liners. In this sense I knew that during my meetings with them, they were looking to me for help. I still wore my whites and as such represented all the EU Governments in Bosnia, albeit most of them had reopened their own embassies in the country by now. Time and time again Ministers would turn my questions around and I learnt very quickly that they were actually looking for advice yet their pride determined that they couldn't directly ask for it. Instead I had to couch my questions in such a way that suggested that it might be a good idea to look at a specific area. So for example, when meeting with the RS Minister of Education, instead of asking what his new platform was or what reforms he would make to the education system, I'd ask instead whether he'd be reviewing the contemporary history syllabus to ensure that derogatory references to the other ethnic groups were removed from text books, or whether he'd allow the use of the Latin alphabet in schools and not just the Cyrillic one which was an obstacle for Muslim and Croat students? In effect I was helping to shape the new Government's policies and priorities, something that I found far more rewarding than just writing reports for the HQ who in the absence of any proper Feedback were probably still not doing anything with them anyway. That said, other people were more than interested with what we were doing and by Spring time, Robin and I were having to brief at least one high level EU delegation a week. These briefings were hard work, took a lot of preparation and were an additional burden to Robin and me as the French DHCC still took no active part in anything operational whatsoever despite now having an admin NCO to do his work for him. Nevertheless the briefings were extremely rewarding, as we knew that we were helping to shape European policy towards Republika Srpska. Most visiting delegations still looked upon the Serbs as the bad guys and wanted to see for themselves what was really going on in the new RS. On one occasion Robin and I briefed the Norwegian Secretary of State for Foreign Affairs, Mrs Janne Haaland-Matlary for several hours one afternoon and then for several hours more over dinner in the evening. Before the visit she had been against giving aid to the RS but we were able to point out that whilst the RS parliament was inexperienced and only a nascent democracy, it was in fact the only democracy in the whole region and was therefore worth backing. Indeed, in Serbia, Milosevic was still firmly in power. In Croatia, President Tudjman was just as bad whilst even in the Federation in Bosnia, both the SDA and HDZ, the two hard-line nationalist parties that had taken the country to war, remained firmly in power, something that contrasted sharply with the fall of the SDS in the RS. We also learnt several days after the meeting from the Norwegian Charge d'Affaires that as a result of our meeting, the Norwegian Government had given fifty million US dollars in aid to the RS – better feedback than anything we ever had from HQ ECMM.

Interspersed with attending the periodic sessions of the newly elected RSNA, holding meetings with newly appointed Government Ministers and trying to sort out and force through an equitable implementation of the previous September's municipal election results on the RERIC, I spent the rest of my time with ECMM monitoring and reporting on many of the smaller issues of peace implementation and post-war recovery, and there were many. The Americans were still conducting the Train and Equip Programme and so Slobodan Jelicic, the Bosnian Serb Deputy Minister of Defence wanted the RS to be a part of it in order to, 'Ensure a proper balance of forces between the Federation Armies and the VRS.' As usual, HQ ECMM did nothing other than forward my Special Report with Jelicic's request on to Bruxelles and so we approached the Military Cell in OHR to raise the issue instead. In the end I spoke directly with Joseph Allred, the Director of Public Affairs for MPRI who simply listed a series of prerequisites imposed by Ambassador James Pardue, the American

Special Envoy for Regional Stablisation (Military Matters) and by Robert Gelbard, the US Special Envoy for the Balkans. The demands were pie in the sky and reflected the inequities in the American perception of reality. It was clear that both would never entertain the idea of training the VRS but instead preferred to live in their fairytale world in which the ABiH and HVO were fully co-operating with each other and with all the American demands, and were for example forming a united Ministry of Defence, something that still hadn't happened over three years later. It was frightening to listen to what Allred had to say and what he believed to be the truth. Then there was the whole issue of free trade and FoM. Both were inextricably linked to each other and their resolution multifaceted. It took months for the High Representative to force through legislation that scrapped the system of three ethnic vehicle number plates and replace them with a single plain white number plate which did not indicate where the owner lived thus facilitating better FoM. Similarly it took huge efforts to force through legislation to introduce a new Bosnian Flag, a new Bosnian Passport and then a new form of currency called the Konvertable Mark, which was linked one-to-one with the Deutschmark. All of these measures were necessary to rekindle trade between the entities and neighbouring Croatia. The Serbs even opened their Northern border to all traffic allowing Muslims and Croats to trade freely across the international crossing, yet for months the Croats refused to allow any Serb across their own bridge citing insurance problems as the reason whilst the IC stood idly by and did nothing to help the Serbs and resolve the issue. In the RS, economic experts working with the US Agency for International Development (USAID) drew up plans to privatise the economy and create capital markets and I was repeatedly able to advise the US Chief of Party on the subtleties of Bosnian politics. In a totally different area I was able to help Marko Pavic with his request to reopen Banja Luka's airport which had remained closed whilst Sarajevo airport had long been open to commercial airlines. NATO's Southern Air Command in Italy had refused to grant air traffic clearance to the airport having decided that Pavic's request wasn't valid. Before they would grant clearance to open the airport, which was technically ready and waiting to start operations, the Bosnian Civil Aviation Authority and not just the RS Civil Aviation Authority had to make the request. Pavic had shown me his letters to both the Muslim and the Croat members of the joint authority but neither would sign the request effectively denying the RS trade with the outside world. Pavic had therefore made the request on his own, only to have it rejected. It was another example of inter-ethnic obstruction that I was able to bring directly to the attention of the OHR who quickly resolved it by forcing the Muslim and Croat members to sign a joint request.

Whilst I was able to assist with these any many other issues, innumerable others still needed to be addressed and continue to be so even seven years after Dayton. By June 1998, I had been in the Former Yugoslavia for three whole years. I had achieved much although there was still much more to be done. Yet

I was not to continue to do it, at least for the moment since as the end of the UK Presidency drew near, the Delegation had to reduce its numbers from around fifty back down to the pre-presidency total of around twelve or thirteen. Those of us who had been in the core team beforehand were to be 'released' and sent back home. Some of us would find other work in new missions elsewhere. I was tired and beginning to loose my objectivity having spent a long time in the field, indeed the equivalent of six full military 'Roulemont' tours back-to-back without a break, and that was an extraordinary feat in itself. I had been shot at, had numerous guns put to my head in café bars and had even had my house blown up. I needed to go home and perhaps I needed someone to tell me that; for dealing with Presidents and Prime Ministers, and helping to rebuild a country as well as people's lives and livelihoods ravaged by the most destructive war seen in Europe since 1945, was a bug and I had been bitten. My family needed me too and that was to be my next challenge, as settling back in to domestic life wasn't ever going to be easy for me or for them. So finally, when the brown envelopes came and we all opened our letters that set out our futures, it was with mixed feelings that I read that it was time to go home. Sadness, anger, relief and concern all swept through me. I reflected on the quantum changes that had occurred in Bosnia and how much things had changed since I first arrived in Montenegro back in 1995. In ICFY I had lived off pickles and pizzas and in my first few months amidst the destruction of Sarajevo I had scrounged rations off the Army simply to survive. Now as I contemplated returning home, I was sitting in café bars eating and drinking amongst the Serbs I had once feared watching the '98 World Cup casually listening to the celebratory gunfire when someone scored a goal as if firing Klasnikov's in to the air was the normal thing to do on such occasions. I had helped stop the war by ensuring that the Bosnian Serb Army was starved of its vital supplies and then I had been instrumental in creating the institution envisaged by Dayton to lead the peace implementation process. I had put the OHR on the map working from its very inception to provide Carl Bildt with the tools he needed to rebuild the country. I had then moved on to take a more active and far more political role working in and amongst the Serb hard-liners in infamous Prijedor directly influencing the decision of that municipality to turn away from nationalism and join the reformers despite the poor judgement of Ramsey and the inopportune timing of the SAS raid. I had pulled it off and then gone on to help the new RS Government in Banja Luka to formulate its policies and to raise awareness across the IC of Plavsic's and Dodik's attempts to democratise the entity. It had been a struggle. A struggle to determine the truth and reality from that which countless interlocutors told you. And it had been a struggle against the ECMM. I had achieved so much despite the efforts of the HQ and not because of them. Now that the time had come to finish my mission, I would not be sad to put them behind me although I was sad at the thought of leaving the country, my friends, and the way of life and excitement that I had become so accustomed to. I was also angry at the FCO for their thankless attitude and the thought that all my knowledge and experience was now going to go to waste. But on the other hand I was relieved that I was finally going home, even if that decision had been made for me. I was also concerned what I'd do next. I had come to Yugoslavia having had a terribly mundane and pointless job in 'civvy-street' and now my attitudes had hardened even further. I was already unimpressed by many people back home who were content to sit back and watch the world go by without even a care or thought for the huge suffering so prevalent around the rest of the world. Having walked the killing fields of Srebrenica standing among the decaying bodies of old men, women and small children murderously slaughtered by Serb guns, I was now even more intolerant as it seemed that the UK had become a nation of moaners who got excited about the smallest things, such as my children playing in the street, which in the big picture of things simply didn't matter. I would have to cope with all this and perversely I would also need to adjust to life with rules, regulations and responsibilities. I wasn't even used to stopping at red traffic lights – what was the point in a country blown to pieces by four years of war? But now I was returning to the most proscribed country in the Western world, a thought that I found quite claustrophobic and in complete contradiction to what most British people believed to be the truth about their country. It was clear that my attitudes to life had changed dramatically and permanently. I was returning to my family but I would not be the same person who had left them three years previously. I would never be able to stand by in the face of human suffering or injustice without needing to act and to speak out. I had learnt many lessons and new values. Values that placed people, family and hospitality at the top of one's priorities and not wealth and possessions, and I had started to reject the Western model of modern living centred around power and materialism, forever rushing around planning every aspect of one's life. Instead I had learned from the Bosnians that it is life itself that is important and that one should take time to enjoy it and to act spontaneously rejecting the need for micro control and planning of almost every aspect of one's life. The Bosnians and especially the Bosnian Serbs all live for the moment, they are passionate about the here and now and they take every opportunity to enjoy life for they know not what tomorrow might bring. As a people, they have endured centuries of occupation, brutality and oppression and this has had a profound influence on their culture and their behaviour. As my Romanian friend Stefan said to me once when we were discussing precisely this issue, 'When you leave, you take something of that from them. But in return they keep something from you. They steal your heart.'

In reality I knew that I'd be back sooner or later and indeed I would return, first to Kosovo in 1999, and then to Bosnia for another set of elections in 2000, once I'd finished my Masters Degree. But for now I was leaving and so it was amongst the incessant Serb celebratory gunfire during the '98 World Cup, that I said my goodbyes, packed my bags and, flying from the transformed and newly civilianised Sarajevo airport, I finally departed Bosnia leaving part of my heart behind.

Notes

Chapter 1

1. The term Bosnia is used throughout the book to refer to and mean the same as the whole territory of Bosnia i Hercegovina.
2. Slovenian war of secession 1991. Croatian war of secession 1991-1995. Bosnian 'civil' war 1991-95. Kosovo war 1999.
3. The Balkan Wars 1912-13, the First World War and the Second World War.
4. Malcolm, N. 1994. *Bosnia, A Short History*, Papermac (London).
5. Sandzak refers to an Ottoman Region into which the Balkans was divided for administrative purposes.
6. Malcolm, N. 1994. *Bosnia, A Short History*, Papermac (London). pp 147 - 149.
7. Malcolm, N. 1994. *Bosnia, A Short History*, Papermac (London). p 174.
8. Tito declared Yugoslavia's independence at Jajce in 1943.
9. At the beginning of 1990, inflation was running at 2,600% p.a.

Chapter 2

10. JNA: Jugoslovenska Narodna Armija (Yugoslav People's Army).
11. Croatian Serbs were actively supported in their territorial acquisitions by the JNA which was largely officered by ethnic Serbs.
12. Hv: Hrvatska Vojska. Croatian Army.
13. Tito's 1974 Constitution recognised the Muslim religious group within Bosnia i Hercegovina as an equal 'ethnic' group. From this date, the Muslim population were no longer simply a third religious group along side the Orthodox 'Serbs' and Catholic 'Croats,' but were a recognised third national group with full 'national' status.
14. Malcolm, N. 1994. *Bosnia, A Short History*, Papermac (London).
15. The Federal Republic of Yugoslavia consists of Serbia and Montenegro, the only two out of the original six republics which chose to remain in a federal system.
16. Malcolm, N. 1994. *Bosnia, A Short History*, Papermac (London).
17. SAMCOM Teams were European Customs Officers who enforced sanctions on the FRY by sealing its borders with surrounding countries. SAMCOM Teams did not operate within the FRY.

18. Cultural and sporting links were re-established. This included air travel.
19. YAT: Yugoslavian Airlines.

Chapter 3

20. Zastava means 'Flag' in Serbo-Croat and is also the name of an indigenous car manufacturer producing mostly old FIAT and Lada designs.
21. Bar is a small port on the Montenegrin coast from where the car ferry runs to Italy.
22. Glenny, M. 1992. *The Fall of Yugoslavia*, Penguin (London). p. 132.

Chapter 4

23. Podgorica was named Titograd from 1946 until 1992.
24. The last secular Prince of Montenegro resigned in 1516 and transferred civil authority to the Greek Orthodox 'Vladika' – Bishop of Montenegro.
25. Cetinje became the Montenegrin capital in about 1484.
26. Bey: A Muslim nobleman within the Ottoman system of government.
27. Originally the position of Bishop had been an elected office but in 1697 it had become hereditary.
28. A rough brandy, often home made.
29. The Treaty of Berlin, signed on 13 July 1878, ended the Russo-Turkish War of 1877-1878 and also provided for an autonomous principality of Bulgaria.
30. The First Balkan War was concluded by the Treaty of London on 20 May 1913.
31. The Second Balkan War was concluded by the Treaty of Bucharest on 10 August 1913.
32. Jelevich, B. 1983. *History of the Balkans Vol I and Vol II*. Cambridge University Press (Cambridge).
33. Glenny M. 1992. *The Fall of Yugoslavia*, Penguin (London). p. 133.

Chapter 5

34. The Contact Group consisted of Britain, France, Germany, Russia and America. The Group was created to try to solve the problems in Bosnia and first proposed a peace plan in May 1994.
35. VJ: Vojska Jugoslavije – The 'Army of Yugoslavia' was formed from the old JNA after the creation of the FRY.
36. UNPROFOR: United Nations Protection Force.
37. CAPSAT. Usually a 'Thrane & Thrane' satellite data communications system linked to the International Marine Navigation System (INMARSAT).
38. A Sporet is a wood burning stove or range, used for cooking and heating the house.
39. Glenny, M. 1992. *The Fall of Yugoslavia*, Penguin (London) p. 242.
40. VIREP: A Violation Report was the means of alerting the UN Security Council that sanctions were not being applied correctly.
41. The VW Iltis is a small and very basic 4x4 soft-top jeep used by the Bundeswehr.
42. OP: Refers to an Observation Post used to watch over an area.
43. Vehicles carrying empty Jerry cans were recorded to ensure that the cans were still empty on the return crossing.
44. Banate: An area of territory run as a feudal fiefdom and ruled by a Ban.
45. Ragusa refers to the ancient walled city of Dubrovnik, which like Venice, was a major power during this period.
46. The Zastava Fica is a copy of the old Fiat 126.
47. Vinjak: Grape Brandy.

48. Kasarna: A small garrison or military barracks, often no more that a large house with a walled courtyard housing about a platoon sized unit.

Chapter 6

49. The Russian Intelligence Service, Military Intelligence Service and Special Forces respectively.
50. The three main Serbo-Croat dialects are ijekavica – spoken mainly in Bosnia, ekavica – spoken mainly in Serbia and jekavica – spoken mainly in Croatia and Montenegro.

Chapter 7

51. DPs: Displaced Persons refers to those people who have been displaced from their homes but remain within the borders of their own country and are therefore still subject to its sovereignty. There is a distinction in international law between DPs and refugees, the latter will have been displaced from their homes but will have crossed an international border and are therefore protected by the 1951 UN Convention on the Status of Refugees and the 1967 Protocol.
52. Malcolm, N. 1994. *Bosnia, A Short History*, Papermac (London) p. 248.
53. ABiH: Armija Bosna Hercegovina.
54. HVO: Hrvatska Vijece Odbrane (Croatian Defence Council) – the Bosnian-Croat Army.
55. Dual Key: Joint UN/NATO – control of forces.
56. IHL: International Humanitarian Law is the governmental term used to cover the four 1949 Geneva Conventions and the two additional 1977 Protocols policed by the International Committee of the Red Cross. Within military circles, IHL is commonly referred to as the 'Law of Armed Conflict.'
57. Several USAF 'Heavy Drop' webbing parachute strops were evident in the immediate area.
58. Extracts from an interview with Brigadier Mirsad Selmanovic, Chief of Staff ABiH 5th Corps in the Sarajevo weekly political paper: *Ljiljan*, 2 June 1997. (reporter Isnan Taljic) p. 57-60.
59. The Bosnia Serbs denied responsibility for this attack. Throughout the whole period of my time in Sarajevo, the argument continuously raged as to whom was actually responsible.
60. British Battalion assigned to the UN.
61. President Milosevic of Serbia was the chief negotiator for the Bosnia Serbs at Dayton since the Bosnian Serb President, Radovan Karadzic was unable to travel outside of Bosnia as he had already been indicted by the International Criminal Tribunal for the Former Yugoslavia (ICTY) in the Hague.
62. Within months of leaving Whitehall, Dame Pauline Neville-Jones and her old Foreign Office colleague and former Foreign Secretary Douglas Hurd, were arm and arm with Milosevic in Belgrade celebrating a business partnership between his regime and their new employer, NatWest Markets.

Chapter 8

63. A provision which came remarkably close to realising the original war aims of both Presidents Milosevic and Tudjman!
64. The process to enable both refugees and displaced persons to return to their pre-war homes.
65. CSCE: Part of the Cold-war Helsinki negotiations.
66. The EU Presidency rotates every six months.

Chapter 9

67. Serbia is not a member of the international Green Card insurance system.
68. Commercial shipping 'containers' had been strategically placed on the road across each junction and filled with rocks and stones to act as bullet catchers to protect the population from the Serb snipers up in the surrounding hills who constantly attempted to pick off the unwary as they crossed the road.
69. 4 x 4 wheel drive vehicles such as Toyota Land Cruisers and Land Rovers.

Chapter 10

70. Despite being the largest and most powerful Army in the world, the American obsession with not taking any casualties has arguably rendered their ground forces 'non-operational.' This argument will be explored later in the book.
71. Both COS and DCOS are military terms used to describe the senior officer responsible to the commander for operational matters and for administrative/logistics matters respectively. In OHR the term COS was retained throughout but the term DCOS was replaced with the standard UN terminology of Chief Administrative Officer once I had secured that post.
72. Sir Arthur Watts had been appointed to oversee the division of assets belonging to the SFRY.
73. http://www.ohr.int
74. President Krajisnik was the subject of a 'Sealed Indictment' and later arrested by SFOR for alleged War Crimes.

Chapter 11

75. The SAS positions were overrun by the BSA who were actively being helped by the VJ 63rd Paratroop Brigade from Nis.
76. Banja Luka is the largest town in Republika Srpska and in 1997, replaced the village of Pale as the Bosnian Serb capital.
77. CIMIC is military terminology for Civil Military Co-operation. It became normal US policy to attach as many serving CIMIC officers (wearing civilian clothes) to the various civil pillars of the peace process as possible, thus being in the position of having US paid employees under American military law within the decision making process of these 'impartial international organisations.' Readers can draw their own conclusions about such policy.
78. Jock had already engaged a Full Colonel as his personal assistant in Sarajevo and a small CIMIC Team in Banja Luka to 'help out.'
79. Cited in the BBC. *The Reckoning*, 1999.
80. The Guardian. *Language of Torturers*, 14 May 99.

Chapter 12

81. Sealed indictments were secretly issued to the IPTF and IFOR/SFOR so that arrests could be conducted without the person charged being aware that they were on the wanted list. This policy was introduced to deny PIFWCs the opportunity to evade capture.
82. 'Conditionality' was the American 'expression' for applying/attaching conditions to the distribution of the vast sums of donor aid being pledged by the contact group and other international donors. It was therefore by definition, a set of restrictions placed on the delivery of humanitarian aid albeit the policy could not be applied universally to NGOs who were still able to adhere to basic humanitarian principles and provide aid where they saw a 'humanitarian imperative' free from political constraints.

83. It was envisioned that all civilian aid workers including OHR staff would be evacuated prior to any military action by IFOR.

84. See Chapter 15 for further details on Brcko.

85. See Chapter 16 for further details on Krajina Serbs and their influence on the 'returns' process.

86. The expression D+45 was used to mean 'Dayton + 45 days.'

87. The GFAP proscribed both the HVO and the ABiH and specifically demanded that the Muslim-Croat Federation had a single combined and fully integrated army complete with a single unified command structure.

88. Taken from *OHR and Economic Reconstruction briefing paper*, 1996.

89. See Chapter 21 for further details on Economic Reconstruction.

90. Visiting Bosnia i Hercegovina some five years later, the author was sad to observe that outwardly little had changed. The Black and Grey Economies were still rife. The only new businesses visible consisted of no more than corner kiosks and café bars, and many inefficient and unprofitable industries continued to be subsidised by the State. Bosnia continued to remain starved of foreign investment due to a lack of international confidence and by a shift in the political centre of gravity in the Balkans away from Bosnia i Hercegovina, first to Kosovo and then subsequently to the Federal Republic of Yugoslavia.

91. UNCHR is now known as the UNHCHR (UN High Commission for Human Rights).

92. At first appearance, it seemed that the Bosniak plate was the only multi-ethnic plate since it had 'BiH' written on it. In fact the plate was synonymous only with the Muslim population.

Chapter 13

93. OHR. 1996. *The Constitution of Bosnia and Hercegovina*, (Sarajevo)

94. The main nationalist political parties in Bosnia in 1996, which had taken the country to war in 1992, were the 'Serbian Democratic Party' (SDS), the Bosniak 'Party of Democratic Action' (SDA) and the 'Croatian Democratic Union' (HDZ).

95. These 'provisional' Rules and Regulations were still in use during the April 2000 municipal election and the Nov 2000 national and presidential elections since neither entity had agreed upon and passed a joint BiH election law.

96. The Washington Agreement 1994, created a Muslim-Croat military alliance to fight the Serbs.

Chapter 14

97. The CSCE was the forerunner to the OSCE.

98. The European Community (EC) was the forerunner to the current European Union (EU) however the ECMM has retained its original title throughout these changes.

99. An ECMM helicopter carrying four monitors was deliberately shot down by a Yugoslav airforce jet in 1992, with the loss of all life.

100. The Ferhadia Mosque was built in 1580 by Ferhad-Pasha Sokolovic, the last Bosnian Sanjak-Bey, and was perhaps the greatest piece of Turkish architecture in Bosnia of all times. At the time of writing, not even the rubble remains to mark its former position.

Chapter 15

101. There were three concentration camps in and around the Prijedor area which were exposed by the investigative journalist Roy Gutman in 1992. These were located at Keretern, Trno Polje and at Omaska. Gutman, R. 1993. *A Witness to Genocide*, Element Books (Shaftsbury).
102. See Chapter 16 for further details on the 'returns process.'
103. http://www.ohr.int/1997/cal-1997.htm

Chapter 16

104. CIMIC: Civil Military Co-operation. Efforts by the military to co-ordinate their efforts and knowledge with those of the civilian agencies operation within the same theatre.
105. The expression 'two-way returns' process is used to denote the return of both Serb and Muslim populations to their pre-war homes.

Chapter 17

106. This international crossing was only open to diplomatic missions.
107. The Krajina Serbs had formed their own militia, the VRSK, back in 1991 to fight in the Krajina but this had long since melted away.
108. Report of the High Representative to the UNSG dated 14 April 1996.
109. Report of the High Representative to the UNSG dated 14 April 1996, paragraph 68.
110. Biljana Plavsic voluntarily handed herself in to the ICTY in the Hague on 11th January 2001 having been indicted on nine counts of genocide and crimes against humanity
111. 21 SAS is a Territorial Army Volunteer Reserve unit.
112. AMIB: Allied Military Intelligence Branch.
113. JCO: Joint Commission Observers.
114. Both American and British Military CIMIC Doctrine encourages the military to partake in small scale humanitarian aid projects in order to win over the hearts and minds of the population. There is currently much debate within the humanitarian community as to whether the military should be allowed to play a partnership role with civilian aid agencies who reply for their freedom of operation on their impartiality. As the military by definition represent their governments, they can never become impartial and so taint by association those with whom they work. In practice, both British and American military CIMIC teams in Bosnia and later in Kosovo were not capable of providing the military commander with appropriate political analysis of events and so project management was often the only meaningful role they could fulfil.

Chapter 18

115. Stakic has since been captured and brought to justice in the Hague where he is currently serving life for Crimes against Humanity.
116. 22 SAS is the regular army SAS unit and in military circles is usually referred to simply as 'two-two.'
117. The Spanish diplomat, Carlos Westendorp, replaced Carl Bildt on 18th June 1997.
118. Banski Dvor: 'Palace of the Ban' and main cultural hall in the city. The building housed the Office of the RS President, the main offices of the SDS, the regional editorial offices of SRT and had two concert rooms and a bar-restaurant.

Chapter 19

119. A Contact Report is the standard NATO terminology for reporting an incident that involves a 'contact' with the enemy. Use of the word 'contact' on the radio is expressively forbidden in any other context other than one in which life is at risk. When used, all other radio users will automatically stay off the radio until the incident is cleared.

Chapter 20

120. Republika Srpska did not have Cantonal level local government authorities.
121. The ODIHR is based in Warsaw, Poland.
122. The IC eventually woke up to Alagic's corruption a year later and finally saw fit to remove him from office.

Chapter 21

123. In the Army of the Irish Republic, a Commandant is the equivalent rank to a Major in the British Army.
124. Jon in fact volunteered for duty and was sent to Kosovo during 1998 where he played a key role in monitoring the activities of the Serbian Police, VJ and the ethnic Albanian 'Kosovo Liberation Army' (UCK).